# REMEMBERING

*Studies in Phenomenology and Existential Philosophy*

# REMEMBERING

## A Phenomenological Study

EDWARD S. CASEY



INDIANA UNIVERSITY PRESS
BLOOMINGTON AND INDIANAPOLIS

Manufactured in the United States of America

**Library of Congress Cataloging-in-Publication Data**

Casey, Edward S., 1939-
Remembering : a phenomenological study.

(Studies in phenomenology and existential philosophy)
Bibliography: p.
Includes index.
1. Memory. 2. Phenomenological psychology.
I. Title. II. Series.
BF371.C33 1987 153.1'2 85-45889
ISBN 0-253-34942-7
ISBN 0-253-20409-7 (pbk.)

1 2 3 4 5 91 90 89 88 87

*To The Memory of*
*My Parents*
*Catherine J. Casey   Marlin S. Casey*

*And in Remembrance of*
*the Vanished World of*
*My Grandparents*
*Daisy Hoffman Johntz   John Edward Johntz*

# CONTENTS

# PREFACE

> through spiral upon spiral of the shell of memory that yet connects us. . . .
>
> —H.D., "The Flowering of the Rod"

> The fact is that we have almost no systematic knowledge about memory as it occurs in the course of ordinary life.
>
> —Ulrich Neisser, *Cognition and Reality*

In the case of memory, we are always already in the thick of things. For this reason there can properly be no preface to remembering: no pre-facing the topic in a statement that would precede it and capture its essence or structure in advance. Memory itself is already in the advance position. Not only because remembering is at all times presupposed, but also because it is always at work: it is continually going on, often on several levels and in several ways at once. Although there are many moments of misremembering and of not successfully recollecting, there are few moments in which we are not steeped in memory; and this immersion includes each step we take, each thought we think, each word we utter. Indeed, every fiber of our bodies, every cell of our brains, holds memories—as does everything physical outside bodies and brains, even those inanimate objects that bear the marks of their past histories upon them in mute profusion. What is memory-laden exceeds the scope of the human: memory takes us into the environing world as well as into our individual lives.

To acknowledge such a massive pre-presence of memory is to acknowledge how irreducibly important remembering is. If we need to be convinced of how much memory matters to us, we have only to ponder the fate of someone deprived of its effective use. Consider, for instance, the case of the unfortunate "M.K.," a high school teacher who at age forty-three was suddenly struck by an acute episode of encephalitis. Within hours, he lost access to almost all memories formed during the previous five years. Worse still, he had virtually no memory of anything that happened to him afterwards: since the onset of the illness, "he has learned a few names over the years, a few major events, and can get around the hospital."[1] This laconic summary, tragic in its very brevity, conveys the empty essence of a life rendered suddenly memoryless by a microscopic viral agent. Such a life is without aim or direction; it spins in the void of the forgotten, a void in which one cannot even be certain of one's personal identity. Not only does it show that what most of us take for granted can be abolished with an incomprehensible rapidity; it also poses the problem of how anything that permeates our lives so deeply can be lost so irrevocably.

How much memory matters can also be seen in the quite different case of "S.," a Russian mnemonist with an astonishing capacity to recall. When asked, as one of myriad tests, to repeat several stanzas of *The Divine Comedy* in Italian (a language he did not know) some fifteen years after having the stanzas read to him just once, he was able to recite them word for word and with perfect intonation. As A. R. Luria has observed, "the capacity of his memory *had no distinct limits*."[2] Envious as we might be of such a capacity, it is noteworthy that S. suffered greatly from it; so overburdened by it was he that he had to devise techniques for forgetting what he would otherwise irrepressibly remember, no matter how trivial it was: "This is too much," he lamented, "each word calls up images; they collide with one another, and the result is chaos."[3] Where forgetting was M.K.'s curse, it was S.'s salvation. But in the end, it is not clear that S., with his gift, was any less oppressed than was M.K. in his afflicted state.

These two figures are limiting cases of what the rest of us, as more or less normal rememberers, experience. On the one hand, each of us has undergone moments or even entire periods of acute amnesia. Whether such amnesia is contingent and occasion-bound (e.g., failing to recall the name of a friend or, more drastically, the circumstances immediately preceding a concussion) or systematic and symptomatic (as in forgetting dreams or incidents from early childhood), it is embarrassing and discomfiting and sometimes even disabling. On the other hand, it is a fact that eight percent of elementary school children possess practically perfect eidetic recall.[4] Moreover, many adults can recover deeply repressed memories in vivid detail even though they have never been recollected before; and, generally, our powers of hypermńesia (i.e., ultra-clear memory) are much more extensive than we usually suspect.[5] Just as we have no difficulty in grasping the devastating consequences of M.K.'s memory loss, so we connect immediately with S.'s prodigious feats of memory through certain of our own inherent, if distinctly more modest, capacities.

Nevertheless, even if we do not find M.K. or S. utterly alien, most of the remembering that most of us do falls between the poles of hypomnesia and hypermnesia. Thus the question becomes: what can we say with confidence about our own remembering as it occurs spontaneously and on a daily basis? Short of total recall and yet beyond amnesic vacuity, how does human memory present itself? What basic forms does it assume? With what content is it concerned? How much is it a function of the human mind, how much of the human body? In short, *what do we do when we remember?*

*Remembering: A Phenomenological Study* attempts to answer such questions as these by taking a resolutely descriptive look at memory as it arises in diverse commonplace settings. In these settings we rarely attend to what we are doing when we remember; we just let it happen (or fail to happen). How can we begin to notice what we so much take for granted—except precisely when we hear of extraordinary cases such as those of M.K. and S.? This book undertakes to help us notice what has gone unnoticed or been noticed only marginally. In this respect the book is a work in phenomenology, an enterprise devoted to discerning and thematizing that which is indistinct or overlooked in everyday experience.

*Remembering* represents a sequel to my earlier study of imagination.[6] But there is a critical difference between the two inquiries, which are otherwise closely affiliated. This difference follows directly from the multifarious incursions of memory into the life-world of the rememberer. These inroads are such as to resist complete capture in the structure of intentionality, which served as a guiding thread in *Imagining*. In remembering, there is an unresolvable "restance"[7]—resistance as well as remainder—which calls for a different approach. Intentional analysis remains valid for much of ordinary recollection (e.g., in visualized scenes), and I devote chapters 3 and 4 to the exploration of remembering insofar as it can be construed on the model of the mind's intentionality. But once we realize how forcefully many phenomena of memory take us out of mind conceived as a container of ideas and representations, we can no longer rest content with intentionality as a leitmotif.[8] That is why in Part Two I consider various "mnemonic modes"—i.e., recognizing, reminiscing, and reminding—each of which can be seen as contesting the self-enclosing character of strictly intentionalist paradigms. In Part Three I depart still further from the narrow basis established in Part One; I do so by describing body memory, place memory, and commemoration. In spite of their central position in human experience, these latter have been curiously neglected in previous accounts of memory. Their description leads me to discuss memory's "thick autonomy" in Part Four: an autonomy which is to be contrasted with the equally characteristic "thin autonomy" of imagination.

A descriptive account of remembering will help us to recognize that we remember in multiple ways: that the past need not come packaged in the prescribed format of representational recollections. To fail to remember in this format is not tantamount to failing to remember altogether. When one memorial channel to the past becomes closed off, others often open up—indeed, are often already on hand and fully operative. I may not retain a lucid mental image of an acrimonious quarrel with a certain friend—I may have successfully repressed it—and yet the same scene may be lingering in an inarticulate but nonetheless powerful body memory. The point is not that there is a meaningful alternative in every case: the sad circumstance of M.K. warns us of dire limits. But plural modes of access to the remembered past are far more plentiful than philosophers and psychologists have managed to ascertain.[9]

Remembering returns us to the very world lost sight of in the language of representations and of neural traces. Indeed, remembering reminds us that we have never left the life-world in the first place, that we are always within it, and that memory is itself the main life-line to it. For memory takes us into things—into the *Sachen selbst* which Husserl proclaimed to be the proper objects of phenomenological investigation. In remembering, we come back to the things that matter.

But memory is not just something that sustains a *status quo ante* within human experience. It also makes a critical difference to this experience. The situation is such that remembering transforms one kind of experience into another: *in being remembered, an experience becomes a different kind of experience*. It becomes "a memory," with all that this entails, not merely of the consistent, the enduring, the reliable, but also of the fragile, the errant, the confabulated. Each memory is unique; none is simple repetition or revival. The way that the past is relived in memory assures that it will be transfigured in subtle and significant ways.

If this is indeed the case—if memory matters in our experience by making a difference in the form our experience itself takes—then a detailed description of remembering is called for. Such a description will not only aid us in distinguishing remembering from kindred phenomena of imagining and perceiving, feeling and thinking; it will also lead us to realize that it was always misguided to propose that remembering could be regarded as a mere offshoot of mind or brain, fated to repeat what has already happened elsewhere. Remembering is itself essential to what is happening, part of every action, here as well as elsewhere: "remembrance is always now."[10] It is also, thanks to its transformative force in the here and now, then and there. Not only is nothing human alien to memory; nothing in the world, including the world itself, is not memorial in nature or in status. And if this is so, it follows that "whatever we know exists in proportion to the memories we possess."[11] Thus far reaches remembering: it stretches as far as we can know.

# ACKNOWLEDGMENTS

To acknowledge adequately the help of so many colleagues, friends, and family members during the decade in which this book has come to birth would itself be a considerable feat of memory. Let me single out only those who offered the most important intellectual and personal resources during this protracted period of time—resources without which this book could not have been written.

First of all, I would like to thank my colleagues and students at the State University of New York at Stony Brook. They have provided a most congenial and exciting atmosphere in which to teach and write. A primary inspiration at Stony Brook has been Marcia K. Johnson, now in the Psychology Department at Princeton University. Together, we taught a graduate course on human memory in which I worked out a number of my fledgling ideas against the backdrop of current cognitive psychology; informally, we discussed many of the themes that appear in this book. In the Philosophy Department at Stony Brook I am especially grateful to Mary C. Rawlinson for her searching remarks on Proust and the subject of involuntary memory. Contributing in diverse ways have been Patrick Heelan, Donn Welton, Eva Kittay, Hugh Silverman, Antonio de Nicolas, and Don Ihde. In Religious Studies I owe much to Peter Manchester's magisterial understanding of ancient Greek philosophy and its late Hellenistic heritage. His colleagues Robert Neville and Thomas J. J. Altizer have been guiding presences. With Janet Gyatso I have discussed to my great profit the semiological aspects of memory, especially the nature of reminders; she also commented valuably on several parts of the manuscript.

Every author should be so fortunate as to have a reader as mercilessly critical, and yet as imaginatively constructive, as J. Melvin Woody of Connecticut College. He saw through most of my rhetorical ruses and inept formulations and led me to rewrite virtually the whole book during a semester's sabbatical leave. If the book as it stands has finally begun to approach coherence, it is very much thanks to my friend's concerted scrutinies.

I am also indebted to Calvin Schrag for his meticulous reading of the entire manuscript at an early stage. His suggestions for reductions in a manuscript that was twice the present length have proven very useful. I also profited immensely from the close readings of Deborah Chaffin; her ideas for revisions have been taken into account in many places. Laura Jerabek was helpful in discussing several chapters of the evolving book. Indispensable to the completion of this project has been Catherine Keller. Not only has she commented on most of the text, she encouraged my recourse to Whitehead at a crucial juncture. Her extensive knowledge of mythology and her subtle sense of style have been gratefully received gifts during the time in which this book assumed its final shape.

Of the numerous people who read determinate parts of the manuscript at various points I wish to mention here Drew Leder for his pertinent remarks on the neurophysiological aspects of memory and for his critical perusal of the chapter on body memory. Glen Mazis also contributed insightfully to my understanding of body memory and its ramifications. Charles Scott set me straight on basic features of place memory in a memorable talk in Perugia, Italy. The role of landscape in place memory was illuminated by David Strong in several discussions. I am especially indebted to Véronique Fóti for her expert guidance in grasping Descartes's conception of memory as well as for talks in which we profitably explored assorted topics in the realm of remembering. Her rigorous standards of scholarship as well as her considerable critical acumen have been of inestimable value in the last nine years.

Friends in the field of psychology—which has devoted more attention to memory than has philosophy in this century—have been inspiring figures in the course of this book's gestation. James Hillman and I have debated, in public and in private, the respective features and virtues of imagination and memory. He also generously provided a place of retreat several summers ago in Botorp, Sweden, where I was able to think out the second half of the book. For many years Stanley Leavy and I have engaged in virorous discussions on psychoanalysis and related matters. His seminal book, *The Psychoanalytic Dialogue*, has been of central significance in my efforts to bring psychoanalysis to bear on my own project. JoAnne Wallen contributed significant insights from the practice of psychotherapy and from her own remarkable psychological sagacity. I also learned much from Dan Reisberg's scintillating lectures at the New School for Social Research on the status of current research on memory in cognitive psychology. Henry Tylbor provoked me to rethink aspects of remembering that I had taken for granted.

For their ongoing support in differing contexts I would like to express my deeply felt gratitude to William Earle, a continuing mentor and friend; Hans W. Loewald, steadfast and untiring in his invaluable assistance; Jan Larson, a most discerning Diotima for more than thirty years of friendship; and especially Brenda Casey, who created an ambiance in which writing could be pursued even into the latest hours. Eric and Erin Casey were movingly memorable presences in that same ambiance. My sister, Constance J. Casey, kept me in vivid touch with important childhood memories. Reed Hoffman, my esteemed cousin of Enterprise, Kansas, apprised me of details concerning the vanished world cited in the dedication to this book.

Virginia Massaro typed several versions of chapters with grace and skill. Others who helped in the typing of the manuscript include Sally Moran, Mary Bruno, and above all Jean Edmunds in the final stages. I received excellent editorial assistance from Lila Freedman, who combined sensitivity concerning style with intelligent critique of content. Librarians at the Guildford Public Library aided me in numerous ways.

I wish finally to thank the American Council of Learned Societies for a fellowship that allowed me to write the first chapters of this book in the fall of 1977 and to the State University of New York at Stony Brook for granting me a year's leave of absence in 1984–85, during which time the book was completed.

# REMEMBERING

# *INTRODUCTION*

# REMEMBERING FORGOTTEN

## THE AMNESIA OF ANAMNESIS

> I come into the fields and spacious palaces of my memory, where are treasures of countless images of things of every manner.
>
> —St. Augustine, *Confessions*

> I convince myself that nothing has ever existed of all that my deceitful memory recalls to me.
>
> —Descartes, *Meditations*

> We moderns have no memories at all.
>
> —Frances Yates, *The Art of Memory*

### I

Nietzsche's essay "On the Uses and Disadvantages of History for Life," first published in 1874, opens with the following fable:

> Consider the cattle, grazing as they pass you by: they do not know what is meant by yesterday or today, they leap about, eat, rest, digest, leap about again, and so from morn till night and from day to day, [are] fettered to the moment and its pleasure or displeasure. . . . A human being may well ask [such] an animal: "Why do you not speak to me of your happiness but only stand and gaze at me?" The animal would like to answer, and say: "The reason is that I always forget what I was going to say"—but then he forgot this answer too, and stayed silent: so that the human being was left wondering.[1]

Not wholly unlike the bovine beings here described by Nietzsche, we have not only forgotten what it is to remember—and what remembering *is*—but we have forgotten our own forgetting. So deep is our oblivion of memory that we are not even aware of how alienated we are from its "treasures" and how distant we have become from its deliverances. Memory, itself preoccupied with the past, is practically *passé*—a topic of past concern. Despite its manifold importance in our lives, it is only in unusual circumstances that remembering remains an item of central concern on contemporary agendas. These circumstances themselves tend to be distinctly self-contained and removed from ordinary life, whether they are found in psychoanalytic sessions, Eastern visualization techniques, or experiments in cognitive psychology. Philosophers have come to despair over finding a constructive approach to memory; they have discredited and discarded a number of existing theories, especially those that make representation of the past the basic function of remembering; yet they have rarely offered a positive account of memory to take the place of rejected theories.

The fact is that we have forgotten what memory is and can mean; and we make matters worse by repressing the fact of our own oblivion. No wonder Yates can claim that "we moderns have no memories at all." Where once Mnemosyne was a venerated Goddess, we have turned over responsibility for remembering to the cult of the computers, which serve as our modern mnemonic idols. The force of the remembered word in oral traditions—as exemplified in feats of bardic recounting that survive only in the most isolated circumstances[2]—has given way to the inarticulate hum of the disk drive. Human memory has become self-externalized: projected outside the rememberer himself or herself and into non-human machines. These machines, however, *cannot remember;* what they can do is to record, store, and retrieve information—which is only part of what human beings do when they enter into a memorious state. The memory of things is no longer in ourselves, in our own discerning and interpreting, but in the calculative wizardry of computers. If computers are acclaimed as creations of our own devising, they remain—whatever their invaluable utility—most unsuitable citadels of memory, whose "fields and spacious palaces" (in St. Augustine's phrase) they cannot begin to contain or to replicate. Although certain non-human things can indeed bear memories—as we shall see toward the close of this book—computers cannot. Computers can only collect and order the reduced residues, the artfully formatted traces, of what in the end must be reclaimed by human beings in order to count as human memories. In this respect, *our memories are up to us*. But for the most part and ever increasingly, we have come to disclaim responsibility for them.

In the same essay as that cited above, Nietzsche suggests one of the motives for our amnesia concerning memory: "Even a happy life is possible without remembrance, as the beast shows; but life in any true sense is absolutely impossible without forgetfulness."[3] Nietzsche himself advocates the concerted practice of "active forgetfulness"—all the more imperative if his doctrine of eternal recurrence is ultimately true. For if everything recurs an endless number of times, we would be well advised to avoid remembering anything that has happened even (apparently) only once! To recall what has happened an infinite number of times—including our own acts of recollecting—would be to assume a crushing burden. As Milan Kundera has put the matter:

> If every second of our lives recurs an infinite number of times, we are nailed to eternity as Jesus Christ was nailed to the cross. It is a terrifying prospect. In the world of eternal return the weight of unbearable responsibility lies heavy on every move we make. That is why Nietzsche called the idea of eternal return the heaviest of burdens *(das schwerste Gewicht)*.
>
> If eternal return is the heaviest of burdens, then our lives can stand out against it in all their splendid lightness.[4]

"Splendid lightness" is fostered by forgetting, an active forgetting of that which becomes intolerably heavy when remembered. Kundera continues:

> But is heaviness truly deplorable and lightness splendid?
>
> The heaviest of burdens crushes us, we sink beneath it, it pins us to the ground. But in the love poetry of every age, the woman longs to be weighed down by the man's body. The heaviest of burdens is therefore simultaneously an image of life's most intense fulfillment. The heavier the burden, the closer our lives come to the earth, the more real and truthful they become.[5]

Could it be that in following the path of forgetting, we have indeed missed one fundamental form of "life's most intense fulfillment"? Have we perhaps lost touch with the "earth" of memory itself, its dense loam? Is not the way of forgetting a way of obscuring, even of renouncing, the sustaining subsoil of remembering? As Kundera also remarks: "The absolute absence of a burden causes man to be lighter than air, to soar into the heights, take leave of the earth and his earthly body, and become only half real, his movements as free as they are insignificant."[6]

The half-reality induced by forgetting, its oblivious half-life, tempts us to attribute the full reality of remembering to machines. As if by a rigid law of compensation, the logic seems to be: the less responsibility I have for my own remembering, the more I can forget—ultimately, the more I can forget my own forgetting. And the more I can forget, the more responsibility I can ascribe to other entities: most conveniently to computers, or to my own brain or mind regarded as computerlike. Thus my own alleviation exists in inverse ratio to their encumberment. As I become more like the happy unremembering beast, free from the "dark, invisible burden"[7] of remembering, machines or machinelike parts of my own being become burdened with the heavy tasks formerly assigned to my unassisted self. Like Nietzsche's Last Man, I smile and blink in my memoryless contentment as I come to rely on data banks and mass media to hold and transmit memories for me. Not only do I not do my own remembering, *I have forgotten to remember*. I no longer know how to remember effectively or even what I want to remember. In this state I am failing to remember remembering.

> What then shall we choose? Weight or lightness?[8]

For us moderns, Kundera's question comes to this: what will we choose—the way of remembering or the way of forgetting? Perhaps it is already too late to answer this fateful question meaningfully. We may already have lost our anamnesic souls to the collective amnesia embodied in machine-memory. Such a loss might be acceptable if eternal return were truly to obtain. If Nietzsche is correct, relief from the heaviest of burdens might well lie in the frivolity of forgetting, a frivolity that follows upon handing over responsibility for remembering to machines.

But what if Nietzsche's doctrine of *die ewige Wiederkehr des Gleichens* is itself moot? What if it is (therefore) not too late to choose? What then? Might we then take seriously once more the genuine weight of memory instead of mindlessly opting for the spurious lightness of forgetting? Can we remember to remember? Can amnesia give way to anamnesis?

## II

Before we can begin to answer such questions, we must undertake two tasks in the remainder of this Introduction. First, concrete evidence of memory's decline in prestige needs to be adduced if the claims just made in section I are not to seem merely dogmatic or rhetorical. I will set forth such evidence in this section and in section III, while remarking upon certain counter-currents in section IV. Second, a look back to an earlier time, when memory was highly valued, is called for—not only as a foil to the modern plight but as itself an important part of the very background that we have forgotten. This backward look will occur in sections V to VII, which will consider the fate of memory from ancient Greece to the Enlightenment.

Given our defensiveness before the weight of the past—which, as a direct consequence, we tend to regard as something merely "fixed" and "dead"—it is not altogether surprising that we have turned in recent times to machines as repositories and models of memory. If the past can be reduced to a dead weight, then it can be deposited in machines as just one more item of information. Our most commonly employed current metaphors for memory betray this action of consignment along with a scarcely concealed denigration: "memory machine," "machine memory," "photographic memory," "memory bank," "storage system," "save to disk," "computer memory," "memory file," and so on. What is most noticeable in any such list of descriptive terms is the way in which memory is construed by reference to an apparatus or procedure that is strictly mechanical and nonhuman in nature: above all, the computer with its extraordinary powers of compression and retention of discrete units of information. Indeed, the currently most influential models of memory in experimental psychology are those based on "information processing" as enacted and exemplified by computers. I shall not here debate the claims of advocates of "AI" that "natural" human intelligence can be successfully replicated and even improved upon by computers.[9] I wish only to call attention to how readily memory has become assimilated to a machine as paradigm—to its own disadvantage. Precisely because the machine in question is viewed as endless in its resources and all but miraculous in its operations, "merely" human memory comes to suffer by comparison: subject to more severe constraints in its quantitative capacity than a computer, such memory is also subject to more extensive errors in its functioning. No wonder that human memory is impugned, implicitly or explicitly, by being analogized to something that remembers more efficiently than do human beings themselves.

The problem lies not in computerization as such. Computers may well have superior memories—so long as they are dealing with expressly chunkable, bit(e)able information—and they deserve recognition on this score as enormously effective prototypes of how the form of remembering we call "memorizing" might operate. That is, if such remembering were itself mechanical, which it is not! The problem resides, rather, in the tacit undermining of the authority, scope, and value of human memory in its own domain—in its ongoing performances in everyday life. Just what these performances are and exactly how they take place, will represent the major preoccupation of the present book. "What is wanted," as Freud remarks, "is precisely an elucidation of the *commonest* cases."[10] It is ironic and revealing that to undertake a detailed description of just such cases is to accord to remembering a form of respect that is rarely granted in this age of artificial intelligence.

Concomitant with the current metaphorization of memory—the *translatio* or "transfer" of its basic sense or structure into the very different sense and structure of computing machines—we find the singularly striking fact that the lexicon of currently used terms for memory has dwindled considerably in the last two centuries. How many of the following words, all of them employed by writers of English in earlier times, do you recognize, much less use yourself?[11]

—"memorous" (memorable)
—"memorious" (having a good memory; being mindful of)
—"memoried" (having a memory of a specific kind)
—"memorist" (one who prompts the return of memories)
—"mnemotechny" ("mnemonics," itself hardly a familiar word today)

—“mnemonize” (to memorize)
—“mnemonicon” (a device to aid the memory)

The contemporary rarity of such terms, terms once familiar to ordinary speakers of English, should give us pause. Where have all the words for memory gone? The impoverishment of our vocabulary for (and about) remembering goes hand in hand with the general decline in esteem which memory has suffered in modern times and is, indeed, its first symptom.[12] Presaged in the replacement of orally transmitted memories by handwriting and (especially) printing, the disappearance of an earlier and richer vocabulary has left us with considerably diminished verbal resources.[13]

## III

Further evidence for memory's declining prestige is found in several other areas that merit brief examination here. Memorizing, once a standard pedagogical tool in primary school, is no longer emphasized in the early years of education. True, children are still occasionally required to memorize a poem or a brief prose passage; but this serves more as gesture than as substance, reminding us of a period, only several decades past, when memorizing was a much more integral part of the curriculum. At that time, educators believed that students learned certain texts best by committing them to heart (i.e., “memoriter,” another word fallen into disuse) and that the very activity of memorizing, beyond furnishing a shared cultural tradition, was beneficial to a child's mental development. We need not defend these practices, which were sometimes over-rigorously applied in an oppressive zeal for achieving the exact repetition of prescribed material.[14] The point is that such practices, however misapplied they may have been, are now conspicuously absent from contemporary curricula.[15] Their very absence reflects a general devaluation of memory.

Consider in this connection the steadily decreasing interest in mnemotechnical devices and systems through which to improve one's powers of memory. Although “mnemonics” retains a certain curiosity value—as is witnessed in the popularity of Lucas and Lorayne's *The Memory Book*[16]—it is no longer the object of assiduous study on the part of ordinary people. In the first half of the nineteenth century, thousands of New Yorkers flocked to hear such mnemotechnical experts as Fauvel-Gounod, Aimé Paris, and Dr. Pick, all of whom promised vastly improved memories to their handsomely paying auditors. By 1888, however, William Stokes could complain in the ninetieth edition of his popular tract *Memory:* “In spite of all that has been said and done [in the past], we may say comparatively—almost absolutely—that the art [of memorizing aided by technical devices] is a thing unknown!”[17] This lament rings still more true today, nearly one century later.

Not even the eloquent efforts of Frances Yates in *The Art of Memory* to reconstruct the early history of a distinctive mnemotechnical tradition and to indicate its now largely forgotten importance in the ancient, medieval, and Renaissance worlds is likely to revive a widespread interest in mnemotechnics *per se*. The author herself revealingly disowns any personal stake in the memory method she so lucidly recounts: "There is no doubt that this method will work for anyone who is prepared to labor seriously at these mnemonic gymnastics. *I have never attempted to do so myself*."[18] The most eminent expositor of the *ars memorativa* tradition chooses not to use this art to improve her own memory. This choice is symptomatic not just of the decreasing employment of mnemotechnics but of a still more momentous loss of interest in cultivating memory for its own sake.

Still another sign of the times is the regrettable fact that reminiscing as a central social practice has faded from style. By "reminiscing" I do not refer merely to a stray recounting of times past, but to those particular social situations in which older, more experienced persons recollected past events in the presence of younger auditors. These occasions endowed memory with a decisively communitarian dimension. Moreover, reminiscing was often the only way in which an otherwise unchronicled part of the past was reclaimed for others, especially if the person who did the retelling was the last surviving witness. In a more leisurely age—for instance, before World War I in the Middle West—reminiscing was a frequent feature of family gatherings and other social settings. It is now, by the late twentieth century, an increasingly uncommon phenomenon—doubtless due to the disintegration of the extended family structure and to a concomitant lack of veneration for the elderly in our culture. Whatever the exact causes, the clear result is that memory has been driven still further into retreat.

One of the most telling evidences of the marked decline in the prestige of memory can be found in the notable fact that four of the leading theoretical treatments of memory undertaken in the last one hundred years have approached remembering through the counterphenomenon of *forgetting*. It is as if a more direct approach would be futile and question-begging: memory is best understood via its own deficient mode. Let us consider in cursory fashion the four cases in point.

### NIETZSCHE

As we have seen in section I, Nietzsche stressed the virtues of "active forgetfulness," that is, the capacity to forget not merely by *lapsus* but willfully and for a purpose—so as to erase, or at least to cover over, the scars which repeated remembering would only turn back into open wounds. Such willed forgetting is the counterpart of the enforced remembering which Nietzsche detects in societies anxious to ensure rigid conformity to law on the part of their members.[19] But, for the individual, forgetting is by far the more crucial of the two activities: the individual "wonders at himself, that he cannot learn to forget but clings relentlessly to the past; however far and fast he may run, this chain runs with him. . . . He says 'I remember' and envies the animal, who at once forgets and for whom every moment really dies."[20]

FREUD

It is a fact worth pondering that psychoanalysis, so often regarded as a form of "memory therapy," was originally much more concerned with forgetting. Although Breuer and Freud proclaimed the cure of symptoms by the abreactive or cathartic recall of traumatic experiences in their *Studies on Hysteria* (1895), Freud himself backed away from this therapeutic optimism only two years later when he became persuaded that his patients' apparent memories of seduction were actually fantasies disguised as memories. By 1899, he had become profoundly skeptical of the validity of *any* purported childhood memories, since such memories are likely to be "screened" in various ways;[21] and he came to believe in a generalized childhood amnesia which represents the involuntary (but still purposive) forgetting of large tracts of one's early experience.[22] The aim of psychoanalysis became, accordingly, to "fill in the gaps in memory,"[23] to undo the baneful, pathogenic effects of forgetting wherever this is possible. In 1909, Freud could say almost cynically that "the weak spot in the security of our mental life [is] the untrustworthiness of our memory."[24] More generally, what Freud called "the blindness of the seeing eye"[25] may be taken as referring to the forgetting that shows itself to reside actively in the heart of remembering like an insidious virus, ready to do its destructive work there—with the result that psychoanalysis can be said to consist in a continuous struggle against the forces of forgetfulness.

HEIDEGGER

The inner dynamic of all of Heidegger's philosophical work may be said to consist in a prolonged effort to deal with the forgetfulness of Being. This forgetfulness has afflicted the Western mind from Plato onwards and continues in the present in the form of an ontological blindness which Heidegger terms "subjective presence" in the wake of Descartes, and which reaches an apogee in the idolatrization of modern technology (including, as a paradigm case, computers). Thus, *Being and Time,* Heidegger's *magnum opus* of 1927, opens with the plaint: "*The Necessity for Explicitly Restating the Question of Being*. This question has today been forgotten."[26] Later, in *Being and Time,* forgetfulness, even in its ordinary forms, is interpreted as more primordial than remembering: "In the 'leaping-away' of the Present, one also forgets increasingly. The fact that curiosity always holds by what is coming next, and has forgotten what has gone before, is not a result that ensues *from* curiosity, but is the ontological condition for curiosity itself."[27] The many works which have followed *Being and Time* can be considered as sustained, if often oblique, attempts to overcome the forgetting of Being in order to induce an adequate remembrance of it which Heidegger comes to term *Andenken*, "commemorative thought."[28]

EBBINGHAUS

In 1885, Ebbinghaus inaugurated the experimental study of memory with the publication of *Über das Gedächtnis*.[29] This slim volume gave the results of numerous experiments involving rote remembering which Ebbinghaus performed upon himself in the early 1880s. The remembering was of nonsense syllables that were as free as possible from semantic ambiguities. Nevertheless, what emerges from a close reading of this seminal monograph is that Ebbinghaus was in fact measuring *the rate at which he had forgotten a given group of nonsense syllables*. As a consequence, the famous "Ebbinghaus curve of memory"—shaped roughly like this: ∩ —is in fact a curve of forgetting, mapping out the precise amount of material that failed to be remembered at particular points in time. Thus, even within a fastidious laboratory setting that was the first of its kind in Western psychology, remembering ceded place to forgetting.

It is a striking coincidence that Ebbinghaus's fateful study was published just three years before the final edition of Stokes's *Memory* appeared. At the very moment when the demise of the art of memory was announced, the science of memory was born. What had been left to amateur teachers of memorizing, minstrels of memory and sometimes its sophists as well, was now to be given over to the quantitatively precise, experimentally expert hands of laboratory psychologists—psychologists very different in kind from those whom Freud was to inspire. In the aftermath of Ebbinghaus, the ranks of the experimentalists are now legion; their approaches to memory are widely disseminated and discussed in professional journals, where they are regarded as providing the most exact and reliable penetration into the mysteries of memory. What began as an isolated attempt to measure forgetting with a new precision has spawned an entire industry of research into the nature of remembering itself.

Despite the undeniable ingenuity of this research and its many methodological merits, it remains yet another symptom of a pervasive subsiding of interest in memory. What has faded from focus in the eyes of the common man has been scrutinized ever more minutely behind the closed doors of the psychological laboratory.[30] And concurrently with memory's withdrawal from display as a standard method of public education and as an object of public exhibition by professional mnemonists, technology has supplied publicly available (but entirely mechanical) mnemotechnical aids that displace the burden of memory from individuals to machines. These machines, whether they be hand-held calculators or room-size computers, sound recorders or video playback devices, offer practically irresistible aid and comfort to the imperfect individual rememberer. Easily available, usable, storable, or disposable, these prosthetic memories have become indispensable instruments of modern living.

In the end, the scientific study of memory and the presence of elaborate electronic *aides-mémoire* are only the currently most manifest symptoms of the declining interest in "remembering in the old manner."[31] Whatever the ultimate reasons for this decline, we must acknowledge it as an established fact, an intrinsic feature of ever-increasing proportions within Western culture. It has become such a deeply entrenched tendency at the level of *praxis* and theory alike that it would be Luddite-like to try to reverse, or even to lament, the trend. At the most, one can hope that a detailed, dispassionate description of human memory itself—one that neither subjects it to experimental treatment nor turns over primary responsibility to machines as models—will aid in restoring a long-neglected concern for remembering construed in its own terms and given regard for its own sake. In keeping with Husserl's dictum "to the things themselves!" such an account is what the present study purports to offer. And in this admittedly nonscientific but nonetheless descriptively rigorous way we may begin the difficult process of remembering memory for what it is and can be.

## IV

In any effort to unforget our own forgetting, we need all the support we can find. Strangely enough, it can be found close at hand. Beneath the amnesiac flood tide of indifference toward remembering are distinct undercurrents of respect. This respect is observable in certain everyday attitudes toward memory. Notice, for example, our irritation at someone who continually repeats himself or herself: why doesn't this person *remember* that he or she has told us the same thing before, indeed, just yesterday? Standing in contrast with this banal circumstance of disappointment—which nevertheless betrays definite expectations about the use of memory—is the amazement we experience upon reading such a book as Luria's *The Mind of a Mnemonist*.[32] Whatever its untoward effects upon individuals who possess it, "photographic memory" remains in our spontaneous judgment an enviable and extraordinary gift. When such a memory-for-minutiae is combined with intelligence of the highest order, as in Homer or Seneca the Elder, Milton or Freud, the prospect of such genius redoubled strikes us as awesome. In yet a different way, there is a haunting sense that something abidingly important has been lost in the near-elimination of memorization from education, as is reflected in the often-heard complaint that our memories have become slovenly and unreliable in comparison with those possessed by our forebears only a few generations back.

These various attitudes, pallid as they may appear in the face of the massive decline just described, nevertheless attest to a considerable lingering concern with the role of memory in ourselves as individuals and in our civilization generally. We do seem to care, at some level, about memory's sinking fortune; its subsiding fate over the past century—indeed, since the Renaissance—does matter to us, even if we feel personally powerless to stem the tide toward diminution in esteem and enfeeblement in use. Stymied in the present and altogether uncertain of the future, we are naturally led to look back—not without envy or nostalgia—to a time when memory was deeply revered and rigorously trained, as it was in ancient Greece.

## V

Memory was a thematic, even an obsessive, concern of the early Greeks. The very survival of the rich oral culture of the Archaic Period (twelfth to eighth centuries B.C.), depended on concerted, disciplined remembering: "Language and thought for the early Greeks grew out of memory."[33] Until the introduction of alphabetic writing—that "recipe not for memory, but for reminding," as Plato says in the *Phaedrus*[34]—the Greeks were forced to rely on the memorial powers of individuals, especially on those who had received special training.[35] The *mnemon*, for example, was someone who kept track of proceedings in law courts without the benefit of written documents. In mythical representations, the *mnemon* was a servant of heroes who reminded them, at crucial moments, of divine injunctions. Thus Achilles was accompanied by a *mnemon* who was enjoined to warn him that if he were ever to kill a son of Apollo, he would be put to death. But this appointed reminder failed in his function and was himself put to death.[36] The bards who chanted the *Iliad*, in which this particular tale is recounted, were themselves mnemonic masters who had no written texts to aid their memories. They were almost certainly required to undergo memory training in which they learned to employ mnemotechnics of various sorts, including the use of systematic meters (e.g., hexameter) and internally varying epithets. Such artifices were sorely needed in view of the taxing tasks to which the bard's memory was submitted. Many verses of the *Iliad* are little more than copious catalogues of names of warriors (including their place of origin and their exact form of military strength), the most important horses, names of servants, etc. The memorization of such verses was not intended merely to impress audiences with virtuoso performances. It was the sole means of keeping an entire body of collectively held lore alive. As Jean Pierre Vernant remarks, it was by the recitation of these seemingly unending compendia that:

> there was fixed and transmitted the repertory of knowledge which allows a social group to decipher its 'past'. [Such recitations] constitute the equivalent of the archives of a society without writing: purely legendary, they correspond

> neither to administrative demands nor to an attempt to glorify royalty nor to a historical concern.[37]

Memorization in the Archaic Period was therefore more than a mere device for keeping facts straight—more than an efficient storage and retrieval system. It was a way of getting (and staying) in touch with a past that would otherwise be consigned to oblivion; it was a fateful fending off of forgetfulness.[38]

The past to which the bard transported his audience was more mythical than historical: "The 'past' is an integral part of the cosmos; to explore it [in epic poetry] is to discover what lies dissimulated in the depths of being."[39] To be conveyed into this past is to be able to forget, however briefly, the anxieties of the present. Here forgetting and remembering work hand-in-hand, each helping the other to realize an optimal form—in contrast with the conflictual relationship that we have witnessed in the thought of Freud and Nietzsche, Heidegger and Ebbinghaus. Indeed, for the early Greeks generally, forgetting and remembering form an indissociable pair; they are given explicit mythical representation in the coeval figures of Lesmosyne and Mnemosyne, who are conceived as equals *requiring* each other.[40] Or, more exactly, the two co-exist, but in this co-existence Mnemosyne, the pole of remembering, incorporates Lesmosyne, the pole of forgetting:

> 'Lesmosyne' derives from the same root as 'Lethe' and means exactly the same thing [i.e., forgetfulness]. The sphere of the Muses, which arises from the primordial Goddess Mnemosyne, also has the benefit of Lethe, who makes everything disappear that belongs to the dark side of human existence. It is only both the elements—giving illumination and letting disappear, Mnemosyne and her counter-pole, Lesmosyne—that make up the entire being of the Goddess, whose name comes solely from the positive side of her field of power. This [is a] *union of the opposites under the dominion of the positive*.[41]

"Mnemosyne": if this name is remembered at all today, it is as "the Mother of the Muses," a formal (and formidable) figure who stiffly receives a sceptor from her daughters, the nine muses. Just as there is little that is inspired or inspiring in this traditional depiction, so we moderns are not inspired by this Goddess. We have forgotten, if we ever knew, that it is she who enthuses poets:

> She first makes [poets] inspired, and then through these inspired ones others share in the enthusiasm, and a chain is formed; for the epic poets, all the good ones, have their excellence, not from art, but are inspired, possessed, and thus they utter all these admirable poems. So is it also with the good lyric poets.[42]

As poets are thus enraptured by the instreaming of Mnemosyne, so their "rhapsodes" or recitants are likewise possessed or "held"[43]—and so too are those who listen raptly to their impassioned readings. Altogether, three rings are suspended from the loadstone who is Mnemosyne and who, "through all the series, draws the spirit of men wherever [she] desires, transmitting the attractive force from one into another."[44]

Mnemosyne is a source not only of inspiration but of knowledge as well. It is due to her infusion from above that the poet is able to know how the mythic past really was: how things were in *illud tempore* (that former time). Mnemosyne possesses a *sophia* or wisdom that is in principle omniscient. This is why Hesiod can describe her as knowing "all that has been, all that is, all that will be."[45] Hence the parallel between the poet who is informed by Mnemosyne and the prophet or seer who is guided by Apollo: both poet and prophet know more than they know, more in any case than they could know by their own unaided efforts. Whereas for the prophet this knowing is primarily of the future, for the poet it is mainly of the past—it is a knowing that is, in Heidegger's word, a commemorative "thinking back":

> When it is the name of the Mother of the Muses [i.e., Mnemosyne], 'memory' does not mean just any thought of anything that can be thought. Memory is the gathering and convergence of thought upon what everywhere demands to be thought about first of all. Memory is the gathering of recollection, thinking back . . . Memory, Mother of the Muses—the thinking back to what is to be thought is the source and ground of poesy.[46]

An echo of this view is detectable in the Romantic definition of poetry as "emotion recollected in tranquillity." We need only substitute "knowledge" for "emotion" in this formula of Wordsworth's to be in full accord with the ancient Greek vision of Mnemosyne's unique gift of recollective knowing. It is a striking fact that Mnemosyne is the only deity in any Western pantheon whose name explicitly denotes memory; the Greeks' general veneration of memory finds expression in her status as a Goddess, the highest honor it was within their collective means to bestow.[47]

## VI

The deification of Mnemosyne, and with her of an entire mythical past, could not survive the emergence of philosophy in its specifically Platonic form in the fifth century B.C. For Plato, recollection *(anamnesis)* is less of any particular past—personal or mythical[48]—than of eidetic knowledge previously acquired. The highly personified figure of Mnemosyne disappears; not named in the few myths which are allowed to survive in Platonic dialogues—where myths are designated "second-best" accounts—she is foreign to the austere dialectic that Plato proposes as the unique mode of access to philosophical knowledge. A premise of this dialectic is that the knowledge being sought is *already possessed* by the individual inquirer, who therefore requires no inspired infusions from a presiding Goddess.[49] Even the very highest level of knowledge, *epistēmē* proper, is to be gained, or rather regained, "from within" *(ex hautou)*—from within the individual's already acquired cognitions. The fact that these cognitions have been forgotten makes the process of inquiry recollective in character; the remembering, however, is not undertaken for the sake of reviving past experiences *per se*—not even learning experiences—but only for the sake of bringing knowledge as such back to mind.

Plato represents a critical moment of transition. The exaltation of memory and the attribution to it of divine powers give way to a view of it as an instrument of dialectical inquiry—an indispensable instrument but an instrument nonetheless. Granted, Platonic *anamnesis* does point beyond an individual's finite existence in time; it helps him or her to cohere to a greater whole (namely, the universe of Forms). Nevertheless, the primary role of memory is to aid in bringing inquirers from a state of ignorance to a state of knowledge. Or more exactly, memory itself becomes a function of knowledge: "Mnemosyne, supernatural power, has been interiorized so as to become in man the very faculty of knowing."[50] Important as memory is in this capacity, it is difficult to avoid viewing its growing secularization in Plato's hands as marking a first moment of the decline in its prestige in the early Greek world.

By the very next generation the secularization of memory was complete, thanks to the diligent labors of Aristotle. This transformation was accomplished in three steps. First of all, Aristotle effectively undermines the transcendent aspects of memory—whether these be mythical or metaphysical—by simply ignoring them. He distinguishes two forms of remembering, "memory" and "recollection,"[51] and in so doing he restricts memorial phenomena to a finite, sublunar realm. In this realm remembering yields no eternal verities about Gods or Forms, but only empirical truths about happenings within the compass of an individual's life. Second, Aristotle's account insists on the intimate link between memory and the *personal* past: "Memory," he says laconically, "is of the past,"[52] where it is clear that he means a past which I have experienced or witnessed *in propria persona*. Not only am I constrained to revive this particular past, but I must do so by taking account of the "time-lapse" between its original occurrence and my present remembering; indeed, Aristotle offers a detailed discussion of just how this lapse of time is to be calculated.[53] Third, this time-bound, first-person past comes contained in an *image*. Since images belong exclusively to the perceptual part of the soul, any attempt to link remembering and eidetic knowing in the manner of Plato is placed in question. At the same time, any residual claims concerning memory's liberating influence are undercut, for images are conceived exclusively as *copies* of past experiences, internal replicas resulting from a mechanism of isomorphic imprinting in the soul. Memory, in short, is "the having of an image regarded as a copy of that of which it is an image."[54]

Image, perception, time: these had been the very things that remembering, in Plato's vision, helped us to escape or overcome. Images are the lowest level of experience, belonging to the abject realm of reflections and shadows, *eikasia;* perception is linked with *pistis,* one level upwards in the epistemic ladder; and time is for Plato the "moving likeness of eternity,"[55] an *eikon* of what is cosmically ultimate. Therefore, in construing memory in terms of the imagistic, the perceptual, and the temporal, Aristotle is conceiving it unremittingly under the aspect of *seculae seculorum;* he is bringing it down to earth—down to the domain of the finitely rememberable.

## VII

The finitizing of human memory so evident in Aristotle's seminal treatise *De Memoria et Reminiscentia*—a work whose very brevity may be said to symbolize the diminishment to which memory is submitted in its pages—had for its outcome a dramatic splitting in future considerations of the phenomenon. On the one hand, in keeping with Aristotle's own primary bias, there emerged an entire tradition of what may be called "passivism," in which remembering is reduced to a passive process of registering and storing incoming impressions. The passivist paradigm is still very much with us, whether it takes the form of a naive empiricism or of a sophisticated model of information processing. In fact, since Aristotle's position was first formulated, passivism has been the predominant, and typically the "official" (i.e., the most respected and respectable), view of memory. On the other hand, and as a consequence of this very fact, there has grown up a countervailing tradition of "activism," according to which memory involves the creative transformation of experience rather than its internalized reduplication in images or traces construed as copies. Echoes of activism are detectable in Plato and Aristotle themselves, especially in the shared conviction that recollection takes place as a search[56]—a conviction still resounding in notions of "rehearsal" and "retrieval" as these have arisen in cognitive psychology. But it is not until recent times that full-fledged activist models of memory have been developed: e.g., in Janet's idea of the retroactive transformation of memories by means of their narration; in Freud's praxis-oriented concepts of interpretation and construction in psychoanalysis; in Bartlett's theory of the evolving character of memories as these are reconstructed by various memorial schemata; and in Piaget's similar theory that memories directly reflect changing schemes of accommodation to and assimilation of experience.[57]

The traditions of activism and passivism have remained remarkably independent of each other from Periclean Athens to the present day. Perhaps only in the case of Plato and Freud—those curious *confrères* in so many matters—do we witness a meaningful working alliance between the two traditions. Each thinker likens memory to imprinting (whether this be on a wax tablet or within specifically "psychical" neurones in the brain); but each also comes to adopt a more activist position, evident in Plato's metaphor of searching for memories in an "aviary" of the soul as well as in Freud's stress on recollection in psychoanalysis as a process of active "working through."[58]

Short of these creative compromises, we are left with the extremes of passivism and activism, exemplified respectively by such antithetical figures as Aristotle and Piaget. In between, there is a history of the repression of memory's potentially transformational role. This is not to deny that, along the way, various valiant efforts have been made to give back to memory some of its lost allure—most notably, in the magical and mystical uses of mnemotechnical systems in the Middle Ages and the Renaissance. But Yates, who traces the rise and fall of these efforts so movingly, ends her study abruptly in the seventeenth century. After Leibniz,[59] the transformative powers of memory, when they were noticed at all, were accorded a distinctly marginal position. Much as Platonism survived at critical moments only in the form of a subterranean and subversive Neoplatonism, so the art of memory (itself the sole context in which memory was still venerated) continued only as a hermetic discipline.

When mnemotechnics was revived in the eighteenth century in a nonhermetic form it had become a merely pragmatic discipline, suitable only for aiding in the memorization of masses of facts—for instance, geographical facts of latitude and longitude, which became of special concern in the wake of the explorations of the world undertaken in preceding centuries. In this practical setting, as distant from Athens as could be imagined, memory was valued merely as a means of arranging and preserving facts efficiently. Even if some of the techniques employed in training memories (e.g., the system of places) were identical with those used by the ancients, they were no longer learned for the sake of *sophia* but only to render one's memorial powers more capacious and retentive. The model of human memory as a computer was already beginning to take shape in dim outline, and it is telling that Leibniz was at once the last philosopher to take the art of memory seriously and the first to have envisaged the real possibility of computers in his search for a "universal calculus."

The mathematization of nature so prominent in Galileo and Newton as well as in Leibniz meant that memory, too, would eventually become mathematized, whether in "computer language" or in some other equally formalized symbolism. Before this began to happen in any thorough fashion (and it still has not occurred in a format that can pretend to general acceptance), memory's fate was one of constant disparagement by philosophers. Descartes dismisses memory in the *Meditations* as one of the most dubitable of human capacities: "I convince myself that nothing has ever existed of all that my deceitful memory recalls to me."[60] When the methodological doubt introduced in the first *Meditation* is lifted later in the text, Descartes does not even bother to restore his (and his reader's) confidence in memory by any specific argumentation.[61] In much the same spirit, Spinoza writes off memory in his *Ethics* with the derisive remark that it is "*simply* a certain association of ideas involving the nature of things outside the human body, which association arises in the mind according to the order and association of the modifications *(affectiones)* of the human body."[62]

Hume, arch-empiricist, echoes Spinoza, arch-rationalist, by emphasizing that "the chief exercise of the memory is not to preserve the simple ideas, but their order and position."[63] "Order and association," "order and position":[64] these strikingly similar formulae reinforce a common point. If memory is constrained[65] to depict past events in the precise order in which they occurred, it is thereby compelled to mimic them, to offer an image or copy that is related to them by isomorphic representation of position or form. No less than in Aristotle, indeed even more vehemently in the agile hands of Hume, memory has become a copying machine, a mere replicator of experiences.[66]

This resolutely passivist view of memory is in no way altered by the many *epigoni* of Hume who carried forward the enormously influential movement of associationism.[67] Nor is it overturned even by Kant, formidable critic of Hume in so many other respects. On this matter uncharacteristically timid and traditional, Kant treats memory in *The Critique of Pure Reason* only under the evasive heading of "reproductive imagination," which is held to be strictly empirical in status and to operate by association alone.[68] With Kant, we reach the point at which memory has lost, not only its former attraction and power ("productivity" belongs to imagination alone), but also *its own name*, since the term "memory" does not occur once in the entire *Critique*.[69] Here, *in extremis*, is a deeply defensive denial of memory's importance in human experience, constituting in effect a radical philosophical put-down.

## VIII

Despite the earnest efforts of Bergson and James at the end of the nineteenth century, of Husserl at the beginning of the twentieth century, and of cognitive psychologists in the last few decades, memory has not received anything like the recognition it was given in ancient Greece or in the Renaissance. It is altogether characteristic of the present situation that the most recent extended philosophical treatment of memory in English, Norman Malcolm's *Memory and Mind*,[70] is almost entirely critical and polemical in nature. Malcolm's book tells us very effectively what remembering is *not*, showing up the contradictions and inconsistencies in many current conceptions. It does not, however, tell us in any adequate way what memory *is*—what its consists in, how it operates, what its origins and limits are. Perhaps the time has come for a careful description of the positive features of remembering, its operation in everyday life and in natural contexts. Perhaps, too, on the basis of such a description, we can come to remember memory anew, recapturing some of the depth and vitality which early Greek poets and thinkers appreciated so fully and which we have just as fully forgotten. Such remembering—such re-viewing and re-valuing—does not require a re-divinization of this elusive power; it is not a question of resurrecting Mnemosyne in person or in name. But it is a matter of reinspiring respect for what the Greeks called *mnēmē* and the Romans *memoria*. As *memor* means "mindful," so we need to become re-minded, mindful again, of remembering described in its own structure and situated in its own realm—a realm neither mythical nor mechanical but at one with our ongoing existence and experience. Then memory might reassume its rightful place in the pantheon of essential powers of mind and body, self and other, psyche and world.

By attending patiently to memory's many infrastructures and thereby respecting it as a phenomenon in its own right, we can begin to undo the self-forgetful forgetting that has led to such disrespect for its fields and spacious palaces. Rather than fleeing its dark embrace—its heaviness—and handing it over to machines, we can start to apprehend its intrinsic lightness, its own luminosity. Or more exactly, we may come to realize that its heaviness is not altogether "deplorable" nor its lightness simply "splendid." We may even be able to choose both its lightness *and* its weight, its power to alleviate and illuminate as well as its capacity to embroil and bog down.

If this is indeed a genuine option, we need not envy the beast in its bovine oblivion. Setting aside our own self-inflicted forgetting, we can look forward to remembering in the old manner—and in many new ways as well.

Is there, then, a freedom in remembering, a freedom unknown to animals and machines alike? Perhaps. But we cannot possibly answer this last question until we know more about the character and course of human remembering itself.

# *Part One*
# *Keeping Memory in Mind*

# *I*

# FIRST FORAYS

> It is so difficult to find the beginning. Or better: it is difficult to begin at the beginning. And not try to go further back.
>
> —Wittgenstein, *On Certainty*

## I

It is evident by now that if we are to question such an entrenched tradition of neglecting memory as has just been outlined in the Introduction, a more complete grasp of the phenomenon itself is required. Without this grasp, we run the risk of spinning in free space, speculating as to the right direction in which to move. Like Kant's dove of metaphysics, we shall cleave the air in vain unless our random groping can succeed in finding a more certain way. Just as metaphysics for Kant must become a metaphysics of experience if it is to cease to soar in sheer speculation, so we likewise shall touch earth by following the "secure path" *(sicheren Gang)* provided by ordinary experiences of remembering.[1] It is only by the careful examination of such experiences that we shall be able to discern what is basic and distinctive about memory as we enact it unselfconsciously (and for the most part unwittingly) every day.

Indeed, it is just because remembering is so ubiquitous in our lives—so pervasively present there—that we must make a special effort to excavate it from its deeply embedded position in human experience. It has been claimed by cognitive psychologists that "recent research has made it increasingly clear that there is almost no conscious awareness of perceptual and memorial processes"[2]—at least in their everyday enactments. This conclusion is unduly pessimistic, especially if it is taken as implying that any effort to describe remembering as it occurs consciously is foredoomed to failure. Nevertheless, it does underscore the need for a cautious and detailed assessment of memory—just the sort of assessment which we do not trouble to make in the throes of daily demands. In these throes, we make use of memory unquestioningly, treating it as stock-in-trade, as something ready and reliable. So ready and reliable, indeed, that we do not pause to consider what it is and how it performs—and usually it performs so well that we lose explicit awareness of its very operation within us.

Let us suspend the well-oiled mechanism of memory for a while, plunging into the midst of things so as to capture consciousness of what it is that we do when we remember. In this way we may begin to achieve that "conscious awareness" which psychologists have decried. I shall begin at the only place where one can effectively begin in trying to obtain a full account of the phenomenon—namely, with my own experiences. Since I have attempted to justify this reliance on first-person description elsewhere,[3] I will plunge into the task unabashedly here by citing several instances of my own remembering. These are not proffered as definitive, or even as strictly representative, of my own (much less of others') experiences. They are exemplary only in the sense of providing preliminary samples of memory at work. Rather than a systematic conspectus of types of remembering, they constitute a loosely knit cluster of cases—but a revealing cluster nonetheless.

## II

### Example #1

While putting together the above preparatory reflections, I found myself suddenly remembering a visit to Yosemite National Park which I made at the age of nine or ten in the company of my family. We had come over to Yosemite from San Francisco, and my expectations were very keen as we approached the park in our car. My first distinct recollection is of a breathtakingly panoramic vista of the park from a roadside viewing point. I can recall rushing from the car (a green Buick?) over very dry and dusty ground to look out at the valley below. (I also now recall a photograph of myself and my sister taken at precisely this point—a photograph displayed for a number of years afterward on my mother's dressing table. It showed us two children eagerly occupying the foreground while Yosemite beckoned in the background through pine trees.) Concerning what followed this entry to the park, my memory is discontinuous and yields only several seemingly isolated episodes, presenting themselves in no definite order. First, there is a view from below of the "Dome" (is this the correct name?), accompanied by a feeling of awe at viewing the massive protuberance. (This memory is suddenly interspersed with a much more recent memory of hearing about a group of four or five mountain climbers who had scaled the face of the formation.) Second, there emerges a vague image of the cabin where we had spent the night (or nights—I do not recall how long we stayed in Yosemite). Even in the absence of definite images, I feel certain that the cabin itself was situated low in the valley, was surrounded by fir trees and near a stream, and was a place where bears might roam (this last thought mixing fascination with fear). Third, I have a comparatively distinct recollection of approaching and viewing the great waterfall in the park—of running ahead of my parents and sister along the path of approach and suddenly being confronted by the cascading fall in all its breathtaking height and power. I recall being overwhelmed and standing staring at it for some time, until my family finally caught up with me. And that is all. Following this last scene there is a decided fading-out, and I can remember nothing more—not even the departure from Yosemite, a departure which I must have found difficult after such an exhilarating experience there.

REMARKS

(1) What stands out first of all is the contrast between the perspicuousness of a number of parts of this memory—e.g., the initial scene of first viewing Yosemite, the appearance of the "Dome," the spectacle of the waterfall—and the equally striking indefiniteness of so much else in the same memory. This indefiniteness extends to at least four different parts of its content: place (e.g., the vaguely located and unspecified overnight resting place); time (how long the visit lasted; what my exact age was when it occurred); objects (the make and color of the family car; the clothes I wore); names (the proper name of the "Dome" or of the waterfall); and sounds (e.g., that of the crashing waterfall).

(2) It is to be noticed that such indefinitenesses are not so radical as to vitiate the memory altogether; with the possible exception of the overnight site, they all possess some minimal determinacy. I was somewhere between nine and eleven years old, since I am certain that the trip took place in the period 1948–1950; and I am reasonably sure that the trip occurred in July or August, since my family always vacationed in one of these two months. Similarly, my guess that the family car was a green Buick is based on other memories of our having such a car at approximately that period of time. And I can safely conjecture that the visit to Yosemite was less than a week and more than a day in duration when I think of other comparable visits while on vacation. Notice that in each of these cases the probable range of indefiniteness is established by recourse to material not contained in the memory itself—most typically, to *other memories* from the same general period of my life—and to simple inductive and deductive modes of inference (inductive in the case of the probable length of the visit; deductive in the case of the year of the visit, since I know that it *could not* have occurred before 1948 or after 1950, when distinctly different vacations, explicitly remembered now, were undertaken). Of course, in the act of remembering itself I did not choose to employ these reasoning procedures, nor was I even aware of their operation. I simply remembered objects and events as being located at such a place and at such a time, and as having such and such a character—without yet considering the probability or verifiability of these claims.

(3) There was another, and this time wholly intrinsic, role of other memories within my remembering of the visit to Yosemite. At two points, a quite

differently based memory intervened: that of the photograph taken at the time of the visit and prominently displayed later, and that of hearing about a recent scaling of Half Dome (such is its correct name). Each of these intersecting memories played a distinctive, though mostly unnoticed, role in my primary act of remembering. The dramatic news story of the scaling underscored, at the moment of remembering, the precipitous and sheer structure of Half Dome which had so impressed me at the time of my first seeing it; I suspect it also linked up with a wish or fantasy of climbing it myself, which I may have had at the time, though I don't remember that at present. The memory of the photograph, in contrast, had the effect of confirming and fixing the moment of approach to Yosemite and thus of underlining my excited anticipations. Indeed, one might venture that the photograph played a very special and complex role in my experience. Not only did it offer documentary proof of the historical fact of the particular moment in question, but it itself very likely contributed to the survival of my own recollection. Seeing the photograph on my mother's dressing table in later years regularly reminded me of the episode photographed and thus of the visit as a whole. The photograph and its memory may have become emblematic of the trip to Yosemite, so much so that I can now recall relatively few other incidents that took place after the photographing of that first scene.

(4) The sense of *myself* in this recollection is somewhat peculiar. On the one hand, I have a very clear sense of my own place and role, of being present and active in the first scene of the memory—of myself scrambling to get a view of the long-awaited valley. This sense of self-presence was perhaps again strengthened by the photograph's having been taken at just this point, since the iconic image of myself in the photograph bespeaks the fact of my having been personally present at the initial scene. On the other hand, my felt presence in the other remembered scenes was considerably diminished in comparison. I was always *there*, somehow *in* the remembered scene, and never wholly absent from it; but I was there in a curiously diluted and dispersed form: faceless and almost bodiless, a mere onlooker who observes not himself but what is spread before him in nature.[4]

(5) My sense of *other persons* in such a memory is closely related to my sense of self-presence. My sister has a pronounced presence in the memory of the first scene—no doubt aided once more by the photograph. But after this she fades from focus almost entirely. So do my parents, although I have an attenuated sense of their co-presence with me and my sister in the same initial scene. They are implicated as our spectators or on-lookers, just as, in now remembering that unrepeatable moment, I look onto all four of us together.

(6) "Looking" is the appropriate term here, since the memory in question presents itself in almost entirely *visual* terms. I do not "hear" again the talk that must have attended the taking of the photograph, the expressions of awe that I and the other members of my family probably emitted at various

points during the visit, or even the deafening roar of the waterfall. All is silent—so silent as to be somewhat eery, otherworldly, a world apart. The visual imagery itself is discontinuous and inconsistent, sometimes bright (though not brilliant) and delineated (though not as fully delineated as objects in a comparably complicated perceived scene). But some of the images are very dim, to the point of lacking color, and shapeless, as if lacking contour and even depth. The overall effect is of a moving *montage* of visual contrasts.

(7) The temporality of the recollection is also peculiar, and seems to consist of three quite diverse components. First, the memory exhibits an inbuilt successiveness as its scenes unfold with a certain rhythmic regularity. The regularity is pronounced enough for the same succession to appear on re-rememberings—and yet not strong enough for me to be certain that the order of succession in the memory exactly corresponds to the order in which the original events took place. Did I really gaze upon Half Dome *before* seeing the waterfall? Probably—since Half Dome is so prominent a feature of Yosemite valley. But all that I know for certain is that *within my memory* there is a self-regulated progression from the Dome scene to the waterfall scene. Second, while thus moving *along* in a quasi-linear fashion, the memory also seems to draw me *in*. I sense that I am, in some inexplicable way, re-entering the past, being taken up by it, even becoming, to some degree, at one with it: temporality here is not chronological or linear but a matter of absorption in a measureless depth. Third, I nevertheless retain a distinct sense of being still anchored in the present—precisely the present of the act of recollecting itself. I am now remembering this sequence of past scenes, and I do so from a temporal vantage point that does not belong to these scenes themselves. Here I sense the enormous gulf between the present moment of remembering and the scenes remembered: these latter almost seem to belong to another life and certainly to another part of my life.

(8) The emotional tonality of this memory deserves brief mention. Throughout the remembering there was a sense of muted exhilaration at having been in such a magnificent setting. This exhilaration modulated into awe when I was facing Half Dome and the waterfall in memory. Also felt was the mounting excitement of the first scene, an excitement fueled by expectations of what was to come as the park was entered. I notice that it is difficult to determine exactly where such emotion as originally experienced ends and where the same emotion as now felt-in-the-remembering begins, though I am convinced that the former is more acute in tenor and less worked through. On the other hand, a faint nostalgia, a subtle mixture of longing and pleasure, arises; it attaches itself less to the elapsed contents of the memory than to the present experience of remembering, lending it a poignant if subdued character.

(9) The nostalgia and poignancy no doubt reflect the origin of the memory in childhood and in a particularly pleasant moment of childhood at that. It is

worth noting how spontaneously I reverted to this particular memory as a first example—as if to say "here is a paradigm for other memories, a memory of memories!" Despite the ambiguous and problematic nature of such a memory—as revealed, for instance, in its temporality and emotionality—it seems capable of assuming a privileged position among all the myriad memories accessible to me at a given moment. What is it about this portion of the past that makes it such a suitable and tempting subject for recollection?

### Example #2

A memory of a relatively recent event comes to mind. I recall going to the movie *Small Change* a few weeks ago—exactly when, I am not certain. After dinner nearby at Clark's, my two young children, my wife, and I had walked briskly over to the Lincoln Theater, stopping briefly at a paperback bookstore on the way. Anticipating a large crowd, we arrived early and were among the first to purchase tickets. There ensued a wait that seemed much longer than the ten or fifteen minutes it actually was. The children were especially restive and had difficulty staying in the line that had formed—Erin attempting some gymnastic tricks on the guardrail by the entrance, Eric looking at the posted list of coming attractions. Finally the doors were flung open, and we entered at the head of what was, by then, a considerable line. Once inside, we sought seats approximately in the middle of the theater, settled there, and interchanged positions a couple of times to adjust to the height of those sitting in front of us. The lights dimmed, and *Small Change* began directly. (Or was there not a short feature first?—I cannot say for sure.) The film was in French, with English subtitles. I have only a vague recollection of the spoken words; in fact, I cannot remember any single word or phrase, though I certainly remember the characters *as speaking*. The same indefiniteness applies to the subtitles, at which I furtively glanced when unable to follow the French. Of the music in the film I have no memory at all—indeed, not just of *what* it was but *whether* there was any music at all. In contrast with this, I retain a very vivid visual image of the opening scene, in which a stream of school children are viewed rushing home, seemingly in a downhill direction all the way. Two other scenes also stand out in my present recollection: an infant's fall from the window of a high-rise apartment (the twenty-nineth floor?) and the male teacher (whose name, along with all others in the film, I have forgotten) lecturing passionately to his class about child-abuse. Interspersed between these scenes is a medley of less vividly recalled episodes, ranging from fairly distinct (the actions of a child-abusing mother) to quite indistinct (e.g., children's recitations in the classroom). While I am recollecting this uneven and incomplete sequence of filmic incidents, I find myself at the same time remembering my own children's ongoing reactions to the film. I do not remember their behavior in detail but only as a kind of generalized response consisting of laughing, whispered questions, outright comments, and the like. These reactions are as intrinsic to the memory as is the unfolding of the film itself; so too is the mixture of pleasure and exasperation which I felt in being located, as it were, *between* children and film. Suddenly my memory of *Small Change* comes to an end: the lights go up, and we leave through a side exit near us, overhearing expressions of amusement and satisfaction from those around us as we walk out into the night.

REMARKS

(1) Notice, to begin with, how this memory comes structured into several major episodes—meeting for dinner; waiting to get into the theater; watching the film (itself subdivided into a discontinuous series of scenes); leaving the theater. These episodes serve both as points of punctuation (as places of greatest interest or stress) and as interconnected components of the memory as a narratized whole. Nevertheless, the details remain indefinite in many respects, e.g., as to just when I saw the film, the role of music in it, the precise content of my children's remarks, etc.

(2) It is evident that the nature of this indefiniteness differs significantly from that found in the Yosemite memory. Where in the latter instance, the exact year and month were in doubt, now it is the exact day that is in question: the recentness of the experience has narrowed the range of indefiniteness as to its date. Moreover, unlike the memory of Yosemite, in this new memory a number of intermediate incidents serve to bridge the gaps between the major events recalled and thus make what was remembered a more continuous whole. The effect of this increased continuity is that the main episodes are somewhat less dominant; the felt "surface" of the memory is smoother and gives rise to an account that, having fewer lacunae, is significantly closer to a continuous narration or retelling. In addition, the greater availability of detail in the *Small Change* memory manifests itself in an augmented describability of any given incident or episode. The dinner just before the movie, for example, could have been set forth in considerably more detail: what was eaten, in what order, what the subject of conversation was, which other customers were present, etc. Where the detail given in my actual description above is detail *in extenso*—drawing together diverse parts of the memory—the detail recalled in this description is detail *in pleno,* that is, detail that deepens the high points of cursory recollection.

(3) One of the most revealing features of this memorial experience is that of "memory-within-memory." By this I mean that the memory as a whole includes a portion, i.e., that occupied by the movie, which could very well be remembered alone and in isolation from the rest of the experience. Frequently, in fact, we speak of "remembering a movie" in such a way as to mean a memory of the movie *by itself,* that is, what we perceived on the screen in isolation from associated experiences of viewing it, going to see it

in the first place, etc. This strict memory of the movie itself is highly developed in film critics and film buffs, to the point that a mere mention of a title is capable of triggering a quite intact and accurate recollection of an entire sequence of scenes. (In my case, I fell far short of such full recollection.) Often, however, the memory of the movie (whether partial or full) will be embedded within a more encompassing memory that includes details not directly related to the movie itself. This occurs in the memory under examination—which exhibits the further feature of embedding a "movie-within-the-movie" within the memory as a whole.[5] Such compounding and double compounding of memory components presents no problem in principle, for it signifies only that within a given remembered experience there may be parts (and parts of parts) that can be recalled separately and without reference to the original experience in which they were situated.

(4) What is more problematic, however, is the fact that during the movie portion of my memory there was, in addition to a memory of the film as such and of my silent experiencing of it, a distinct memory of my children reacting to the movie by speech and gestures. The result is what we may call a "two-track" memory, a memory with two foci or epicenters. Does this mean that I have two different, but simultaneous, memories—or a single, but internally bifurcated, memory? In my original description I said that the two centers of attention arose "at the same time." Nonetheless, I am not able to focus, *with exactly equal concentration,* on the two events in remembering them. Both are intrinsic and valid components of my recollection—to this extent we need not resort to two rememberings—yet one must be peripheral if the other is central to my attention and vice-versa. The two-track, and theoretically the n-track, character of remembering is therefore found in its capacity to be multiply, though unequally, focused within a given segment or part.

(5) Another kind of multiplicity is also inherent in this instance of remembering. Such multiplicity derives from the fact that I have attended many movies in the same Lincoln Theater in which I viewed *Small Change*. It is difficult to believe that my previous viewings did not influence my present remembering in some fashion. In particular, they have so familiarized me with this theater and with viewing films in it that my remembering of a film seen recently there did not need to include any reference to the theater itself, its interior or exterior, or to the way it feels to be seated inside while watching a movie there. All of this circumambient detail was taken for granted; it is not *un-remembered* or forgotten, but rather so pervasively certain that it does not have to be explicitly represented in the manifest content of my present memory, thereby no doubt serving interests of economy and selectivity.

(6) Finally, I want to consider a variation on the above-reported experience, namely, that I remembered this experience of remembering itself a day after the remembrance originally occurred. My recollection of going to

the movie occurred yesterday. Today, I can remember that experience of remembering. Not only is such remembering of remembering possible, but the result is curiously comparable to what was just termed the "two-track" effect of contrasting but concurrent features within a given memory. On the one hand, I find that I can indeed call back the original memory as such—that is, the very same mnemonic content as I first described it—but that this content is now present to my mind in a considerably more condensed or schematic form. Only the primary episodes of the original experience come back to mind, e.g., standing in line, being seated in the theater, a few major scenes from the film. Even these episodes appear in such a scanty form that I am tempted to say that I am presenting myself with a *digest* of the memory—as if my mind were declaring: "no need to run through all of this memory in detail again; here is a convenient summary of the most crucial contents." On the other hand, there is now, a day later, an entirely *new* phenomenon, namely, a memory specifically of my yesterday's activity of remembering. This new memory does not force itself on me; it is an essential possibility, something that I can activate if I so wish. If I do, I suddenly have an image of myself at my desk, bent over a yellow legal pad on which I am writing in rapt absorption. This image, which does not develop, is accompanied by the half-articulate thought "myself-recounting-a-recent-memory." There is something peremptory and programmatic about this last remembering. Moreover, I soon discover that I cannot effect the remembering proper and the re-remembering simultaneously: *either* I remember myself remembering yesterday *or* I remember the memory that I remembered at that time.

### Example #3

I am discussing with my neighbor the possibility of having a water softener installed in my house. Suddenly the single word "Culligan" comes to mind. I immediately realize that this is the brand name of the water softener that was situated in the basement of my childhood home. Along with this instantaneous recognition, and persisting for a few moments afterward, come very indistinct images of that basement and of a Culligan service truck.

#### REMARKS

The very brevity of this example lends itself to a thorough description of its structure, a structure which is at the same time quite lacunary.

(1) Its mode of emergence is striking. The word "Culligan" and the memory-images associated with it arose not just spontaneously—i.e., without effort or rehearsal, as in the previous two instances—but suddenly. So suddenly in fact that it took me quite by surprise, finding me unprepared for this semi-startling event. Beyond the suddenness, what contributed to the sense of being startled was the fact that I had not consciously thought of the proper name "Culligan" or of the water softener in my boyhood home for a very long time—certainly not since the home was sold, which was some

twelve years ago. Here is a case of a memory that, deriving from a fairly distant past period, has lacked direct reinforcement or repetition in the interval between that period and the present.

(2) Equally striking were the duration and development of this momentary memory itself. It was indeed *so* momentary that there was very little sense of its unfolding as such. The word "Culligan" seemed to disappear almost as soon as it appeared. Even the images that accompanied it persisted so briefly as to be virtually untrackable. In neither case was there any sense of *sequence*, of one incident or episode leading to another as in the first two memories above. In fact, there were no incidents or episodes at all, nor was there anything like the consecutiveness characterizing memories that have a quasi-narrative structure.

(3) Also missing altogether was any felt *self-presence*, any sense that I was myself somehow involved in the content of the memory. Of course, my presence was presupposed insofar as I must have perceived the water softener in my childhood home, doubtlessly on many occasions. But there was not the slightest vestige of myself-as-previous-perceiver in the memory's consciously entertained content. Nor were other persons present in this content: they too had vanished, leaving an utterly personless presentation of the past.

(4) What *was* present, dominating this content, was the word "Culligan." This word stands out, especially in contrast with the mostly muted role of language in the previous examples. Now language predominates, and it does so in a highly specified form. The fact that "Culligan" is a proper name, the most particular and rigidly designating of noun forms, takes this specificity to its limit: there is (so far as one may reasonably guess) only *one* brand of water softener called "Culligan." By the same token, to remember precisely this word is itself the most economical and direct way of referring to the object of this memory, namely, the actual water softener in my parents' basement. For in remembering "Culligan," I am remembering not only the word but what it stands for—or more exactly, the word-as-standing-in-for the very thing which it designates. *The memory constituted by "Culligan" is a memory mainly composed of one word, one thing: one word-thing.*[6]

(5) "Mainly," but not entirely so composed. For my memory, one-worded and transitory as it was, also included an imagistic component. The imagery was visual—as indeed the word was too.[7] "Visual" seems almost too strong, since the two images were so radically indistinct. The first was identifiably of a basement, though I could not precisely identify any details within the basement because of its shadowy nature. The second was still more diffuse: so diffuse that I could not say for sure that it was of the "Culligan truck," as I tended to suppose. It might also—with equal plausibility and in the absence of definitive evidence to the contrary—have been of the "Culligan man" who actually serviced the water softener. It is due to just such imprecision that both images were able to play a framing role; they provided a nebulous

setting within which the much more distinct word-thing "Culligan" could stand out. At the same time, I suspect that it is also due to their indistinctness that they seemed to linger slightly longer in my memory, as if calling for a scrutiny that might overcome their very vagueness.

(6) There is a last noteworthy feature of this memory experience. This is its direct precipitation by the immediately surrounding situation—a situation that is much more intrinsically involved in the remembering than in the preceding two cases. Each of those arose from a largely indifferent context—in each instance idle musing at my desk. But in the present case I was in the midst of discussing water softeners when I so abruptly and swiftly recalled the water softener of my youth. Instead of unfolding before me on its own (an unfolding that may itself be a function of the very lack of specific context),[8] it seemed by its very condensed and cursory quality to be a mere response to the ongoing discussion—to be its momentary addendum or appendage, a kind of comment on it. Hence its wholly involuntary character and its suddenness. Hence too its lack of detailed content or continuous development as well as its conspicuous datelessness. It served more as an interjection, a precipitous exclamation, than as a revival or scanning of the past: if it was *from* the past, it did not seem to be *of* the past in any sustained or sustainable manner.

## Example #4

I was just—a moment ago—sipping a cup of tea and eating a piece of fruitbread. I now remember this event as if it were still present. The taste of the tea seems to be still in my mouth; it is slightly astringent and tempered only by the sugar I had put into it. Its smell simultaneously pervades my nose. Also, my very gulping—both the feel within my mouth and throat and the dim internal sound—is a distinctly lingering presence. The flavor of blackberries in the fruitbread and the bread's familiar texture are just as present, though in a somewhat more muted form. At the same time, I am aware of the peculiar wailing sound of a garbage truck crushing its new load of garbage somewhere beneath my tower office. And a dim visual impression of my desk, the tea cup, and the fruitbread in a plastic bag stays on as I write these words.

### REMARKS

(1) This memory is still less of the past than was the case in the last example. Indeed, we may even wonder if its content stems from the past in any strict sense. The experience remembered was not only closely juxtaposed to my act of remembering (the lapse of time between the two was no more than one minute) but appeared to *persist* into the very act of remembrance—into the present in which remembering was taking place. There was no sense of revival or retrieval, since the remembered content was *already* available to my apprehension. Or more exactly, *still* available, for the experi-

ence had never faded fully from view. If it was past, it was part of a past which was continuous with the new present of the activity of remembering: just as the latter was thereby deepened, so the former was correspondingly lengthened.

(2) In contrast with all of the experiences so far reported, which have been predominately visual and secondarily verbal, this experience was genuinely *synesthetic*, involving all of the primary senses. Not only was there *sight* (of my desk and a few objects on it), but *taste* (of the tea and the fruitbread), *touch* (in relation to the texture of the bread and the feel of the tea in my mouth), *smell* (a faint aroma of the tea in my nostrils), and *hearing* (both internal and external: my gulping and the garbage truck). What is most striking in this pluri-sensorial situation is that all of these sensory modalities were operative together. Each had its own distinctiveness and clarity, and none was markedly subordinate to the others. Indeed, if any single modality was slightly subordinate, it was the visual one: I thought of the visual arrangement last, and it contained only a few barely sketched items. Thus the usual preeminence of vision in long-term memory—as exhibited in the way in which the euphonious word "Culligan" became almost entirely a visual phenomenon upon recollection—is supplanted and even reversed in this instance, where all sensory modalities are given expression.

(3) What we witness here, then, is a case of genuinely *multi-modal remembering*. Whereas previously, two sensory modes (i.e., visual and verbal) had presented themselves in a single memory and were not fully simultaneous, now, several are present at once. Moreover, at least three of these are experienced as strictly simultaneous with one another: the taste, smell, and touch sensations caused by the tea. These sensations do not form the content of separate memories but present themselves as components of one and the same memory. Within this memory, they are inseparable but distinguishable from each other.

(4) Notably absent from this experience are any of the emotions or moods that so frequently attach themselves to long-term remembering: nostalgia, remorse, or even the peculiar pleasure that characterized two of the examples described earlier. There was a certain *sensation* of pleasure which lingered from the agreeable taste of the tea and fruitbread, but this is not to be confused with the special pleasure of recalling this taste at a subsequent point. Pleasure *at* tasting is not at all the same pleasure as pleasure *in* remembering this tasting, even though the former can itself be remembered *with* pleasure.

(5) It should be stressed that an example such as this would not normally be an object of attention or description; in fact, it might not even be considered a case of remembering at all! This experience occurs so frequently and yet so unobtrusively that we tend to pass it over as inconsequential or as the mere "rearward portion of the present space of time."[9] But when we do attend to it, we realize that it is an essential and distinctive form of

remembering—"primary memory," as psychologists from James to contemporary researchers have called it.[10] We shall return to this point in more detail in chapter 3. For now it is sufficient to note that the mere fact that a description of the present example was possible—and that it included features not evident in previous descriptions—bears out the importance of regarding this kind of remembering as worthy of further study.

### Example #5

I have been talking on the telephone with an acquaintance. We agree to meet at my office before going to lunch together. He asks, "What is the number on your office door?" Without hesitation I answer "902."

REMARKS

(1) This banal example, of which there are many equivalents in everyday life, nevertheless illustrates a fundamental form in which remembering often occurs. Every time we remember that $6 \times 8 = 48$, our home address, our ages, our social security numbers, and so on indefinitely, we enact such remembering of basic information. The acquisition of this information typically arises from sheer repetition, as in the rote memorizing of multiplication tables or the routine of providing our social security number. In the present instance, I learned my office number through simple habituation; I have resided there for five years and thus have perceived "902" innumerable times on entering; and I have given this same number to others on countless occasions. The effect of such repetition is to make "902" a quasi-permanent part of my empirical knowledge. Even should I leave this office, I suspect that I will not lose this item of information for quite some time.

(2) It is just because such an item has been so fully acquired and so thoroughly sedimented into my present stock of knowledge that I retrieve it so effortlessly and spontaneously. Like my own name, albeit to a lesser degree, it has become part of my memorial repertoire—so much a part that I need not search for it, or reflect upon it, when asked to specify it. The result is a peculiar *emptiness* in the experience of recalling it. When someone inquires about my office, I come up with the correct identification immediately: "902" springs to mind so unfailingly that there is no sense of residuum or unfulfillment. The number fills my mind so completely as to leave it blank in other regards, i.e., with respect to emotion, sense of suspense, etc. The very success of such a cut-and-dried case as this renders otiose various concomitant or contextual factors that might otherwise be prominently present—e.g., a certain melancholic mood I experience in remembering my boarding school days.

(3) If we compare the present example with the last two, we notice that all three arose instantaneously and in an unsolicited fashion. Moreover, in particular contrast with the first two examples, there was in the last instance no further development of the initial presentation—no sequel, however

brief or inconsequential. But the instance of "902" is to be distinguished from that of "Culligan" and of my tea-tasting by the fact that, unlike these two, it has no particular point of anchorage in the past. My memory of tea-tasting was based on a particular experience of the moment before; and, although "Culligan" was acquired by repetition, that memory had a firm base in a fully determinate past period in my life which it even symbolized in part. "902" may someday gain the same status—perhaps by signifying my years of teaching in a particular place—but at present it has the very different status of being an item of information about my current environment, an environment which is not yet fixed and finished in the manner of my childhood years. Thus there is a peculiar *lack of discrete referentiality to the past* in the memory of "902," which in this respect (though perhaps only in this respect) resembles the memory of a recurrent fantasy whose origin we cannot determine: both seem to float upon a sea of temporal indifference.

## Example #6

For the first time in over a year I enter a pair of connecting rooms housing philosophy books. It is late in the evening; no one else is present. Suddenly I am overcome by memories of former visits to these rooms situated high in the stacks of Sterling Library and overlooking the university below. These memories are not wholly distinct from each other and they seem to gravitate around a central memory of having worked on an article in this very place in evenings several summers ago. I try to think of which article I was writing then and which summer it was. The latter is easily inferred from the fact that my evening vigils in the library took place during the only summer in which I lived in New Haven near the library itself: 1969. But it proves more difficult to determine which article I was working on, since I was writing several closely related essays at that time. By process of elimination this narrows the field to two or three candidates, and I have a strong suspicion, though no strong conviction, that the article in question was entitled "Man, Self, and Truth." As if to confirm this hunch, a quite explicit memory of studying Brentano's *The True and the Evident*—of sitting at a certain table in this very room and taking notes on Brentano's book—comes suddenly to mind, and I feel reassured that my guess is correct.

REMARKS

(1) This is a sample of what we might call a place memory.[11] It is very strictly tied to a particular place, and it emerged only when I returned to that very place. Thus it is at once a memory *of* a given place (as was the Yosemite memory) and a memory occurring *in* that place (which was not the case with the Yosemite memory). This place, in other words, evoked memories of itself—of one and the same place as frequented at various times. The result is a sense of stability and self-replication in the experience; the two rooms are somehow doubly present: present as perceived and

present as remembered, but in each case the selfsame rooms. Reinforcing this perduring character of the experience is the impression that by merely being back in these rooms I had gone *halfway to meet* memories of them. This is more than a matter of bare recognition, which could have been possible by simply looking at a photograph. It is rather a situation in which my actual revisiting of the physical rooms themselves was itself revisited by memories of previous visitings. The latter would not, I think, have made the impact they did unless I had been bodily present there.

(2) A curious and yet characteristic feature of this experience is the arousal of a number of memories that were fused with one another in an amorphous mass. Since they did not present themselves as separate memories, it is convenient to think of them as "semi-memories." I call them this merely on the basis that, while they do make reference to former experiences in the rooms in question, they do so only by conveying fragmentary details of these experiences (e.g., "once helping to shelve books here," "being unable to find a copy of some journal here," "being frustrated by the others who were talking here," etc., none of which presents itself as a complete memory in itself). What is most striking about such semi-memories is not their occurrence as such but the way in which they merge to form an overall sense of having-been-in-these-rooms-before-on-many-occasions. Diffuse as it is, this is a genuine mnemonic experience. It is the sort of experience we have whenever we say that the past returns to haunt us in a certain place, pervading the present in a somewhat insidious and less than wholly definite form.

(3) It was just such a pervasive, unpinpointed past that gave my remembering its nostalgic cast on this occasion. I was not simply remembering for the sake of remembering, much less for any utilitarian purpose. I was quite overcome, emotionally moved, by these *revenants* of a comparatively calm and productive period of my past. Their very return signified to me that this period no longer existed, and was not likely to be repeated in the future. Although I was indeed back in the same place, I could not work there again as I had once done—in carefree and yet committed abandon, heedless of the uncertain future ahead. My nostalgia reflected this implicit knowledge of unrepeatability, the conviction of not being able to recapture this portion of the past fully: the recognition that it can be represented, but not repeated. The very flooding back of these memories brings with it the tacit acknowledgment that the experiences they recapture are unique and not to be undergone again as such. Hence my nostalgia: it is just insofar as they are unrepeatable that these remembered times beckon so movingly and powerfully to me in the present.

(4) In contradistinction to the loose aura of miscellaneous semi-memories discussed just above was the much more distinct memory of having worked on a specific article in the library rooms. This latter memory emerged as a *focus memorious* around which the vaguer memories circulated. It seemed

at once the most important and the best organized of everything that I remembered, as if it were somehow the prototype of all my memories of these rooms. It possessed a significance and durability that the others lacked. It conveyed, in short, the single most memorable experience undergone in that particular place and, as such, was paradigmatic of my other experiences there.

(5) Yet as I first received it, even this memory was by no means fully determinate in detail. I could discern only its general format, i.e., working-on-an-article-in-these-rooms. As a consequence, I had to search out further specification of it. At first, I resorted to inference: "it *must have been* in the summer of 1969 *because*"; and "it was certainly one of three or so articles which I was writing at that time." Not only did these inferences seem valid in themselves, but they provided the setting for the sudden return of the confirming memory that I had studied Brentano's *The True and the Evident* in these rooms at that time. This supported my hunch that I was working on "Man, Self, and Truth" because (and here was a final, seemingly certain inference) this latter article, in fact, discusses Brentano's notion of truth. The result was that my central memory, thus filled out, became even more pivotal in my mind—so much so that as I reflect upon it now, several hours after the initial memory report was written, it still further obscures the peripheral memories. The very fact of my having searched for additional specification, and then having found it, acted to accentuate this particular memory, giving it a privileged position in relation to the other memories, which were vaguely specified to begin with and not further specified in the course of remembering.

The foregoing six samples of my recent remembering help us to appreciate at once the diversity and the mystery of memory. My mere "random groping" has not yet indicated anything like the "secure path" of reliable insight into the macrostructure of remembering. But it has revealed a phenomenon that proliferates before our very eyes, engendering many species with no single supreme genus. On close inspection, moreover, each of these species shows itself to have intrinsic peculiarities, microstructures that are paradoxical (e.g., memories-within-memories) or at least puzzling (e.g., semimemories). The mystery only deepens when we realize that we have few if any clues to the bodily basis of multisensory memories, or when we ponder the fact that the past need not be dated—or perhaps even be dateable—to be remembered. Clichés about "remembering the past" begin to sound hollow when we become aware that we can remember something even when the "past" remembered is not significantly separated from the present in which we are remembering; indeed, is immanent in it. In other words, the flora and fauna of remembering which we have encountered even in this cursory first engagement manifest themselves as quite exotic, despite the fact that they are drawn from the quotidian consciousness of one "approximately normal"[12] rememberer. There is no need to resort to the exceptional when the very memories that we are most familiar with and take most for granted involve an unsuspected complexity and, on this very basis, possess an uncommon interest. What more can we learn from such memories? To answer this question, we must move from a first immersion to an analysis of eidetic, structurally inherent, features.

# *II*

# EIDETIC FEATURES

Let us consider which basic traits of remembering emerge from the brief tour of examples which we have just taken. I shall single out a series of these traits for mention and divide them into primary and secondary. Just as the examples themselves do not pretend to comprise anything like a comprehensive survey of remembering—crucial additions will be made in Parts Two and Three—so the traits discussed below are not intended to illuminate human memory in its entirety. They are designed instead to convey certain of its fundamental features as these arise in a first appreciation of its multiplex and sinuous structure.

## I

## Primary Traits

By this designation I mean those traits of certain forms of remembering that are either always in fact present or are at least potentially present on many occasions. For reasons that will become apparent as I proceed, I shall group these traits into pairs.

### SEARCH/DISPLAY

"Search" refers to a number of allied moves or procedures which are employed in the effort to remember something better or just to remember it in the first place. As Aristotle says, "recollection is a search in something bodily for an image."[1] Searching is closely correlated with forgetting, but the scope of the searched-for is broader than that of the forgotten. For we can search out experiences or aspects of experiences that we have not so much forgotten as simply allowed to become marginal—"out of thought but *not* out of mind." A case in point was my failure to recall the musical soundtrack of *Small Change*. I searched my memory in vain, and yet I would not want to say that I had ever forgotten the music: I had never paid any special attention to it in the first place.[2] In other cases, however, there is genuine forgetting and the corresponding search is then more focused, more protracted, and more prone to rely on inference (as happened in my experience in the philosophy library).

"Display" alludes to an actually recovered memory. It may occur at the end of a search, in its midst (as with the Brentano memory), or in the absence of any search at all. Several of my foregoing examples involved displays that arose of their own accord, without any specific solicitation. I think here of the quite sudden appearance of "Culligan" or of the equally sudden but less surprising emergence of "902." Even such comparatively prolonged cases as those found in examples #1 and #2 displayed their content spontaneously and without bidding.

It is important to stress that search and display may occur within the same mnemonic experience—as occurred in example #6, which arose unprompted, led to a search, and ended with a resolution of this search by the unexpected intervention of a pertinent display. It also needs emphasizing that the display itself does not have to be visual. It may be multisensory, as was evident in my tea-tasting memory. And it may even be nonsensory, as became clear in the case of remembering "902." Indeed, it may be at once sensory *and* nonsensory—as in "Culligan," which was both verbal and visual at once. The polymorphous character of mnemonic displays is something that we shall have to explore at greater length.[3]

### ENCAPSULMENT/EXPANSION

Whereas search and display tend to follow and replace one another in remembering—to be alternatives to each other—the members of this new pair of terms tend to complement and match each other. "Encapsulment" is the more striking of the two traits and is found in many forms, of which only four will be mentioned here. First, there is an intrascenic encapsulment—for instance, when I remembered a movie within a movie in the case of *Small Change*. I remembered both films, and one precisely as belonging to the very content of the other. Such emboîtement, however, is relatively rare in remembering; it depends on the presence of a self-representing medium such as film, which can convey versions of itself on its own terms. Second, an encapsulation by amorphous amassment of previous experiences of a similar kind was present by implication in the same memory (i.e., my former visits to the Lincoln Theater) and explicitly in the philosophy library memory (where I recalled fragments of earlier experiences). Third, and closely related to this last mode of encapsulment, is emblematic encapsulation, in which a single memory comes to stand surety for a series of other less well-defined memories. I have in mind here the way in which the verbal-visual display "Culligan" condensed a whole group of unretrieved (and yet in principle retrievable) memories of a water softener in my boyhood home. Finally, encapsulment may occur by *re*-remembering, as when I recalled the memory of seeing *Small Change* the day after first having it. Such remembering of a memory is reiterable several times over: we can remember ourselves remembering . . . ourselves remembering. This reiterability is not realizable so fully or so easily in other mental acts, and its strictly self-enclosing character is the most encompassing encapsulation of which remembering is capable.

"Expansion" is a crucial, though often unnoticed, co-feature of remembering. The contractive power of encapsulment is matched only by the distending power of expansion. A first form of this latter is found in the way in which one memory so frequently branches out into other memories. Typically, the new memories will be continuous in content or format with the initial memory, e.g., in my sudden remembering of the photograph of myself and my sister at Yosemite Park in example #1. But this need not be so; in states of reverie, an entire sequence of disconnected memories can arise.[4] Whether continuous or not, the chain of memories thus formed constitutes a significant expansion of the delimited remembering from which it takes its departure. A second mode of expansion occurs not by the addition of new memories but by the dilation of an original memory, its filling out *from within*. This is frequently the product of search: of seeking for a more complete memory, as occurred in the course of example #6. (It is noteworthy here that the expansion of my initial memory by the intervention of the specific recollection of reading Brentano enabled the thus-clarified memory of working on a particular project to be more fully representative of still other memories. In this case expansion also served the interests of encapsulment.) Third, expansion can arise via the multimodal potential of remembering. The otherwise indifferent tea-drinking episode of example #4 was expanded in my immediate memory of it to include sensory features not explicitly noticed in the original experience itself. Fourth, a specifically temporal expansion is also evident in the same example: by remembering it as I did, and by describing it in the way I did, I was extending its half-life within the psyche. The same is true of my other acts of remembering, though less obviously so: whenever memory is viewed under the aspect of survival or revival, it is seen as playing an expansive role.[5]

### PERSISTENCE/PASTNESS

This dual dimension of memory was implicit in the discussion just above. To speak of remembering as temporally expansive is already to invoke the pastness of the remembered experience as it extends into the present; and to talk of encapsulment is to refer, overtly or covertly, to the persistence of such an experience within an abbreviated form. But persistence and pastness are generic traits that call for specification on their own terms. "Persistence" is a matter of prolongation: prolongation of the past into the present. This is most directly and dramatically effected in primary memory, whose very *raison d'être* seems to consist in its conservator's role. Through primary remembering of the kind evident in the immediate memory of tea-tasting, a just-elapsed experience is conserved in the present, allowed to persist there. But the past is permitted to persist in every other case of remembering as well, though differently so in each instance. It may persist, for example, by virtue of the rote learning that lay at the basis of my spontaneously recalled office number; "902," learned through repeated routine encounters, endures in my present recollections as a piece of quasi-automatically remembered information. Its persistence is habitual in origin and in present operation. The persistence of "Culligan," on the other hand, is anything but habitual. My initial exposures to this word may have been habitual in character, but since I had not thought of it in many years it had lost the habitual status which it may once have had. It is not remembered routinely, as is "902," but unpredictably and sporadically. Yet it *is* remembered; and by being remembered even once, it persists. Persistence in this limiting case is just the fact of being recalled from "the bottomless abyss of oblivion"[6] on some occasion subsequent to its origin in time. In many other cases, e.g., in examples #1, #2, and #6, persistence consists in a tendency to be recalled on a number of subsequent occasions, often (as in #6) occasions of simply returning to the very place in which the remembered experience occurred. This place serves to remind us of what once occurred there, and our being reminded in this fashion is the vehicle of persistence.[7]

Persistence in memory is persistence *into* the present, but that which persists also derives *from* the past and is itself a persistence *of* the past. "Pastness" names that quality of what is remembered which places its origin and provenance in a period preceding the present. Without this origin and provenance, it could not be remembered in the first place: we cannot remember the present *qua* living present or the future *qua* yet-to-come future. Each of these latter has to become past in some sense and to some degree in order to be rememberable. And to become past is to be situated or situatable in a period of time now elapsed or elapsing, even though the time in question need not yet be entirely traversed. My tea-tasting was not wholly over with when I remembered its savors and sounds, tastes and touches, since these latter still lingered as fading sensations. But it was sufficiently elapsed to fall away from the central focus of my ongoing sensing and thus to be recapturable as *just-having-been-experienced*. It had acquired enough pastness to be remembered as such, that is, as an experience or a phase of an experience that was no longer coincidental with my consciousness of the present. In the other examples, the pastness was more well-established and pronounced, even if I could not locate the particular point in the past from which the memory derived. I do not know exactly when I first heard or saw the word "Culligan," but I am certain that it was at *some* period of my childhood. To know this is to know the word as belonging definitively to my past; it is to acknowledge its inherent pastness.

Acknowledging pastness is also acknowledging another dimension of the remembered. What we remember not only has its origin in the past but is now completed, finished, or ended—or on its way to being so. Just how this is the case once again differs from instance to instance, from the dead-and-done-with to the still tingling. My Yosemite experience is now so remote, so long since finished, that it is gappy and hazy at a number of points and has about it the sense of being almost out of reach. I am tempted to say that it is so complete as an experience that it is incomplete as a memory. But the other, less remote experiences we have examined are also expired or expiring experiences and rememberable as such. For unless an experience has become (or is becoming) genuinely an *ex*-perience, something standing *out* as lived through, it cannot begin to be remembered. The fact that it is remembered in the present, and thus persists into this present as its point of retrieval, in no way eliminates or even diminishes its pastness. Only that which is now past can *per*-sist, i.e., last through the vicissitudes of intervening time and be revived in the present. Thus pastness and persistence imply each other: the past alone truly persists, and only what persists is genuinely rememberable.

### ACTUALITY/VIRTUALITY

It is but a short step from pastness to actuality. For the past is populated with actualities—with what has actually been the case. We remember just this: former (and sometimes still surviving) actualities. Many of these actualities, whether objects or states of affairs, are observable and recordable in an objective manner, e.g., by a camera, as in the instance of the Yosemite photograph. But many others are not publicly presented events of this sort at all. They are feelings (e.g., of awe before Half Dome) or thoughts (e.g., of how distracting my neighbors were at my viewing of *Small Change*), and may not be evident, much less expressed, to others at all. Yet they are no less actual in status—i.e., actual as events—than the perceived positions and movements that can be objectively documented. Though not as easily locatable in space as are, say, Yosemite National Park and the Lincoln Theater, they may be quite locatable in time. My feeling of awe when confronting Half Dome is no less datable than my standing at its base and peering upward at it; indeed, in this case the date is the same.[8]

Beyond datability, actuality in memory involves the specific factor of "finishedness" as I should like to call it. What we recall is finished to the point of possessing a certain minimal coherence or intelligibility; otherwise, it is not identifiable as *a* memory, a memory of something in particular that *has* happened. The degree and kind of coherence varies from instance to instance; "902" serves as a valid memory in the context of being asked my office number, but would be quite incoherent if it arose in the midst of my *Small Change* memory. In fact, if it were to arise in the latter context, I would question whether it was a memory at all and not an interpolated fantasy. The actuality of the remembered therefore brings with it what Husserl calls "the unity of the remembered,"[9] that is, the sense that what is being remembered hangs or holds together as an experience or group of experiences[10]—as a single actuality or group of actualities.

A final facet of the actuality of what we remember has to do with self-presence. The actual is here not only a matter of the datability and finishedness of the remembered but concerns the role of the rememberer himself or herself: what is actual is what he or she undertook, learned, or witnessed *in propria persona*. The remembered calls for the presence of the rememberer at its original happening. This presence is first-person presence, the only kind of presence in which actuality is experienceable and hence rememberable. As James says:

> Memory requires more than mere dating of a fact in the past. It must be dated in *my* past. In other words, I must think that I directly experienced its occurrence.[11]

We find a sense or trace of self-presence in almost all of our examples, whether in the form of active participation (as in #1, #2, and #6) or as a still lingering experience of passive participation (in the tea-tasting episode). In these cases, the present actuality of remembering—in which we are at one with our own activity—revives the past actuality of having been present at the scene remembered. Even if this scene reduces in some cases to a "scene of instruction" of which the remembered precipitate is a mute residue, it is no less essential that we were then present, however uninvolved we may have been in any personal way. For only as present at that time, or in a series of such times, are we in a position to become rememberers of what was then experienced.[12]

"Virtuality" names quite another aspect of remembering. It designates, first of all, a readiness of former experiences to be reactivated in memory. In Ingarden's term, it is a *Parathaltung*, a "holding ready" which corresponds to the neurophysiological notion of memory trace.[13] Descriptively considered, it refers to our frequent conviction that more, and often considerably more, could be recalled than what we have so far succeeded in recalling: there are things about a particular object or event that are held ready for remembering, though they are not actually being recalled at the time. Thus, although my Yosemite memory was extremely thin to begin with and although I could not then (or now) recall a single additional detail about that visit, I still felt that much more *might* be remembered, if only my memory were "jogged" in the right way. This was not just true of the memory as a whole, but of every incident in it, each of which presented itself as being further fathomable. I felt that such fathoming was also possible in my more proximate memories as well: much remained virtual even in my recollection of seeing a movie recently (e.g., details of the theater, of people around me, of the movie itself) and indeed in my immediate memory of tasting tea. Admittedly there are fewer virtualities to contend with in this last case, and the same holds for the "902" and "Culligan" memories. Yet even these latter carried with them a thin penumbra of virtuality: I could have plummeted more deeply into the diverse origins of what was actualized so distinctly in each case.

Virtuality manifests itself in various kinds of inchoateness. For example, the surroundings of my remembered tea-tasting almost totally lacked definition; beyond my desk and a few objects on it, nothing stood out. But a very different lack of form invaded the memory of working in the philosophy library: here not only the background but the foreground itself of the remembered scene lacked definite detail, and the indefinite permeated not only space but time. In my recollection of Yosemite, in further contrast, the indefiniteness was situated *between* episodes as well as within them. And, of course, entire memories can be quite formless, as when I realize that I have only a very "hazy" recollection of my great aunt Leone, not being able to recall much of anything beyond her name and her approximate position in my family tree.

All such indefiniteness is not merely a necessary correlate of the selectivity inherent in any form of focused attention.[14] It is also, and more importantly for our purposes, a quite concrete way in which the virtuality of what we remember insinuates itself into remembering. Even if this virtuality is not experienced as such, its presence is made evident in the areas of the inchoate that pervade, riddle, or surround remembered content. Being less than crystalline in their clarity, these areas seem to solicit exploration: to beckon to us as virtually there. Much of what we experience as memory's pervasiveness in the present—its mysterious infusion in all ongoing experience and thought ("there is no perception that is not full of memories," said Bergson)[15]—is attributable to this aspect of the virtual. But the same aspect of virtuality also accounts for the vanishing quality of so many memories, their rapid retreat once scanned. The retreat is into still greater indefiniteness—into the state of being unremembered. Yet this state is characterizable not just negatively (as when we say that memories are "lost") but positively as well: and precisely by that being-held-in-readiness which is the basis of memory's virtuality.

## Secondary Traits

These are traits that are only optionally present in any given experience of remembering. They may or may not characterize this experience, but if they do they can become important and not merely incidental features. There are several such traits, of which I shall single out three for discussion here.

### QUASI-NARRATIVE STRUCTURE

Many memories manifest themselves in a quasi-narrative form. They seem to constitute a story or part of a story. A tale of sorts is told. Such memories have an identifiable beginning point; a certain development of motifs or themes then takes place; and there may even be a decisive conclusion. One of my sample cases easily fits into this pattern. In remembering my viewing of *Small Change,* I began by recalling several preliminary events (dinner, stopping at the bookstore, waiting in line), then described incidents that took place within the theater (mainly watching the film but also being distracted by others around me), and ended with a brief allusion to exiting from the theater. The result was a peculiarly well-rounded memory, one that closely approximates to a simple narrative account of the main events which occurred on that particular evening.

A less exemplary version of the same basic narrative structure was evident in my memory of visiting Yosemite National Park. A distinct beginning (the initial viewing of the park) was followed by a series of incidents within the park. Despite sharing a common setting, however, these incidents had no genuine continuity with each other. They unfolded independently of one another. And there was no conclusive ending or rounding-off, just an abrupt cessation after I had recalled the waterfall scene. This truncated narrative structure was nevertheless much more complete than in any of the remaining examples. These latter were all predominately non-narrative. In the case of "Culligan" and "902" there were no distinct actions or episodes to remember as such, hence no basis for narration. The same holds true for the tea-tasting episode regarded as a primary memory.[16] But there were at least implicit narrative elements in my memory of working on a particular essay in the philosophy library, since it involved the central action of researching-and-writing—an action that naturally called for a narrative-like description.

The "quasi" in "quasi-narrative" has two primary meanings. The first refers to the *implicitly* or *possibly* narrative form that a memory, or a portion of a memory, may possess even though the manifest form is non-narrative. The tacit hypothesis here is that *if* more detail could be recalled, *then* a narrative description would be appropriate. This is, however, only a hypothesis, for it does not always happen that when additional details are remembered they assume a narrative form: on the contrary, they may be so dispersed and disjointed as to resist this form. For this reason we cannot claim that all remembered content has even an implicit narrative structure.[17]

In a second sense, "quasi" in "quasi-narrative" refers to the narrative-*like*, yet still not strictly narrative, nature of remembering. By this I mean that even in the most propitious cases such as the *Small Change* memory, there is something notably lacking when comparison is made with story-telling, which is the embodiment of full narration. What is lacking in memory is a proper *narrative voice*, the voice of an authoritative narrator who spins out the tale. Whether actually spoken or present in written form, this voice commands the course of the tale in story-telling, reflecting the fact that the narrator knows the entire story in advance. ("Narrate" and "know" are cognate in origin.) Nothing strictly comparable to such a voice is found in remembering. Not only does the rememberer not always know the entire course and content of a given memory, but even when he or she does (as in frequently repeated memories) there is no need for a commanding voice delineating and directing the memory and distinct from it. Not even the rememberer's "inner voice"—i.e., the expression of a self-commenting internal agency—plays the requisite role. Memories are not narrated by anything like an authoritative voice; if anything, they tend to *narrate themselves;* for we possess them so intimately, so much from within our own life-histories, that there is no need for a separate source of articulation to recount them to us.

Therefore, even though some memories have an explicitly narrative structure—that is, a content which falls spontaneously into an ordered sequence of events (and prototypically into beginning, middle, and end)—they still lack a distinct narrative voice and are thus not fully narrational in nature. They are at best, and then not always, quasi-narrative in one of the two senses just discussed; and if this is so, Ryle is misguided in claiming that "being good at recalling . . . is a narrative skill."[18]

SCHEMATICALNESS

By "schematical" I mean abbreviated in such a way as to be sketchy or blurred—not fully presented. It can be argued that all memories are schematized in that they embody affective or cognitive schemes of various sorts.[19] But not all memories are schematical in the sense of indistinct. Some come to us in utmost clarity: "902" arrived without ambiguity of any kind. It was not only the correct answer to the question "what is the number on your office door?" but it presented itself in a quite crystalline and transparent form. It was not just beyond the shadow of a doubt but lacking in internal shadow as well, *sans ombre*, and thus a strictly unschematical memory. At the other end of the spectrum were the shadowy images that accompanied "Culligan." These were so schematical that I had difficulty identifying and describing them in any coherent way. And yet the fact that they appeared in the same memory as the clearly articulated element, "Culligan," testifies to the compatability of the schematical and the unschematical within the same experience of remembering. A given experience need not exhibit exactly the same schematicalness throughout. I have, for instance, a very vivid recollection of coming into port in Bergen, Norway, along with a very sketchy remembrance of my visit to the home of Sibelius outside Bergen, and yet both scenes are part of the same overall memory that could be labeled "visit to Bergen, 1958."

Not only the degree but the *kind* of schematicalness can vary in a given instance. My memories of having worked in the philosophy library at different times had a condensed and loosely overlapping schematicalness which contrasted with the much more compressed and definite schematicalness of the particular memory of having worked on a certain essay in that same library. The result is a somewhat bewildering *montage* structuring one and the same memory sequence, a situation in which one sort of schematicalness is juxtaposed with another. Just as we were earlier forced to acknowledge various forms of the virtual within remembering, now we must admit the co-existence of different schematicalnesses.

## RUMINESCENCE

To capture the special mood or emotional state that remembering may occasion I have coined the word "ruminescence," which combines "reminiscence" with "rumination." Remembering may give rise to a whole spectrum of emotions, ranging from exhilarating joy to despondent remorse. Poets have movingly described most of the feelings which thrust themselves on our awareness when we remember. But the peculiar phenomenon of ruminescence has been neglected. This neglect is all the more curious in view of the way it pervades so much of our remembering. What has impeded its full recognition is its ambiguous origin and its tendency to be present in such mild forms as often to be barely detectable.

Ruminescence ranges from active nostalgia to tepid wistfulness. I experienced the former in the philosophy library memory—indeed, I was overcome by it as I entered the library rooms high in the stacks of the enormous building in which they were housed. It is important to consider this nostalgia more closely, for it reveals itself to be more than a mere longing for "the good old days." On the one hand, it was supported by rapidly returning reminiscences: the "semi-memories" that came flooding back as soon as I stepped into the room. Their vagueness did not detract from their considerable power to move me—and may even have contributed to this power by reinforcing their basic wistfulness. A reminiscence can dampen emotion as well as enliven it. In the present case, moreover, it was not merely the indistinctness of detail but the very indistinctness in the *number* of memories that helped to bring about the effect in question. Not knowing just how many memories I was dealing with, I was more moved than if I had known how many were in fact at stake. On the other hand, a quite different facet of this situation was my incompletely formulated thought that the experiences I was recalling were unrepeatable. This thought also contributed powerfully to my mood at the time, and it did so as a form of rumination. I was not so much entertaining this thought (much less expressing it overtly) as *ruminating* it, "chewing it over," reflecting upon it, albeit inexplicitly and unselfconsciously. Such rumination helps to bring about the complex state of ruminescence.

Another factor is the special pleasure we take in the very combination of reminiscence and rumination. This pleasure arises more from the *activity* of reminiscing-*cum*-ruminating than from its content *per se*. The contemplation of the content, as such, can be quite painful, as when I think about the gruesome details of an accident I have just witnessed. But the ruminescent remembering of this same content is a very different matter. It may not ever become positively pleasurable, yet it can come to involve the subsidiary but distinct pleasure arising from the act of remembering in a ruminescent mood. As Virgil says in the *Aeneid:*

> Someday, perhaps, it will be a joy to remember even these things.[20]

At stake here is the role of time in the peculiar pleasure taken in recollection: the more distant the event recalled, the more pleasure we tend to experience in remembering it. As Freud remarks, "It seems, moreover, as though the recollection of the remote past is in itself facilitated by some pleasurable motive."[21] This motive stems, I believe, precisely from the way in which events of the remote past encourage a ruminescent attitude on the part of the rememberer. Just because these events are so distant and so undemanding—and also because they frequently belong to (or suggest) an earlier period of life that we later regard as an uncontaminated mixture of innocence and spontaneity—we become ruminescent in reflecting on them. But, once again, the pleasure we gain in this way derives much more from our *present* activity of remembering than from the events themselves; indeed, these latter may be so dimly apprehended as not to be clearly discernible or even identifiable as such.[22]

It is a striking fact that the very first recollection that came to mind when I sought examples of memory in general was one from my remote childhood. In view of Freud's remark and my gloss on it this fact cannot be regarded as wholly accidental. There is a special yield of pleasure in recalling such a memory—a pleasure that is tinged by a wistful quality. Wistfulness is hardly an intrusive mood; it is often so unobtrusive as not even to be expressly noticed by the rememberer: hence its absence from my explicit descriptions of the Culligan and Yosemite memories, both of which also stemmed from my childhood. It was not a prominent feature in either instance, being present more as a hazy emotional atmosphere than as a specific mood. Yet its presence was nonetheless detectable and gave to these rememberings an emotional flavoring lacking in most of the other examples cited. With the exception of the philosophy library memory, these latter were not wistful, much less nostalgic. They were experienced without any trace of ruminescence, indeed were uncolored by any precisely delineatable emotion or mood. Thus we are warned that ruminescence is not a constant or primary trait of remembering. It is inherent only in certain instances and then quite differently from case to case. However moving its presence may be on particular occasions, it remains optional in status and is thus, along with quasi-narrativity and schematicalness, a secondary trait of remembering.

# III

# REMEMBERING AS INTENTIONAL

## ACT PHASE

Remembering, regarded as a mental act, is intentional in structure. It can therefore be analyzed into an act phase and an object phase—roughly, into *how* we remember and *what* we remember. Each experience of remembering is thus diphasic, but the two phases are simultaneous and not successive.[1] It is *while* we are engaged in the activity of remembering that what we remember presents itself, and conversely when something emerges in memorial form we are at that moment and to that exact extent involved in an act of remembering. The act and object phases thus call for one another and are strictly correlative: no activity of remembering lacks an object remembered, and vice versa. Each phase is equally essential, since an actless memory is as unthinkable as a contentless remembering.[2]

Despite the fact that the experience of remembering is always act and object at once, I shall treat these two phases in successive chapters. The two phases are inseparable in experience, but they may be distinguished at the level of intentional analysis. Such analysis views the mind as oriented in different basic ways—thanks to various act-forms—toward particular "contents" or immanent objects. Even if they are always in fact conjoined, acts and objects call for separate descriptions.

To analyze the act phase is to concern ourselves with the actual process of remembering, with how remembering is accomplished or realized on specific occasions. Such enactment can be distinguished from the capacity and from the disposition to remember, both of which pertain to "memory" construed as an inherent faculty or tendency rather than as an occurrence.[3] The capacitative and dispositional dimensions of remembering are of crucial import—of more importance, for example, than their counterparts in imagining. Individual acts of remembering not only exercise the capacity and disposition to remember at particular points in time and space but in so doing draw upon (and thus depend upon) what is contained or stored in memory. Such keeping or retaining—whether long-term or short-term in status[4]—would not be possible without the functioning of inbuilt memorial capacities and dispositions.

There are problematic borderline cases in which the distinction between capacity or disposition on the one hand and occurrence on the other is difficult to discern: e.g., those unconscious or preconscious memories which are continually active and yet not currently remembered as such.[5] Such cases notwithstanding, an analysis of the act phase of remembering on its own terms remains both possible and desirable. It is possible insofar as the act itself and the capacity or disposition that makes it possible manifest themselves so differently: the former directly in our conscious experiences of remembering, the latter indirectly through a variety of instantiations, normal or pathological,[6] unconscious or conscious. It is desirable insofar as an ability or disposition to remember is fully actualized and known only by its particular occurrences.[7] In fact, we shall never learn anything significant about memory as capacity or disposition unless and until we begin with a study of how it actually arises in human experience.

How then does remembering occur? What are the forms that human memory assumes in its enactment? These forms are multiple, exhibiting what I have elsewhere described as "the multiplicity of the mental."[8] It is as if the very proliferation of act-forms in which remembering arises somehow compensates for its determinacy of content—compared, for instance, with imagining, which has relatively few act-forms but a quite indeterminate content. In view of this proliferation and for the sake of clarity, I shall divide my analysis of the act-forms of memory into three groups.

## Primary and Secondary Remembering

These are generic forms of memory to which a number of other types of remembering may be assimilated, including certain of the basic types to be considered under what I shall call "Main Types of Remembering." As primary and secondary memory have already received the lion's share of attention from philosophers and psychologists alike, I shall be brief in my own treatment. Moreover, precisely because they are so broadly generic in status, they do not lend themselves to the detailed specificity at which I am aiming in this book.

### PRIMARY REMEMBERING

This is a form of remembering that occurs so continually and often so imperceptibly that we rarely notice it at all; and even when we do notice it, we are not inclined to consider it a form of remembering.[9] I refer to the way in which we remain aware of what has just appeared or happened in our experience. In my tea-tasting memory, for example, the event of tasting was no longer present as such—no longer occupied the central 'now' of my conscious attention. Yet it was still held in mind in the margins of my awareness. I say "held in mind" because primary memory cannot be identified with the actual, psycho-physical reverberations of the just-past experience.[10] It is a question of a momentary "retention" by the mind as this experience subsides or "sinks away" from explicit awareness.[11] Such an experience is *maintained in mind* even as it vanishes from explicit consciousness. In this way, it forms a penumbra around any newly appearing or happening content of consciousness; in James's striking formulation, it is "a vaguely vanishing backward fringe."[12]

Primary remembering can be construed in either of two ways. On the one hand, it can be regarded as the prolongation, the "persistence" as we called it earlier, of a previously present moment of experience—its gradual, rather than precipitous, demise. The amount of prolongation varies from experience to experience and from person to person, but it appears to range from several milliseconds up to half a minute.[13] Whatever the exact duration, "primary memory" refers to the way in which what was just experienced (the "*soeben gewesen,*" as Husserl terms it) is drawn out and allowed to remain accessible. (My memory of tea-tasting is once again a case in point. The entire experience, with all of its synesthetic coherence, was describable immediately after its occurrence as still smoldering in my consciousness, though also as rapidly vanishing from it.) On the other hand, the fact of primary remembering—its omnipresent, though often unnoticed, operation—can be viewed as deepening the *present* present, the new present which has taken the place of the present of the experience now sinking back or down in mind. This latter experience forms what Husserl calls a "comet's tail" trailing off from the nucleus of the ever-new "now-point."[14] Seen in this perspective, primary remembering is a way of enriching present experience by adding the dimension of the *soeben gewesen,* the just-having-been, to an otherwise purely punctiform present. What has just been *shadows* what is now appearing or happening, thereby constituting what E. R. Clay named the "specious present" and Husserl the "living present."[15]

### SECONDARY REMEMBERING

Except for the tea-tasting incident, all of the examples given in the first chapter were cases of secondary remembering, the remembering of experiences that had lapsed from my consciousness after their initial occurrence. As is the fate with all contents of primary memory, they had become immersed in the waters of Lethe and had to be remembered in a decisively different manner. In ordinary parlance, such remembering is termed "recall" or "recollection," and its operation is conceived as that of rescuing former experiences from oblivion. These experiences require rescue insofar as they have run their course; they are entirely elapsed as events—in contrast with their partial lapsing as the content of primary remembering. James has described this salvaging operation in graphic terms:

> An object which is recollected, in the proper sense of that term, is one which has been absent from consciousness altogether, and now revives anew. It is brought back, fished up, so to speak, from a reservoir in which, with countless other objects, it lay buried and lost from view.[16]

The "secondary" of secondary remembering, then, carries no connotation of being lesser in importance or status. Rather, it describes an act of remembering that is subsequent, that follows upon primary remembering—as is suggested by one of the main German words for recollection, "*Wiedererinnerung*," literally a remembering *again* or *re*-remembering.

The new activity of remembering is not, however, a mere repetition of its predecessor. It is a distinctively disparate activity, which psychological experimentation shows to differ from its forerunner in such ways as probability of recall, means of encoding content, effects of distraction or interference, and the internal relationship between the various materials being remembered.[17] This is just what we might expect, since secondary remembering does not draw upon essentially unchanged and still-conscious experiences, but upon no longer conscious experiences that have been held in long-term storage—and thus made vulnerable to transformations unknown to the rememberer himself or herself.

Secondary remembering is a two-fold activity. First, it involves the *retrieval* of items not now in conscious mind; that is, the recapturing of experiences no longer extant in perception or in primary memory. As "stage analysis" in psychological treatments of memory suggests, retrieval is to be distinguished both from acquisition and from storage. Accuracy or ease of retrieval does not necessarily correlate with accuracy or ease of acquisition, and each of these stages must be distinguished from the distortings and forgettings that may occur during storage. In particular, we have to distinguish between the general *availability* of content previously acquired-and-stored and its actual *accessibility* at a given point in time.[18] Whatever is available in principle—and a staggering amount normally is—it actually becomes accessible only in discrete, particular acts of secondary remembering by which we retrieve items from the long-term storage where they have been held in "death's dateless night."[19] The retrieval itself may be instantaneous (as when I was asked to recall my office number) or labored (as when I am asked to recall the name of my second grade teacher), but in every instance of successful retrieval we manage to recuperate something that has entered into a memorial limbo. In other words, accessibility entails availability but not vice versa.

A second aspect of the basic action of secondary remembering is found in *revival*. The retrieval of items vanished from view is not a merely mechanical procedure of "decoding" information that has been "encoded" upon being "placed in storage" (and sometimes recoded thereafter).[20] It is also a resuscitation of previously experienced objects, events, and circumstances—a re-experiencing of them, albeit in representational or symbolic form. The "re-" of secondary *re*membering takes on special significance in this activity of mnemonic re-enactment or re-presentation,[21] a significance lacking in primary remembering. Just as the latter involves no factor of retrieval (for the contents of primary memory have not been sufficiently forgotten to require being retrieved), so it does not include revival either; its contents are still alive in consciousness, are still being experienced (however dimly), and hence have no need of being *re*-experienced: "An object of primary memory is not thus brought back; it never was lost; its date was never cut off in consciousness from that of the immediately present moment."[22] But for that material whose date *is* cut off, the resuscitation effected in secondary remembering is required; and the resuscitation is of more than the date alone: at the limit, it is a revival of an entire experience, of our whole stance and attitude, the way we *were* in confronting and engaging the objects of our concern. To revive such an experience and these objects in secondary remembering is to give them a second chance, a second life. This second life is not the strict equivalent of the first, and Husserl is right to caution that "I can relive the present, but *it* can never be given again."[23] But secondary remembering does make possible an after-life within the current epoch of the remembering mind. It is a main means by which the present and the non-immediate past rejoin each other in human experience.

## Main Types of Remembering

Granting the pervasiveness of primary and secondary remembering, can we make out more particular forms in which we remember? Such forms would not only subtend but cut across the generic forms. In describing them, I shall concentrate on those that are exemplified in long-term memory, but there are short-term counterparts to practically all of the phenomena discussed below.

### REMEMBERING *SIMPLICITER*

We can, and frequently do, remember single things in isolation from other things and events. Such "things" include mountains and mice, faces and flowers, houses and highways, while "events" vary from birthday celebrations to commencement exercises, from doing banal chores to moments of creativity, from being teased to teasing, from running to ruminating. In each instance, something is remembered in a more or less isolated state—as *just* this or *just* that. The "this" or "that" remembered need not be perceptual or public in status. I can very well remember *simpliciter* an itch or an idea, a feeling of chagrin or a sense of calamity, a fantasy or a formula known only to me. Take, for example, the bare remembering of a person, say, my friend Jan. I can remember her *as such* in a remarkable variety of ways. I begin by recalling her face as a whole, shift to a single feature such as her delicate chin, then to the characteristic expression of excitement which can illuminate her entire physiognomy. I remember, too, events in which Jan's face figured and which it reflected revealingly. Beyond such concreta as the perceived face or these events, and beyond even the feelings and thoughts registered in this face or experienced in myself, there is the *person* "Jan," whom I remember as a vivacious, brilliant, and endearing being. When I remember this person *simpliciter*, I remember her in her very uniqueness: as unreducible to any given set of qualities or events.

There are other objects of memory which, unlike my friend, are neither perceivable *per se* nor unique. These form a class that can be designated as "items of information"—where "item" denotes any piece of information that is not an episodic fact. Isolated numbers and words are the most prominent members of this class, and they were represented respectively by "902" and "Culligan" in my original examples. Groups of numbers or words taken as single sets can also be remembered *simpliciter:* "the even numbers," "all words starting with re-," etc. So also, concepts and laws (and their classes) are rememberable in their singularity, e.g., "the transcendental unity of apperception," "the second law of thermodynamics," "the equator," etc. Such abstracta may make implicit allusion to complex facts or situations—as do "1066" or "$E = Mc^2$"—but this does not prevent us from recalling them *simpliciter*, that is, in their strict singularity. Nor does their greater or lesser internal complexity preclude their being remembered in such straight-on fashion, for it is not this complexity that is being recalled. To recall "$\pi$" *simpliciter* may be equivalent to recollecting "3.1415 . . .," but it is not equivalent to recalling the mathematical operation by which I derive this transcendental number, much less any use to which it may be put. It is just to recall a symbol, or a number, *as such* and without additional complication.

Granting that what we remember *simpliciter* need not have been given to the senses originally, can the display in which the remembered term now appears be *non*sensuous? It is often just this when we recall a particular bit of information, including certain objects and events,[24] in a rapid and unselfconscious manner—typically in the context of an activity that involves these remembered things only incidentally.[25] Nevertheless, there is a pronounced tendency for that which we remember *simpliciter*, however abstract in nature it may be qua number, word, concept, or law, to sediment itself into a sensuous format of presentation. Unless I am caught up in an analysis of the very sort I have been performing just above, I usually remember Jan by her face (or voice, or bodily movement), the word "Culligan" by an appropriately visualized word, "902" by a sensuous representation of these very numbers, "$\pi$" by the visualized symbol itself, "$E = Mc^2$" by the visualized formula,[26] "the even numbers" by their internally pronounced or quasi-pronounced names or by a string of visualized numbers ("2, 4, 6, . . ."), and so on. In each case there is a definite proclivity to employ a self-presentified symbol or set of symbols as the vehicle of memory and thus to render the mnemonic display sensuous.

### REMEMBERING-THAT

In addition to objects and events, we remember states of affairs—whole circumstances in which subjects (or subject-terms) are implicated in actions or endowed with qualities (active or attributive terms). The implication is the nodal point of such remembering. To remember *that* x did y or *that* x was a is to remember neither x, nor y, nor a in isolation; nor is it to remember their mere juxtaposition, which is still a matter of remembering *simpliciter*. It is to remember their very interaction, the way they are implicated in each other through a shared "predicational crease."[27] The effect (or better, the expression) of such interaction is a state of affairs, that is, a situational structure in which the component terms are subordinated to the architectonic of the objective complex constituted by their interaction. What we remember is more the structure than the terms—or rather, the structure as manifested in and through the interinvolvement of the terms, the crease they conjointly constitute.

Much remembering occurs in this form. Whenever we recollect a scene in which something was happening or a process in which properties of various kinds were acquired, we are remembering-that. Such remembering is by no means restricted to recalling sequences of events possessing what I have called a "quasi-narrative" structure (e.g., my memory of viewing the movie *Small Change*). It extends to any remembering of any state of affairs, whether narrational or not. When I remember a single episode such as my VW suddenly crashing into the car in front of it—an episode so barren of complication or detail as to resist a narrative account—I am remembering *that* this incident happened: that it constituted a more or less coherent state of affairs, however momentary or fragmentary it may have been. Nor can this act of remembering-that be reduced to remembering *simpliciter;* in the present case, the latter would be the mere remembering of the event qua event ("the car crash") and not of the event as entering into an objective complex ("my-VW-crashing-into-another-car-in-front-of-it"). It is evident that "crashing" is the crease of this complex, that around which subject- and object-terms revolve in the constitution of a single, but internally articulated, state of affairs. When we remember this state of affairs, we remember *that* it occurred.

Just as multiple episodes are not necessary for remembering-that something was the case, so what was the case need not be present to mind in a sensuous guise. The instances of remembering-that investigated in chapter 1 all possessed such a guise. But this need not have been so. I can very well remember-that nonsensuously. Here are some examples: remembering that Uncle Ralph retired from the family business in the 1930s; that the Popular Front came to power in France before World War II; that Caesar crossed the Rubicon. In none of these cases of "factual memory"[28] do I experience a sensuously specified mnemonic display. If such a display *were* to arise, upon analysis I would find it to be mainly of illustrative value, an adventitious fleshing-out of the bare fact being remembered. For in such cases I am remembering *situations that I never witnessed myself*. Since I did not witness them, i.e., was not present at their occurrence, I *cannot* remember how they happened in their sensuous specificity.[29]

We must be careful to distinguish this kind of nonsensuous remembering-that from another quite different kind.[30] In this latter, I may very well have been present at the state of affairs being remembered, but *the state of affairs was itself nonsensuous*. When I remember that my grandfather doubted that human beings would ever reach the moon, I am remembering a state of affairs which I first grasped by listening to verbal utterances but which was not itself auditory or even quasi-auditory in status. "My-grandfather-doubting-that-man-would-ever-reach-the-moon" describes an objective complex that includes an opinion or thought yet is not intrinsically sensuous, even if it is normally expressed or represented in some perceptible form. Of course, I can also remember that I once *heard* my grandfather express his doubts on the subject. But "my-hearing-my-grandfather-express-his-doubts" is a very different state of affairs from that designated just above, and this is so even though my hearing of my grandfather or of someone else telling about my grandfather's views (or my reading written accounts of his views) is a necessary condition for my being able to remember that he was skeptical concerning man's capacity to land on the moon. Here the nonsensuousness of remembering-that is not so much predetermined as inherent. In the one case I *cannot have been* a witness of what I remember in this way; in the other, I *must have been*—yet to no avail.

### REMEMBERING-HOW

Beyond remembering an object or event *simpliciter* and remembering-that certain things were the case, we can remember how to effect a given movement. Although we may not have singled it out—or even recognized it as a separate species of our remembering—remembering-how is a distinctive and quite pervasive way in which we remember. As such, it cannot be reduced to other forms of remembering, or regarded as their mere extension. But it actively collaborates with these forms, making use of remembered objects, events, and states of affairs in its own actualizations. Thus I may remember how to do X where X itself is the event of, say, swinging a golf club correctly. Yet it remains a very different thing to remember *how* to swing such a club in the right way and to remember *that* I have once so swung it. As in the parallel case of knowing how versus knowing that, each is independent of the other.[31] I can remember how to perform the action in question *without* recalling any specific episodes of past swingings; conversely, I can recollect such episodes—even in considerable detail—and still not remember how to swing successfully in the present. No more than in the case of imagining-how and imagining-that can we assimilate one activity to the other.[32]

Remembering-how is not a single, simple act-form but exists in two primary modes.[33] Let us look at these in succession:

*Habituating/habituated remembering-how to do*

By this I mean all the instances in which we remember how to do[34] something as they arise from the early stages of habituation. "Habituation" refers not only to repeated action (though this is usually required) but to becoming familiar with doing the action itself in appropriate circumstances. An example is remembering how to drive to a friend's home after several previous visits. Although I may now have successfully learned how to get there, my remembering how to do so is not yet *habitual*. It has not reached the point where I could attain my destination mindlessly, "on automatic" as it were. Inasmuch as I am getting habituated or am freshly habituated, I must pay heed to various perceptual cues along the way—e.g., crucial corners, the lay of the land, a sense of how far I have come at certain points, etc.—and I may also have recourse to cues in my mind's eye or ear.[35] Still, once I take advantage of these diverse points of reference, I do generally manage to reach my destination: I have remembered how to do so on the basis of habituation. Such remembering is equivalent to *knowing how to get there,* even if getting there has not yet become altogether habitual. This form of remembering-how is invaluable not just in situations of navigating and of becoming acclimatized or oriented to new environments but also in changing circumstances where it is a matter of "learning my way around" more adequately.

*Habitual remembering-how to do*

By "habitual" I mean fully routinized—so much so that attending to or heeding my own remembered doing is no longer necessary. I just "do"; I act without having to think about acting. This does not mean, however, that such action is the direct or simple result of voluntary efforts. It may have come about by sheer immersion in my surroundings—as when, after months of living in a new house, I come to know my way around its interior "without a moment's reflection." Nor need it be strictly bodily in character:[36] I can slip, all too easily, into habitual patterns of thought or of feeling, indeed of remembering itself. Habitual remembering-how to do encompasses a vast portion of our lives, so vast that we may find it alarming to admit to ourselves as voluntary agents. And our disavowal is quite justifiable, since the saving in heedful reflection thereby achieved frees us for much in human experience that would not otherwise be possible, including the acquisition of new habitual actions!

Habitual remembering-how to do has a correspondingly capacious range of actualizations, from facial grimaces to resolving equations in advanced algebra. It is most often found in the form of skilled actions. Once again, these latter need not be corporeal; but bodily skill tends to provide the most prominent paradigms for this sort of remembering-how to do: e.g., remembering how to swim, how to ride a bicycle, how to swing a tennis racquet with the proper form. Since my original list of examples did not include a case of skilled action, let me cite an instance from recent experience.

> I was returning to a house I had not visited in over a year. The key had been given to me by the owner without comment, even though he had once emphasized how difficult it was to open the front door with it. Nevertheless, and without any premeditation on my part, I inserted the key in the lock, made a full turn to the left and returned a half circle to the right—and the door opened immediately.

The banality of this example should not mislead us. With the exception only of the highest-order skills, most instances of skillful remembering-how to do are humdrum in character; their value is found almost entirely in their practical usefulness—here, in entering the house where I was planning to do some writing during the next week. Hence our tendency to deride such skills as "merely mechanical," along with the consequent temptation to locate them not just in bodily behavior but in those least developed reflex actions that we dismiss as mere "*re*actions." However understandable this tendency may be when it is a question of "motor memories" wholly immanent in the body, it does not take into account the considerable interest to be found in many cases of the habitual remembering-how to do that informs skilled actions. Consider only the following three points:

1. Such remembering may be taken as behaviorly equivalent to *not having to relearn* the skill in question. Whereas I might need to be given directions again in order to find my way to my friend's house even after I have become habituated to the right route there, this is not the case with genuinely habitual actions or movements, which have become so thoroughly learned ("sedimented") as not to have to be relearned, or even to be thought about during their actual performance. This was precisely what happened when I performed the unlocking movements at my friend's house: no relearning, or even rethinking, was required for this learned skill to be correctly re-performed.

2. Involved in this kind of remembering is a sense of *personal agency* directed to an end or purpose that is attained by means of the skill in question.[37] This sense can be quite explicit, especially when I have just mastered a new skill (giving me an enhanced self-image, a feeling of new personal *élan*) or when I am blocked from enacting my skill (forcing me back upon my own resources). But it can also exist in an implicit form—e.g., as the basic conviction that this action or movement which I am remembering how to perform is my action or movement, *my doing*, even though I do it "mechanically" and with my mind wholly on the goal

of my movements. That was what happened in the above example: my thoughts were directed exclusively toward entering my friend's house that night; yet I was aware, however dimly, that *I* was executing the skilled action that would make it possible for me to get there.

3. Habitual remembering-how to do is not a matter of repeating an action or movement in every detail; it is a question of of re-enacting a *pattern* or *structure* of an action or movement. So long as one keeps within the large lines of this structure, considerable latitude is allowed—and sometimes even encouraged. In the case under discussion, the fact that I may have varied my hand movements somewhat from previous occasions did not undermine my remembering how to turn the key in the right way: where "right way" means precisely "in accordance with this particular key's pattern of unlocking." The same holds true for skilled movements in sports: I can remember how to perform the breast stroke in several ways provided only that my stroke conforms to a significant degree with the official version, the standard structure, of the stroke.

As in the case of remembering-that, both modes of remembering-how to do can occur sensuously or nonsensuously. Whether as merely habituating/habituated or as fully habitual, I can remember how to do things in engrossed sensory concreteness or in a quite abstract manner. Thus, I can remember how to do logarithms as well as how to swing a tennis racket. Moreover, variation is possible even within a single kind of action. Remembering how to drive to my friend's home may be something I can effect only in the presence of particular perceptual cues *en route;* but I can also recall how to do so entirely "in my head" by rehearsing a series of turns (e.g., "three rights, one left, then a final right"), none of which is visualized, much less perceived. Similarly, I can remember how a habitual action such as doing the breast stroke goes by flailing my arms (in or out of water) in the proper sequence; or I can remember how to do the stroke by visualizing myself or someone else effecting it in my mind's eye; or, at the limit, I can remember how the stroke goes *in abstracto*, as a set of directions that possess neither imaginal nor perceptual instantiation.

### REMEMBERING-TO

I want finally to take up a type of remembering rarely recognized by previous students of the subject.[38] Yet it is both distinctive and important. Its varieties include remembering to act, to reflect, to feel, to play, to work, etc., in certain ways and in certain circumstances. Consider the example of remembering to return books to the library on their due date.[39] Although I am somewhat notorious for *not* remembering to do this, when I do manage to remember, the following situation normally obtains. First, I already know the due date and now recall this date, even if it is specified as vaguely as "toward the end of this week." Second, I may be actually in the process of returning the books ("You see, I am remembering to return these books"), on the verge of doing so, or may merely project their possible return. Third, what I remember to do is an action that I normally carry out myself, but that may be delegated to someone else—in which case the delegating then becomes the relevant remembering. Fourth, the action itself is delimited in duration and can be concluded, or at least terminated, by my own voluntary efforts.

These characteristics of the example indicate three basic aspects of remembering-to. (1) As in remembering-how to do, previous learning is presupposed. In addition, however, there is a commitment or promise implicit in remembering-to, e.g., to return books I have checked out from a library. Moreover, this learning and this commitment are not idle, but exist to be acted on at a particular place (the library) and time (the due date). Thus, the spatio-temporal circumstances in which remembering-to is enacted are essential and not merely contingent: I can remember how to do sums in my head in almost *any* situation, but I cannot effectively remember to return books to the library in any way that is comparably oblivious to time and place. (2) The temporal dimension is especially crucial in remembering-to; it is also unique among basic types of remembering. For I remember to do, undertake, feel, think, etc., not in turning toward the past (the past is only presupposed as the period of learning and commitment) but in being directed toward the *present or the future*. On the one hand, I may remember to do *just now*, that is, simultaneously with my carrying out of what is thus remembered. (Sometimes we have already made the initial motions, e.g., started walking toward the library, when we suddenly "remember to do" what we are already in the process of doing. Here remembering-to precedes the conscious act of remembering, much as remembering how to do the backstroke may precede the act of explicitly remembering how one did it on former occasions.) On the other hand, what we remember to do may equally well lie in the future. Although this future is typically the near future (i.e., when a task or duty is expected to be performed), it can also be relatively remote (e.g., "I must remember to make mention of Sorabji's study of Aristotle in my course on memory next year"). Such present- and future-oriented remembering is rarely found in other types of remembering, which tend to be resolutely retrospective.[40] (3) As with remembering-how to do, personal agency is an important feature of remembering-to. But this agency takes a more delimited and determinate form in the present instance. The action, duty, thought, etc., which I remember to carry out is indeed something that I alone am to do; but I do not explicitly (or even implicitly) think of myself *as doing it*. Nor do I necessarily envision myself doing so in the future. Even though I could not meaningfully deny that I am (or am to be) the active doer of what is thus remembered-to-be-done and not its mere witness (as in remembering-that something appeared in a certain way), I take myself to be more the *vehicle* of remembering-to than its *agent*. It is *through* me that what I remember to do will get done. Every "through" indicates a "beyond," and here that beyond refers to what I am to effect *after* remembering-to proper. The status of remembering-to is accordingly that of a pre-action or (if every human undertaking is to be viewed as an action)[41] of a preparatory action. In remembering-how to do, I help to effect the action-to-be-accomplished by the very memory of it: acting and remembering become contiguous with one another. Nevertheless, I remember to undertake an action that is not itself part of my remembering since I need not have witnessed what I am to do, or even have learned to carry it out.

Remembering-to rejoins the other main types of remembering in being enactable in either nonsensuous or sensuous form. When I remember to think certain thoughts or to feel in a particular way, I enter into a nonsensuous mode; but I am sensuously engaged when I remember to perceive something or to execute a concrete action such as returning books to a library. In this respect the range of remembering-to is commensurate with that of remembering *simpliciter,* remembering-that, and remembering-how. This is so despite the otherwise striking disparities we have found between these four major types of remembering. Moreover, we can *remember to remember*—just as we can equally well remember that or how we remembered on a previous occasion. The reiterability may extend yet further, so that we can remember to remember . . . to remember; or we can remember that we remembered that we remembered . . . that we remembered; or remember how we remembered . . . how we remembered. Only in remembering *simpliciter* does such self-expansion fail to exfoliate.

## Subsidiary Types of Remembering

Besides the major types just explored, there are other act-forms in which we remember. They are "subsidiary" only in their comparative infrequency of occurrence, their relative rarity. But they are not necessarily less important than the kinds of remembering discussed above. I shall limit discussion to four instances:

### REMEMBERING-AS

On some occasions we say that we remember someone or something *as* exhibiting or having a certain attribute or quality. This attribute or quality may be regarded as residing in the thing remembered ("I remember my cousin 'Topper' as exuberant last summer") or as having affected us or others in some way ("I remember that year abroad as having changed me profoundly"). In either case the as-structure serves as a nodal point for the act of remembering. It brings together the subject or topic of ascription and the ascribed property. What is remembered is the complex thus formed: 'S-as-P'. This is to be contrasted with the skeletal content of remembering *simpliciter* ('S', 'P', or 'S-P'), remembering-that ('that-S-was-P'), remembering-how ('how-to-do-S'), and remembering-to ('to-carry-out-S at time t and place p'). It is clear that 'S-as-P' most closely resembles 'that-S-was-P'. To remember my cousin as exuberant is very like remembering *that* my cousin acted in an exuberant way. In both cases emphasis is placed upon manifest action, looks, and the like. But there is a crucial point of difference. In remembering-that something was the case, the "I" of the rememberer is involved as the onlooker or witness of what is recalled: its essential mirror. In remembering-as, however, the rememberer's self has no such well-defined role to play. It may play no particular role at all (as in the memory of my exuberant cousin); and it is not always conspicuous even when the as-structure consists in something's being-affected rather than a property's residing-in—for its effect can be upon *others* as well as upon myself. I can remember a year I spent abroad with someone else as influencing that person in certain ways, without taking note of any comparable changes in myself. The consequence of such a suspension of the remembering self is a correspondingly more emphatic focusing upon the character and quality of what is remembered via the as-structure itself. This is so even when what is remembered are the effects of this structure rather than the structure itself. Throughout, the stress is placed upon the "it" and not upon the "I." To remember-as is to remember S as P, where 'P', the property, is attached exclusively to 'S', qualifying *it* primarily and my own experience of S only secondarily.

### REMEMBERING-WHAT

When I remember what happened on last July 4 or what make of car I used to have, I am engaging in a form of remembering-that, since these two acts of remembering can be analyzed respectively as "I remember that X happened on the last 4th of July" and as "I remember that I used to have a Cricket." Although the exact propositional content may be identical in the two kinds of remembering, there is a felt difference between them that answers to the "what" and the "that" forms of expression. To remember *that*, as we know, is to recall a state of affairs, a situation in which the members of an objective complex interact with, affect, and modify each other in an internally articulated fashion around a central predicational crease. To remember *what*, in contrast, is not to summon up an entire objective complex, but a summary version of it in the form of a what-structure. This structure represents the *nominalization* of the complex, its subsumption under a description that is itself singular and without internal complication (e.g., "what happened," "what make"). Thus, a step in the direction of remembering *simpliciter* is taken to the extent that we are now remembering a singularity. But the step is not complete; the what-structure remains linked intrinsically to a state of affairs, of which it is in fact a condensed surrogate. In remembering-what, we are remembering a state of affairs through its own abbreviated, nominalized core.

### REMEMBERING ON-THE-OCCASION-OF

Remembering often arises on special occasions, especially recurrent ones such as holidays, anniversaries, and birthdays, though also when we are in particular places (e.g., my home town upon my return there). The act itself of remembering which occurs at such moments may not be exceptional; in fact, it is most typically a form of remembering *simpliciter* or remembering-that: a childhood scene rises before me as I perceive the house in which I grew up, or a memory of a previous anniversary upon the occasion of a present anniversary. But, as with remembering-to, such remembering is strictly circumstance-bound, giving to the experience a particular savor. Whether its emotional tonality be nostalgic or painful, this savor is an expression of our sense of *being back* at a given point in space or time, of *once more* experiencing something (usually something especially meaningful). We have encountered an instance of such remembering in my philosophy library memory: on entering the library I was suddenly overcome by a nostalgic sense of having worked there on many previous occasions. Characteristic of this experience was the haziness of my actual recollections at this poignant moment. These recollections were not brought back to mind in detail, but as a vague series of amassed similar experiences, all tied to a particular place. Such remembering on-the-occasion-of is even more dimly present at other times. On Christmas day, for example, one may experience an atmosphere of "Christmas past" without being able to specify *which* Christmas, or group of Christmases, one is thus indistinctly recalling. It is as if the significance of the occasion precludes more explicit acts of remembering or at least renders them difficult, replacing them by a diffuse familiarity in which the past is present not in person but by insinuation only.[42] We should also notice, finally, the considerable commemorative power of remembering on-the-occasion-of.[43] Such remembering is not necessarily an express act of commemoration (e.g., as it might be on Memorial Day); but it often plays this role because of the very nature of the situation: to remember in this way, at this place and time, is *ipso facto* to commemorate past experiences that occurred in this same place at other times.

### REMEMBERING THE FUTURE

At an antipode from such commemorative remembering is the very different act of remembering the future. In remembering-to, we have already encountered a case in which the future was explicitly at stake (e.g., as the time in which a duty is to be met). But there are other situations in which remembering relates to the future even more expressly. These occur when we remember a meeting, a trip, indeed any project that we have planned for the future: "I remember my dentist's appointment tomorrow." Notice that, as in the case of remembering-what, this statement is analyzable as "I remember *that* I have a dentist's appointment tomorrow." But the temporal modality differs radically from the normal instance of remembering-that, in which what we remember is unequivocally located in the past. We are now remembering a future situation not in its detail (this will not become possible until after we have experienced it, i.e., when it will have become the content of a normal case of remembering-that) but as something which we *expect to happen, or to experience ourselves, at some subsequent point.*[44] We have posited this point as existing sometime beyond the very moment in which we are right now remembering. As thus posited, it is futural; but as something that we must first recall in order to posit at all, it is tied to the past. The future *is* remembered in such a case, yet only as a projection from a past that is itself subject to remembering *simpliciter* or remembering-that. To remember my dentist's appointment I must be able—in principle, if not in fact—to recall when I made this event this appointment in the first place. Only on this basis can I remember it as an event that is to take place at a time yet to come.[45]

* * * * *

This completes the analysis of the act phase of remembering. I have not sought to be exhaustive but only to present several centrally important (and several other less important) forms of remembering, beginning with primary and secondary memory, extending through remembering *simpliciter*, remembering-that, remembering-how, and remembering-to, and ending with a number of subsidiary modes. Incomplete as this intentional analysis is, it nonetheless provides vivid proof of the multiplicity of the mental. This multiplicity is such as to resist attempts to encapsulate remembering into just two main forms (as James, Husserl, and Bergson tried to do) or even three such forms (as has been essayed recently).[46] Rather than endeavoring to contain the act-forms within such strict limits, it is more salutary to remain open on the issue of the exact number of basic ways in which remembering realizes itself as an act. The fact that I have discerned four major and four minor forms of remembering in this chapter should not lead us to regard these forms as constituting anything like a dense series of species that, taken together, exhaust the genus of remembering qua act. They are simply salient sorts of remembering that emerge frequently in our ongoing experience.

Nor should we suppose that each act-form is pristine and independent of the others. Just as (in Bergson's classification) habit memories are often infused with recollective imagery while recollections themselves can become sedimented into habitual actions,[47] so we constantly encounter hybrid cases of primary memory seeping into secondary memory, of remembering-that mixed with remembering-how, of remembering-to *cum* remembering *simpliciter*—and of the subsidiary forms merged with each of the foregoing. When it comes to matters of memory, we almost always have to do with commixture rather than with separation. And not surprisingly in view of the fact that remembering is a paramount, perhaps *the* paramount, connective power in our lives! Nevertheless, for purposes of analysis, especially intentional analysis, I have had to enter into a separative mode of discourse.

The same thing will obtain in the next chapter, which will complete the intentional analysis of remembering. Throughout, I am driven to distinguish what remains unseparated, and often inseparable, in the experience of remembering itself. In this experience act-forms and object modes actively collaborate with each other—especially on those occasions when we are inclined to say that we have had a particularly rich or rewarding time in remembering something.

# IV

# REMEMBERING AS INTENTIONAL

## OBJECT PHASE

The act of remembering is never entirely empty of content. To be remembering at all is to be directed, however deviously or indistinctly, toward *that which* we remember. This may seem so obviously true as to render redundant any claim that "we cannot remember without remembering something."[1] But we shall soon discover that this "something" is considerably more complex than may appear at first glance, consisting as it does of a number of different elements.[2] These elements in their interaction with each other constitute what we often simply term "a memory." Experiencing a memory is equivalent to being conscious of what may be designated as the "object phase" of remembering. I prefer the latter term at this stage of analysis because it serves to remind us that to speak of what we remember, i.e., the total object, is to presuppose an act or activity by means of which we remember this object. There is no such object without an act by which we attain it, and, conversely, no such act without the compresence of some such object. This circularity of act and object phases is the very circularity of intentionality itself—of that which holds the mind together in its very self-transcendence and makes it into one self-cohering whole. But in becoming a whole it is built up from components that together constitute the full intentional correlate of remembering. Let us consider these components in succession by reflecting on the structure of this correlate.

### The Mnemonic Presentation

The mnemonic presentation is *all that* we remember on a given occasion. I italicize "all that" to emphasize that I mean to include everything we then remember—everything save for the particular *way* in which what is remembered manifests itself (this will be treated under "Modes of Givenness" below). The mnemonic presentation is another way of describing the "total object" of remembering: all that we experience as presented to us, set before us, in a given case of remembering. This presentation may be divided into three importantly different elements: the specific content, the memory-frame, and the aura. Though distinguishable from each other in a descriptive account, these elements are often so intertwined in actual experiences of remembering as not to be noticed separately in their structural differences from one another.[3]

### SPECIFIC CONTENT

It is upon this that attention normally fastens when we remember—often to such an extent that the aura and the memory-frame remain in the background of our awareness. Indeed, our focus on the specific content may be so intent that we also tend to lose track of the particular act-form through which we are attending to this content. My first-hand reports of various experiences as given in chapter 1 illustrate this tendency to favor and stress specific content at the expense of other basic aspects of remembering. These reports concentrated almost exclusively on the details of what was remembered: "my first distinct recollection is of a breathtakingly panoramic vista. . . ." Here the object of the "of"—a particular vista-as-recollected—is such as to restrict the description of the object phase to its specific content. Such a tendency is not deplorable; it may even be inevitable, since *what* we specifically recall is typically more conspicuous than *how* we recall it. Indeed, there is no reason why we should not employ the "what" as a *fil conducteur* in a phenomenological description of human experience. But we must not thereby take the part for the whole, and suppose that our descriptive work is done once we have delineated the specific content of what we remember.

But what *is* this specific content? It is anything and everything that can be remembered, only *in its barest format*—that is, shorn of all features that are not crucial in its description and/or identification. It is thus *just what* we remember and no more; it is what we would be inclined to give in the sparsest, most economical, account of an experience of remembering. That does not mean, however, that this account need be monosyllabic or even short-winded. It can be quite detailed indeed, most notably in the case of recent experiences such as my remembered viewing of *Small Change*. And there is even sometimes the sense that a given description could continue indefinitely, so complicated or many-leveled is the experience being recollected, as in the opening of Robbe-Grillet's *Le Voyeur*. But in every instance, simple or complex, remote or recent, the specific content is *precisely* what is remembered, where "precisely" means with just that form and amount of detail with which what I remember presented itself to me. The exact degree of detail will therefore vary from case to case, but the necessity of being able to specify *some* detail holds constant throughout. If I cannot specify to myself or to others *in any way whatsoever* (including the use of admittedly indefinite descriptive predicates) what it is that I have remembered, then I cannot justifiably claim to have remembered at all. As Aristotle asserts, "Whenever someone is actively engaged in remembering, he always says in his soul . . . that he heard, or perceived, or thought *this* before."[4] The "this" is the specific content, and as such it must be specifiable by some form of "saying," whether this takes place in the soul or not.[5]

Now that I have indicated what sort of thing the specific content of remembering is, the main kinds of such content can be considered.

(1) First of all, we can discern "singular" objects and events, actions and persons. Here we remember particular things, things that are specifiably discrete: a particular face or gesture, a given gait or glimmer, a momentary mood or state of mind. It is a matter of what we remember *simpliciter*. The specific content of the "what" of remembering-what also belongs under this first heading. Even though such content is ultimately analyzable into an objective complex, *as experienced* it is singular in structure: it is just this particular thing or set of things.

(2) States of affairs represent a second kind of specific content in remembering. Here we remember specifically that certain events took place—that certain circumstances obtained, or that certain happenings arose. Instead of remembering things in isolated singularity, we remember that certain things *were the case;* we remember not just the objective complex they form but their internal articulations within this complex. Putting it differently, we can say that the specific content consists in a "situation" or, more precisely, in the skeletal structure of a situation—in its pure "thatness." I remember *that* such-and-such occurred and in so doing I remember the lineaments of this situation, the way in which certain qualities, relations, or actions inhered in it as its correlated constituents.

(3) A third sort of specific content is that involved in experiences of remembering-how. Here I recall a habituated or habitual *doing*, as when I remember how to exercise a certain learned skill, such as rowing a boat. In this case, what I am remembering explicitly is not just the exercise of the skill, but how this performance impinged, and may still be impinging, upon myself as agent. The specific content is articulated around myself-the-rememberer as expressly re-enacting the skill, which (in contrast with the objects of remembering *simpliciter* and remembering-that) is not remembered for its own sake.

(4) Finally, the content remembered may emerge in the form of actions to be carried out immediately or in the near future. These actions are often designated as duties—e.g., to feed the dog, to turn the light out, to talk in a louder voice, etc. Unlike many instances that fall under (3) above, however, they need not involve any particular skills in their enactment. For they are simply actions that we remember to undertake. Since as actions *per se* they can figure into various kinds of content, their specificity consists rather in the way they are bound by past commitments, promises, or vows. Thus, part of

the specific content of remembering to speak in a louder voice may be my vow to make myself better understood. I need not remember this vow as a particular past experience in order to remember to act upon it in the present.

Two brief remarks are in order here. First, the close correspondence between kinds of specific content and the major act-forms is not at all surprising but, indeed, just what we should expect in view of the strict correlativity of act and object phases. A particular kind of remembering will call for, and dovetail with, a particular kind of content; otherwise, the experience of remembering would fall into disarray instead of being the more or less cohesive whole that it presents itself as being. Second, each of the kinds of specific content discussed above can be presented in a sensuous or a nonsensuous guise, even though there is often a bias in favor of the former.

### MEMORY-FRAME

Although we can thus single out the specific content of what we remember for description and discussion, on closer examination we find it to be embedded in a "memory frame," that is, the setting within which specific content is presented to us. Such a setting is not of uniform appearance but varies from one experience of remembering to another. Indeed, it varies precisely in accordance with the character of the specific content itself, providing a unique ambiance for this content in each case. Moreover, we do not always apprehend the memory-frame with the same perspicuity. Sometimes it is only dimly manifest, and often it is not thematized. Nevertheless, it is always operative to some degree, as the main means by which specific content is situated. When we are not at all aware of any such frame, we may be led to doubt that we are remembering at all. This can happen in the memory of dreams. When I cannot "place" the content of a dream that flashes back into mind, I may very well apprehend this content as a present fantasy. But when I can say to myself, implicitly or explicitly, that "I dreamed that last night," I have found a setting (a strictly temporal setting in this case) that helps me to identify the presentation as a memory rather than as a fantasy.[6]

The primary function of the memory-frame is therefore evident: it serves as a setting by which the specific content of a memory may be situated and, as situated in a certain way, identified as mnemonic in character. The nature or inherent structure of the memory-frame is far from evident, however—due to its changeable appearance and to its equally changeable apprehension. Despite this variability, we can make out four basic factors in its composition.

#### *Worldhood*

This is not a constant or universal factor in the constitution of memory-frames. There is little, if any, sense of world present in the immediate recall of items of information learned by rote, such as dates or historical facts.[7] But in many full-blown memories we do experience—or better, *co*-experience—the embrace of an environing world. Even if it lacks the massive solidity and the unendingness that we find in the perceived world, the world of the remembered does exhibit consistency and persistence as part of a given memory-frame. It acts as an underlying field of presentation for the specific content remembered, and in this respect it is more fully worldlike than the momentary mini-worlds of imagination.[8] We may therefore speak of the "worldhood"[9] of the memory-frame—a worldhood which has two major components: scene and surroundings. The *scene,* taken in a strict sense, is the scene of action, that wherein a remembered object, event, state of affairs, performance, etc., appears or occurs. The scene may be spatial or temporal—or both at once. It forms the *immediate* setting for the specific content remembered. As such, it is this content's place of presentation, the locus where it is given.[10] The *surroundings,* on the other hand, refer to the nonimmediate setting, the general vicinity that surrounds the scene. Just as the scene situates the specific content, so the surroundings situate the scene. They do so by providing an arena in which the scene and the specific content can emerge and unfold. This arena may itself be void (i.e., in the manner of an empty field) or filled with content of its own. Such content is made up of co-remembered (versus focally remembered) things—"contiguous associates" in James's apt phrase[11]—which form with the specific content a loosely knit constellation. The contiguous associates are not normally singled out or even mentioned in a verbal description, since they remain at the edges of what we remember.[12]

*Self-presence of the rememberer*

Like worldhood, self-presence is not an inevitable concomitant of all remembering. Yet precisely where there is such worldhood within the memory-frame, the self-presence of the rememberer may become a noticeable component of the object phase of remembering. For the presence in question is that of the rememberer himself or herself *at the scene remembered*. In other words, we may recall not only the scene and its surroundings—and the specific content set within this scene—but also *ourselves* as present to all three of these constituents (and they to us). Then our own role in the experience or event recollected becomes integral to what we remember. We have internal evidence that *we were there*—there in the very midst of the remembered.

The exact way in which we remember ourselves as having been there can vary considerably. It may be a dominant part of remembering. This was clearly the case in my nostalgic remembering of having worked in a particular philosophy library: my working there formed the nearly exclusive focus of that set of related memories. Or one's self-presence may be simply one item among others, as was evident in my Yosemite and *Small Change* memories—where others were co-present and shared the remembered scene with me. Or, again, such self-presence can be quite muted, as in my very dim "Culligan" memory.

In whichever way and to whatever degree self-presence is an ingredient in the memory-frame, it can be of cardinal importance in remembering. For it is mainly responsible for that special sense of familiarity—that cozy "warmth and intimacy"[13]—which pervades many of our returning memories. In contrast, no such familiarity figures prominently into most of our imaginings, which are often quite impersonal in comparison.[14] But it would be a mistake to make familiarity into an indispensable attribute of remembering—as Russell tried to do.[15] Not only are there extraordinary instances of remembering in which familiarity is not felt where it would otherwise be expected (e.g., in what are technically termed "*jamais vu*" memories), but many ordinary memories do not include any factor of self-presence. The latter is especially evident in nonsensuous remembering-that (i.e., when we remember facts that were never experienced by us in the first person) and in routinized remembering-how (i.e., when we recall skilled actions which are not accompanied by distinct recollections).[16] We may conclude that when it is an active ingredient in the memory-frame, self-presence bears importantly on the fate of remembering; but it need not be present at all for *bona fide* remembering to arise.

*Remembered space*

In actual experiences of remembering, the spatiality and temporality of the mnemonic presentation are often correlated to the point of becoming indissociable. The "when" and the "where" are inextricably linked—so that, for example, to remember a scene from my grandparents' home is *ipso facto* to remember a scene that took place at a certain period of my childhood. Whenever such a scene is recalled, I know almost for certain that it comes from this period, despite the fact that I may have had other, later experiences at the same place. The converse situation can also obtain: a given period of one's life may always, or most characteristically, be remembered in terms of a given location: a room, a building, a landscape. Such a strict correlation between one particular stretch of time and one equally particular location in space does not, of course, always occur. But even when it does not, we can discern specifically spatial and specifically temporal structures that are ingredient within what we remember. These structures are the primary means of situating specific content, anchoring it more or less securely. Without such anchorage, this content would be cast adrift; it would be worldless.

The spatiality inherent in the mnemonic presentation appears in quite diverse forms, several of which I shall pick out here. (1) The most minimal space is that in which isolated items of experience or information appear: the face of my friend Jan, the visual symbols for "902," or "Culligan." Here there is neither scene nor surroundings—just a bare presentation in which the remembered item, and this item alone, figures. The presentational space lacks any articulation with an environing space; its only configuration or structuration is internal, e.g., among the various features of Jan's face, the numbers of "902," the letters of "Culligan." This constricted space excludes all else, leaving just enough room for presenting the specific content recalled, as if to say: this and no more. (2) A somewhat more capacious space was evident in my short-term memory of tea-tasting. The multiple items in this memory brought with them a correspondingly variegated spatial presentation. Not only did this presentation appear as having a circumambient space (albeit only dimly specified) and as containing more complex internal relations, but the *order of complexity* was increased by the multisensory nature of the experience. The space remembered was not visual alone but also auditory, haptic, gustatory, etc. Each of these modalities of remembered space has special features: the readily penetrable character of sound-space, the billowy and fragile quality of olfactory space, the decidedly buccal location of gustatory space, etc. In spite of this complexity and multiplicity—which reflect the complexity and multiplicity of the synesthetic experience itself—such a primary memory includes an effect of diminished involvement in the spatiality of the remembered content. (3) This sense of remove—of distance between myself as rememberer and what I remember—becomes more pronounced in relation to long-term memories of episodes from the distant past. Some such distance can be observed in almost all of one's childhood memories. Even the most distinct and seemingly indubitable memories from this era are experienced in the present as if through a screen or sieve. Indeed, in just such cases there may be an actual *Entfremdungseffekt* as we are struck by such a vastly different earlier self of ours engaged in apparently innocent activities. Yet much the same alienation-effect may also arise in the remembering-that of events in which we played no part at all; here too we seem to remember through a glass darkly and at a considerable remove. (4) At other times, however, there may not be any sense of such distance but, on the contrary, a merging of the rememberer (i.e., of his or her self-presence) with the remembered. This occurs above all in cases of remembering-how to do, e.g., when we remember how to perform a certain tennis stroke. In such an instance, the spatiality is normally confined to that of our own skillfully moving body in its goal-directed and yet self-circumscribed activity.

When we confine ourselves to the spatiality immanent in long-term, recollective memories with discernible scenes and surroundings, we find several basic characteristics of remembered space:

(*a*) First of all, we can discern a *clustering* tendency, i.e., a tendency for the specific contents of these memories to coagulate around particular points or locales rather than to distribute themselves evenly over a total field of presentation. Thus the entire series of memories that flooded in on me as I entered the philosophy library had as their locus a particular set of two rooms. The scenes they presented—even those only adumbrated—came securely implaced in these rooms, which thus acted as an anchorage point in space around which the specific contents of several recollections could cluster.

(*b*) A second characteristic of recollective space is its condensing or *compressing* effect. This occurs when a number of past locales become telescoped into the single locale of a given mnemonic presentation. These locales may all be the same, as in the case of the Lincoln Theater in my *Small Change* memory. But the locales can also be quite different from each other. In the latter case, a single spatial expanse condenses within it various other expanses, "summating" them as it were. This occurs, for example, in a memory I have of sweeping my grandparents' porch. This porch, I strongly suspect, is remembered not only for its own sake but as standing in for other parts of my grandparents' house where chores were carried out as well. There seems to be a factor of economy, sometimes to the point of elegance, in this compressing of several locales into a single privileged place of enactment. But there is a price to be paid for this very minimalization of means, and it is to be seen precisely in a third characteristic of remembered space.

(*c*) This is the *gappiness* found within many memory frames. Between and around the stably situated and relatively well-defined locales of memories are undefined and unlocalized patches of space. These are not so much empty as simply unspecified. We witnessed such areas of "dead space" in the Yosemite memory, each of whose episodes was securely located in relation to the park (i.e., as occurring on its edge, in its valley, etc.) but *between* which there was a sense of suspended space, a kind of mnemonic Erewhon. The patchiness of remembered space may also extend to the internal features of each such episode or scene, as was especially evident in my failure to recollect just where (in what spot) we had spent the night in Yosemite, whether *in* a cabin, *at* a campsite, etc., although I could certainly remember that I was in the valley of the park. Even in the most distinctly and fully recollected memories such spatial gaps can appear as sudden and often unsurmountable lacunae: what exactly was situated between the restaurant and the theater in my *Small Change* memory? However much I scrutinize this memory, I cannot detect the appropriate intermediate objects, which have now entirely vanished from my mind. I cannot therefore count on the memory-frame to furnish me with a gapless continuum of remembered space. On the contrary, both this frame and its contents are characteristically patchy: spatially indeterminate, "schematical" in the term I used in chapter 2. Thanks to their very gappiness, memories can be considered *pastiches* of the past—never its full spatial re-presentation.

*Remembered time*

When we turn to the temporality of the remembered, we notice first of all a phenomenon reminiscent of that just discussed under the heading of spatiality. This is the presence of considerable indeterminacy in regard to location in time. We often specify this location by such locutions as "last year," "in the past few weeks," "in my early childhood," etc. These locutions are often less than fully focused; instead of pinpointing the event or experience remembered, we posit (or better, retroject) a vaguely delimited framework *within which* we feel reasonably certain that the event or experience occurred. But we balk at tying down the precise moment of occurrence within this framework. Even when we are recalling something that happened as recently as "yesterday" or "this morning," we use these inexact terms as temporal indices rather than the more precise designations of "10:01 p.m." or (if a clock is not available) "when the shadow cast by the sun reached just this particular point." Now this is not merely a matter of being slothfully unobservant. We might very well have tried to be much more exact—for instance, had we been cross-examined as a witness of an accident or a crime. But since we do not usually make this effort except on occasions when the precise time must be known for extrinsic reasons, one begins to suspect that the memory-frame resists full specification *so as to allow for maximum temporal latitude*. This is not just to cover up possible mistakes in our estimates as to when the remembered event took place but, more importantly, to suit the inherent temporality of remembered material itself—especially its duration, which can be very difficult to determine with precision. Thus, even for those events about whose general time of occurrence we are quite certain (so that the possibility of error is not at issue), we still project a less than fully definite temporal setting. We say that the Battle of Hastings took place in 1066 instead of citing (unless we are historians of the subject) the very days in 1066 during which the battle lasted.[17]

What we call the "date" of an event or happening is nevertheless the most precise format in which the temporal matrix of the memory-frame crystallizes itself. Despite the remarkable range which a given date may allow for—"1986," "January 1986," and "January 25, 1986" are all dates—it is still an effective way of demarcating one period of time from another. "1986," however capacious it is qua date, still does exclude "1985" and "1987" on either side of its considerable extent. Indeed, a date affixed to a memory characteristically exhibits a basic ambivalence of being unspecific with regard to what lies *within* its limits but quite emphatic as to what is to be excluded as lying *beyond* these same limits.[18]

In fact, it is only in exceptional cases that we remember a past event or experience *along with* its date as a temporal marker.[19] For the most part, we are not aware of any appropriate, much less exact, date for what we remember but only of what James calls "a general feeling of the past direction in time."[20] Such a feeling arises most conspicuously in the case of those memories which emerge suddenly and which we cannot place at any particular period in the past—most notably in *déjà vu, déjà faite,* or *déjà raconté* experiences where we feel convinced that we have encountered their specific content before but cannot say where, not even within very large parameters. Even if we do not succeed in determining which precise part of the past they stem from—and thus which symbolic designation, which date, could be suitably affixed to them—we remain convinced that they originated *somewhere* in the past, at some prior point that has already occurred. Despite its vagueness, this conviction suffices for the purposes of the memory-frame, whose situating function is fulfilled in such instances by the very belief that what is remembered took place *sometime* in the past. The fact that this past is so dimly adumbrated—lacking even the liberal limits which a generic date such as "1986" would impose upon it—does not prevent it from acting as a framework for the specific content we remember.

Beyond date and general past-directedness there is a third way in which what we remember becomes characterized in temporal terms. This is found in the relationship between the specific content remembered and *other* past objects or events. These latter, which can aid our return to the past considerably, may have occurred either at the same time as the specific content—as when I remember where I was *at the time of* John Kennedy's assassination—or at some different time, as when I recall this assassination in association with that of Robert Kennedy. In the former case we have to do with simultaneous events that coincide or overlap in time with the focally recalled event. Such *co*-events or "contiguous associates" are particularly useful as forms of *aide-mémoire,* and we frequently rely on them as helpmates when we are searching for a particular memory or for a detail within a memory.[21] They constitute the proximal neighborhood—the temporal version of what I earlier called the "immediate setting"—of specific content that is remembered. In this capacity they serve to stretch out remembered time sidewise beyond the delimited moment in which the specific content *per se* is held to have arisen or to have lasted.

The *non*simultaneous objects or events which we recall in conjunction with focal content, on the other hand, have the function of situating this content in a larger context: e.g., "the tragic fate of the Kennedy family," or "modern assassinations." This function is realized thanks precisely to the lack of simultaneity—which leaves successiveness as the relevant ordering principle. An ordered series is set up, even if not deliberately; and the focally remembered event is placed in it in a before and/or after relation to the other events recollected. This can also serve as an effective mnemonic device, one that we may employ on purpose when we reconstruct an entire sequence of events so as to aid the remembering of a particular event located within this sequence: we find the particular event more readily because it has been nested in a series whose other successively arranged members act as alternative cues for its retrieval. A consequence of this strategy is to extend time in a linear, forward-and-backward, way.

The experienced quality of remembered time possesses much the same range as we have found to obtain in the case of remembered space. It varies from being apprehended in a sudden flash—as seemingly instantaneous and without any appreciable duration of its own (e.g., in my memories of "902" and "Culligan")—to being experienced as quite protracted (e.g., my memory of viewing *Small Change*). In the latter case, as I noted, time often assumes a quasi-narrative form: it unfolds in the manner of a story that is being recounted. Incidents are "strung out" over time—a time that is not, however, homogeneous in its unfolding.

The resulting heterogeneity is a basic feature of memories having a consecutive character. In parallel with the clustering phenomenon observed in the instance of remembered space, there is a tendency for memories whose content has the same or similar period of origin to *knot themselves together* in groups and to be remembered in relation to each other. We see this phenomenon at work whenever we speak of "memories of being a student at the University of X," "memories of summers spent on Cape Cod," or "memories of working late into the night."[22] Along with such clustering goes *compounding*—that is, the tendency to compress a group of temporally related memories into a single composite memory or a single emblematic memory—as well as *distending*, the thinning out of the temporal intervals between nodal memories or groups of memories.[23] All this knotting, compounding, and distending is more extreme than in remembered space, with the consequence that the temporal matrix is more discontinuous and disjunctive than its spatial counterpart—as well as more concentrated and deep-going at critical points. Hence the frequent sense that spontaneously arising memories emerge from a more complex, manifold origin in time than in space. Our memories are typically rooted in comparatively few *places* but in many different *times*—more times than we could begin to recount. While places *situate* events and to this extent are characteristically isolated and few in number, times serve instead to *connect* remembered items and in this capacity tend to be more numerous.

A different kind of heterogeneity arises from the contrast between the time of remembering and the time remembered. This contrast can be quite poignant. For we know that we shall never again experience the previous point or period in time in its aboriginal form—"I can relive the present, but it can never be given again [i.e., *as present*]"[24]—whereas I might well return to a perduring place: indeed, even if it has changed its character in certain ways, it will remain *the same place*.[25] Moreover, we are particularly prone to an alienation-effect when we become aware of a profound temporal gulf existing between the self who is presently remembering and the self being remembered (albeit only indirectly or implicitly). The time in which the latter self existed has elapsed definitively and forever; it is a *temps mort*. Even if I am expressly remembering myself as, say, exercising a skill that I still possess, I experience the memory of myself-as-pristine-performer as estranged from this still-skilled but now-older self who is doing the remembering.

Underlining this difference is the basic fact that the period of time in which I do my remembering is subject to quite exact chronological measurement—I need only look down at my watch to pin down the moment of remembering—in contrast with the time being remembered, which we have seen to be resistant to any such measurement even when it possesses a date. This is not the difference between a punctiform present and a nonpunctiform past—none of experienced time is strictly punctiform[26]—but between a form of duration that allows, and even invites, interpretation in terms of the point, the instant, and the line and one that obstinately refuses any such interpretation. The difference—and the mystery of the difference—is nowhere better revealed than in the everyday circumstance of recalling what happened during a whole year, its major events at least, in a thrice—the thrice of time occupied by the act of remembering itself—whereas the recalled events themselves may contain and exhibit considerable temporal spread.

### AURA

In addition to specific content and the memory-frame, the mnemonic presentation contains a third component. This component, the aura, is much more difficult to describe than the content or frame because of its intrinsically diffuse nature. It is what Bergson would call a "zone of indetermination."[27] Nevertheless, I shall attempt a brief description in order to acknowledge the important role of the aura in many memories and its presence to some degree in all memories.

We may begin by noting that the aura characterizes the mnemonic presentation in two distinguishable forms, each of which deserves description at this point:

(1) It appears first of all in the form of a blurred fringe or *margin* surrounding specific content and its memory-frame. It is the vanishing of these beyond the point of precise determinability in terms of time, space, worldhood, objecthood, eventhood, etc. As Minkowski claims, "Whatever the slice of the recalled past may be, whatever the depth of the recall that characterizes it, there is always a vast but obscure zone around it, from which it emerges and which serves as its support."[28] Thus the aura is not just unthematized—as anything else in the presentation may be at a given moment—but unthematizable. It is radically inchoate, in contrast with, say, a date, which may always be made more definite, at least in principle. (That is,

we can always further specify a given date: from day to hour, from minute to second, etc.) Such a fringe factor is the equivalent of what I have elsewhere called the "imaginal margin."[29] Both can be said to be resolutely nondescript—to be "an obscure perspective without horizons, without limits"[30]—yet to represent the very way in which the specific content of imagining or remembering evanesces of its own accord by dispersing and disappearing within an act of apprehension. For what we imagine or remember does not simply present itself and then come to an altogether abrupt spatio-temporal end. It tends, rather, to fade out, to dissolve, and it does so even in a brief imagining of "Pegasus" or a peremptory remembering of the name of the street on which one once lived. But these highly abbreviated displays dissolve quite rapidly compared to the much slower dissolutions of quasi-narrative imaginings and rememberings.[31] In every case, however, the aura or margin is that which the imagined or remembered content dissolves into, its *terminus ad quem*—albeit a terminus without determinate dimensions.

The differences between the imaginal and rememorative margins—insofar as one can still speak meaningfully of differences between what is so indistinct to begin with—are of two general sorts. On the one hand, the marginal region of imaginative presentations is usually more *noticeable* than in the case of mnemonic presentations, where we tend to overlook marginal factors altogether. This difference reflects the fact that imaginative presentations are often experienced in considerable isolation from immediate surroundings—i.e., in their "context-independence"[32]—whereas what we remember is typically more continuous with its context. On the other hand, even when the margin is quite noticeable in both cases, it tends to assume a more *pronounced* form in what we imagine than in what we remember. Compare, for example, the visualization of a wholly imagined friend with the visualization of a remembered friend. The imagined friend will normally appear encircled by a prominent and even conspicuous margin of indefiniteness, while the remembered friend appears with a significantly less discernible margin. Why is this? It has to do with the differing ontic status possessed by the two kinds of content. Remembered content is actual in status; it is something that we assume has in fact appeared or occurred on some previous occasion (even if we cannot now recall the precise moment). Imagined content, in contrast, is purely possible in status; it is something that, at most, *might* have appeared or occurred previously or that might yet do so in the future.[33] Positing imagined content as only possible, I am not as engrossed in it as such; my attention wanders more freely beyond this content to its immediate environs and more particularly to its margin, where still other possibilities might emerge. When I posit remembered content as actual, however, I tend to remain riveted to it, and I am correspondingly less tempted to transcend it toward a marginal region that lacks such sturdy actuality.

(2) The second form in which the aura of the mnemonic presentation appears can be called its *atmosphere*.[34] Unlike the margin, which encircles the specific content and the memory-frame, the atmosphere is experienced as pervading the presentation itself. Where the former rings *around* what we remember, the latter is given as a presence felt *throughout*. Moreover, our present remembering self often becomes beguiled and caught up in the same atmosphere.[35]

In this way memory and desire merge, much as Plato described in the *Philebus*.[36] Desire is in turn linked to emotion as its most expressive and overt manifestation. The atmosphere pervading the mnemonic presentation and ourselves as rememberers is characterized by a particular emotion or group of emotions, lending to this atmosphere its dominant tonality. It is not accidental that we speak of memories as "sad" or "joyful," "heart-rending" or "exhilarating." But when we do so, we are referring more to the atmosphere than to the specific content—or more exactly, to the atmosphere *of* and *for* this content. The character of such an atmosphere is emotional, and it is experienced in undisguisedly emotional terms: as rememberers, we tend to become sad or joyful in the act of our own remembering.[37] Yet just this infectious emotional assimilability between the rememberer and the remembered is what is most characteristic of the aura-as-atmosphere: it dissolves dualities and fuses otherwise disparate terms.

Although the aura thus takes two discernibly different forms within the mnemonic presentation, these forms combine and co-operate in the basic task of *unifying* this presentation. Without an aura as margin and as atmosphere, the presentation might risk becoming a mere congeries of dispersed parts—or else a bare monogram that is difficult to distinguish from a fantasy or image.[38] Since what we remember always presents itself as something more than a monogram and as something internally unified, it must contain a factor beyond what inheres in the specific content or even in the memory-frame. The frame unifies in terms of time, space, and world; but what holds the frame itself together and allows it to play its situating role is the aura. The latter unites the mnemonic presentation as a whole by its distinctive two-fold action of surrounding the presentation as its margin and permeating it as its atmosphere. The very diffuseness of the aura in both of its forms aids in this process. The result is the com-position of the mnemonic presentation as a coherent experiential unit: as *a* presentation with its own identity and stability.

## Modes of Givenness

The foregoing account of the object phase is not yet complete, however. In focusing on the constitution and unification of the mnemonic presentation, I have stressed the "what" at the expense of the "how"—how, namely, this presentation is given to us in remembering. It is given to us in many ways, not one only. One and the same *rememberatum* can be given to us differently at different times or in different circumstances. As Husserl says, "we can carry out remembering 'more quickly' or 'more slowly', clearly and explicitly or in a confused manner, quick as lightning at a stroke or in [a series of] articulated steps, and so on."[39] Whether this variability proves the "freedom" of remembering as Husserl also claims is a question beyond our immediate concern.[40] How then is the mnemonic presentation given to us? In four major ways:

### CLARITY

A particular presentation may offer itself to us with varying kinds of clarity. These are of two sorts. First, there is the steadily diminishing clarity with which an experience sinks back in primary memory; as it fades away in retentions, and in retentions of retentions, it becomes gradually dimmer (unless we focus upon it again expressly).[41] Second, there are variations of clarity that do not arise from such quasi-automatic fading—or even from the "veiling" to which so many secondary memories are prone[42]—but from the differential effects of various parts of the mnemonic presentation. The consequence of such effects is a series of instances differing mainly in degree. The sudden recollection of "902" was utterly distinct in presentation, appearing transparently and without any ambiguity in its mode of givenness. My "Culligan" memory displayed considerable distinctness too, though it was beclouded by the attendant images that accompanied it. The result was a hybrid clarity that was present in most of the other examples as well. In the Yosemite memory, the initial view of the park was given quite lucidly (aided, no doubt, by later perceptions of the photograph taken of this view); but the visual details of subsequent scenes were much more dimly given. Lack of clarity can also occur by omission, as happened in the philosophy library memory, in which the unclarity concerned less the particular details of remembered scenes than what exactly I had been doing there at certain previous points. In this instance, dimness of fact is more crucial than dimness of detail. The aura of a particular memory will often be of decisive importance in this regard, serving to obscure (as when an atmosphere of anger obfuscates what the anger was about) or to make luminous (as when the joyfulness of the atmosphere acts as a clue to the precise nature of what is remembered). But a basic variation in clarity may also be due to the memory-frame, especially with regard to the definiteness inhering in remembered time or space: despite the comparative clarity of "Culligan" as a visual display, it was highly ambiguous with respect to its temporal matrix. Indeed, the specific content itself may predetermine the clarity with which a presentation is given; I can remember a severe siege of sickness when I was a child; but since I was delirious at the time, the specific content of this memory is exceedingly blurred in my recollection of it.

### DENSITY

By "density" I mean the felt compactness or solidity of what we remember. Once again the range of variation is considerable. On the one hand, certain memories present themselves to us as intrinsically ephemeral—not just in the sense of being short-lived but as diaphanous, light, porous. What we term a "passing memory," typically composed of a single image, often presents itself as having a low degree of density. Here the mnemonic presentation seems so thin, so depthless and floating, that it may even be difficult to distinguish it from a passing fancy, which has much the same ethereal character. On the other hand, some memories present themselves as high in density—as concentrated, heavy, solid—from the very beginning. Prominent here are memories of highly charged or quite solemn occasions. But density is not decided by specific content alone. It can also result from the telescoping of many memories into a central memory whose density is itself an expression of the extreme compression that has occurred. Also, the sheer fact of recency tends to increase the density of a memory—as in the case of my short-term memory of tea-tasting in which the taste of the tea, the look of the objects, sounds, etc., all were held in mind as dense presences having considerable sensuous solidity. Density can also reflect stationing in temporal and spatial frameworks: the more specific the date or the location of what we remember is, the denser its presentation is likely to be. It is around such spatial or temporal nodal points that *other* remembered material tends to gather and coalesce, increasing the density still further. A single pivotal date, which comes to stand for an epochal event, may gain a remarkable density over time: "1492," "1776," "1945." So too may our date of birth or, for that matter, our home address or the number on our office door. Thus density is not dependent on the sensuousness of the mnemonic presentation, but can consist in the echoes or resonances—the influx of connoted material—which lend to something nonsensuous a characteristic weight, a consistency and impact which it would not otherwise possess.

### TEXTURALITY

This mode of givenness is closely related to density and is often correlated with it. But it is distinguishable from it by virtue of referring specifically to the way in which the *surface* of the mnemonic presentation is experienced as given. It is a question of the particular "feel" of this surface, its implicit palpability. Texturality may be such a prominent mode of what we remember that it comes to dominate its description—as was the case with the tea episode (an episode in which, moreover, there was a correlation between density and texturality). In other instances, it may be so faintly operative as hardly to merit mention, e.g., in the case of my remembering "Culligan" and "902." Nevertheless, numbers and words are not entirely lacking in texturality, as is sometimes dramatically evident in remembering lines of poetry: "Lilacs last in dooryard bloomed. . . ." The vast majority of cases, however, fall in between the two extremes just mentioned. In them, texturality plays a subdued but nonetheless distinctive role, being the way in which the various surfaces of remembered items are presented to us as coarse, uneven, smooth, silken, etc. Whenever we are inclined to use one of these latter words in our description of a memory, we are referring to texturality.[43]

DIRECTNESS

Finally, and quite crucially, the directness with which a mnemonic presentation is given must be considered. The main kinds of directness, each with its own differences of degree, are as follows. First, there is the directness of personal participation in the action being remembered, that is, self-presence in the form of enactment. Such participation reaches an extreme point in cases of habitual remembering-how to do, in which the rememberer and the remembered become one with each other: I, who am now executing a skilled action, am at one with the very self who first learned how to perform this action, and former performings are strictly continuous with my present performing, which represents their remembering. Second, directness of presentation may occur in the guise of my having been the witness of an object, event, or state of affairs that is being remembered. These latter, as the specific contents of memories, are what is most focused upon. One's own self-presence as witness is given along with them in a tandem mode, as *co*-present—as having been there too, albeit on the margins of the scene remembered. Third, a genuinely indirect givenness arises in instances in which facts are remembered of which one could not have been a witness: the signing of the Magna Carta, the outbreak of the Franco-Prussian War, etc. Although we may recall such facts with complete clarity, they are not remembered as directly given to us: I do not remember the *scene itself*, much less my witnessing of it, in which the Magna Carta was signed. I only remember *that* it was signed (and perhaps at a particular date), where the "that" signifies that the event itself is quite outside my personal experience—and hence must be remembered in the indirect form of a learned fact. Fourth, still another mode of indirectness is found in remembering-by-proxy. I can remember the Oklahoma Land Rush *as told to me by my grandfather*, thus remember it through him as my stand-in. To the extent that I identify with my grandfather in his recounting of this event, I remember it "with his eyes." But these eyes are only on loan; my memory remains vicarious and its full description cannot avoid reference to my grandfather as a mediating figure: "As my grandfather told it to me, 'no one could cross the line until. . . .' " The introductory clause underlines the indirectness, and what is put in single quotes is in effect my memory of my grandfather's direct memory. My own role is necessarily that of preserver or transcriptor of my grandfather's reminiscing, and my own recollection of this reminiscing (e.g., in the form of perceiving how he looked when recounting the incident, etc.) is the only form of direct remembering of which I am capable in such a case.

With this discussion of four major modes of givenness we have reached the end of our description of the object phase of remembering. This phase harbors considerable complexity—more complexity in any case than most of us care to pay attention to in the ordinary course of remembering. Remaining riveted to the specific content for the most part—many "memories" are described in terms of this content alone—we tend to overlook the other facets of the intentional correlate of remembering. So that we may keep the full picture more clearly in mind, it may be helpful to summarize the overall structure of the object phase in a formulaic and graphic way:

*Object Phase,* or Full Intentional Correlate of Remembering

A. Mnemonic Presentation: what we remember
   1. Specific Content: what we remember in particular and as such: objects, actions, persons, states of affairs, etc.
   2. Memory-Frame: that which situates specific content
      a) Worldhood
      b) Self-presence
      c) Remembered space
      d) Remembered time
   3. Aura: the indefinite setting of the presentation
      a) margin
      b) atmosphere

B. Modes of Givenness: how the mnemonic presentation is given
   1. Clarity
   2. Density
   3. Texturality
   4. Directness

* * * * *

The analyses undertaken in this chapter and in chapter 3 have attempted to discern the intentional structure of remembering. To the extent to which they have succeeded, these analyses have shown remembering to be an experience that exhibits the two closely intertwined dimensions that I have called "act phase" and "object phase." The preceding chapter examined basic ways in which we carry out the act of remembering; it disclosed four major act-forms along with several subordinate modes of enactment. The present chapter has picked out four main components of the object phase and has given a detailed description of each component. Although the act and object phases of remembering have been treated in separation from each other, I have pointed to a number of conjunctions and correlations between them—for instance, between a certain kind of specific content and a particular act-form. In this way the intentionality of remembering has emerged as a central feature of what we term generically "human memory." Such memory reveals itself to be much more orderly in its internal structure than we usually take it to be in our unrehearsed and unreflective immersions in it. If the reader has become convinced of such an inner regularity of remembering, an important step toward a full assessment of remembering will have been taken.

This step becomes still more decisive when we take into account the results obtained in chapter 2. There we singled out four pairs of traits that deserve to be designated "eidetic": search/display, encapsulment/expansion, persistence/pastness, and actuality/virtuality. Each of these pairs designates a fundamental parameter of human memory. Moreover, such pairs bridge over the intentionalist bifurcation of remembering, since (with the exception of search/display) each can characterize both act and object phases.

As Part One draws to a close, we are left with a question of how to coordinate the eidetic analysis of chapter 2 with the intentional analysis of chapters 3 and 4. One way of doing so is by means of the accompanying chart, which admittedly is highly schematic. It presents correlations only and these often with less than complete certainty. The correlations are between eight eidetic traits identified in chapter 2 and eight intentional structures that have been singled out in chapters 3 and 4. Nevertheless, the chart helps to situate eidetic features of memory within an intentional framework. It also indicates, by its own multiplex character, the nonsimple nature of memory even at this early stage of analysis. Despite the diversity which it represents, however, the chart reveals certain definite patterns: search and display are seen as exclusive alternatives vis-à-vis act and object phases (and there is a symmetry in regard to whether these traits are conspicuous or muted within these phases); remembering *simpliciter* and remembering-that embody the other six eidetic traits in a steady, "normal" appearance, whereas remembering-how and remembering-to are internally divergent in this respect; and in the object phase, there is a pronounced tendency for seven of the eight traits to emerge either conspicuously or normally in the specific content or memory-frame, while the same traits are much more muted in the aura and in modes of givenness.

However striking they may be, such patterns do not bespeak *causal* connections; the chart is strictly correlational in status and significance. Its very tenuousness—its sheerly diagrammatic character—reflects the limits of any purely phenomenological analysis that restricts itself to the eidetic and

| Intentional Structures | Eidetic Traits | | | | | | | |
|---|---|---|---|---|---|---|---|---|
| | Search | Display | Encapsulment | Expansion | Persistence | Pastness | Actuality | Virtuality |
| *Act Phase* | | | | | | | | |
| 1. remembering *simpliciter* | c | | n | n | n | n | n | n |
| 2. remembering-that | c | | n | n | n | n | n | n |
| 3. remembering-how | m | | c | c | c | m | c | m |
| 4. remembering-to | m | | c | m | n | m | c | m |
| *Object Phase* | | | | | | | | |
| 1. specific content | | c | n | n | n | n | c | n |
| 2. memory-frame | | c | c | m | c | c | c | n |
| 3. aura | | m | m | c | n | m | m | c |
| 4. modes of givenness | | m | n | n | m | m | c | m |

m = mute appearance or occurrence
n = normal appearance or occurrence
c = conspicuous appearance or occurrence

intentional aspects of memory. A more complete analysis is called for, an expansion of the project beyond these initial and tentative steps.

For it must be emphasized that the journey undertaken in this book has only begun. Much remains to be done in Parts Two and Three. At this point, let me only note that we have thus far accomplished what a traditional phenomenological approach necessarily seeks to accomplish: to provide an investigation of a given phenomenon in its eidetic and intentional features. That this investigation is formal by its very nature cannot be denied. The formality is only reinforced in any mere listing of traits or in the drafting of a chart such as that presented above. But the same formality means that such an approach cannot claim full adequacy to the phenomenon under scrutiny. Beyond the form of memory there is its matter; beyond its surface, its depth. As a consequence, there is something undeniably and almost literally "superficial" about the descriptions given in the last four chapters. These chapters have largely confined themselves to conveying what Bachelard calls "sudden salience[s] on the surface of the psyche."[44] As an effort at the pure description of such saliences, this Part has confined itself to conveying the results of a first look at memory's surface structures.

Moreover, this first viewing has considered memory as an almost exclusively mental phenomenon: as "memory in mind," in keeping with the origin of the word "memory" itself in the concept of mindfulness. It is only appropriate and expectable that in this enterprise an intentional analysis would assume prominence. According to Brentano's archetypal credo, *all* mental phenomena, and *only* mental phenomena, are intentional.[45] Yet remembering is more than a matter of mind alone, and we must move beyond the surface of the psyche if we are to grasp memory in its full amplitude. We need to move beyond the narrow (if nonetheless useful) framework set forth in preceding chapters. If this takes us beyond the intentional, it will also take us more completely into the phenomenon of remembering itself—into the heart of our existence as rememberers.

# *Part Two*
# *Mnemonic Modes*

# PROLOGUE

> I will make a suggestion as to how we should proceed. Imagine a rather short-sighted person told to read an inscription in small letters from some way off. He would think it a godsend if someone pointed out that the same inscription was written up elsewhere on a bigger scale, so that he could first read the larger characters and then make out whether the smaller ones were the same.
>
> —Plato, *Republic*, Book Two

With the investigations of Part One we have taken a decisive first step toward providing a comprehensive description of remembering. Moreover, we have done so in accordance with traditional phenomenological categories of "eidetic features" and "intentional structures," achieving a certain closure in the process. But such closure can bring with it a foreclosure of neglected aspects. Just when we think we are becoming clear about the basic structure and forms of human memory, it still manages to elude us. Like the fabled statues of Daedalus, we need to keep tying memory down by describing it in ever more adequate terms that respect its multiple modes of appearing.

At this turning point, foreclosure threatens in two closely related ways. First of all, an unexamined mentalism has been subtending almost all the analyses given in Part One. By "mentalism" I mean the view that human minds—or surrogates for these minds, most notably computers—furnish the ultimate locus as well as the primary limit of human experience. A critical consequence of this view is that all that we undergo must come to be represented in the container of the mind if it is to count as an "experience" at all. This is not the place to pursue the difficulties attendant upon mentalism, which has dominated Western epistemology from Descartes to the present. Ryle and Rorty have tried to lay its ghost to rest,[1] and I return to the issue myself in the Prologue to Part Three. What matters now is merely to notice how pervasively mentalistic my treatment of remembering has been thus far in this book. I have talked unabashedly of "acts" and "presentations" in ways that make sense only if these are understood as specifically *mental* acts and presentations. Even "objects" have been construed specifically as intentional objects: that is, as objects of and for the mind. It was only as an exception that I spoke of remembering-how as an activity that may require habitual and skilled actions of the *body*. Otherwise, the preceding four chapters have been written in mentalese and openly invite being read in this same idiom.

The danger inherent in adopting such an idiom is not only that of subscribing to a model of remembering as strictly self-contained within the human mind. It also consists in the fact that the mind itself is notoriously opaque in its own self-disclosure. It did not take Freud's assiduous efforts to tell us how intricate and shadowy, indeed deceptive and misleading, the mind can be to itself and for other minds. In Book Two of the *Republic*, Plato remarks on the considerable difficulty of dealing with the inner psychology of justice. In the same spirit of honesty, we must acknowledge that the inner workings of memory are deeply veiled; they are as unknown to ourselves in the course of daily remembering as are the workings of our own spleen or pancreas. As Wittgenstein, an especially keen critic of mentalism, has remarked: "Memory, therefore, is certainly not the mental process which, at first sight, one would imagine."[2] Despite the supposed lucidity of mental phenomena, it is precisely when it is construed as a "mental process" that memory shows itself to be something other than what one first takes it to be.

What shall we do in this impasse? We cannot turn to the analysis of ordinary language, as so many philosophers have done in the wake of Wittgenstein and Austin. The language of memory is saturated with mentalistic biases: the word "remembering" itself is normally construed as a mental act in a wholly unclarified sense. Furthermore, as I pointed out in the Introduction, nuanced terms and expressions for memory have for the most part become archaic and obsolete in the English language. When dealing with the vocabulary of remembering, whether this vocabulary be mentalistic or not, we are skating on thin ice indeed. Although we can gain clues from existing taxonomies and especially from ancient etymologies, we are cast adrift on a virtual Sargasso Sea of linguistic confusion and oblivion when it comes to the exact description of human memory. Where then may we turn for clarification and inspiration?

Here we may take a clue from Plato himself in the above epigraph. If human beings cannot reliably observe the internal structure of justice in the depths of the human psyche, he suggests that they look to where justice appears in "larger characters." This is in effect what we shall do in Part Two by examining three distinctive mnemonic modes in which remembering is writ large. Each of these modes involves outstanding factors that cannot be contained within the meshes of mentalism: factors that are external to mind itself such as physical reminders, the concrete discourse of reminiscing, and other human beings as objects of perceptual recognition.

Mnemonic modes are therefore forms of remembering whose adequate description cannot be confined to an exclusively mentalistic analysis. By pursuing these modes, we will be taking a crucial first step beyond the mentalism that has underwritten so much of the preceding investigation. We will be engaging in a journey whose destination will not become fully apparent until considerably later in this book.

# V

# REMINDING

> There is an active and aktuall Knowledge in a man, of which these outward Objects are rather the re-minders than the first Begetters or Implanters.
>
> —Henry More, 1653

## I

The very multiplicity of the mental that has been operative in Part One threatens us with a special form of forgetfulness. We have witnessed a proliferation of types and subtypes, of primary and secondary traits, which brings with it the distinct danger that the overall shape of remembering will become lost in the minute traces of detailed descriptions. In facing this danger of descriptive immersion, it is advantageous to consider a mnemonic mode that is concerned specifically with the *limits* of memory. Reminders are expressly designed to draw us back from the edge of oblivion by directing us to that which we might otherwise forget. As reminding by its very nature delimits forgetting by constraining and diverting the waters of Lethe, so our consideration of reminding itself may help to delimit the present inquiry and to rescue it from submersion in an ocean of descriptive detail.

Reminders are also among the most dramatic instances of memory "writ large." They exhibit a quite determinate structure, as we shall come to observe. Thanks to this very structure, reminders literally stand out in our lives. Indeed, we find ourselves in their midst at practically every turn, whether they appear as written or spoken warnings, as book reviews or grade lists, as recipes or train schedules. Precisely because we are at all times threatened by engulfment in forgetting, we have arranged about us an encompassing armamentarium of reminders. It is as if reminders constituted a gigantic exoskeleton of memory, serving to protect it from oblivion by their determinacy, their unique combination of noticeability and reliability. As an important sector of what Heidegger calls generically the "ready-to-hand,"[1] reminders surround and support our ongoing existence in countless manners. As such they give point and purpose to the often bewildering onrush of our lives, signaling to us what we should remember to do or think as well as how we might remember more effectively.

## II

As I sit at my desk writing these lines, I cannot help but notice an array of objects randomly disposed before me:

1. A post card from Athens: this acts as a double or triple reminder. Viewing its picture of the Parthenon, I am reminded of my visit to this building twelve years ago; I am also reminded of "the glory that was Greece," a glory for which the Parthenon has become a standard symbol but which I cannot experience in the first person. On the other side of the card is a letter from a former student, of whose flamboyant face and uneven academic career I am suddenly reminded by his handwriting and his signature. It is not without interest that the first three sentences on the card run:

   > The origins of Western thought are indeed difficult to find in this extraordinary world of rubble and stone. But if we should forget the hidden nuances, alas, [nevertheless] such obvious *reminders* as the magnificent temples persist. How true that everything dates back to antiquity. (my italics)

   Here the very word "reminders" is used to remind me (and no doubt my student himself) of that about which the building depicted on the post card's opposite side reminds us wordlessly, demonstrating the interchangeability of the medium in which reminders may operate.

2. A single sheet of paper marked "*Memorandum*": here a reminder announces, and literally underlines, its own function—in this case to remind absent-minded professors of their bounden duty to hand out course evaluation forms. Note that the heading of the memorandum is tripartite, each line specifying a different aspect of reminding:

   To: ("remindee")
   From: (remitter of the reminder)
   Subject: ("remindand")

   This curt format could suffice by itself; but since the action in question is likely to be forgotten, the remitter adds a fairly lengthy prose statement in which reminding is done by way of pointing to an order: "This fall the departments have been directed to do their own evaluations in lieu of a university-wide evaluation" and then by a thinly veiled threat: "All

Ph.D. students and faculty seeking tenure or promotion are mandated to do this evaluation every year." Further reinforcing this memorandum are three words I have added at the top in pencil: "Bring to class"; these words act as a reminder to myself to carry out the request (i.e., the remindand) contained in the original reminder.

3. A small slip of cardboard on which is written: "Put rest of notes on 'The Problem of Perception and Imagination' here—then back in the folder below." This is a message which I had hastily scribbled to myself in the midst of preparing a lecture for a course in the philosophy of perception. The notes, about whose proper place the message was to remind me, had been made a couple of years ago in connection with another course, one on perception and imagination. Thus, the proper place for storing the notes in question is in the folder for the course for which they had originally been prepared.

   The imbrication of past and future is striking: the note was written as a reminder of a future action to take place at some point after my coming lecture, but the aim of this action was to return the notes to a place determined and established at a past point—a point to which I will no doubt continue to refer in subsequent uses of the same notes. Here one cannot help but wonder: how can there be such a thing as a reminder of the future? If reminding is not restricted to the past, can it be considered a mode of memory?

4. A slightly larger slip of paper: this represents information taken down during a recent telephone conversation bearing on plans for a summer institute in archetypal psychology to which I had been invited. Here is the sequence of things that were noted down:

| remuneration for the session | — dates of the session | — daily schedule | — others invited | — phone number of the organizer |
|---|---|---|---|---|
| money | time | | people | |

All of these components of the reminder point to a future event whose status at the moment was only possible when I made the note. Neither the institute itself nor my coming to it was yet definite, in contrast with the future but definite action indicated by the previous reminder. The only reference to the past is indirect: I had attended a meeting of archetypal psychologists the year before. Writing their names down, I am reminded of the earlier meeting. Here a part of the total reminder serves to remind me of something disparate in time and structure from the event for which the rest of the reminder was expressly designed *as* a reminder. And, once again, the future (even as indefinite) is seen to be just as implicated as the past in the full process of reminding: how can this be?

With these examples before us, we must now ask: how does a reminder remind? What is its *modus operandi?* By what procedure does it do its work? Answers to these questions will be forthcoming if we first consider what its basic work is. This work, the work of reminding itself, is *to induce the actual or potential remindee to do or think something that he or she might otherwise forget to do or think*. At stake here is a considerable range of actions—from putting notes back in their proper place to handing out course evaluation forms, from receiving a possible remuneration to making certain telephone calls. The action indicated by the reminder is typically one step removed from the immediate present in which I apprehend the reminder itself. I am being reminded of a possible action which I may undertake very soon or eventually, though not precisely when and as I am perceiving the reminder. The action itself,[2] the remindand proper, is thus situated not in my present as such but in the future, whether this future be near-term or more distantly projected.

One might well ask at this point, where do the *past* and therefore *memory* enter into this picture? It is important to realize, first of all, that the very phrase "the past and *therefore* memory" is by no means unambiguous, since the two items thereby conjoined are not as indissolubly linked on all occasions as the "therefore" suggests. I can, as we have seen, remember that I have an appointment with my dentist *tomorrow*. It may be retorted that I must then remember that I made the dentist's appointment at a particular moment in the past. Yet this is simply not so: I certainly did make the appointment, but I may not be able to remember how or when I did. To remember a future commitment is to presume, but not necessarily to recall, a past event of committal. In this way, the earlier act is implicated by the commitment even when it is not expressly recollected. When I am reminded of something to *do*—something I ought to do, may do, can do, will probably do, etc.—I am remembering to undertake a future action mandated or sanctioned by a past action which I may not recall as such but which I must nonetheless presuppose. The reminder is thus a point of connection between past and future, a *Janus bifrons* which is apprehended in a present moment situated *between* the past of engagement and the future of enactment.

But there are also cases in which reminding engages the past more directly. We have posited that the work of reminding is "to induce the actual or potential remindee to do or *think* something that he or she might otherwise forget to do or think." The thinking in question may take many forms: thinking of one's duty, health, or family, thinking of mathematical or philosophical truths, or thinking of future actions to be undertaken. One of its primary forms, however, is *thinking of the past*. Remindful thinking of the past is itself a basic way in which we remember the past.[3]

When I am being reminded of the past by being led to think of it as such, the remindand is neither a future action nor the past moment of engagement implicated thereby, but a past event or state of affairs that I have witnessed or come to know from various sources. The picture postcard of the Parthenon reminded me of my own previous perceiving of this same building some twelve years ago.[4] The postcard provoked me to think of this perceiving in the format of certain determinate recollections. It also reminded me directly of my erstwhile student and of "the glory that was Greece."

The above analysis of stray reminders on my desk helps us to appreciate the considerable range of reminding. It also serves to focus attention on the several components of reminders themselves. But it does not tell us anything substantive about the relationship between these components, especially in regard to the question: How does the reminder remind me of the remindand?

## III

In order to find our way to an answer to this last question, let us examine a classic and apparently simple example of reminding: a piece of string tied around a finger. Suppose that I tie a string around the little finger of my left hand early one evening to remind myself to turn down the heat in the living room later that evening: I regularly forget to turn down the heat when I go to bed. Such a failure of memory calls for instituting a reminder. Nevertheless, I frequently forget to establish one—even when I explicitly resolve to do so in advance. Once when I did set up such a reminder, I could not recall its purpose when I gazed at it later on! This time, however, let us assume that the reminder functions successfully. It does remind me to turn down the heat in the living room late one very cold night. How does this take place? The three components at work are readily identified: the *reminder* is the string tied around my finger (or more exactly the string *as* tied around my finger); the *remindand*, what it reminds me of, is the clear-cut but all too easily forgettable action of turning the heat down later that night; and I, the potential heat-reducer but also the potential forgetter of heat-reduction, am the *remindee*. As it happens, I am the one who sets up the reminder by tying the string around my finger, even though a friend might have tied it for me. The institution of the reminder on a given occasion must therefore be distinguished from the activity of reminding itself—as must any unintended effects of this activity (such as the frozen water pipes that might result if I turn the heat too far down).

One traditional model of reminding stems from Aristotle. In *De Memoria et Reminiscentia* Aristotle maintains that reminding takes place because (and to the extent that) the reminder *(mnēmoneuma)* is construed not as a pure figure *(zōon)* but as a copy *(eikon)* of the remindand—where the remindand is not singled out for separate description but is conceived simply as that of which the figure is to be regarded as a copy. Aristotle goes on to assimilate memory to this model of the reminder as a copy:

> For the figure drawn on a panel is both a figure and a copy, and while being one and the same, it is both, even though the being of the two is not the same. And one can contemplate it both as a figure and as a copy. In the same way one must also conceive the [memory] image to be something in its own right and to be of another thing. In so far, then, as it is something in its own right, it is an object of contemplation or an image [*phantasma]*. But insofar as it is of another thing, it is a sort of copy and a reminder . . . if one contemplates the image as being of another thing, and (just as in the case of the drawing) as a copy, and as of Corsicus, when one hasn't seen Corsicus, then . . . [it] is a reminder.[5]

Aristotle's account is not tenable as a general explanation of reminding. For not all reminders are icons or likenesses of their respective remindands. This is especially evident in the paradigm case at hand. What conceivable resemblance is there between a piece of string tied around my little finger and turning the heat down? There is no resemblance between the action of tying the string around my finger, or even seeing it tied there, and turning down the heat. Nor is there any similarity between the perceived or pictured contents of these actions. As the configuration of the knot does not resemble the posture of my body in adjusting the thermostat, it is clear that the form of the reminder need not bear any likeness to that of which it is the reminder.

Of course, some reminders *do* resemble their remindands; indeed, the likeness may be very exact, as in the case of the postcard depicting the Parthenon. The iconicity of such a reminder doubtless aids its effectiveness as a reminder, since on first perception I can hardly think of anything *other* than that of which it is the exact copy. Nevertheless, the isomorphism such reminders display in relation to their remindands is not *indispensable* to their role as reminders. Other, wholly non-pictographic reminders can put me in mind of the very same thing, as does the single word "Parthenon" printed on the reverse side of the same postcard. Though entirely lacking in pictographic resemblance to the ancient temple, this word brings my mind to my experience of this monument as expeditiously as does the photographic reproduction of the same building. Aristotle's copy theory must be discarded, then, because reminders need not resemble their remindands in order to remind us of them.

But if the relation between reminder and remindand is not that of resemblance, what is its essential nature? What *is* indispensable to it? One model that suggests itself is that of *indication*. The string around my finger is not a copy of an action, but it may be a sign that indicates a past or future action. As an indicative sign, the string picks out such an action by signaling its actual or possible presence. Put in terms of our ongoing nomenclature, the string as reminder indicates to me as remindee a past or future action as remindand. This offers a more promising model than Aristotle's, since we are not bound by any requirement of resemblance. Moreover, the role of the remindee, neglected in Aristotle's treatment, is here brought explicitly into play.

As if to confirm the correctness of this view, Husserl singles out reminders as leading instances of indicative signs *(Anzeichen)*: "Signs to aid memory, such as the much-used knot in a handkerchief, memorials, etc., also have their place here. If suitable things, events, or their properties are deliberately produced to serve as such indications, one calls them [indicative] 'signs' whether they [successfully] exercise this function or not."[6] Husserl also recognizes the essential role of the remindee: "a thing is only properly an indication if and where it in fact serves to indicate something *to some thinking being*."[7] Included in this latter statement are the equivalents of all three components of the reminding situation: reminder ("an indication"), remindand (the "something" which is indicated), and the remindee ("some thinking being"). Further, Husserl conceives of indication in such a way as to avoid any commitment to a copy theory of reminding. This is evident in his formal definition of the "common element" in all species of indication:

> In these we discover as a common circumstance the fact that certain objects or states of affairs of whose reality *(Bestand)* someone has actual knowledge indicate to him the reality of certain other objects or states of affairs, in the sense that his belief in the reality *(Sein)* of the one is experienced (though not at all [self-] evidently) as motivating a belief or surmise in the reality of the other.[8]

Nevertheless, Husserl's conception of the common element present in all indication ranges too broadly to enable us to isolate the *specificity* of reminders as a particular species of indication. In Husserl's own reckoning, indicative signs include brands on slaves, Martian canals, fossil vertebrae, volcanic eruptions, chalk marks on blackboards, and much else besides.[9] We are not told what specific differences there may be between these various species, nor even where (or how) to start looking for them. On the other hand, the very same conception is too narrow. It excludes many cases of reminding, including our own exemplary case of tying a string around one's finger. The constriction is due to Husserl's emphasis upon the notion of "reality" in the above definition. Granted, the reminder itself is a reality of some sort, whether perceptual (as in string-tying) or cognitive (as in those cases in which a thought acts as a reminder: this thought has reality as an actual occurrent in the mind). And in many cases the remindand is also a reality—above all, when what we are reminded of is a past object or event, since this object or event is real by virtue of having already occurred. But what of those no less numerous cases, including our paradigm, in which the remindand proper[10] is a future object or state of affairs, one that has the status of being merely optional, would-be, should-be, etc.? How can we claim reality, however loosely construed, for that which is not yet in being? *There are no future realities*—the very phrase "future realities" being a blatant contradiction in terms—and yet many reminders evoke future actions, including that of lowering the heat on a wintry evening when I have not yet lowered it and need to be reminded to do so by placing a string on my little finger. I certainly do not actively believe in or presume the reality of such an action. If I *did*, I wouldn't bother to put the string around my finger! From the standpoint of the present, what I am being reminded of is only *possible*—for I may *not* carry out the action in the end, even if the string successfully reminds me to do so.

We must therefore reject Husserl's conception of the indicative sign as a model for reminding. Although this conception is an improvement over Aristotle's account, it is at once too broad and too narrow. As a result, we still do not have an adequate idea of how the string around my finger exercises its reminding function. I would suggest that we consider this function to reside in *the figurative and schematical adumbration of an object, action, or state of affairs*.

The cursory formula I have just underlined calls for several comments:

(1) If I am reminded of an object or state of affairs, it is necessarily located in the past, in the future, or in a contemporaneous present that is not identical with my own present (e.g., I am reminded of my cousin's bypass operation in Kansas City as I notice that it is now 10:00 a.m. in St. Louis). To be reminded of an action is to be put in mind of a doing or thinking that occurs at some point in the past, present, or future. Moreover, I can be reminded of actions or situations in which I am the initiating agent (e.g., turning down the heat, putting my notes away), in which I serve as observer or witness (my viewing of the Parthenon), or in which I seem to play no role at all ("the glory that was Greece," of which I can be reminded only if I have once learned of this same glory, my agency as a learner here being presupposed).

(2) The term "figurative" in the above formula refers to the fact that, in order to function effectively, a reminder is normally presented to the remindee in a sensuous or quasi-sensuous format. This format is not to be confused with a strictly iconic representation since, as we have seen, reminders need not be structurally isomorphic with their remindands to remind us of them. Indeed, they need not *represent* them in any explicit or readily recognizable way at all. They may be pure figurations which convey only their own figurative structure, as in the case of most written reminders and of the piece of string tied around my finger. It is odd to speak of this piece of string, or of a group of reminding words, as representing, much less as iconically depicting, any specifiable action, object, or state of affairs. They

are sheer presentations, and as such they need not be given to our physical senses at all but may appear as mental images or words of inner speech. But such images and words still present themselves as *quasi*-sensuous; they are *appearances*—to the mind if not to the senses.

(3) It is a striking fact that "appearance" is the original meaning of *schēma* in Greek.[11] If a schema is an appearance or shape—a "figure"[12] in the rich sense given to this latter term by Gestalt psychologists—then a reminder *qua* schema will be inherently figurative in status. But "schema" has also come to connote what is figurative in a specifically *condensed* or sparse form. Notice in this regard the structure of the string around my finger: the simplicity of this structure is distinctly schematical, and its very knottedness seems to symbolize the schematicalness of all reminders.[13] Indeed, think of almost any reminder—including the four cases with which I began this chapter—and a definite economy will become apparent. In part this is a practical consideration: who would devise reminders that are more elaborate than that which they remind us of? In part, however, the schematical aspect of reminders subserves their adumbrative dimension.

(4) What, then, is adumbration? In the context of perception, adumbration (literally, "shadowing forth") is a mode of manifestation in which the already perceived parts of an object suggest to the perceiver the presumptive character of those parts that have not yet been perceived.[14] Since a reminder need not be a perceived object,[15] however, its form of adumbration is not identical with this perceptual paradigm; it is more a type of relation than a mode of manifestation. What is shadowed forth in the adumbration of reminding is not some hitherto concealed part of the reminder taken as a singular object. What is adumbrated is no part at all of the reminder *qua* sensuous or quasi-sensuous object—which is to say, *qua* schematical figure—but something else to which the reminder is itself related. This something else is, of course, the *remindand*. This, and this alone, is adumbrated by the reminder in the process of reminding.

It is important to underline that such an adumbrative relation is not indicative, much less iconic, in character and that it differs, therefore, from the models proposed by Husserl and Aristotle. Although reality and resemblance—which characterize the respective models of these two thinkers—may play a role in reminding, we have found that neither trait is a necessary feature of reminders. Instead of copying the remindand or motivating a belief in its reality, reminders adumbrate what they remind us of. They shadow it forth or suggest it to us as remindees by any number of means (including iconic and indicative means themselves on occasion). The adumbrative relation thus set in action is best understood under the headings of "evocation" and "allusion."

(a) The *evocation* consists in a summoning-up of the remindand from a state of actual or potential forgetfulness. The reminder is established to combat such forgetfulness in the first place, and it does so by presenting to the remindee a sensuous or quasi-sensuous configuration conspicuous enough to draw attention to itself. I don't usually tie a knot on my little finger: thanks to its more or less striking appearance, the knot stands out and distinguishes itself in my everyday environment. But I do not attend to it for its own sake; instead, when I apprehend it as a reminder I grasp it for the sake of what it evokes. This is true even of aesthetically appealing reminders such as the post card from Greece. I may admire the photograph of the Parthenon, and find myself lingering over its purely formal properties; *as a reminder,* however, it sends me beyond its own aesthetic surface by calling up in me experiences or objects not part of this surface. That which is evoked in such cases is the remindand, but it is crucial to stress that it is *e*-voked: called forth from obscurity and often still partaking in some of the same dark Lethic indistinctness from which it arises. Indeed, it is this indistinctness that allows the remindand to possess the status of the possible, the hypothetical, the probable, etc. These modal characters, in their very indeterminacy, cannot be indicated in Husserl's strict sense, and they often defy iconic representation as well. Yet they can be evoked, that is, summoned into mind in their very lack of existential determinacy, called up like shades momentarily escaping immersion in the waters of Lethe.

(b) The remindand is not only evoked by the reminder; it is also referred to by it. This reference occurs by *allusion,* which must be distinguished from denotative designation. This latter is in fact a form of indication, since we can designate only that which exists, has existed, or (presumably) will exist. In the case of allusion, on the other hand, we may make reference to what does not exist and may never have existed, and we are not at all restricted to employing proper names as we are in the case of strict designation. We can allude to what is purely possible, to fictitious actions and characters, even to contradictory states of affairs. We are sanctioned to do so because of the indirect and somewhat indefinite nature of this mode of reference: its literally "allusive" quality. The echo of *ludere* (to play) is to be heard in the root word *alludere;* one of the earliest meanings of "allude" in English was to refer by way of play or fancy. In its most general contemporary sense, an allusion is a "covert or implied reference" *(Oxford English Dictionary),* and it is just such reference that occurs in much reminding, where the remindand is only allusively suggested by the reminder: obliquely suggested, as it were. The obliqueness itself arises from the fact that the reminder is an artifice established by convention. Whether the convention is idiosyncratic (e.g., my way of making notes to remind myself to put back other notes in their proper place) or publicly sanctioned (the string around the finger), the reminder is (i) arbitrarily related to the remindand (i.e., is not intrinsically associated with it by virture of relations of similarity or contiguity), and is nevertheless (ii) an essential third term standing between the mind of the remindee and the remindand. Arbitrary and intermediary, and thus doubly oblique in its very constitution, it refers to the remindand by allusion and hence indirection.[16]

Both aspects of adumbration, evocation and allusion alike, must be acknowledged as constitutive elements of the operation by which the reminder accomplishes its function. When the adumbrative relation, thus constituted, conjoins with the reminder's own figurative-schematical format, the work of reminding is made possible.

## IV

In concluding this account of reminding, several additional points need to be made:

(1) I am not claiming that the adumbrative model fits every case of reminding. It remains true that much reminding occurs by means of a strictly iconomorphic relation between reminder and remindand (e.g., between the photograph of the Parthenon and the building itself) or via an indexical relation (as when my memo to myself signifies a particular place in which to put my course notes). Nevertheless, many remindands are neither indicated as actual existents nor are they pictured; instead, they are evoked and alluded to. As a consequence, the adumbrative relation has a very wide application in the realm of reminders. Not only strings around fingers but any reminder that sets forth an action, object, or state of affairs which is intrinsically indeterminate as to date of appearance or performance, or as to setting, will be captured by the model that I have outlined.

Consider in this connection two very different cases in point: being reminded by a perception and being reminded by a thought. On the one hand, a sensory perception can, by its mere occurrence, remind me of another perception—or of a memory, a fantasy, a commitment, etc. Husserl even claims that "*everything* perceived 'reminds' one of something past that is similar or like even though temporally separated."[17] If the factor of resemblance is removed from this assertion, it implies that the range of perceptual reminding is vast indeed. For a virtually unlimited number of things that I may perceive at any given moment can adumbratively remind me of other parts of my experience. The bird perched before me on a limb can evoke/allude not just to birds of a similar feather but to my conviction that life is precarious and subject to precipitous risks; or it may suggest a certain lightness in my body when I am in high spirits. On the other hand, any passing thought—however ephemeral it may seem in contrast to a sensory perception—may also serve as a full-fledged reminder. Without having to rely on similarity or functioning as an indexical sign, it can adumbrate a considerable array of remindands that are indeterminate in status. I include under "thought" not only pure, nonsensuous cogitations, inferences, and the like but also *memories themselves*. For a given memory can be as effectively remindful as any perceived object; and the memory qua reminder may itself be of various sorts: e.g., a recollection, a body memory, even a primary memory.[18]

(2) Once it is considered in its adumbrative as well as its iconic and indexical dimensions, the field of reminders is seen to be capacious in another basic respect: degree of conventionality. Here we may discern three natural groupings. (*a*) Some reminders function without any detectable conventional features; these include unalloyed perceptions and thoughts serving as reminders in the manner just discussed. It is the perception or thought itself that maintains an adumbrative, iconic, or indexical relation to the remindand without receiving any aid from a pre-established social practice of construing it *as* a reminder. (*b*) A middle range group of reminders relies on convention for establishment and continuation, yet with considerable latitude being allowed as to the exact forms assumed. The string on my finger can be tied in any number of ways so long as it is permitted to appear in a fairly conspicuous manner. The same principle obtains for the temporality of many reminders: guilty thoughts remind me of my being remiss during a time interval lasting from several minutes to several months after I have failed to carry out a promise.

(c) Those reminders most thoroughly conventional in origin and status are typically (though not exclusively)[19] verbal in character. Every memorandum I write employs words whose meaning and syntactical formation are quite conventionally established. But it should be observed that the message such words convey may have meaning *as a reminder* only for me as its instigator: as its self-assigned remindee. The role of remindee thus remains integral to the full situation of reminding: not everyone who speaks my language is able or willing to assume this role. Further, the meanings of the words I employ in written or spoken reminders are often far from perfectly determinate. They are frequently open to interpretation, and may be as much evoked as strictly designated. Although the use of language is itself ineluctably conventional, such conventionality need not eliminate the adumbrative relation from the structure of verbal reminders.[20] "The glory that was Greece" is at once entirely conventional (i.e., as a syntactically well-formed phrase intelligible to all speakers of English) and effective as an adumbration of a golden age of Western civilization that was never to be repeated.

(3) We began by observing that reminders present themselves at first glance as massively external: as the protective outworks of memory in its vulnerability to forgetting. We were struck by the proliferation of reminders that so often characterize our everyday life—beginning with my daytime desk and continuing into the night as I try to remind myself to turn down the heat. In between, I pay bills, return books, read the newspaper, buy

groceries on the basis of lists I have written out, etc. Each of these mundane activities either is a reminder in its own right or requires one for its successful performance. My life, then, is awash in a sea of externally presented, constantly impinging reminders that answer to (and defend against) an at least equally encompassing sea of forgetting.

Yet amnesia itself—against which I have constructed such a formidable array of admonitions—is not an external matter. It is *I*, this person or self, who forgets; it is my mind that goes blank or (in paramnesia) thinks of something else when I should be remembering a particular object or task. Hence it is not surprising that we also make use of an entire set of specifically *internal* reminders: thoughts, fantasies, even memories themselves. These psychical reminders are, as it were, the "deficient modes" (Heidegger), the soft underlining, of reminding—not because they are ineffective or without value, much less because they have a defective structure (they are as effective and as fully structured as the string on my finger), but because they are somewhat more difficult to establish as conventional practices. Only in mnemotechnics do we witness anything like a collective, conventionalized employment of mind-inherent reminders: e.g., the various prememorized *loci* that constitute the basic grid in the ancient *ars memoria*. Yet such purely psychical cues are not deficient as reminders, whatever their natural nonconventionality; and our study of reminders must acknowledge them as such. Mind, in short, remains a pertinent ground for reminding, which for all of its natural affinity with the external and public world of perception and language, cannot claim to transcend the mental sphere completely.

It is only appropriate to end by reverting to Plato, who was unusually sensitive to the internal and external aspects of reminding. In fact his doctrine of recollection *(anamnesis)* makes the experience of being reminded *(anamimnēskesthai)* indispensable to gaining knowledge of the Forms. As Socrates says in the *Phaedo:*

> I suppose that you find it hard to understand how what we call learning can be recollection? . . . I look at it in this way . . . if a person is to be reminded of anything, he must first know it at some time or other. . . . Are we also agreed in calling it recollection when knowledge comes in a particular way? I will explain what I mean. Suppose that a person on seeing or hearing or otherwise noticing one thing not only becomes conscious of that thing but also thinks of something else which is an object of a different sort of knowledge [i.e., properly eidetic knowledge]. Are we not justified in saying that he was reminded of the object which he thought of?[21]

Thus (in Socrates's own example), equal things, sensuously perceived, remind one of absolute Equality. Reminding is here more than a mere analogy to the acquisition of eidetic knowledge: it is *part and parcel of such acquisition*, integral to it. Far from being subordinate to recollection, reminding is critical to its very realization. This becomes evident when we reflect that in his account of knowledge-as-recollected Plato includes each of the basic ingredients of reminding: the reminder (primarily sensuous for Plato),[22] the adumbrative relation of this reminder to the remindand (this is twice termed "suggestion"),[23] the remindand (which is ultimately eidetic), and the remindee (who is any philosophically-minded learner).

Moreover, on Plato's account, what we are reminded of is something eidetic that has its seat *within the soul:*

> This knowledge will not come from teaching but from questioning. One will recover it for himself. . . . And the spontaneous recovery of knowledge that is *in him* is recollection.[24]

If reminding is most frequently precipitated by the perception of external objects, its end-state is nonetheless situated in the soul of the remindee. In being reminded of the Forms by perceiving particulars in one's external environment, one comes to recover "from within" *(ex hauto)* a secure knowledge of the eidetic structures.

In beginning this Part, we were drawn to reminders in their externality because of a growing concern about having become engulfed in the shadowy reaches of mind in Part One. In making this step away from the sheerly mental, we cited Plato's advice to look for things in "larger characters" before grasping them within our souls in their own proper stature. Now we are again following Plato: this time in returning from the external manifestness of perceived reminders to the tacit realm of recollection within the soul. For in being reminded we are drawn into ourselves by what is outside ourselves.

But Plato also makes it clear that in the recollection made possible by reminding, we are drawn out of ourselves once more—though only because we have gone so fully into ourselves in the first place. We must pass by body (as the ground of perception) and mind (as the locus of philosophical dialectic) in order to know what is more than either. If reminding is mainly a matter of externality in its most efficacious public use, it needs to be in touch with the internality of mind if it is to lead eventually to objects that transcend any strict dichotomy of body and mind, of self and other—and of internality and externality themselves.

In this way reminding, despite its dual origin, allows us to draw things together. It is a force of unusual unifying power. What Plato attributes to its role in philosophy we can discern in the midst of ordinary life. Reminding brings together and unifies the *disjecta membra* of human experience: past, present, and future, duty and desire, the forgotten and the remembered.

# VI

# REMINISCING

> Memory . . . at my time of life is gradually becoming one of her own reminiscences.
>
> —James Russell Lowell, "Democracy" (1884)

## I

In *Absalom, Absalom!* we read:

> It seems that this demon—his name was Sutpen—(Colonel Sutpen)—Colonel Sutpen. Who came out of nowhere and without warning upon the land with a band of strange niggers and built a plantation—(Tore violently a plantation, Miss Rosa Coldfield says)—tore violently. And married her sister Ellen and begot a son and a daughter which—(Without gentleness begot, Miss Rosa Coldfield says)—without gentleness. Which should have been the jewels of his pride and the shield and comfort of his old age, only—(Only they destroyed him or something or he destroyed them or something. And died)—and died. Without regret, Miss Rosa Coldfield says—(Save by her) Yes, save by her. (And by Quentin Compson) Yes. And by Quentin Compson.[1]

Faulkner here presents a scene of remembering. But the remembering is notably different from anything that we have thus far encountered. To begin with, it is not a matter of recollecting—where this means remembering in visual images to and for oneself. Instead, two people, Rosa Coldfield and Quentin Compson, are remembering certain things *together*, and they are doing so *in words*, not in images. Something at once social and verbal is happening: and therefore something we have not yet considered explicitly and for its own sake. Nor does what is happening here involve any of the other forms of memory discussed in chapter 3: primary memory, remembering-how, remembering-as, remembering-on-the-occasion-of, etc. The two interlocutors are engaged in an activity so thoroughly conjoint that none of the models considered in Part One—each of which presumes enactment by a single, discrete rememberer—is applicable. As if to signal this fact, Faulkner alternates parenthetical thoughts and remarks in a complex interplay that echoes and intensifies the deeply dialogical character of the situation.

At the same time, there is a noticeable absence of any trace of what we have come to call "mentalism" in the co-remembering realized by Quentin and Rosa. Whatever remembering occurs arises *between* them, not within their minds taken in isolation from each other. Memory enters in the form of what the German language designates as *Zweisprache*, literally "two-talk." Rather than minds spinning and projecting recollections, remembering occurs in and as colloquy, common discourse; and this circumstance is further reinforced by its conveyance to us in the written format of Faulkner's graphic two-person dialogue.

No less than in the case of reminding, we here transcend a paradigm whose exclusive focus and vehicle is the human mind. As reminders move us resolutely into our professional and personal environs, so reminiscing takes place primarily in the interpersonal domain of concrete language. But in the case of reminders the extra-mental appears in and through iconic, indicative, and (especially) adumbrative signs that need not have any strict social basis—any foundation in consensus or convention. We have seen that reminders can be established and maintained entirely by individual remindees. Reminiscing, in contrast, is much more consistently social in origin and operation; it belongs to the realm of what Heidegger would term *Mitsein* ("being-with-others"). For in its central cases it arises as discourse in the company of others: Quentin with Rosa, you with me, and (as a limiting case) myself with myself. It is a matter, in short, of remembering *with others*.

It is a striking fact that whereas the verbs "to remember" and "to recollect" both take a direct object, "to reminisce" does not. We do not reminisce something, we reminisce *about* it. In this regard, reminiscing is comparable to reminding: we are reminded *of* X or Y. But there remains a critical difference. In a circumstance of reminding, I am characteristically in a passive position, as is signified in such expressions as "I am reminded" or "that reminds me." I am always dependent on a particular reminder, even if it is one of my own devising. In reminiscing, I assume a more active posture: *I*, or more typically *we*, reminisce about Z. I or we get in touch with the past actively, thanks to concerted efforts at talking about it, musing on it, and so on. Such a difference between reminding and reminiscing is not just a verbal matter. It reflects the fundamental difference between being thrust into a world of the ready-to-hand—where I am willy-nilly parasitic on the pre-existence of given reminders arranged around me—and being a participant in an ongoing conversation in which I am responsible for articulating the past in quite particular ways. The difference is as basic and perspicuous as that between being put in mind of a trip I once made to the Parthenon by merely receiving a postcard from Athens and talking about this same trip with the person who accompanied me. As the former situation is instantaneous and involuntary—it emerges by virtue of my mere apprehension of the post-card—the latter is both diachronic and voluntary: it takes time and effort (at least the effort of speaking) and is *ipso facto* an activity or performance.

## II

If reminiscing thus contrasts revealingly with reminding—as well as with recollecting and other fundamental forms of remembering—it is more difficult to distinguish from two activities with which it is quite often allied: recounting and telling a story. It is tempting to subsume reminiscing under *recounting*, itself a form of the still more generic activity of retelling, under which both recounting and reminiscing fall. To recount is to retell by giving an account of events and experiences in written or spoken words. Recounting almost always involves a regulative narrative form, a form that allows the original order to be preserved while permitting diversions along the way.[2] The narrative order is crucial; if no semblance of it persisted, the recounting would dissolve into a purely random relating. Reminiscing, however, need not be narrative in format, nor is it constrained to repeat the original order of events it sets forth. A reminiscer may pick out events in any order and does not have to retell them in the sequence of their actual occurrence. When we speak of "the springing up again of reminiscences," we are pointing to this uneven, unconsecutive, and unpredictable dimension of reminiscing, a dimension which contrasts markedly with the regular reliability of recounting.

*Story-telling* is itself a special form of recounting, but one that is not confined to the relating of actual incidents. Stories bear not only on the real but on the imaginary, which they help to create. Their verbal-*cum*-narrative format, which they share with all recounting, is correspondingly freer, particularly with respect to observance of chronological order. By means of such techniques as flashback or flashforward, they may upset this order, not only reversing it but confusing it to the point of unrecognizability—as Faulkner himself so masterfully demonstrates in the above passage. Nevertheless, *within the story itself*, an order is respected, however irregular it may appear to be when measured by continuous, chronometric world-time. Or more exactly, the manifest *order narrated* may be irregular, but the latent *narrative order* itself (i.e., beginning-development-end) remains intact and recognizable.[3]

In reminiscing, there need be neither a manifest nor a latent narrative structure. For one thing, a given reminiscence may be too brief or too condensed to allow for anything like the distension required by narrative time. For another, even when there *is* considerable continuity in, and prolongation of, a given reminiscence, it can rarely be considered a matter of sheer development, that is, of steadily increasing insight, tension, or complication. Instead, when we reminisce, a certain laxity of direction or purpose abounds that disallows, or at least discourages, the kind of intensified build-up which is so characteristic of story-telling and which, under the designation of "drama," is what produces and holds our interest as listeners or readers. A skilled storyteller relies on this build-up within the story line because of its gradually augmenting dramatic intensity, whereas a reminiscer may adhere to his or her own reminiscing through motives as disparate as the simple joy of re-experiencing the past, the challenge of confronting the past *as* past, a specific need for catharsis, etc.[4]

This is not to deny the presence of deep affinities between story-telling and reminiscing. Indeed, the very telling of one's reminiscences to others induces or encourages a storylike form, and few can resist the temptation to embroider storywise upon otherwise banal reminiscences. But the existence of the temptation or tendency does not establish the equivalence of the two activities. The truth of the matter is that everyone—even someone as concerned with story as Faulkner—can reminisce without telling stories and tell stories without reminiscing.

## III

It is one thing to say what reminiscing is not. It is quite another to determine what it *is* as a distinctive phenomenon in its own right, especially in the case of something so open-ended and even tenuous in its presentation. Let us single out four of its basic characteristics: reliving the past, *reminiscentia,* wistfulness, and its communal-discursive aspect.

### Reliving the Past

To remember is to relive the past. But isn't this true of all remembering? By no means! Some remembering is undertaken in order to recover information, either for its own sake or as an aid in various projects, e.g., those that involve relearning how to do something. But some remembering has no such utilitarian purpose; it just arises involuntarily and is savored as such: as sheer reliving of the past. Or if it is self-induced, it is undertaken for the simple joy of being able to recall something, quite apart from any given use or value: "I just like recalling those salad days, or that multiplication table," etc. Reminiscing, whether involuntary or self-induced, is rarely undertaken for the sake of any particular concrete aim or gain. Insofar as it has any stateable aim at all, it is that of reliving the past.

To relive the past in reminiscence is not merely to re-present to ourselves certain experienced events or previously acquired items of information. Nor is it a question of searching for these things in memory or having them displayed there spontaneously. Rather, it is a matter of *actively re-entering* the "no longer living worlds"[5] of that which is irrevocably past. In reliving the past, we try to re-enter such worlds not just as they were—which is, strictly speaking, impossible—but as they are now rememberable in and through reminiscence. That we do not aspire to their full reinstatement is indicated by the fact that adequate and satisfying reminiscing can occur without our having any explicit images of that which is reminisced about.

This happens especially when we reminisce by just talking about the past. But it can also arise mutely when we re-experience a certain ambiance, emotion, or mood for which there is no corresponding image. Moreover, we do not even need to re-feel the original affective elements *per se*.[6] Reminiscing can occur in the absence of exactly answering imagery *or* any corresponding emotion:

> It may be said that two old soldiers are reliving the past when they are discussing and joking about some terrible events which they lived through. These old men may be having neither mental imagery of the events, nor may the original horror be, as it were, felt again.[7]

It would be misleading to claim that reliving the past and reminiscing are two *separate* descriptions of such a case as this. Rather, the two comrades are reliving the past *by* reminiscing: it is their reminiscing together that allows them to relive the past as they do. In reminiscing about it, they are reliving it.

Reliving the past by reminiscing is normally a highly selective affair. In any case it is not a matter of re-experiencing the whole past—not even the entirety of that part of the past, that world, upon which we are momentarily focusing in reminiscence. When two soldiers reminisce about their wartime experiences together, the war-world they relive is by no means the complete scene of which they were the witnesses. Not only has much been forgotten or repressed, but in no way is it requisite that the total scene return in reminiscing. Indeed, a given act of reminiscence may become all the more moving or poignant if it does *not* attempt to scan the whole of the original experience. Concentrating on just a few details may be quite effective enough: "Remember when the weather suddenly cleared?"; "Wasn't it strange how quickly we reached that hill?"; "What a sodden mess that trench was after the initial barrage!" Since reminiscing does not attempt to recount the total action or experience, the existence of considerable gaps in the reminiscing, of glaring discontinuities in time and space, and even of significant inconsistencies in the retelling do not occasion the anxiety or concern they would arouse if the situation were one of straightforward reconstruction—or even if it were a scene of sheer story-telling, which must retain a certain continuity of narration and consistency of detail in order to hold the attention of the storyteller's audience.

Reminiscence, then, can be very "spotty" and yet still count as full-fledged reliving of the past. This is so for the reason that the past is not being relived as it unfolded in strict succession but only as certain happenings stood out and were remarked at the time. Consequently there is usually a marked restriction to two classes of events: what *befell* me or us; or what I or we *accomplished*, or failed to accomplish, in certain circumstances. Hence the tendency to reminisce about calamities of various kinds on the one hand and about diverse moments of triumph on the other. In either case, reminiscing seems to involve a certain *ingrained egocentrism*, a tendency to recount only what concerns one's own being, one's own fate (even if this is a fate shared with others).

Such self-centeredness, far from being a defect, is in fact essential to reliving the past through reminiscing about it. For this reliving amounts to *insinuating ourselves* back into the past—re-experiencing a peculiar cul-de-sac, a pocket of time into which only one's own self, accompanied or not by immediate companions, can possibly fit. Indeed, it is the very snugness of this fit between the present self and its past experiences that we at once need (as a precondition) and seek (so as to strengthen the bond between the two). In this light, reminiscing can be said to be a way, an essentially privileged and especially powerful way, of *getting back inside our own past more intimately, of reliving it from within*.

This effort at infiltration is to be contrasted with ordinary recollection, in which we often seek merely to recall certain experiences, dates, or facts—where "recall" means quite literally to call back to mind again. In this re-collective activity of summoning something back into the state of consciousness, there is no concerted effort to enter more intimately into the specific content of what is remembered; we allow the mnemonic presentation to arise without feeling an urgent need to delve further into it. Reminiscing itself often employs recollected material, but instead of resting content with a contemplative mode of apprehension, it undertakes the very different tactic of revivifying a previous experience. In this way the reminiscer enters into a more active alliance with the remembered past.

By "revivifying" I mean the way in which reliving the past in reminiscence is in fact realized. It consists of three distinguishable factors:

(1) *Myself-as reminiscer:* I enter into reminiscence in the expectation of being refreshed or rekindled by the experience, though I need not do this in any deliberate way.

(2) *The reminisced-about:* This comes back to life (and not just to mind) in the activity of reminiscing, which revives remembered content in a peculiarly vivid way.

(3) *Myself-in-relation-to-the-reminisced-about:* When reminiscence is fulfilling or successful, there is a momentary merging of my mnemonic consciousness with that which is remembered, a sense of becoming one with what I remember.

When all three factors are in play and in animated interaction with each other, revivification occurs in its fullest format: each factor serves to validate the other two in the reminiscential reliving of the past. Thanks to this resuscitative action, I can more easily and spontaneously merge with my past in that intimate intro-involvement that is so characteristic of reminiscing.

It is largely due to the work of revivification that any connection with the past in reminiscing is more than academic—more than "antiquarian" in Nietzsche's term.[8] When we reminisce, we are not going back into the past to reconstitute it as an object of historiological inquiry. We return, rather, as persons whose *present* interests and needs are most fully met by reminiscing. I do the reminiscing not for the sake of the past as past but for the sake of myself: that is, for the pleasure of the good that it will effect in the present. Or more precisely, *the revivifying of the past that occurs so prominently in reminiscing is at the same time a revitalizing of the present in which the reminiscing is taking place*.[9]

## Reminiscentia

It is a revealing fact about reminiscing that although it can take place wholly internally or psychically—as when we "just muse" about the past—it will sometimes be provoked by an external factor acting as a memorial support. Indeed, it may even seek out this support when it reaches an end of its own resources. An example will help to illustrate this point:

> In sorting through some old family papers, I come upon several stacks of documents that bear on the death of my grandmother. Just perceiving a few items in these stacks sets in motion a train of reminiscences concerning circumstances at the time of her death. Seeming to have exhausted my reminiscential supply, I discover that I wish to delve into the documents more completely so as to foster further reminiscing—and this is exactly what happens as I look into the documents more carefully.

This example makes it clear that what can be called "*reminiscentia*" include anything that survives from the epoch reminisced about, including letters and photographs, relics and souvenirs of all kinds, indeed any object or trace of an object that remains and is presently available in perception. Each of these serves as an *aide-mémoire* of a particular kind. Rather than functioning strictly as reminders or as records of the past—that is, as directing us to take some action or as documentary evidence alone—they act as *inducers* of reminiscence. What counts here is not the accuracy with which they reproduce or suggest the past (as it would in the very different context of historical reconstruction); instead, it is their special aptitude for arousing a reminiscent state of mind that matters.

And in what does this aptitude consist? It consists in supplying just those cues that aid the reminiscer to relive the past in the manner described above. In particular, it is a question of providing details that augment revivification by increasing one's sense of personal involvement with the period being reminisced about. In my example, this took quite specific forms, e.g., lists of names of those who had come to offer condolences upon my grandmother's death. Perceiving these lists, I was not merely enabled but actively encouraged to reminisce in a quite definite way about those visitors. A "line" of reminiscence was thus opened up that might otherwise have remained closed off or been pursued much more dimly.

All pertinent cues, temporal or spatial, object-based or situational, deserve the appellation "*reminiscentia*" inasmuch as they offer appropriate supports for reminiscing. As such, they enlighten the present as mementos of things past. To come into more intimate contact with any of them is to be given material assistance in one's reminiscential projects—projects which can be expanded, or at least clarified, with their aid. In this way, they supplement one's already available, and normally quite intangible, resources, providing these resources with a touchstone in the spatio-temporally concrete. One caveat is in order, however. This is that such *reminiscentia* are rarely, if ever, *necessary* to reminiscing. Supplements, however valuable they may be as conducive cues, are not preconditions.[10] We can still reminisce, and reminisce quite satisfactorily, in the absence of their solicitation:

> A soap box covered with green cloth supported the dim little photographs in crumbling frames she liked to have near her couch. She did not really need them, for nothing had been lost. As a company of traveling players carry with them everywhere, while they still remember their lines, a windy beach, a misty castle, an enchanted island, so she had with her all that her soul had stored.[11]

Thus even if we do not really have to have *aides-mémoire* in the form of concrete *reminiscentia,* it is nevertheless characteristically the case that, like the woman here described, we tend to surround ourselves with them and avail ourselves of their help whenever possible.

Recourse to *reminiscentia* has one further significance. We reach out, *faute de mieux,* for fragments surviving from the past as a response to knowing that what is now past has fled forever and thus cannot be recaptured intact in its pristine format. As Husserl says, "I can relive *(nachleben)* the present, but it [the present] can never be given again."[12] If *it,* the forever-flown past moment, cannot last as such, then we will characteristically cling in compensation (or consolation) to what is extant, however superficial or trivial this may appear when compared to past presence itself. Seeking out and holding onto *reminiscentia* is admittedly like clutching at straws cast into the corrosive wind of time. Chaff as they may be, these straws at least signify the fact that there *was* that particular past world from which they stem, and we often treasure them even—and precisely—in this minimalist role.

## Wistfulness

Another aspect of the same circumstance is the peculiar wistfulness it may inspire in us. We are rendered wistful by the nonretrievability of certain experiences, and our reminiscing about them at once expresses this mood and represents an effort to deal with it constructively. One of the main meanings of "wistful" itself is "reminiscently evocative," as in the phrase "deserted buildings above which wistful flags fly bravely."[13] Like brave but ultimately futile flags, our reminiscences evoke the many deserted buildings of past worlds. The acute wistfulness they can occasion constitutes an acknowledgment of the ineluctable transience of human experience: a transience which we often cope with by engaging in reminiscence itself.

It is revealing in this connection to notice that "wistful" derives originally from "wishful." The basic wish at stake is, *per impossible,* to fuse fully with the past we reminisce about. What we know we cannot accomplish in reality, we can still wish for; and this wishing, a wishing in the face of acknowledged impossibility, becomes quite naturally wistful in character. Hence the common meanings of wistful as "full of timorous longing or unfulfilled desire"; "melancholy yearning"; "musingly sad: pensive, mournful."[14] Both sides of the circumstance of reminiscing are captured in these dictionary definitions. On the one hand, the sadness, mourning, and unfulfillment reflect the realization of the past's very pastness, its being irrevocably over and done with. On the other hand, the longing, desire, and yearning point to the refractory presence of a wish to return to, and to be still present in, this now elapsed past. Such a wish, in such a situation, tends to be wistful indeed. If it is true that the present "can never be given again," this is precisely because once it has been given *once*—once it has been lived through and has transpired—it has *eo ipso* become a *past* present. What occurs in any subsequent present can only be its revival in memory or its survival in traces, but it never revives or survives *as* the present, in the first-timeness of an aboriginal experience. Time may well be "the fluid cradle of events,"[15] but it takes away as much as it gives rise to. We respond to its two-sided action with that ambivalent admixture of despair and hope so characteristic of wistful reminiscing.

Confronted with time's permanently "passifying" power, one can hardly help but be ambivalent: sad that certain experiences have ended, even if we are hopeful as to their sequelae. The ambivalence is such that we can be wistful even when reminiscing about difficult or painful events: "Some day, perhaps, it will be a joy to remember even these things."[16] The pain inherent in "these things" is transmuted into the peculiar pleasure of reminiscing about them. Such pleasure, intrinsic to reminiscence, has little to do with hedonism. It is a peculiarly reflective or "ruminescent" pleasure that is composed equally of an acceptance of past pain and of a determination not to be overcome by it. Precisely the finality of the past itself—of the past qua past—comes to our aid as we realize that the pain, however excrutiating it *was,* is now over: now that we can reminisce about it in the present, taking pleasure in this very activity and perhaps gaining a sense of minor triumph as well.

On the basis of just such a realization, we often experience reminiscing as a "bittersweet" activity, one in which sadness, even fear and foreboding, is not unmixed with pleasure. Indeed, the melancholy tenor of some reminiscences, and the anxious or apprehensive character of others, is not only tolerated but may be actively sought. Moreover, the complex phenomenon we call "nostalgia" indulges in much the same ambivalent, bittersweet sentiment: the pain *(algos)* of being absent merging with the pleasure of returning home *(nostos)*.[17] Bittersweetness pervades reminiscing of many kinds and lends body to its wistfulness. It is evident that the sweetness stems ultimately from the basic pleasure we take in recollecting things situated in the remote past—a past we can now afford to savor, thanks to its very distance from the present—while the bitterness bears on the fact of transience, on the past's immutable closedness. It is also evident that in reminiscing wistfully, we combine the bitter with the sweet, cherishing or honoring a past we might otherwise regret or vilify.

## Communal-Discursive Aspect

We tend to think of remembering in general as a mainly introspective affair carried out in the privacy of the psyche. We often consider it to be a search for information stored in some intrapsychic retreat to which the individual rememberer has a privileged, perhaps even a unique, mode of access. Thinking this way, we take the verbalizing and sharing of memories to be an adventitious activity. Why should we bother to put into words and relate to others what we possess so securely from within, at a level of experience that is at once pre-linguistic and pre-social? And yet when we reminisce we find ourselves doing both of these supposedly otiose things—and doing them spontaneously and unselfconsciously. Moreover, we do not feel ourselves to be merely "translating" private memories into public artifacts as if from some compunction to communicate. We sense ourselves to be fully engaged in an autonomous activity having its own formative, indeed transformative, power.

The most immediate, as well as the most telling, clue we have as to the inherently communal-discursive aspect of reminiscing is the mere fact that it *flourishes in the company of others*. Not only does it frequently occur in a specifically social setting, it is also actively solicited by such a setting. Not that any explicit request is then required—indeed, it would be distinctly odd to say "let's reminisce together now"—but just being together suffices, as it also does in the case of story-telling. Unlike the situation of story-telling, however, it matters deeply just *who* is together in the scene of reminiscing. Whether those present be relatives or friends, or mere acquaintances or even strangers, they must all share to some degree the experiences being reminisced about. For what evokes and sustains reminiscence is the possessing of certain common or like experiences. I say "common *or like*" in order to make clear that the reminiscer and those who are co-present with him or her need not have had literally the same experiences. In fact, we may distinguish between the following three circumstances:

### STRICT COMMONALITY OF PAST EXPERIENCES

This is a condition, not of reminiscence in general but only of *co*-reminiscence, in which conjointly experienced events form the very topic of the reminiscence; indeed, one is here quite frequently *comparing* common experiences, sometimes with the explicit aim of making corrections or modifications in the details of the reminiscence ("I seem to remember that Jeffrey was there"; "No, he wasn't since I remember seeing him leaving the building earlier that evening"). Because close friends or family members have more experiences strictly in common, they will tend to co-reminisce more than other groups, although people hitherto unknown to each other may co-reminisce about an event which they all happened to have experienced ("Woodstock," or the Santa Barbara oil spill of 1969). But even where experiences have been quite directly shared by members of a given group, it is not necessary that they all experienced precisely the *same* facts or features of the events in question. So long as all the co-reminiscers were present at the scene, the condition of sharing is met. What each person apprehended may vary considerably in exact detail, as may the memories that each person now recalls. One of the primary motives for co-reminiscing is no doubt that of checking out each other's memories in view of differing experiential modes and perspectives. Furthermore, by reminiscing with others, we may construct a more complete *tableau* than we could ever effect in reminiscing while alone: "I remember him praising Locke's *Essay,* whereas you recall his irony in doing so—now a fuller picture emerges."

### DIFFUSE COMMONALITY OF ERA AND AMBIANCE

Instead of having been present together at precisely the same scene, co-reminiscers may share in a conjointly experienced era or epoch of their lives: "how it was to be a civilian at the time of the Vietnam War," "the political climate in France under DeGaulle," "growing up in Topeka in the 1950's," etc. In such cases there is a common participation not in particular events but in the ambiance or atmosphere attaching to the era in question. However diffuse it may be, this ambiance is at once the medium of the co-reminiscing and its explicit theme. For we are remembering together *how it felt* to imbibe a general atmosphere—to be present in its midst. Of course, this atmosphere is not independent of particular events, about which we can co-reminisce in the sense discussed above. But we can also recall together the atmosphere itself, the pervasive mood of the times.

LACK OF STRICT OR DIFFUSE COMMONALITY

Reminiscing, though not co-reminiscing, is possible in a group some of whose members were neither direct witnesses of an original scene nor participants in its overall ambiance. In this case, those who listen to the primary reminiscer must either actively *liken* the reminisced-about scene or atmosphere to something significantly similar in their own experience, or *imagine* the original scene or atmosphere vividly enough to feel that they *might* have been there, that they could very well have been there had circumstances conspired or permitted. Either way, the listener is drawn into the reminiscing, and assumes its specific content as if it were his or her own experience, though without coming to the point of actually believing that it was (as would be required in full-fledged co-reminiscing). An effective reminiscer is someone who can elicit such likening or imagining on the part of his or her listeners, even if these latter cannot be considered co-reminiscers in any strict sense.

Different as they are in their basic structure, all of the above three situations are *interpersonal* in nature. Each involves a minimal dyadic unit of reminiscer-*cum*-listener, and this unit is indefinitely expandable insofar as both reminiscer and listener may be plural in number. It is also modifiable by the substitution of co-reminiscer for listener—in which case, each party becomes at once reminiscer for *and* listener to the other, thereby realizing an intricate interplaying of roles as well as an equality of status. In the communal context, co-reminiscing may be considered something of an ideal type, perhaps even that toward which all reminiscing tends by its very nature. *Reminiscers naturally seek partners in a common enterprise of reliving the past wistfully*—partners who are not only listeners but themselves active contributors to the process of reminiscing.

However obvious it may seem, this observation nevertheless serves to distinguish reminiscing quite decisively from other forms of remembering so far considered, none of which exhibits any such pronounced communitarian tendency. Some of these forms even eschew an interpersonal setting—for example, primary memory, communion with one's personal past in recollection, and the remembering done in the course of dreaming. Other forms involve interlocutors in various phases of their operation, though not in a manner essential to their structure: thus skillful remembering-how may be done with, in the presence of, and even for the sake of others, while reminding can arise in an interpersonal nexus of relations (e.g., when others leave reminders for us or vice versa). But both remembering-how and reminding can also take place successfully on a strictly solitary basis without any sense of anomaly or loss. In contrast, the primary thrust in reminiscing is *toward others:* so much so that we may even say that *co-reminiscing is normative for reminiscing as a whole*. And if this is so, two corollaries follow immediately:

COROLLARY #1: REMINISCING IS MAINLY ADDRESSED TO OTHERS

As an engagement *with* other rememberers, whether undertaken with others in person or only with them in mind, reminiscences are addressed—with an important exception to be treated in section IV—*to* others. In the ideal case, these others are themselves present, and a circle of co-reminiscers is constellated. But they may be implicated in other modes as well:

(1) as *absent:* when others are addressed *as if* present. This often occurs when those who figure into a particular reminiscence are absent from the actual scene of reminiscing but are nonetheless invoked as quasi-present during the reminiscing itself: "dear departed leader, be with us today as we remember your presence among us."

(2) as *fictitious:* when others who make no claim to actuality even as absent are nonetheless potent presences as addressed in and by an author's reminiscing. Such others may be generalized or typified (e.g., "anyone present at the [imagined] carnival"); or they may be depersonalized altogether (e.g., "a member of the Snopes family"); in these cases, the other may be addressed as judge, muse, or witness of one's reminiscing as well as an equal or co-respondent.

The very diversity of others who can be addressed when we reminisce reinforces its status as an inherently interpersonal activity.

COROLLARY #2: REMINISCING IS MOST FULLY REALIZED IN LANGUAGE

Discourse, as Heidegger claims, is one of the "equiprimordial" structures of human existence and thus never entirely separable from it.[18] Indeed, it is the main way in which human beings convey their experiences to each other: "In discourse Being-with *(Mitsein)* becomes 'explicitly' *shared;* that is to say, it *is* already, but it is unshared as something that has not been taken hold of and appropriated."[19] Reminiscing, especially as co-reminiscing, involves *resharing already shared experiences,* and its discursive or verbal form aids in the full accomplishment of the resharing. It is possible to reminisce wordlessly—as when photographs of a shared-in scene are passed around among the original participants—but we naturally resort to language on most occasions. We do so for two major reasons.

On the one hand, words *facilitate* reminiscing by allowing it to become independent of particular material supports connected with the original scene—supports that can erode and vanish altogether. Words, in contrast, are much less perishable because they are not material entities in the first place.[20] As the most effective and enduring form of symbolism which human beings have devised, words provide a collective and massive framework for communication and expression at many levels. To have recourse to this framework is of inestimable advantage in conveying one's reminiscences to others.

On the other hand, this same system makes possible a considerable *refinement of expression:* an exactitude of reference as well as a subtlety of insight unmatched by nonverbal systems of signification. If it is true that "to significations, words accrue,"[21] it is also the case that words delineate and develop significations far beyond the point at which other forms of *semiosis* leave them. Verbal language has an extraordinary capacity for clarifying and conjoining otherwise dim and disjointed meanings or thoughts. As such, it is an unmatched "articulation of intelligibility,"[22] and it is not surprising that reminiscing, in its zeal to convey itself to others in a maximally communicative manner, assumes a predominantly discursive-verbal format. For the most part, *reminiscing is talking the past out;* it is teasing the past into talk, reliving it in and by words.

There is a final aspect of this matter that deserves our attention. We reminisce not only to savor but to understand, or re-understand, the past more adequately—where "understand" retains something of its root meaning of "standing under," gaining an intimate perspective not otherwise attainable. In reminiscing, we try to get back inside a given experience—to insinuate ourselves into it, as I have said—so as to come to know it better. Better, perhaps, than we knew it in its first flurry, which may well have been more disorienting than clarifying. The sudden onset of the experience—the "immediate rush of transition,"[23] as Whitehead called it—may have been such as to leave us breathless. And *speechless!* Without words to specify various parts and points of an experience, it tends to fuse with other experiences in a flux of indetermination. Thanks to its discursiveness, reminiscing transforms mere experiences into articulate and enduring wholes possessing sufficient integrity to be understood in memory.

"Understanding and discourse," said Plato, "are one and the same thing."[24] However exaggerated this claim may be in certain respects,[25] it is a fitting description of what is accomplished in reminiscing. For our understanding of the past in and through reminiscing occurs mainly by means of its discursive ex-plication: its unfolding in fully articulated words. Such articulation is the primary way a past experience comes to be comprehended in reminiscing. The reminiscential return to the past is a return via discourse—via the word, *logos*—and as such it is an *understanding remembering* of it.

## IV

Just here you may find yourself asking: Can I not reminisce *to myself?* Granting that reminiscing as a discursive and wistful reliving of the past prospers in the company of others, may it not take place in private as well? What do we make of those situations in which I simply "muse" upon the past by myself, pensively reliving it in a ruminescent mood? Would we wish to dismiss this as an inauthentic case of reminiscing? Surely not. Just as we have had to allow that reminiscing can occur between people who have not shared precisely the same experiences, so we must now admit that it can arise in the absence of any others at all. There is such a thing as reminiscing to myself, "auto-reminiscing."

As with psychical reminders—with which it can in fact be closely allied on occasion—auto-reminiscing may be considered as a privative, but quite legitimate, form of reminiscing in general. This is evident when we realize that in reminiscing to ourselves we encounter versions of all four features that characterize more central instances of reminiscing and co-reminiscing. We relive the past wistfully in reflective moments of self-musing. Further, we are provoked to do so by various *reminiscentia* in the immediate environs, including our own memories acting as reminiscential cues: as is signified in the epigraph by Lowell cited at the beginning of this chapter. And there is even, perhaps contrary to our expectations, a communal-discursive aspect of auto-reminiscing. When I reminisce *to* myself, I am treating myself as a reminiscential partner—as an other who listens to himself. Rimbaud's dictum finds striking application here: "le je est un autre."[26] Moreover, in self-engaged and self-engaging reminiscing, I am not falling short of language, whether I auto-reminisce in inner speech or out loud. If all thinking is a "dialogue of the soul with itself,"[27] auto-reminiscing can be considered a matter of proto-communal discourse. When I talk the past out to myself in auto-reminiscing, I establish an intra-dyadic community within my own soul.

The discursive dimension of auto-reminiscing is not limited to speech alone. As with other forms of reminiscing, it can also occur as *writing*. Indeed, writing may even be its optimal mode of realization. Let us consider several cases in point. Thanks to the essentially public status of writing as a graphic and thus fully visible medium—as a matter of tracing, of what Derrida calls "espacement"[28]—we shall see that each of these cases bursts the bounds of strict privacy and pursues, even if unwittingly or unwillingly, a communal *telos*.

### DIARIES AND JOURNALS

Whether destined for publication or not, diaries and journals are instances of auto-reminiscence in which the written form is essential. As written, they fix and stabilize an author's understanding of his or her life, making it available not only to the author but to others as well. Diaries and journals are therefore always at least potentially communal, sometimes against the express intent of those who compose them. Being in principle open to inspection by friends, relatives, or future biographers, they represent a curious blend of *pensées intimes* and *pensées ouvertes*. They are intensely intimate insofar as they record ideas and impressions that would not normally be announced overtly to others,[29] and yet, precisely *as written*, they are something to which these same others ultimately have access. Hence the ambivalence with which many diary or journal entries are written down in the first place and in which one sees at once a desire to reveal and to conceal. Hence, too, a tendency to address the diary as if it were itself an interlocutor: "My diary. I have managed to confide all my thoughts freely to you; you are my best friend on this earth, the most faithful, the most sincere."[30] In the auto-reminiscing of diaries and journals we can therefore detect, in the form of intrapersonal self-address, an essentially *inter*personal tendency toward discourse-with-another, albeit another part of one's own self. Such self-directed discourse is itself a form of reliving the past—reliving it by and in writing—and it differs from other reminiscential types of reliving only insofar as it usually bears on events of the immediate past, much as a dream will incorporate the day's residues into its own manifest content.

AUTOBIOGRAPHIES AND MEMOIRS

Although these two forms of writing are also self-focused—in each case one is giving an extensive account of one's own life—one is now directing one's discourse not to oneself but to others, i.e., those others who will read one's account in print. The communalizing penchant which is tacit and self-enclosed in the auto-reminiscing of diaries and journals here becomes explicit, since "publication," the public disclosure of one's life, is now an express aim. This move into the overtly public domain brings about two corresponding modifications. On the one hand, as an entire life-time is often the subject matter of an autobiography or memoir, the time-scope of reminiscing is characteristically more distended. Hence whole chapters, covering whole years, decades, or epochs, replace the daily entries of diaries and journals; and an effort is usually made to touch upon each significant segment of a lifetime—if not in one volume, then in six or seven![31] On the other hand, a concern for accuracy of detail often manifests itself in this more exposed form of self-revelation, open as it is to public scrutiny and criticism from the very first moment of publication. It is not at all surprising, then, to find that Vladimir Nabokov avidly sought out relatives and other close witnesses of his personal past before publishing his autobiography entitled *Speak, Memory!*[32]

## V

Despite the considerable interest and power inherent in written reminiscences—and apart from their value in showing us how the communal-discursive dimension emerges even in the most private forms of auto-reminiscing—it remains the case that reminiscing in the oral mode is most fully paradigmatic for the phenomenon as a whole. Such a claim is based on the straightforward observation that reminiscing in speech is the most thoroughly dialectical form of reminiscing. In full-blown co-reminiscing, the interlocutors can "trade" reminiscences more completely and more flexibly than in other reminiscential situations. They can do so more completely insofar as they can correct and augment each other, something that is difficult or impossible to achieve in silent or written auto-reminiscing; and this is done more flexibly because of the ebb and flow of the dialogue itself, allowing for more nuanced assessments. The understanding of the past attained in such dialectically structured co-reminiscing is a genuine co-understanding that cannot be accomplished in solitude or by proffering writing to an anonymous public.

The special virtue of reminiscing out loud is evident even in circumstances that lack any intersubjective reciprocity or dialogue. In eulogies, for example, the speaker will often employ reminiscences as a primary topic of his or her discourse. Such overtly unilateral reminiscing can be entirely appropriate and efficacious on the occasion, even though the person eulogized may be absent or dead and members of the audience are reduced to silence. The latter *could* doubtless co-reminisce, and may well do so before or after the formal ceremony; but they need not do so for the situation to be thoroughly reminiscential. Much the same one-sided circumstance obtains in psychoanalysis, in which the patient's open reminiscing is often met with by silence on the part of the analyst. As in the eulogy, the reminiscing that is realized in this apparently inequitable setting is no less forceful or insightful for failing to achieve co-reminiscing in any strict sense. In both circumstances, the past is talked out in a closely-knit (if temporary) *communitas* composed of speaker and listener(s). Even in the absence of dialogical interchange, the reminiscing remains valid and effective.

The psychoanalytic situation, considered as a scene of reminiscence, has yet another significance. It repeats, in considerable intensity and depth, experiences and processes that occur in the course of everyday life, especially in the setting of one's family or close friends. These latter, our proximate associates, are often, perhaps always, reminiscential presences themselves. We reminisce not merely *about* them (in isolated auto-reminiscence) and *with* them (in full co-reminiscence) but *through* them (when they present themselves to us as reminiscent of persons other than themselves). Aspects of all three options are in evidence in the dialogue between Rosa Coldfield and Quentin Compson with which this chapter opened. Any interpersonal situation may include or intimate complexity of this order. But psychoanalysis thrives on it. As in so many other ways as well—some of which will be explored later in this book[33]—the psychoanalytic situation represents a highly condensed, and highly revealing, version of extra-analytic experience. In particular, it is a prototype of reminiscential experience realized in the presence of intimates who not only reminisce together but reminisce in and beyond each other—in the presence and person of one another and beyond the merely conscious cognition and recognition of each by the other.

Reminiscing in this extended sense is at once a transcending of the historical and perceptual limits of the immediate situation—the present discourse and its actual or virtual interlocutors—and a return to a past of which one has been forgetful up to this point. Such a past pre-exists the present, and yet it is resuscitable in reminiscence: in that communalized discourse which relives the past in question, often wistfully and just as often aided by *reminiscentia* of various kinds. As the slave in the *Meno* recovered knowledge he had so thoroughly forgotten that he never realized he possessed it in the first place—the recovery owing much to his dialectical cross-examination by Socrates and to *reminiscentia* in the shape of diagrams drawn in the sand—in psychoanalysis we recover an acquaintance with the past which we have long since repressed. Something similar occurs in the co-reminiscing we do with friends and family; and it also happens in intense auto-reminiscence. Through all these forms of reminiscing, we become reacquainted with the past, gaining an intimacy with it that we may not have experienced when we first encountered it. Retelling this past in discourse of several sorts—Platonic dialogues themselves combine spoken with written reminiscing—we articulate its structure and come to know it from within again. We come to know it better, more completely and more poignantly, than if we had left it unreminisced, un-unfolded in *logos*, un-explicated in "the dark backward and abysm of time."[34]

# VII

# RECOGNIZING

> What is the strange difference between an experience tasted for the first time and the same experience recognized as familiar, as having been enjoyed before, though we cannot name it or say where or when?
>
> —William James, *The Principles of Psychology* (1890)

## I

> I am arriving at the airport in South Bend, Indiana. A figure comes striding toward me, his hand extended. Is it Tom? I cannot recognize him at first, as a large straw hat is drawn down over his face. Then, suddenly, the hat is thrown off, and I just as suddenly recognize who it is: Charles! Although I have not seen Charles since last fall (it is now June), he is instantly recognizable—and clearly distinguishable from Tom, who nevertheless resembles Charles in physique and whom I had expected to meet me on this occasion.

It is striking how much of this experience is present-oriented. One present moment—that of the quasi-recognition of Tom—gives way instantaneously to another present moment, that of actually recognizing Charles. Each moment is all-absorbing, and is occupied without remainder by an act of quasi- or real recognition. The act serves to punctuate the present—to give it its special content and its immediate limits. There is a definite *fixation on the present*, an anchoring of attention there, as well as a felt presentness of the experience itself as it gives itself to me in the moment of recognition.

The presentness is such that the experience here reported lacks an explicit orientation toward past or future. The past in particular is strangely absent from the conscious content of my experience: "strangely" because both Charles and Tom have been integral presences in my past. If they had not been such presences, I could not be said to recognize them at all: *past experience of the recognized object is presupposed even if it is not manifest as such in the experience itself.* It may be that it is just to the extent that this presupposition is at work in recognition that the past experience itself need not be elicited as anything distinct from the present experience of recognizing: and thus not as something to be recollected as such.

This is not to deny that we do recognize some things precisely as *stemming from* the past: when I judge that "I recognize him as a ghost of his former self" I do make an explicit reference to the past. But even here no specific recollection (much less a memory image) of this past needs to arise. Rather, the reference to the past is built right into the presentness of the experience—is part of its very content and is not inferred or posited, much less experienced separately. In Heidegger's terminology, the "as-structure" here is "existential-hermeneutical" and not apophantic in nature; it expresses an *inherence of the past in the present* rather than the reverse; and it does not effect any division into distinct regions of time. This immanence-in-the-present remains operative even when I recognize something *as about to happen*. The "about to" is an intrinsic feature of the recognized object itself—much as protentions of the immediate future form the forward fringe of the "living present" in Husserl's analysis of time-consciousness.[1]

There is still a further level of consideration. Acts of recognition such as occurred in the South Bend airport exhibit presentness not only in the sense of occurring *in* the present, dominating it, and making it prevail over the past and the future. They also *aid in the constitution of the present itself*. How is this so? They do so by contributing two basic factors to the present: "availability" and "consolidation."

*Availability*

Availability names the way in which recognition serves to render items in our experience readily accessible to us—where "accessible" means not just nonproblematically present but positively identifiable, that is, having a distinct, and normally nameable, identity. A recognized face such as that of Charles affords a privileged access to a body that, before the moment of recognition, was an advancing physique posing a question for perception: "Whose body is this?" A flash of recognition resolved this ambiguous situation by making the identity of the owner of this body available to me—available not just in the present but constitutive of it. In fact, we can trace a movement from "this-body-with-unknown-owner-advancing-toward-me" to "Tom-as-possible-owner-of-this-body-coming-toward-me" to "Charles-as-certain-owner-of-this-body." This movement of increasing specificity is the work of recognition. At the same time, a distinct sense of "nearing"[2] accompanies availability and enhances it. Charles's face, once revealed and recognized, no longer keeps the distance of something hidden under a straw hat but leaps forward toward me as a distinctly identified entity that constitutes the present as a scene of recognition. Thus, what remained distant in a state of unrecognized ambiguity draws near to my apprehension. It lets me have a still closer look, puts me on the inside of the phenomenon, and gives me the feeling of immediate access to it.

*Consolidation*

Consolidation is a second, somewhat less obvious, factor. Recognition contributes to the constitution of the present (and thus manifests its own presentness) by allowing the recognized object or event to come forth as itself—to gain its *own* identity and stability. Hence the unidentified and unstable head-with-straw-hat became the solidified head of Charles. Through recognition, what was evasive and shifting became intact and settled; the question as to the identity of this figure was resolved. The ambiguous head belonged to Charles and Charles alone, and it gained in felt density what it thereby lost in mystery. This density or consolidated character is by no means incompatible with the experience of nearing mentioned just above. The two even work closely together: it is just because Charles drew sufficiently close to me that he gained enough density to be recognized as himself. His nearing and his consolidation as an object of recognition went hand in hand.

We have been discussing what can be designated as the *presentness* of recognition: its orientation toward the present as well as its actual orientation of it. As a result of presentness, recognition helps to shape the very stretch of time in which it plays out its own drama. Availability and consolidation play a determinative role in this drama, since each contributes in an essential way to presentness. All this occurs in a curiously suspended state of temporal process. The past, though crucially presupposed, and the future, though undeniably portended, are not permitted to intrude themselves into the heart of recognition, composed as it is almost exclusively of present-making activities.

Reinforcing this same emphasis on the present is the fact that recognition often occurs in the immediate context of perception, itself a deeply present-oriented activity. Where else does perception arise except in the present, and what does it offer to us but various contemporary items arranged and arrayed in the same present? In the South Bend airport, recognition occurred in the very midst of perception; it arose from it and was continuous with it; it was in perceiving Charles that I came to recognize him. More generally, to recognize what I see is to see it "as" something. Wittgenstein has deftly analyzed the fact that recognizing something is seeing it *as* a distinguishable and identifiable thing—as a determinable, and usually an already determined, x.[3] This basic act of seeing-as is perceptual in nature, though it is also sometimes interlaced with imaginings.[4] Even if it is not true that all recognizing is construable as seeing-as—a theme to which I shall return—that which is so construable presents itself as at once perceptual and present-bound: once I recognize him, I see that advancing figure as Charles *now*.

## II

Just as to be present-*making* is not necessarily to be limited to the present, to arise in the midst of perceiving and to occur in the form of seeing-as are not strictly present-confined. Despite the insistent focus on presentness that is so much a part of the experience of recognition, the past must play some role if recognizing is indeed a mode of memory. As Sartre queries:

> But if everything is present, how are we to explain . . . the fact that in its intention a consciousness which remembers transcends the present in order to aim at the event back there where it was?[5]

Even if recognizing does not aim expressly at a past event "back there where it was," it must involve the past in some capacity if it is to count as remembering. This much we have already acknowledged. But how exactly are past and present related in recognizing? This question becomes acute precisely because presentness is so massively evident as a primary feature of recognition.

It is tempting to explain the role of the past in recognizing by positing a subterranean stratum at work beneath what is manifest in the experience itself. The past is then conceived as a suppressed undercurrent. As reported by William James, Höffding espouses such a view:

> His theory of what happens [in cases of instantaneous recognition] is that the object before us, A, comes with a sense of familiarity whenever it awakens *a slumbering image, a, of its own past self,* whilst without this image it seems unfamiliar.[6]

But it is superfluous to posit the past in the form of a subliminal image lurking beneath an experience of recognition when this experience not only contains no conscious trace of such an image but *does not need it* in any adequate accounting. An act of recognizing is self-sufficing, especially in its instantaneous form. That which is recognized, the "*recognitum*" as we can call it, gives itself to us in transparent plenitude. This is an aspect of its very presentness. Thus it does not need the support, not even the subliminal support, supplied by a memory-image of its earlier occurrence. Even if it were to arise, such an image would be distinctly redundant. As James says in critique of Höffding: "[The experience of recognizing a face] is so intense as to banish from my mind all collateral circumstances, whether of the present or of former experiences."[7] Collateral circumstances are banished—not because they are inappropriate, but because they are useless *impedimenta* in a situation in which everything essential is already furnished.

But this leaves unresolved how past and present are in fact related in situations of recognizing. Even if the past does not obtrude into the present overtly in these situations and even if it is otiose to invoke it as a covert factor, its presence is hard to deny: as is clear from the simple fact that we cannot recognize something we have not encountered before at some point and in some way. However difficult it may be to detect as such, there is resonance in the present from this encounter in the past. How is such resonance to be conceived?

It will not help to invoke instances of the past/present relationship that were considered in previous chapters. In these instances, past and present remained easily distinguishable terms. In reminiscing, for example, the reminisced-about past is the very topic of the activity of reminiscing itself; it is even thematized as such: "Those were the days. . . ." In the case of reminding, an item apprehended in the present is related to something past (and sometimes to something future) via a distinctive iconic, indicative, or adumbrative relation; at every moment, past and present are discernibly different. The same holds true for ordinary recollection, which is premised on the distinguishability of the scene recollected from the act of recollection. In all of these cases—and in many others as well (e.g., in biographical or historical reconstruction)—past and present are conjoined in such a way that the very difference between the two terms is constitutive of their mode of relation to each other.

In recognition, by contrast, any such intrinsic difference is annulled or held in abeyance: the two temporal phases rejoin each other instead of being kept apart. They rejoin each other so thoroughly that they cannot even be said to adumbrate, much less to indicate or imitate, each other. At the most, we might say that one term *expresses* the other in the sense of "gives expression to," "makes manifest," or "reveals." Thus the past could be said to be expressed in and by the present of recognition. But the idea of expression has a double disadvantage in the current context. On the one hand, it implies the idea of an *un*expressed remainder—whereas what we recognize, being altogether manifest, carries with it no such residue. On the other hand, expression is naturally allied with verbal language—the paradigm of an expressive sign is a word[8]—while recognizing has no special affinity with linguistic contexts and modes of articulation.

The most adequate model for grasping the relation of past and present in recognition is that of *suffusion*. By "suffusion" I mean the situation in which what is otherwise distinct, or at least discriminable, combines and mixes to the point of indistinguishability. Such is precisely what happens with past and present in cases of recognizing. In particular, the past of the *recognitum* fuses with its present apprehension—so completely that we would be hard pressed to differentiate one from the other. Thus, when I recognized my friend Charles, my past relationship to him was condensed or telescoped into the present of my perception of him *as* "Charles," as just this person (and not, say, Tom or any number of other people who resemble him). Of course, this relationship itself had been built up from discrete episodes, some of which I could recollect separately, reminisce about, be reminded of, etc. But insofar as I was recognizing Charles, these episodes were not at stake; at most, they were contributing factors to the single Gestalt designatable as 'Charles-as-recognized'. What was at stake was a circumstance in which the present of apprehending Charles was suffused with the past of my relationship with him.

It is not altogether accidental that the specific *recognitum* in this exemplary case was a human *face*. For both James and Hoffding, the face is a paradigm of recognizability. In the face—the naked face as fully recognized[9]—the suffusion of past and present is at its most complete. Once I recognized Charles's face, the uncertainty of his identity, an identity at first confused with that of Tom as quasi-recognized, was immediately dispelled, leaving no unrecognized residue. The past pertinent to this experience was made one with the present in which recognition occurred. Indeed, the suffusion was such that not only past and present but the manifested and the manifestation, meaning and vehicle, identity and phenomenon—all merged in the decisive moment of recognition. The two members of each of these pairs of terms interfuse in the terminal point of recognition itself. Much as a finished painting possesses the quality of being finally and fully expressive—and expressive *of itself*, "auto-iconic"[10]—so a recognized face has the same intransitive and self-completing character, the sense of having-come-already-into-its own.

The process of suffusion itself is complex and sinuous. I shall single out only two of its features for comment here.

*Merging*

Merging in its most basic form brings together the perceived with the remembered. A simple example will demonstrate this. When I was working on a summer job many years ago in my hometown, my employer remarked to me one day that he recognized my father in me. When I asked him how this was so, he said that I had "my father's walk"—his very gait, his style of walking. His perceiving of my walking was imbued with remembering; or rather, his perceiving me the way he did *was* his remembering—a remembering that did not require a separate recollection of my father's walking in comparison with my own. The mere perception of my walking supplied both the occasion and the content of his recognitory act.

What is striking about this example, and many others like it in daily life, is the two-way action of the merging. Of such a case, it is equally true to say that the perceived unites with the remembered (my walk with my father's walk) and the converse (his walk with mine). It is not a matter merely of the remembered becoming immersed in the perceived—even if this remains most salient on many occasions. The perceived also loses itself in the remembered. At the moment of recognition, then, there is a thoroughly reciprocal fusing of the two factors. The same is true, *mutatis mutandis*, for the past and the present, the manifested and the manifestation, identity and phenomenon, meaning and vehicle.

Of course there are experiences of partial recognition in which the merging of such factors is far from complete: e.g., my quasi-recognizing Tom in place of Charles. The identification was very tentative ("Is it Tom?" I asked myself) because present perception and past experience merged with each other only imperfectly. The perceived figure (still shrouded by the straw hat as it was) did not fully coincide with any particular remembered figure, and the resulting discrepancy between the perceived and the remembered exhibited itself in a distinct hesitation on my part as well as a need to perceive more of the person advancing toward me so that an act of full recognition could occur. In other instances such hesitation can be even more prolonged. But this does not render the moment of merging any less important. Whether it proceeds gradually or suddenly, implicitly or explicitly, all recognition aims at this moment as at a natural culmination. For it is the moment when we can say that recognition has genuinely taken place. Not to experience such a moment is not to recognize fully—even if the moment itself represents the suspension of basic distinctions on which our lives otherwise depend.

*Clarification*

Clarification names an effect of suffusion rather than part of the process itself; but it is a crucial effect nonetheless. To recognize something is to cast it in a new light—to illuminate it in a way that was lacking when it remained unrecognized in its bare perception. As that which is perceived becomes suffused with the past to produce a recognition in the present, the perception gains a luminosity that clarifies an otherwise ambiguous or attenuated situation: as when the actual recognition of Charles suddenly dissipated the mist of uncertainty that clung to the not-yet-identified person striding toward me in the South Bend airport.

The clarification achieved by recognition need not be so dramatic as this. When I gaze upon the house in which I grew up, I am not looking at an indifferent construction of bricks and boards with an utterly unknown interior. Instead, I am seeing a house known from within and recognized as such. The presently perceived house is clarified by my very recognition of it—quite apart from my having explicit memories of it. Particular memories may also arise, often in the very wake of recognition, but *their* illumination is of a different sort from that which is effected by recognition proper. In the "click" of recognition, my past experiences with a given perceived object are unleashed *en bloc,* as an amorphous mass. The illumination cast by connection with this experiential mass is necessarily diffuse; in place of spotlighting (as occurs so frequently in secondary memory, where what we remember enters "the brightly lit circle of perfect presentation"),[11] there is a suffusion of light—an indistinct but steady saturation of the object recognized. That this clarification results in something indistinct should not trouble us. Vague phenomena are still authentic objects of phenomenological description. As Husserl admonishes:

> We can always bring what is given nearer to us even in *the zone of obscure apprehension*. What is obscurely presented comes closer to us in its own peculiar way, eventually knocking at the door of intuition, though it need not for that reason pass over the threshold.[12]

The very light cast by recognition also casts a shadow. This shadow inheres as much in its source (i.e., the amorphous mass of past experiences in which no particular memory or group of memories stands out) as in its present action of illumination, wherein it is difficult to say just how the now-recognized object has been clarified. Description is here drawn into metaphor: "mass," "mist," "suffusion" itself. In fact there is no more exact description available to us, since suffusion proceeds as much by obscurity as by clarity, by shadow as by light. Nevertheless, the light that *is* at work in suffusion is quite adequate for the task of clarifying the *recognitum,* allowing it to be grasped as something recognized.

Presentness (with its two subtraits of availability and consolidation) and suffusion (characterized by merging and clarification) are the primary features of what we recognize. They complement one another in important ways. Presentness points to the insistence of the *recognitum,* its characteristic manner of insinuating itself into our ongoing experience and of serving as a magnetic pole for our attention. In their presentness, recognized objects become cynosures of our existence, "the stars of our life."[13] In contrast, suffusion singles out another aspect of these same objects, i.e., their manner of combining divergent properties in a seamless whole having its own luminosity. What is accessible and consolidated from the perspective of presentness is by the same token diffuse and vaguely illumined from the standpoint of suffusion. The richness of recognition, the mystery of its working, is reflected in this very complementarity of features whereby what we recognize brings together what we might otherwise consider to be incompatible. No wonder, then, that recognizing so often presents itself as a borderline phenomenon—as located somewhere *between* memory and perception, past and present, myself and another. It negotiates this borderline state not by vacillating between such pairs of terms but by actively conjoining them in its presentness and suffusion.

## III

We have proceeded thus far as if there were only one fundamental kind of recognizing—instantaneous in its happening and having its paradigm instance in the recognition of a human face. Although facial recognition is certainly an indispensable species of recognizing—its absence, "prosopagnosia," is debilitating and leads to such anomalies as "the man who mistook his wife for a hat"[14]—it cannot be regarded as representative of other species. The fact is that recognizing comes in a number of very different shapes and forms, and it takes place in quite diverse settings. Not only can I recognize certain things much more gradually than I usually recognize faces, I can do so when I am in practically any state of mind or body, with corresponding effects on the act of recognition itself. Recognizing occurs in and through emotions as well as by means of perceptions: when I am depressed, recognition even of common objects may differ significantly from recognizing the same objects when I am elated. Just as the circumstances of recognizing vary considerably and may alter the character of the act, so the range of objects I am capable of recognizing is immense: from concrete faces to abstract numbers, from molecular configurations to spiral galaxies, from the style of Monet to that of Mozart. The distinctions between specific *recognita* are also considerable: a painter will recognize the difference between cadmium red deep and cadmium red medium, while a musician can discern differences between hearing a song in C minor and E flat major (even though the key signature is here the same). Anyone is able to tell the difference between a friendly and a not-so-friendly handshake, between the coolness of irony and the coolness of jest, or between the touch of guitar strings and the touch of the strings on a tennis racket. As our lives are generally surrounded by reminders and *reminiscentia* of many sorts, they are also immersed in many kinds of *recognita*. Living successfully—indeed, living at all—depends on our ability to apprehend myriad recognized items and to discriminate among them.

In this section I shall undertake a brief survey of several types of recognizing that deserve recognition in their own right. My intention is not to be exhaustive but merely to suggest the rich array of recognitory possibilities at our disposal.

### Dim and Dawning Recognition

Although many cases of recognition (especially facial recognition) are instantaneous in occurrence and perspicuous in content, it would be a mistake to claim that instantaneity and perspicuity are inherent features of all recognizing. Much recognizing occurs slowly and is murky from beginning to end. We can recognize through a glass darkly as well as with full transparency, and it is important to acknowledge this fact. In *dim* recognition we have to do with those cases in which recognition never reaches a level of complete, or even partial, certainty: we are simply not sure that we have correctly recognized, or even begun to recognize, that which we apprehend. Many of these cases arise in fleeting circumstances, e.g., when we barely catch sight of someone who looks familiar driving past us on a highway. But there are also numerous instances where time is not lacking and yet recognition remains stultified. This happens whenever I encounter someone at a gathering whom I sense I know but whose identity I cannot quite specify: not only can I not recall his or her proper name, but I cannot remember when or where we first met. Even if I linger in the presence of such a person, and even if both of us try to explore the basis of the acquaintance, no further illumination may be forthcoming, leaving me with a recognition that is unremediably vague.

In the case of *dawning* recognition, an incomplete recognition, rather than remaining in sheer suspension, evolves toward explicit recognition. Let me cite an example from recent experience:

> Seating myself in a barroom filled with recent arrivals at a conference, I find myself opposite a figure whom I do not recognize at all at first. Gradually, as the evening wears on, it occurs to me that he may be someone I know—but just how I cannot say. Eventually, I realize that this person is probably the graduate student who once gave me a ride from the Dallas airport to the University of Dallas, where I had attended a meeting the year before. His name, "Randy," which I had kept vaguely in mind since being introduced to him earlier this evening, suddenly seems just right, and I finally recognize him fully for who he is.

In dawning recognition, then, I only gradually come to complete recognitive awareness—an awareness that may itself culminate in a definitive flash of insight.

What is the critical difference between merely dim and actually dawning recognition? The foregoing examples suggest that it may reside in the factor of context. When I merely pass someone by in a car or when I am caught up in the frustratingly vague recognition of a person I have run into at a casual party, an adequate recognitory context is lacking. If I proceed to seek out such a context, this is because I feel that, if found, it will offer a crucial clue for successful recognition.[15] In instances of dawning recognition, by contrast, an identifying context is present from the start. In the case reported just above, it is provided by the conference I was attending—a conference closely related in orientation and theme to the earlier meeting in Dallas for which the as yet unrecognized person in question had served as my escort. The collocation of these historically intertwined factors constituted a valuable recognitory matrix, one which supported my slowly growing recognition. This matrix supplied the context—a context furnishing immediate clues—for my full recognition. It helped to complete a search that began with an initially dim recognition. The "display" of my successfully dawned recognition carried out a task that was implicitly set in dim recognition; the two forms of recognizing coalesced as if they were two phases of one activity.

## Recognizing-in

This is a neglected but nevertheless important form of recognizing. It occurs whenever we recognize one thing *in* another: in its form or on its terms. Let me cite another example from my own experience:

> Every time I see a photograph of my great uncle Emmett, I see my mother's face in his—in particular, in his dark eyes, expressive eyebrows, and high cheek bones. Others in my family claim that they see *me* in his face—as well as in his intellectual interests and activities.

It is not entirely accidental that this example involves a family resemblance. In the context of a family, recognizing one person in the aptitudes, features, moods, even the whole life, of another is an ordinary occurrence—indeed, for some families an absorbing pastime. Just as Galton's celebrated composite family photographs bring out strikingly the facial traits shared in common by diverse family members, so cases of recognizing one relative in the habits or traits of another serve to pick out a commonality often unsuspected by the persons who are being juxtaposed.

But recognizing-in is by no means restricted to such family situations. It arises wherever a significant overlap between any two or more people, places, or things becomes evident to the recognizer. To name just a few such non-familial instances: teachers in pupils; analysts in analysands; owners in their pets; the sense of a certain kind of British countryside in regions of Connecticut; the style of one musician or painter in another musician or painter. Included here is the "influence" of one person on another: witness only certain of Wittgenstein's immediate disciples, who were said to mimic him (often unconsciously) in clothing, gesture, wording, and even smoking habits! In a more mundane context, the two members of a married couple are frequently said to resemble each other increasingly as the years go by. Just as we recognize Wittgenstein in his disciples, so we recognize one marital partner in another.

Is resemblance a requirement for recognizing-in? Doubtless it facilitates it—as is evident precisely in cases of family resemblance. But there are instances of recognizing-in in which no notable or even perceptible isomorphism is at play. For example, Picasso owned several early paintings by Matisse that were painted at the beginning of the century, before the emergence of a style that art critics and connoisseurs would come to label as recognizably "Matisse" in character. Yet Picasso insisted that *he* could readily recognize the mature Matisse—even the Matisse of 20 years later—in these juvenilia. Here is a judgment of recognizing-in that is not based on any overt resemblance—indeed, on its very absence, given the considerable evolution in Matisse's style after these early works. Nor is the example as isolated as it may appear. Art historians often urge us to recognize the imprint of one artist or school of art in another—where before we had perceived only discontinuity and difference.

Such recognizing-in has a distinctly different basis from resemblance proper, and may be described approximately as follows. In what we now apprehend, x, we can recognize the presence of at least some of the significant features of y—not because these latter literally resemble any of the features of x but because they *inhabit* the apprehended structure of x. They do so by a process of subtle ingression whereby they, or their representatives, have come to take up residence in x. Once they find a place there, they are not so much presented as "appresented" (in Husserl's useful term).[16] To be appresented is not to be presented as such, in distinct self-identity (hence as enabling a judgment of resemblance, which exists between two separately identifiable terms), but to be *indirectly* presented. The indirection may assume various forms, including suggestion, allusion, expressiveness, and implicit references of many kinds. In the case of a pictorial-visual object, it often arises in a format in which y, the appresented object (e.g., Matisse's later work), is indirectly presented by the complex conglomerate structure of x (Matisse's early work). Rather than the discrete features of x, it is the global structure of x, its overall configuration, which allows one to recognize y in it. Thus, it may not have been any particular features of Matisse's early paintings—their colors, their brushstrokes, their subject-matter—that led Picasso to recognize the later work in them but instead a diffuse tendency which could not be readily analyzed into discrete elements. In Picasso's perception, the later work resides in the early work—haunts it in advance, as it were—by inhabiting it in this indirect but nonetheless highly effective fashion. We might say that it is present there "by proxy"—the proxy provided precisely by the appresentational structure of the early paintings. This structure, far from being based on actual resemblance, may even be hindered by such resemblance inasmuch as it may induce the viewer to undertake a point-for-point comparison between the resembling terms. Not to be led to do so is to find oneself freer to engage in the more nuanced, more discerning recognizing-in to which Picasso testifies. Such recognizing-in is worth cultivating—not only in the realm of art but in other domains of human experience as well.

## Recognizing-as

Earlier I noted an affinity between much ordinary recognizing and seeing-as. But I also warned that not all recognizing can be assimilated to such a strictly perceptual act as seeing-as. This even includes the phenomenon of recognizing-as. In seeing-as, I pick out certain features in a perceived object:

I see this object *as* green and bulbous and heavy. These features are simultaneously present to me, and the perceptual task is typically to perceive as many as possible at a given moment. In recognizing-as, not only is there no restriction to perceived objects, but the features I recognize need not be simultaneously present. The shadow of the past makes itself felt in the form of a discrepancy between present and non-present constituents: a discrepancy notably absent in the situation of seeing-as. How this is so will become manifest as we consider the three main subtypes of recognizing-as.

RECOGNIZING X AS Y

This occurs whenever something of indistinct, or even mistaken, identity comes to be recognized as *other* than it first presented itself as being; not just as having other features but as being another person or object altogether. This was what happened to me in the South Bend airport: there was a movement from the perception of an ambiguous x (i.e., an as-not-yet identified person) through a transitional phase of quasi-recognition (i.e., of x as possibly Tom) to the decisive insight that this x was actually y (i.e., Charles). A discrepancy between present and nonpresent arose in the very gradualness with which my process of recognition unfolded. Even though this process culminated rapidly with the certain identification of the figure as Charles, the moment of authentic recognition of x as y was preceded by a stage of *coming to* recognize that x was indeed y. This stage of coming-to-recognize was nonpresent, already elapsed, in relation to the actual moment of recognizing-as.

RECOGNIZING X AS HAVING HAPPENED BEFORE

The nonpresent may figure into recognizing-as in a quite different manner: as its very content. For one way of recognizing something is to recognize, not its identity or special characteristics, but the sheer fact that it has arisen before in one's experience. This "before" can be quite indeterminate; no exact dating or even recalling of the specific occasion of occurrence needs to be effected, tempted as we may be to do such things. All that is required is the conviction that the object or event presently encountered has entered one's experience at *some* prior point, whatever its precise determination may be.[17]

Another example will help to bring this out. Upon entering a certain Midwestern bus station after an absence of many years, I have the immediate sense that all this has happened before: that I entered the same station in just the same way (i.e., by debarking from an incoming bus) and looked about in much the same manner, half-expectant that I would see someone familiar (my father); and that I found the same rather desolate arrangement of chairs, lockers, and a ticket counter. More than mere familiarity is involved in such an experience, since I can sometimes find a scene familiar even when nothing is being re-enacted in it. Beyond just being back in a familiar bus station, a place which I can grasp as such in an act of simple recognition, I now recognize it as the scene of former action on my part, of an earlier enactment[18] which I take to be re-enacted as I re-enter the same setting. What I recognize is thus my current action of entering the bus station *as having happened before*.

RECOGNIZING X AS A FACT

Here we move from acts of sheer acknowledgement to acts in which we claim truth. To recognize something as a fact is not merely to have the conviction that one is acquainted with its identity or earlier history but to claim to *know* that the item in question has the identity one takes it to have, or did indeed occur as one suspects it did. The usual idiomatic expression of this truth-claim is the simple assertion "I recognize the fact that . . ." (When one says "I recognize that times have changed," one is acknowledging change only because one has observed that change has *in fact* taken place: the acknowledgment proceeds from the more fundamental act of recognizing-x-as-a-fact.)

One of the most striking characteristics of recognizing-x-as-a-fact lies in its considerable range of application. It extends from cases of quite general recognition—"I recognize [the fact] that he is getting older now," where x equals "getting older" and remains largely unspecified as to just how or at what rate he is getting older—to very concrete instances: "I recognize [the fact] that she is 38 years old now," where x equals "being 38 years old" and is precisely specified, at least in terms of chronology. What is common to all such cases and holds them together as a class is the act of recognizing that a certain state of affairs truly obtains. This act itself need not involve any dramatic sense of confirmation or discovery. Indeed, it can happen in a quite resigned state of mind, as if to say: "I cannot help but aver that x is a fact" since I know that x *is* a fact. Such resignation is not surprising in matters of truth, of which we need only be the witness in any given situation.

We are witnesses of recognized facts as *settled* states of affairs, that is, as already being the case. Once more the discrepancy between the present and the nonpresent asserts itself. Not only is a fact *already a fact* when we recognize it, but this very attestation depends on the fact's precedence of our present judgment. Thanks to its precedence, it can present itself as a fact to be recognized as such—as something there to be witnessed. As in other sorts of recognizing-as, such links to the past, however tacit they may be on a particular occasion, bestow on recognizing-as a peculiar temporal depth that contrasts both with the shallowness of presentness and the indistinctness of suffusion.

## Recognizing the General

A common experience is that of seeing familiar figures or shapes in the world about us: the "man in the moon," a camel or other animal in a cloud, a figure in a crack in a wall, a leering face in the very midst of an abstract expressionist painting. These are cases of genuinely recognizing the objects or shapes in question and not of simply perceiving them; or more exactly, we are recognizing them *as having these shapes* or *as appearing in the form of such objects*. The "as" in these verbal formulations is neither the "as" of seeing-as—we are not seeing the cloud *as* a (real) camel or the moon as an (actual) man—nor the "as" of as-if, i.e., of an act of mere make-believe in which we would be merely pretending to recognize the object or shape.[19] Nor is it even the "as" of recognizing-as, since it is not a question of recognizing any object, event, or fact that has temporal depth as an intrinsic dimension. Instead, we have to do with an autonomous activity which is that of recognizing something general in its very generality. Rather than recognizing what is strictly singular—e.g., a given person or place in its very noncomparability with other persons and places—we recognize a general shape or form of objecthood such as 'camel', 'man', 'leering face' that can be exhibited elsewhere in a quite comparable form. By "general," I mean such as to be shareable or transportable *between* experiences: as happens each time we see "the man in the moon" anew. It would be absurd to claim that we are recognizing the *same man*, much less a given *particular man;* but it is not at all absurd to say that on each such occasion we are recognizing the same, or a similar, shape and that this shape evokes the designation "the man in the moon."

Recognition need not therefore be of particulars in their uniqueness (even though just this uniqueness is critical in the recognition of persons) but can be of generals as well, whether these generals occur as perceived shapes, states of affairs, patterns of thought, artistic styles, or in still other forms. Because it can grasp generals in this way, recognizing ranges over the gamut of human experience. Nothing belonging to that experience is foreign to it, since everything in this experience is subject to some degree of generalization.

## Self-Recognition

Despite the widespread generality of *recognita,* many present themselves as stubbornly particular. This is above all true of myself as recognized by myself. Such self-recognition is perhaps the most spontaneous, the least rehearsed, form of recognition. We enact it so frequently and so unthinkingly that it hardly seems a form of recognition at all. The fact that we do not notice ourselves recognizing ourselves is linked to the absence of anything comparable to a flash of recognition: "Aha! that's me!" is a very rare utterance. Nor is there normally anything like a dim or dawning recognition for which the flash would represent a resolution. For we do not misrecognize ourselves except in unusual circumstances—e.g., when one notices an apparent stranger at a distance in a mirror and then realizes with a start that the figure is in fact oneself.

Recognizing oneself in a mirror is no merely contingent example. It is integral to the very process of self-recognition. Jacques Lacan even argues that the formation of one's first sense of self-identity depends upon seeing oneself in a mirror early in life. According to this "mirror stage" theory, the child of eighteen to twenty-four months sees itself in a mirror and suddenly has the insight, thanks to the coordination of actual bodily movements and mirrored movements, that the onlooker and the looked-at are one and the same entity. Self-recognition is born at this moment—albeit in an idealized form.[20] By the time adulthood is reached, the self-as-mirrored has been so thoroughly interwoven into self-recognition that it has become a deeply immanent ingredient of one's ongoing sense of self. At this later age, self-recognition is at once highly *diversified* (since we recognize ourselves in innumerable ways, in habits and forms of thinking, in feelings and tendencies, and not only in visual images of our body) and radically *internalized:* it is no longer dependent on externally perceived cues but has become intrinsic to our entire personal being.

In short, self-recognition proves to be crucial to self-identity. Were I not able to recognize myself in such diverse and internalized ways, I would lack an essential dimension of my very sense of self. Having a personal identity requires the ability to recognize myself as continually selfsame in whatever I do. We might even say that, paradoxically, *self-recognizing by and large vanishes from the scene of manifest recognition so as to assume a suppressed position in the subterranean scene of self-identity*. By no longer (or only rarely) being an issue in the daytime world of ordinary, overt recognizings, it has become free for covert operations of enormous scope—a scope which is co-extensive with that of the very self it helps to constitute.[21]

## IV

Four final observations are here in order.

(1) The description of types of recognizing could continue almost indefinitely. In the end it is difficult to tell what is *not* recognitory in human experience. Since recognizing of some sort can take place in virtually every context and with regard to any kind of object (including oneself), its typological variety is considerable. Indeed, the variety is such as to induce an almost literal con-fusion of recognition with other human experiences. For recognizing readily conjoins with practically any other activity, e.g., imagining and perceiving, thinking and feeling. In this respect, it is Hermetic in character, a creature of the borderlines.[22] The fate of recognizing is often to find itself precisely at the borderline: to be *between* other, more easily discernible phenomena.

The borderline standing of recognizing brings with it both an advantage and a risk. The advantage is that of enabling disparate experiences to become more continuous with each other. Recognizability bestows on these experiences the cement of the familiar. Even if recognizing cannot be reduced to merely cognizing what is familiar,[23] the general effect of recognition is to enhance the familiarization of the circumambient world: to make us feel more completely at home in it. The corresponding risk is that in its very domesticating-cum-mediating role recognizing may lose any distinct status of its own. This risk has been apparent throughout the present chapter. Even in my initial example of recognizing Charles, I was discussing a situation in which recognizing is difficult to distinguish from ordinary perception. Would we not say that I came to *perceive* Charles, having at first misperceived him as Tom? Indeed. And yet we would also rightly say that I came to *recognize* Charles, having first quasi-recognized him as Tom. The situation was at once perceptual and recognitory: both, though neither in isolation from the other. The same ambivalent logic—of being somehow both A and B and yet neither simply A nor simply B—can be detected when we think of recognizing in relation to imagining, thinking, feeling, and still other basic human activities.

So polymorphic is recognizing that it even attaches itself to other, nonrecognitory forms of remembering itself. On the one hand, I can recognize myself recollecting or reminiscing, remembering-how, or remembering-on-the-occasion-of. In such cases I recognize myself in the act of remembering. On the other hand, I can also recognize what I recollect (i.e., its specific content) as well as what I reminisce about, remember how to do, or recall on a certain occasion. I recognize in and by remembering—just as I remember in and by recognizing itself.

(2) It is a fact worth pondering that the only comparably polymorphic memorial activity is that of recollecting. Recollecting, too, has numerous types and subtypes, and their description led me to adverbial and prepositional designations as convoluted as those I have devised to fit recognizing. In their shared polyvalence of realization and expression, recognizing and recollecting are brothers under the flesh. Perhaps this helps to explain why these two forms of memory have been subjected to such intensive comparative scrutiny in experimental psychology: as if detecting their "objective" differences might stave off any threat of confusion with one another. In addition to these efforts—whose results are far from unified[24]—Piaget has attempted to argue that recognition and "evocative memory" (i.e., ordinary recollection) represent respectively the first and the last stages in the development of human memory.[25]

Piaget also offers a working definition of the difference between recognition and recollection: "by 'memory in the strict sense', we shall refer to reactions associated with recognition (in the presence of the object) and recall (in the absence of the object)."[26] However pithy and practicable Piaget's formulation may be, it overlooks critical cases in which the "presence of the object" is not explicitly or fully operative and yet full recognition nevertheless occurs. This happens precisely in certain combinations of recognition and recollection:

(*a*) *Recognizing in recollecting*. We would not consider ourselves to be genuinely recollecting at all unless we were able to recognize, to some significant degree, that which we are in the process of recollecting. Such recognizing not only bears on the act and content of recollecting, but may include a distinct sense that we have undertaken a comparable action of recollecting before. Moreover, we can *recognize that we have recognized* such an action. The interaction between recognizing and recollecting is such as to allow for continual reiteration.

(*b*) *Recognizing by recollecting*. A quite different avatar is that in which recognizing takes place *by* recollecting—by its aid or means. Rather than appearing in the very midst of recollection, recognizing here calls on the latter for the special help it can offer. This arises, for example, in situations of dim or dawning recognition when the presently proffered material (even if it is given in perception) is either highly ambiguous or simply insufficient. Recourse to the "absences" of recollection is then a way of elucidating or expanding such "present" material. I ask myself, "Where have I seen this object before?" "What part of the past does it stem from?" To recapture in recollection the same object in an earlier appearance helps to establish this object as genuinely recognized in the present.

Given such possibilities of interchange, it is not altogether surprising to realize that recollecting and recognizing have in effect framed this book's analysis thus far. What was inaugurated in Part One with recollection has now culminated in Part Two with recognition. Moreover, each form of remembering represents a borderline: in the former case, a borderline for conventionally conceived "remembering in the old manner,"[27] i.e., as a mentalistic activity; in the latter case, a borderline for less frequently acknowledged or researched mnemonic modes. As recollecting takes us decisively into the mental domain—being the very paradigm of "reproduction in the psychical field"[28]—so recognizing places us no less decisively on the margins of the same domain, a borderline that is contiguous with reminding and reminiscing, both of which exceed recapture in recollective terms alone.

(3) It is becoming evident that recognition enjoys in many respects a distinctly *intermediary* position in matters of memory. As we have just seen, not only does it stand between various basic human experiences; it also insinuates itself between particular recollections. At the same time, it mediates between reminding and reminiscing, each of which regularly relies on

recognizing for its own accomplishment. Both the reminder and the remindand must be recognized by us as aspects of an already constituted situation of reminding; and in reminiscing I count on myself and my co-reminiscers or listeners to be able to recognize what I am reminiscing about: to identify its subject matter as shared among us.

Still more importantly, recognizing is actively inter-mediating by virtue of thrusting us into the presence of a nexus of *recognita*. This nexus is even vaster than the domains of reminders and of *reminiscentia* to which I have pointed in the previous two chapters. For it includes all manner of objects, not excluding reminders and *reminiscentia* themselves. Indeed, it even includes the world of Platonic Forms, which we must recognize if we are truly to know them. If Plato does not speak expressly of "recognizing," this is only because recognition is so deeply presupposed in his thinking. What else does the dialectician do but recognize Forms in particulars? Plato's general preoccupation with the realm of *metaxu* ("intermediaries") and with the issue of *methexis* ("participation") finds in recognition an invaluable if not explicitly acknowledged ally.

(4) Recognizing is intermediary in still another way as well: a way that helps to account for its literally intermediate location in this book. In recognizing, I find myself midway between my mind and my world. As a recognizer, I am rarely confined to mind alone: even in intra-psychic recognizing I discover pathways into the surrounding world by way of the content recognized or through the historicity of previous enactments. But, by the same token, I am not trapped within the circumambient world when I recognize; I retain access at all times to what Whitehead would call the "mental pole,"[29] thanks to the freedom with which I can shift attention and refocus in the process of recognizing.

As a result, recognizing engages us in a basic two-fold action. On the one hand, it plunges us willy-nilly into the unyielding perceived world regarded as a source of what Piaget calls "perceptual indices."[30] What could be more obdurate, more determinately *given* than such indices taken as recognitory cues? On the other hand, recognizing draws us back into the interiority of our minds, where its complicated liaisons with recollecting reveal it to be capable of subtle psychical involutions. Its undeniably public face—its manifest and above-board character when it is allied with perception—is counterposed with its equally incontestable (albeit less manifest) private side when it is tied to recollection. The tension between these two directions or dimensions of recognizing is at once more dramatic and more consequential than the corresponding tension between external and psychical reminders, or that between co-reminiscing and auto-reminiscing. All three kinds of remembering exhibit both poles, mental as well as physical—indeed, just this homology helps to constitute them as a coherent group of "mnemonic modes"—but in recognizing the disparity between the two poles is most fully highlighted.

# CODA

There remain other, more deep-going differences between reminding, reminiscing, and recognizing. In part, these differences inhere in the peculiar *medium* of each mode. While reminding arises from the operation of various kinds of signs that constitute a specifically semiological medium, reminiscences favor words, that is, a distinctively verbal format: which is not to deny a significant overlap between the two media. *Recognita*, in contrast, occur in a (prototypically) perceptual context or else in an intrapsychic sphere, neither of which is strictly semiological or linguistic in status. Further, the three modes differ noticeably in their characteristic forms of *temporality*. We have seen that reminders send us either backward or forward in time—or both at once—while in reminiscing we are cast back into the past by virtue of reliving it. In recognizing, on the other hand, I am imbued with an irrescusable presentness and linked to the past only through its shadow in the present. Everywhere, then, differences abound among the mnemonic modes.

But they abound only in the face of the basic fact that all three modes operate by intermediation between mind and world. Each in its own distinctive way is a mediatrix between mental and physical poles, an effective go-between connecting mind with body and body with world (including the world of others). If their connective capacities are not as powerful as the kinds of remembering to be explored in the next Part, the modes are nonetheless first forms of memory writ large and as such merit our closest attention. Together, they compose a dense, massive, and yet nuanced "instrumental complex"[1] which mediates between my present self and everything that is not an immediate component of this self. Between themselves, and precisely as beings-of-the-between, reminders, reminiscences, and recognitions co-constitute our proximate environment—the domain of our commitments and tasks, of our musings upon our diverse pasts, and of all that has recognitory value. The mnemonic modes build up an interworld of things to be done, of communication to be shared, of recognition to be accomplished. In exercising these modes of memory, we are already beyond the confinement of mind considered as the exclusive receptacle of remembering. At the same time we are on the way to still more radical ways of remembering in and through the world.

# *Part Three*
# *Pursuing Memory beyond Mind*

# PROLOGUE

> In this closet of Memory the Soul treasures up the Ideas of things, making use of a clear and subtil Spirit. . . .
>
> —Marius D'Affigny, *The Art of Memory: A Treatise Useful for All, Especially Such as Are to Speak in Publick* (London: Darby, 1706)

We have been witnessing the emergence of memory from within the encasement of mentalism. In viewing it as writ large in recognizing, reminding, and reminiscing, we have observed its indispensable, overt position in the world of perception, signs, and communal discourse. From containment and privacy within the mind of the individual rememberer, we have seen it take up a much more public stance—a stance on the borderline of self and other. Or more exactly, we have realized that it has always already occupied this very stance. If it has been thought to be anywhere else—in the mind in particular—this has been the result of presuming that the paradigm for all remembering is recollecting. Construed as the summoning up of past experiences in visualized scenes, recollection has been conceived as occurring exclusively within the closely containing canopy of mind. In the interest of simplification and in the context of a pervasive mentalism, other forms of remembering have been systematically neglected. The actuality of memory, however, comprises all such forms.

We have taken important steps toward acknowledging this actuality by ascertaining reminding, reminiscing, and recognizing to be intermediate in status. Each of these mnemonic modes is situated midway between mind and the environing world. While each serves as a forceful ingression into this world, each remains tied to a mental pole, whether in the guise of psychical reminders, auto-reminiscences, or the inward recognition of one's own mental acts. But just here we are led to ask: are there forms of remembering that do not retain even such tenuous ties as these to a mental pole? Are there ways of remembering that manifest an abiding and uncompromising implacement in the world? That there are such ways will be shown in this new Part, where we shall pursue memory beyond mind by recovering its roots in the world itself.

In doing this, we will be in effect retracing the history of phenomenology. Part One relied on the classical model of intentionality as it arose in the mentalistic formulations of Brentano and Husserl. It was therefore not surprising that recollection or secondary memory loomed so large in the examples and discussions offered in that Part. In Part Two, in contrast, emphasis was placed on aspects of what Heidegger might call "the worldhood of the world."[1] Implicitly at work was a species of intentionality which is Heideggerian rather than Husserlian in orientation and which is concerned with particular modes of being-in-the-world (including explicitly instrumental modes that would be ascribed to the realm of "readiness-to-hand" in *Being and Time*).[2] Now, in opening Part Three, I begin with a consideration of body memory that quite naturally invokes Merleau-Ponty's notion of "operative intentionality" in his *Phenomenology of Perception*.[3] But I also want to explore certain topics that were not expressly in Merleau-Ponty's purview and that take us beyond the culminating phase of phenomenology which his work is so often taken to represent. These topics are place memory and commemoration, both of which bring us still more radically into the very heart of world implacement. But they do so only as guided by a prior understanding of body memory—to which we must now turn.

# VIII

# BODY MEMORY

> I think that all the nerves and muscles can serve [memory], so that a lute player, for example, has a part of his memory in his hands: for the ease of bending and disposing his fingers in various ways, which he has acquired by practice, helps him to remember the passages which need these dispositions when they are played.
>
> —Descartes, Letter to Mersenne, April, 1640

## I

The centrality of body memory comes home to us most vividly precisely when such memory fails us. This is evident even in comparatively trivial cases. When I settle into the chair in which I have been accustomed to do most of my reading and writing for the past several years, I am shocked to discover a different cushion pressing against me: suddenly my ongoing existence is destabilized, disoriented. So too, I am perplexed upon finding that the keyboard of the typewriter I have used for the last decade has lost its felt familiarity after I have been away for a month in a place where I was forced to rent a different machine. As I fumble to reacquaint myself with the keyboard, I feel *myself* to be a different person in the circumstance—an awkward being, unable to perform efficiently even a quite simple mechanical operation. Indeed, it is often in the suspension of just such a basic and taken-for-granted operation—a suspension whose significance for our sense of instrumentality has been singled out by Heidegger[1]—that we are reminded of how pivotal and presupposed body memory is in our lives. These lives depend massively on the continued deployment of such memory. Even someone as deprived of the normal functioning of every other kind of memory as is an extreme temporal lobe epileptic is still able to find his way around the hospital to which his brain-damaged state has consigned him.[2] As proper names are usually the first items to be systematically forgotten by almost everyone following mid-life, body memories are among the very last to go. This suggests that their role in our remembering is at least analogous to that of space and time in Kant's Transcendental Aesthetic: *a priori* in status, constantly at work in one capacity or another, never *not* operative. Just as eliminating space and time as the indispensable parameters of our intuition would mean the undermining of human experience itself, so the absence of body memory would amount to the devastation of memory altogether.

I speak of "body memory," not of "memory of the body." Body memory alludes to memory that is intrinsic to the body, to its own ways of remembering: how we remember in and by and through the body. Memory *of* the body refers to those manifold manners whereby we remember the body as the accusative object of our awareness, whether in reminiscence or recognition, in reminding or recollection, or in still other ways. The difference is manifest in the noticeable discrepancy between recollecting our body as in a given situation—representing ourselves as engaged bodily in that situation—and *being* in the situation itself again and feeling it through our body. Nevertheless, the difference is not always easy to discern or to maintain. What Jonas calls the "nobility of sight"[3]—the tendency of vision to reassert itself at every turn, including the visualization that subtends most acts of recollection—has the effect of blurring the distinction between body memory and memory of the body. Indeed, at a number of points in the present chapter I fall prey to the all too natural temptation to substitute a recollective consciousness of the body as I remember it "objectively" for the way the body itself, in its sinews and on its surface, remembers its own activity.

Submission to this temptation has been indigenous to Western philosophy. It is a quite remarkable fact that there has been no sustained recognition of body memory from Plato through Kant. Bergson is the first philosopher to have devoted concerted attention to it; but he took a part of such memory (i.e., "habit memory") for the whole of it.[4] Merleau-Ponty, very much inspired by the example of Bergson, speaks of the body as "habitual" in the *Phenomenology of Perception;*[5] and yet the otherwise admirable project of this book—which succeeds in according to the body a prominence that it has never before received in philosophical treatments in the West—fails to underline the importance of body *memory* as such. If Merleau-Ponty fills the void left gaping in Heidegger's *Being and Time*—where the role of the body, though implicit throughout, is never thematized—his own text exhibits a no less glaring lacuna in its bypassing of body memory.

This chapter proceeds by first distinguishing three major types of body memory (and thus avoids Bergson's *pars pro toto* approach), followed by a discussion of the overall significance of body memory (in this way attempting to compensate for Merleau-Ponty's silence on the subject). In so doing, I am not proposing that the body is a cause, directly or indirectly, of human memory generally: whatever the merits of such a claim, it is the proper concern of physiologists, not of philosophers. But I am proposing that the body is of centralmost concern in any adequate assessment of the range of remembering's powers. For this reason, we cannot afford to neglect it any longer. If the body is indeed "the natural subject of perception" and the "point of view on points of view,"[6] body memory is in turn the natural center of any sensitive account of remembering. It is a privileged point of view from which other memorial points of view can be regarded and by which they can be illuminated.

## II

Consider a concrete instance of such remembering:

> I am on an isolated island in northern Sweden with several other people. The only available means of transportation is a 1926 Model T Ford. Although I have been assured that this ancient automobile is in "mint" condition, I cannot make any sense of how to drive it. The situation looks bleak. What to do? Suddenly, a friend, "JH," stations himself in the seat, and begins to drive off—to the astonishment of all the rest of us. Later JH confesses that he had driven the Model T frequently in the past—in the course of several summers a decade or so ago, just after the car had been thoroughly rehabilitated.

What is particularly striking in a case like this is not only the sudden, unpremeditated return of the relevant body memory—for which no express relearning or review was required—but the fact that no explicit recollection of past learning was called for. Even if my friend had happened to recall specific occasions on which he had learned (or relearned) to drive the Model T, specific recollections were not necessary to his successful driving.[7] Nor was there required even a minimal re-familiarization at the level of the ready-to-hand: JH did not have to become reacquainted with the odd assortment of levers and knobs when his hands went unhesitatingly to the correct instruments at the right moments. If the habitual body memory is suitably active, one need not have recourse to other levels or kinds of experience beyond that in which one is presently engaged. All that is called for is that one exist bodily in the circumstance where a given body memory is pertinent.

This sort of bodily remembering might usefully be termed "performative" remembering. My friend's habit-based remembering of how to drive a Model T just *was* the performance of such actions as: cranking the engine; adjusting the hand choke; releasing the handbrake; putting the car into gear; etc. This remembering does *not* consist in the various mental manoeuvers (some of which may even be expressly mnemonic) which may accompany the bodily movements that effect turning on the ignition, shifting gears, braking, blowing the horn, and so on. Even if certain mental operations were in fact constant accompaniments of such movements, this is in no way required for the remembering which the body's spontaneous actions execute. Nor would the occurrence of such operations constitute an adequate indicative sign of this remembering;[8] JH might possess an appropriate set of thoughts (including perfectly accurate recollections of past bodily executions) and yet utterly fail to remember how to drive the car.

It is evident from this example and many others like it that habitual body memories are at once pre-reflective and presupposed in human experience. As pre-reflective, they form a tacit, pre-articulate dimension of this experience. My friend neither reflected on nor articulated his body memory of driving a Model T; he simply *enacted* it. As presupposed, habitual body memories serve as our *familiaris* in dealing with our surroundings—as a constant guide and companion of which we are typically only subliminally aware. They are always already in operation in our ongoing lives. We could not initiate actions, much less continue them, unless we could count on such memories. Even the most probative, trial-and-error operations call for them—much as the body itself is presumed in all higher-order cognitive acts. We may even say of them that they constitute "the body of the body," the connective tissue of the corporeal intentionality that ties us to the world in the first place. As such, they provide the actual ontological ground for Kant's forms of intuition and are not merely analogous to them.

The privileged position of habitual body memory did not emerge in earlier discussions of remembering in its act phase. There, remembering-how was only one in a series of act-forms.[9] This is an expectable result of any purely eidetic enterprise, which seeks a listing of the basic structures of experience without regard to their genesis, goal, or comparative importance. So too the treatment of mnemonic modes in Part Two refused to address the question of whether some modes are more fundamental than others. When we come to habitual body memory, we can no longer afford to be so neutral on this particular issue. For such memory establishes just *how* we are in the world—much as place memory determines *where* we are in it. Even if explicit body memories vary greatly in terms of detail and frequency of occurrence, such memories are continuously at work in our experience and are constitutive of its very fabric.

Reflection on the above example and its implications suggests the following compact definition of habitual body memory:

> an active immanence of the past in the body that informs present bodily actions in an efficacious, orienting, and regular manner.

Let us explicate this formula by looking closely at its three major parts:

(1) Habitual body memory involves "an active immanence of the past in the body." In such memory the past is *embodied* in actions. Rather than being contained separately somewhere in mind or brain, it is actively ingredient in the very bodily movements that accomplish a particular action. It is undeniable that JH's habitual body memory was deeply rooted in the past period during which he learned the action of driving a Model T. Otherwise,

except by sheer random luck, my friend could not have successfully executed this action. Without prior experience or practice, there would be no body memory at all, for there would be nothing to be re-enacted. In the case in point, a moment of instruction preceded—both logically and chronologically—the current capacity to drive the car successfully. But the past thus presupposed became active only as a sedimented force in the immanent present of habitual bodily movement.

The activity of the past, in short, resides in its habitual enactment in the present. This means that the habitual is far from passive in character: as we can see from JH's alert responsiveness. Beyond such a readiness to respond, in what does the active being of habit consist? *Hexis*, the Greek root of "habit," connotes a state of character for which we are responsible, especially in its formative phases.[10] In fact, the early stages in the creation of anything habitual—whether it be character or virtue,[11] or body memories themselves—are definitive for establishing the form that will be continually re-enacted. Not unlike the "primacy effect" that favors the retention of the first members of a list of items to be remembered,[12] the habitual in human affairs represents the continuing triumph of the early-established: not just its survival but its active continuance at later stages when its thorough establishment will help to guarantee its ongoing power.

That habitual action is an active matter is also evident from the Latin root of "habit": *habēre*, to have, to hold.[13] To be habitual is to have or hold one's being-in-the-world in certain ways, i.e., those determined precisely by one's settled dispositions to act in particular patterns. The presence of these dispositions means that our habitual actions help to constitute us as reliable actors within the world—to be counted on by others as well as to count on ourselves. Habituality means consistency in action, the ability to stay the same over time. Thus, my friend, thanks to an intact habitual body memory, remains a driver of his Model T over decades, even gaining part of his identity for others from this fact.

(2) The active immanence of the past also "informs present bodily actions." A "habitude" (as we may call any habitual tendency toward re-enactment)[14] becomes an active ingredient in what we are doing in the present. This means that the habitude in-forms present bodily action: it gives to this action an immanent form, an identifiable character as an action of a certain kind. Part of the very activity of habitual body memory consists in this information, a subtle structuring of behavior along the lines of a personal or collective tradition that becomes readily reinstated in certain circumstances. My friend's behavior behind the wheel of a Model T was not a matter of aleatory motion. It was an action that exhibited its own local history—a history that helped to shape its precise form of bodily movement. The same is true of other habitual body memories. They reflect their origins by their precipitation into a quite particular present action.

(3) Habitual body memories operate in "an efficacious, orienting, and regular manner." Let us consider each of these three characteristics. (a) If such memories were not *efficacious*, they would be dead or frozen habits, routines of a sheerly repetitive sort: a matter merely of "going through the motions." Such routines are not without utility; indeed, taken together, they constitute an entire "second nature" on which we count for the ongoingness of our being-in-the-world. But by "efficacious" I mean having a quite determinate impact on the circumambient world as well as being inherently effective within the immediate ambiance of the actor himself or herself. While the circumambient or outward effects create *differences* in the world—e.g., the driving of the Model T versus its inertial undriven condition—the immediate or inward effects[15] seek to salvage *sameness* in the face of change. How is such sameness achieved by habitual body memories? It is achieved by their acting in concert to constitute my lived body as a coherent and customary entity. In this way habitual body memories constitute an "effective-history" within my lived body and are as integral to it as its tissues and organs. Indeed, it is only through habitual memories that my body can have any history internal to itself.[16] The role that "tradition" plays in the constitution of cultural history is here paralleled by a set of habitual body memories that are the unique possession of a given individual.[17]

(b) Habitual body memories are also deeply *orienting*. It is striking that when we arrive in a new place to stay even for a short visit, we tend without any premeditation to establish a group of fledgling habits such as putting the drip grind coffee in a particular spot, our laundry in another, books in still a third, as well as rising at a certain hour, reading the newspaper at a certain time, etc. These are habituating actions: they help us to get, and to stay, oriented. They establish a base of assurance and ease upon which more complicated, or more spontaneous, activities can freely arise. But their value is more than purely utilitarian: they allow us to discern the sense of a situation, to "get the lay of the land," quite apart from practical results to which they may give rise. Getting the lay of the land is a matter of realizing our being in the world in terms of what I shall call its "landscape" character in the next chapter. For now, I want only to point to the basic ways in which such ground-level orienting occurs via habitual body memories.

The main function of orienting is to effect familiarization with one's surroundings. To be disoriented, or even simply unoriented, is to find these same surroundings unfamiliar, *unheimlich:* "Not to know where we are is torment, and not to have a sense of place is a most sinister deprivation."[18] In particular, it is not to know which way to go or to turn—which route to follow. Getting oriented is to learn precisely which routes are possible, and eventually which are most desirable, by setting up habitual patterns of bodily movement. These patterns familiarize us with the circumambient world by indicating ways we can move through it in a regular and reliable manner. Without such patterned movements, we would be lost in an unfamiliar world.

If such path-finding operations are to be more than means of *becoming* familiar—if they are also to serve as ways of *staying* so—they must be more than fortuitous outcomes. In other words, more than what Merleau-Ponty calls the "momentary body"[19] needs to be mobilized. To remain oriented in a given circumstance, the formation of new habits must give way to consistent habitual responses: the unsettlement of the unknown is only finally vanquished by the acquisition of settled propensities to act. And for these latter to inhere in our behavior, habitual body memory is required. How else are we to carry forward our newly gained orientation into other similar circumstances? Lacking memory, we would be in the immensely demanding circumstance of having to rediscover or to reforge pathways on every subsequent occasion. All of our time would be spent in getting oriented again and again: say, each time we enter a Model T.

In its orienting role, it is clear that the operation of habitual body memory consists in its being a reactivatable link between situations that call for consistent behavior. Such memory subtends these situations, allowing them to become familiar scenes in which we feel at home. Or more exactly: it allows them to become sufficiently familiar to be areas of free action. For habitual body memories liberate us from the necessity of constant reorientation. In their very regularity, they allow us to undertake actions lacking regularity—free and innovative actions difficult to predict, much as an organist adjusts quickly to a new organ and performs creatively on it without any sense of inhibition.[20]

(c) "Regularity" names a last basic aspect of habitual body memory, which is efficacious and orienting in a *regular* way. To be a link between spatially and temporally disparate circumstances—to be the very ground of their felt familiarity—such memory cannot be irregularly operative, i.e., unpredictable and merely wayward. But it also need not be restricted to rote repetition, which simply reinstates the same action again and again—as in a strictly controlled stimulus-response learning situation of maximum reinforcement. Nor need it be bound by induction alone (by the inference of like outcomes from like circumstances); induction calls for an extra-cognitive operation of a highly reflective sort that is inimical to the spontaneous functioning of habitual actions. As I have observed, habitual body memory functions at a deeply prereflective level—which is why it so often occurs without premeditation or particular preparation. But it is at the same time something quite regular. How can this be so?

Consider for a last time the example which has served as a prototype in this discussion. JH's successful body memory arose effortlessly in the circumstance, although his friends' hopes that he might be able to drive the ancient car may have helped to prompt his remembering—and his being actually seated in the driver's seat helped even more. Still, the action of driving itself was not necessitated by these encouraging factors. It came back on its own in the circumstance, as if it were re-visiting my friend from a far-away point in time. It was as if his customary body had suddenly merged with his momentary body. Habitual body memory in fact represents the fusing of the settled and the spontaneous in a re-enactive synthesis. The remembering thereby realized is characteristically sudden and precipitate—and yet quite complete. Habitual body memory typically arises *totum simul*, as when the full action of driving a Model T (or doing the breast stroke or whatever) returns unbidden, in a flash.[21]

This structure of habitual body memory goes hand in hand with its regulated character. Rather than opposing spontaneity and regularity, we should realize that the unpremeditated and the regulated are natural allies. As in the comparable case of what Freud called "primary process" thinking, each calls for the other: the spontaneity of dreaming, far from being utterly unruly and chaotic, is *made possible* by formal rules of condensation, displacement, and symbolization. As Stravinsky has said, "In art, as in everything else, one can build only upon a resisting foundation. . . . My freedom thus consists in my moving about within the narrow frame that I have assigned myself."[22] The free movements of dreams and art find their analogue in the unrehearsed return of habitual body memories, which also accomplish their full freedom only within a "narrow frame." Thus the action of driving a Model T, if it is to be at all successful, must proceed in accordance with certain rules of sequence and of timing:

> *rule of sequence:* give gas by operating a choke; turn on ignition; engage clutch; shift into first or reverse; depress accelerator, etc.
>
> *rule of timing:* do not allow too long a period to elapse between turning on the ignition and engaging the clutch; and similarly between this latter and shifting into gear.

Thanks to its habitual memories, the lived body effects such sequence and timing in a regularized way. And it does so all the more successfully as it does not have to focus on, much less to formulate, the rules at play. Indeed, to focus or formulate would not only impede spontaneity; it might well lead to a misperformance of the activity itself. So too might a concentrated effort to recollect scenes of instruction in which these rules were first propounded and learned. Where propositional formulation and pictorial representation (the two main forms of rule-articulation) are of immense value in the cases of memorizing or reconstructing—indeed, they often complement and strengthen each other in just these cases—they are second-level and often quite superfluous in habitual body memory. The peculiar efficacity and orienting capacity of such memory is most freely exercised in its being thoroughly regular and yet not expressly formulated in words or images, much less concretized in recollections.

## III

A second major type of body memory is *traumatic* in character. Traumatic memories assume many forms, ranging from those that are strictly psychical in status (e.g., memories of painful thoughts) to those that are thoroughly interpersonal (as in memories of perceiving someone else in distress). Traumatic *body* memories, however, arise from and bear on one's own lived body in moments of duress. They are themselves multifarious in type, since they include anything from memories of severe injury to alleviating memories of fleeting pleasure. Rather than setting forth a survey of this striking variety, I shall once again focus on a single instance:

> Each time my tongue passes over my right lower molar tooth these days, distinct memories of being in a dentist's chair and, somewhat less frequently, of chewing on a hard kernel of popcorn still earlier, are elicited. In particular, I recall biting down on the kernel and feeling immediately afterward parts of something very hard lying loose in my mouth: at first I wasn't sure whether these were bits of kernel or bits of tooth. I also remember, from a period about a month later, being in a dentist's chair and experiencing acute pain as my dentist drilled deeply into the broken tooth as part of the procedure of crowning it.

Notice, to begin with, how *particularized* this example of remembering is. In both of its closely related incidents, it bears on highly specific body parts—not only my mouth but a discrete part of it lying within a definite region. This part is, of course, my lower right molar, and my remembering is entirely engrossed in it and its fate: its sudden demolition and its subsequent rebuilding. Such a determinate entity gives to my remembering a point of particular attachment. Rather than being identified with an action or movement that links up smoothly with the surrounding world as in so many habitual body memories, this remembering possesses a content centered on a single object whose very breakdown separates it from the world of ongoing action, forcing my memorial consciousness literally inside myself.

Notice, too, that this object, my afflicted molar, is being remembered bodily as subject to events which are unique and which alter its career in time radically. Neither the initial trauma nor the attempt at dental restoration has anything habitual or repetitive about it. Each is strictly episodic and is remembered as such. Each impinges on and interrupts the amorphous history of my body and renders what is indefinite and undated in this history diachronically distinct: *first* the breakdown, *then* the crowning activity several weeks later. As with all genuinely diachronic events, the sequence is irreversible, consisting as it does of episodes existing in what Kant calls an "objective succession."[23] This succession ensures in turn the datability of these episodes, though only in units appropriate to the circumstance: here week and month (I remember the trauma's occurring about two weeks ago, sometime in mid-July) rather than hour or year.

Despite the isolating concentration on the fate of a single tooth, which became a discrete object for me only at the moment of breakdown, there was a discernible setting in both incidents as remembered. The initial trauma occurred in the context of eating popcorn, and is recalled as situated in this context. Likewise, the pain of drilling is set in the dentist's chair: it does not float free of this circumstance. Neither setting need be remembered in any considerable detail; as the bare location of a traumatic event, each can be quite minimal. Yet even when I remember the point of most intense pain during the drilling, my body is not brought back as locusless; this pain was happening *somewhere,* however denuded its description may be.

The emotionality of both incidents is also vividly conveyed: the shock of realizing that my mouth contained bits of tooth as well as bits of popcorn, the peculiar dread that accompanies deep drilling (I asked myself, "Will this pain, already bad enough, become still worse?"). Although I had no desire to re-experience these feelings—quite the contrary!—I found that they nonetheless afforded access to the original scenes of which they formed such a painful part. A few weeks after the drilling had occurred I was in a service station and heard a pneumatic bolt tightener at work. The shrill grinding sound almost immediately evoked the dread of being the hapless subject of my dentist's drill; I felt myself stiffening in anticipation of worse to come just as I had done in the dentist's chair: ushered in by the dread, my body was itself remembering the trauma. This led in turn to a vivid recollection of the scene—which was, I suspected, a defense against a still more engaging body memory than I had so far allowed myself to undergo. Here is an illustration of how recollection is not consistently primary in its operation; indeed in this case it assumed the decidedly secondary role of helping to keep at bay a recently painful body memory.

Another facet of the particularizing proclivity of traumatic body memories has to do with the *fragmentation* of the lived body. Where habitual body memory typically concerns the body as a coordinated whole—indeed, constitutes it as a single *compositum*—a traumatic body memory bears on what Lacan has called "*le corps morcellé*."[24] This is the body as broken down into uncoordinated parts and thus as incapable of the type of continuous, spontaneous action undertaken by the intact body ("intact" thanks precisely to its habitualities, which serve to ensure efficacity and regularity). The fragmented body is inefficacious and irregular; indeed, its possibilities of free movement have become constricted precisely because of the trauma that has disrupted its spontaneous actions. Body memories of this trauma will necessarily reflect the same fragmentation, as will the terms descriptive of such memories: e.g., "particularization," "isolation of object," "concentration." Such terms can be viewed as giving dimensions of the traumatized body, especially as it acts to inhibit action. Although this inhibition is more dramatically evident in cases of, say, dire back pain, it is still quite manifest in my own tooth trauma, which served to inhibit mastication. Much of the trauma and its associated affect consisted in this very inhibition: or, more precisely, in the realization that "I will henceforth not be able to eat as freely as before."[25] The disabling nature of body trauma here stands in stark contrast with the enabling character of bodily habitudes; and just as the former implies the dissolution of the intact body, so the latter implies its continual re-synthesis.

An aspect of traumatic body memory which the above example does not adequately illustrate is what could be called the phenomenon of "afterglow." This refers to the way that some quite traumatic body memories—which may have been devastating at the moment of origin—will come in the course of time to seem acceptable and even pleasurable to remember. As Virgil says in a passage I have cited before, "Someday, perhaps, it will be a joy to remember even these things" (*Aeneid*, I, 203). My molar matter was too recent to be regarded with anything like pleasure. Yet even if I never take a positive pleasure in remembering it in the future, it is at least likely that I will be able to view it with equanimity and perhaps even with humor or irony. The same holds true for many body traumas, including almost all those that stem from childhood: e.g., my falling down the basement steps just before traveling to my grandparents' home for Christmas many years ago. Although in this latter instance I hit my head against a steel girder, none of the pain associated with this fall survives. So, too, with such other traumatic experiences as being assailed by friends, shot in the leg with a B.B. gun, etc.

This is not to deny that some traumatic body memories never lose their painful and even devastating sting, especially when they are accompanied by some form of humiliation of one's own person—of which a ghastly limiting case would be memories of having been in a concentration camp. Precisely such memories, however, we try to repress, replace, or at least bowdlerize. It remains the case that the pain and poignancy of most traumatic memories recede with time. How does this happen?

One main way it happens, as one might well suspect by now, is that a tendency sets in to transform these memories into reminiscences and recollections. All of my childhood memories cited just above were of precisely this nature: they have become stories I tell to others or recollections in which I indulge when I am alone. Doubtlessly defensive in origin, these transformations have attained an autonomy sufficient for me to take independent pleasure in reactivating them in just these comparatively innocent forms. Closely related to this distancing tendency is the operation of what I called "ruminescence" in chapter 2. When memories, even very painful ones, have become remote from their own point of origin, they often acquire a domesticated quality that encourages our ruminating over them—

instead of simply replaying or radically repressing them (i.e., the two most likely ways of treating the memories of recent traumatic events). When we reminisce about them as well (e.g., by narrating them to ourselves or to others), we enter into a ruminescent state; and in turning them over in our minds in this way, we tame them yet further—to the point where they become our own *re*-creation.[26]

The phenomena of after-glow and ruminescence strongly suggest that many body traumas remain threatening to us even, or rather precisely, as remembered. The return to the initial trauma that their bodily remembering entails brings with it an at least minor trauma of its own, which may in turn have to be defended against.[27] One way to do so is to channel the return of the trauma into a specifically somatic form, e.g., as a hysterical conversion symptom. This is an instance of a quite general strategy of *containing* a trauma, whereby we act to restrict its content and scope to a limited part of one's body. Thus, even if the original trauma was an all-consuming fever, we may remember it as it became focused in a particular form such as dizziness. A second strategy for dealing with the revival of trauma is *situating* it, where the effort is to tie down the trauma by locating it fairly precisely in terms of place or time. In situating, the implicit psycho-logic can be formulated in this way: "if the trauma I am now remembering occurred *there* and *then*, it cannot have such a devastating effect on me *here* and *now* as I remember it." Such an attempt to situate the original occurrence is a salient feature of many traumatic body memories and serves to distinguish them once more from habitual memories. These latter tend to be expansive rather than constrictive and, above all, nonepisodic, hence not pinned down as to date and place of origin: just where or when I acquired or reacquired a certain habitual bodily skill is normally a matter of indifference as I come to enact it subsequently. But I am far from indifferent as to the place and moment when I first underwent the body trauma I am now remembering.

## IV

The body retains memories of pleasures as well as of pains. Scrutinizing traumatic body memories, as has just been done in section 3, risks neglecting the fact that we remember many pleasures in and through our bodies. From among these pleasures I shall concentrate on specifically erotic ones—not because these are paradigmatic of all bodily pleasures (they are at once characteristic and exceptional in this regard) but because their memorial recapture is especially revealing for our purposes.

Let me begin once more with a leading example:

> My shirt rubs against my shoulder one warm afternoon and I am suddenly reminded of the way a certain person used to place her hand on my shoulder

> while we were making love. The touch of her hand combined insistence with tenderness, and intimacy with a certain aloofness. The touch was warm but not oppressively hot, and it took place by a gentle grasping action involving the whole hand. I now experience the remembered touch as being subtly thrilling in its immediacy and in its positioning on my shoulder (it fits my shoulder in a very precise way). This particular body memory brings with it a vivid sense of the affection we once felt for each other. It also, by the closeness which it embodies, serves to dissolve the distance that now separates us.

Especially noteworthy in such an erotic body memory are the following features:

(1) There is a sensuously specific *source* of bodily pleasure as remembered. This pleasure occurs at a quite definite site: i.e., the upper surface of my shoulder. This ties the experience down not only to a particular part of my body but to a special sensory modality, since it is my shoulder *as touched* that is at stake in this body memory.

(2) The bodily remembered touch is *intrinsically pleasure-giving:* the pleasure does not follow the experience but belongs to it as ingredient in it. Whereas I can often separate the performance of a skill from the exact movements of the body parts that effect it, it is not an easy matter to identify remembered erotic pleasure in separation from the precise place in which it occurred—a "place," moreover, which may coincide with my body as a whole.

(3) In the same vein, it is difficult to draw any strict dividing line in such a memory between myself-as-being-touched by the other and the other-as-touching me. The two of us form a dyadic pair who collaborate in the experience as it was once lived and is now being remembered. The members of this dyad are so intimately interlocked that I cannot say for sure where one leaves off and the other begins: the touched and the toucher merge in a phenomenon of interpersonal "reversibility."[28] Each of us share in a genuinely common process that cannot be remembered without including both of us. Such dovetailing of self and other is rarely accomplished in other types of body memory.

(4) An important aspect of erotic body memory is found in the way in which this particular body memory arose: namely, by what we could call "memorial mimetism." Just as two lovers often imitate each other's gestures—a move of one calls for a like move of the other—so a non-erotic body experience seems suddenly to resemble an explicitly erotic experience of the body. Thus being touched on the shoulder by my shirt was immediately assimilated to being touched by a lover in the same place. In our natural eagerness to re-experience sensual pleasure we tend to draw together even quite disparate experiences or entities (here a shirt and a hand), provided only that the same

part of the body is at play (in this case the shoulder) or at least the same sense of how it is experienced.

Let us consider certain still more general structures of erotic body memories:

### INTERSENSORY EQUIVALENCE

Merleau-Ponty observed that various bodily parts can stand in for one another to the point of becoming symbolic equivalents. This is dramatically illustrated in many erotic body memories, where there is a fluid interchange of parts of the body and an open movement between them. The interchange occurs to a much more considerable degree than in habitual body memories, which allow for only a limited substitutability of parts: e.g., right hand for left hand, a leg for an arm, etc. It also contrasts with traumatic body memories, in which the focus is often on a single component or aspect of the lived body. Neither in habitual nor in traumatic body memories is there anything like the free transfer of libido that occurs in erotic body memories, in which one body part can be exchanged with almost any other part in a virtually unfettered fashion.

A closely related facet of erotic body memories is the way in which movement between bodily parts can be *summative* and not merely substitutive. In such memories a shoulder can give rise to a hip and the latter to a breast in an exquisitely additive fashion. Instead of existing in competition with, or as compensation for, each other, these bodily parts constitute an erotic chain of heightening delight as their interconnections are taken up again in memory. How can this be? It is due to the fact that erotic pleasure arises from multiple sensory modalities: touch, sight, odor, hearing, etc. These modalities become genuinely *inter*sensory in erotic activity, which serves to connect what might remain merely disparate in habitual or traumatic situations. This is not to deny distinct personal preferences in sensory modality; but it needs to be underlined that such preferences are subserved by a network of intersensory nodal points encountered in the course of erotic activity. These nodal points—i.e., particular touches, sights, and sounds—allow for variation in the pursuit even of the most preoccupying erotic aim, including orgasm itself, one of whose primary pleasures consists precisely in the fact that it is not reached by a single sensory route alone.

### REMEMBERED EROTIC PLEASURE

It is crucial to keep in mind the distinction between erotic bodily pleasure as it was originally felt and the pleasure we are now taking in remembering this proto-pleasure. However vivid the original pleasure may have been, it is exceedingly difficult to recapture. This is apparent in the sense of loss and attendant nostalgia to which we are prone when we remember making love with someone to whom we were formerly close. Thus the "after-pleasure" of an erotic body memory cannot claim to be an adequate replication of its prototype. Such dependent and late pleasure is a pleasure in and by deferment.

Erotic body memory here resembles traumatic body memory insofar as both call for a distinction between a primary and a belated phase. But erotic memories rarely exhibit any significant analogue of the reversal from pain to eventual pleasure that we observed in traumatic memories. Rather than such a reversal (or its opposite, from pleasure to pain), the original pleasure in an erotic experience tends to sustain itself in its bodily remembrance—though it is certainly subject to dilution or even to suspension (e.g., when the personal relationship on which it is based has gone awry). But for the most part traumatic body memories convey to us a diminished sense of well-being, while erotic body memories serve to underscore our sense of robust intactness.

### INTERPERSONAL ASPECTS

Erotic body memories have the peculiarity that they offer two distinct possibilities so far as the self/other relationship is concerned. On the one hand, they may evoke an explicit sense of the other's bodily presence, which is remembered and valued as such: just *this* posture in foreplay, just *that* thigh, just *those* sighs when excited, etc. In such cases, my memories focus explicitly on the other, and I tend to recall this person in terms of distinctive differences between us, whether these differences spring from basic differences of gender, personality, or whatever. On the other hand, instead of focusing on the other *qua* other in my erotic body memories, I may concentrate on the relationship itself: on just how it felt to be with the other in various activities and postures. In this event, the particular contours of the other matter mainly as contributing to a situation of mutual satisfaction. Similarly, my *own* positions and movements are not remembered in isolation but only as part of the interpersonal complex designatable as "myself-*cum*-other-in-erotic-interplay-together." A double transcendence—of myself and the other as separate erotic entities—is effected in the realization of this complex. The result is a bivalent remembering that escapes the radical singularization of so much nonerotic remembering. In its characteristically dyadic and diffuse manner, erotic body memory is located midway between the alienation inherent in an individual's self-safeguarded recollections and the community realized in a group's genuinely collective remembering.

### ANTICIPATORY DIMENSION

One of the most distinctive features of erotic body memories is their actively anticipatory aspect. They propel us forward toward a future of possible sensual satisfaction that is patterned on satisfaction in the past. We rarely bask in such memories idly or innocently: even when they are not being employed expressly as a means of self-arousal, they evoke in us the projection of a possible repetition. This inbuilt futurism contrasts with the implicit temporality of traumatic body memories, where our concern with a point of origin often reflects a dread of recurrence—and thus a future to-be-avoided rather than one to-be-sought. Erotic body memories are in this respect more like habitual body memories, which are realized by the body in the process of carrying out various particular projects—say, swimming the breaststroke, driving a Model T around an island, speaking in a foreign language.[29] The difference is found in the fact that the aim to be achieved in habitual body memories is strictly defined by a practical context of swimming, driving, speaking; the habitual body is exclusively engaged in what Heidegger has called an 'in-order-to' *(um-zu)* relation: I am doing *this* (activity, practice) so as to accomplish *that* (aim, goal).[30]

Erotic body memories are not easily subsumed into any such manifestly instrumental roles in the pursuit of practical projects. Instead of the in-order-to, their characteristic relation is the 'just-as': just as this past pleasure was remarkably (or moderately, etc.) good, to experience it again would be just as good (or still better). The future of re-enactment or continuation is not a final stage in an instrumentally defined process; rather than being valued for its actuality, it is esteemed for its status as a *possibility:* as leading us into an open future of possible pleasures of the same or similar type. We aim at these pleasures in their very possibility, and we do so out of our re-membering of past prototypes—which provide for us the "repeatable possibilities" of our erotic existence.[31] These possibilities are multiplied not only because of the unknown status of the future but also because of the ready transposability of erotic pleasures from one part of the body to another. If we do not know just what to expect, we can eagerly anticipate new avatars of combination and interchange.[32] The anticipatory dimension of erotic bodily memories means, in short, that the actual cedes place to the possible, the habitual to the novel, the uniquely traumatic to the indefinitely pleasurable.

### RECENT VERSUS REMOTE ORIGINS

We tend to divide erotic body memories into those that are *recent* and those that are more *remote* in origin. The two kinds present themselves to us as distinctively different. Recent erotic memories often still resonate or "tingle" in us. No revival is needed, much less any recollection: they are the bodily equivalent of primary memory, both forming an active fringe around the living present. It is as if an entire recent episode were still happening at some margin of our corporeal life; consequently, much of its affective and sensory specificity is also felt to be continuing. Long-term erotic memories, on the other hand, tend to lack such specificity and even to become stereotypical in status: "myself kissing Jan Stewart on the outskirts of Abilene." Such memories can certainly be forceful and enduring—as is this Abilene memory, which happened over twenty-five years ago—but it lives on only in an emblematic format, characteristically compressed into just one episode: kissing Jan on a moonlit night while the two of us were standing by the car I had borrowed for the evening. In view of the paucity of detail in such a case, it is not surprising that we seek to supplement what we remember bodily by conventional recollections, recourse to diaries, and other sorts of testimonial evidence.[33]

NARRATIVITY

The three types of body memory so far distinguished differ decisively with regard to this last characteristic. Habitual body memories are largely indifferent to a narrative account: their being resides much more in their current efficacity than in any narratizable historicity which they may possess. Their strongly repetitive character, moreover, discourages interest in the kind of historical account that calls for narration. Traumatic body memories, on the other hand, call naturally for a narration of their history. This is due partly to their highly episodic character and partly to our concern about their exact origins. As a result, we often find ourselves recounting an experience of body trauma in narrative terms: telling its story from the moment of the original trauma up to the present moment of remembrance.

Neither of these extremes—one deeply resistant to narration, the other insistently calling for it—is characteristic of erotic body memories. These do not resist narration in any tenacious way; indeed, they often suggest stories and may be woven effectively into larger narrative units. Nevertheless, there is no implicit imperative to narrate them, since they are often fully satisfying precisely in a fragmentary format. In fact, the content of much such remembering consists in fragments: this sense of being touched on the shoulder, that move in foreplay, a given body aroma, a particular perception of bodies interacting. Each of these suffices in itself, indeed *is* the memory in question, and does not call for a supervening narrative structure. The detail, in other words, is memorable just *as detail* and not because the detail is part of some more encompassing story. Even when we suspect that it does belong to such a story, our primary interest does not reside in knowing precisely how it does so: we leave any such concern to situations of reminiscence or recollection.

## V

It is becoming clear that body memory is by no means the same thing as the memory of the *perception* of the body, which is a highly mixed form of remembering that includes among other things a component of recognizing (e.g., when one remembers perceiving oneself as younger in some particular physical aspect). This is not surprising: given that the human body is such a richly expressive vehicle, its perception will be anything but simple. The body as perceived, and hence the body *remembered-as-perceived,* will incorporate multiple layers of meaning and structure, calling for a complex mode of apprehension. Not only recognition but also recollection will figure into such remembering; so too will place memory inasmuch as bodies are always perceived as occupying particular places. Here we do not encounter anything distinctively different from other situations of remembering in which mixed modes are called for—say, in remembering paintings one has seen or books one has read.

Body memory itself, however, is a unique form of remembering and not a mere composite entity. It has its own comparatively autonomous operation;[34] it is not a substitute for another kind of remembering or a stage in the realization of some overarching mnemonic *telos*. However much its specific schemata may change over time, and however much it is vulnerable to the incursions of accident or disease,[35] it is present throughout life. It is thus not just something we merely have; it is something we *are:* that constitutes us as we exist humanly in the world.

If this is indeed the case, we should expect body memory to possess its own set of types and its own group of general traits. That it has its own typology has already emerged in the preceding delineation of habitual, traumatic, and erotic body memories. What has not yet emerged is any sense of general traits which qualify these types by subtending each in some significant respect. Let us therefore proceed to consider such traits. Their consideration will help to knit together much that has so far remained scattered.

## Marginality

Body memories tend to situate themselves on the periphery of our lives so as not to preoccupy us in the present. By "periphery" I do not mean to imply that such memories are of peripheral importance; on the contrary, they are of quite central significance: we could not be who we are, nor do what we do, without them. But the fact remains that bodily remembering assumes for the most part a marginal position vis-à-vis our most pressing concerns—and is all the more effective for doing so. A body memory works most forcefully and thoroughly when, rather than dominating, it recedes from the clamor of the present. As marginal, it belongs to the latent or tacit dimension of our being. In the language of Gestalt psychology, it is a field factor, part of the ground of our experience rather than an explicitly highlighted figure. How this is so will become evident upon a brief review of the three types of body memory identified in preceding sections:

### HABITUAL BODY MEMORIES

These are perhaps the most fully marginal memories we possess. Part of the very meaning of "habitual" is to be so deeply ingrained in our behavior as not to need explicit recalling. To become habitual is to become part of the stock of our resources on which we can draw effortlessly. Such is the fate of most of our habits and thus of the habitual body which supports them.

Merleau-Ponty speaks of the habitual body as an "incontestable acquisition," a "general function."[36] Particular bodily activities can be regarded as condensations or precipitations out of the habitual body, which provides a pervasive background layer to our lives. If such a background were to be explicitly remembered, it might well become intrusive and disorienting—whereas, precisely as marginal, it is the immediate basis for all becoming-oriented in the world as well as for all stabilization there. Whether we take the habitual to be the strictly habit-bound or the merely recurrent—or, as Dewey suggests, as the innovatively habituating[37]—the remembering associated with it is in every case an implicit activity working in ways of which we are barely conscious: hence the inappropriateness of applying to it any strictly mentalistic model such as that of act intentionality. Only in situations of breakdown or when expressly retraining ourselves are we brought face to face with the exact form of its operative intentionality. The very efficacity and regulated character of this intentionality prosper in a situation of twilight consciousness—when we remember very well how to undertake certain actions without necessarily remembering that we did so successfully on any particular occasions in the past.

### TRAUMATIC BODY MEMORIES

These are marginal for the readily understandable reason that making them thematic is to remind ourselves of pain once undergone—and perhaps undergone again upon its very remembrance. It is only too natural that we seek to avoid the full replay of such memories by confining them to the most peripheral position possible in our conscious life. Or we may attempt to transform their initial sting into an after-glow that calls for a complacent contemplation. Either way, we try to forestall a situation in which such memories might become preoccupying; a set of defenses, and sometimes an elaborate system of avoidances, is constructed so as to isolate, deny, split, project, or outright repress the painful content of these memories: all of which can be considered strategies of marginalizing.[38]

### EROTIC BODY MEMORIES

These, it would seem, have no basis for being or remaining marginal. Why would we wish to hold in abeyance anything so inherently pleasurable as these memories? I have already remarked on how much less overtly defensive we are toward erotic activity as remembered—indeed, often less so than toward such activity as currently encountered! Nevertheless, apart from those occasions on which such memories would be distractions from work or other concerns, there is one important sense in which they are indeed marginal: a sense that leads us to expand the scope of marginality itself. I am thinking of the fact that erotic body memories have more to do with the possible than with the actual. They bear, as I have tried to indicate, on what is indefinite and undetermined in erotic experience. Rather than merely recapitulating what has gone before, they suggest to us new dimensions and new directions in our bodily being: this is why, beyond their purely pleasurable aspect, they can play a liberating role. Their comparative indifference to questions of efficient historical causality, most directly manifested in the spontaneity of their contents, makes possible that anticipatory dimension that we found to be so critical in our experience of them; and this dimension is itself arrayed with branching possibilities. For erotic body memories lead us into the marginal *qua possible:* into a horizon of the not-yet encircling our actuality-bound lives. In contrast with the margin provided by the habitual—a deeply sedimented layer of the permanently possessed—the margin adumbrated by the erotic (indeed, by the hedonic broadly speaking) is projective of the still-to-come: the always-already-there is supplemented by the marginality of the ahead-of-ourselves, where certain possibilities *might* be realized. Much as I enjoy basking in erotism already accomplished, this very basking takes me into a future of so far unfulfilled pleasure.

A general remark suggests itself here. In the realm of body memory *almost everything is marginal* from the very start. Even if the lived body is the center of our active experience, as remembered it is continually being displaced into a dim backland of apprehension. The paradox is that body memory is rarely *of the body* as an explicit *focus memorius*. Contrast this situation with that obtaining in recollection, which is often expressly aware of itself as an act of mind. Even when such self-awareness is itself marginal, little else is. It is a striking fact that only one aspect of what I called the "mnemonic presentation" in Part One is marginal in status: namely, the "aura." The aura alone is permitted to be radically indistinct, whereas the expectation is that the remainder of what we recollect will be lucidly set forth before us in clear mnemonic consciousness. This is a far cry indeed from the circumstance we encounter in body memories, which are pervaded by marginality at every significant level.

## Density and Depth

Closely related to marginality is the singular fact that most body memories come to us as notably dense in felt quality: as bearing a high specific gravity. This density is experienced in such qualities as the massive, the opaque, the involuntary, the inarticulate. It is as if the density of body memories, their rootedness in the heft, the thick palpability of the lived body, rendered them mute. My own efforts above attest that they can be put into words, but it is also evident that they do not lend themselves to facile verbalization.

One basic reason why it is so difficult to tease out the structures of body memory—and a reason why the subject has been so conspicuously neglected by writers on memory—lies in their initially inchoate form as well as in their recalcitrance to further specification. Now we must confront their very mutism, which is a feature in its own right and not merely the absence of articulate speech.

To begin with, the felt density of body memories is itself a direct reflection of the body's own densely structured being. Quite apart from its role in memory, the lived body possesses an inner opaqueness in all of its activities. Never wholly transparent to itself—even when it is self-focused—it is so deeply engaged in its various involvements as to be virtually self-transcending and thus unknown to itself. Consider only the way in which my hands and entire upper body are just now involved in typing these words: They seem to belong more to the typewriter than to my own torso. Even if these bodily parts become expressive for an observer or for myself on reflection, they do not take themselves to be such. They are so absorbed in the activity of typing itself that they are not felt to have any identity separate from that which their task calls for. Except in illness—when I am forced to pay attention to the body in and by itself—my body is continually engrossed in the world in much the same self-effacing way. This leaves it as an unreflective core at the heart of its own actions.[39]

Body memories share in this sense of self-opacity which does not even know its own name. Their remove in time from the moment of origin does not endow them with any reflective advantage, much less any tendency to articulate their specific content in words. But their density is not entirely without direction or structure. It is felt as a *density in depth*. Body memories manifest themselves as continually vanishing into the depths of our corporeal existence—and just as continually welling up from the same depths. This is particularly evident in the case of habitual body memories, which arise from and disappear into the dark interiority of our own bodies. But it is also true of erotic and traumatic memories, each of which exhibits an underside of depth: hence the sense of mystery that attaches to the origin of erotic impulses as well as to the unchartable course of a given trauma. Body memories of all sorts possess an essential dimension of depth.

By "depth" is not meant Berkeley's notion of the distance which we infer we would have to travel to reach a predesignated point.[40] This is the external depth *through* which our physical body moves. What is at stake in the density of body memory is the interior depth *in* which the lived body resides—in short, its own depth. Such depth, as Erwin Straus says, "is not a purely objective phenomenon."[41] It is a felt or phenomenal dimension that is not measurable in any metric units; it is, in Merleau-Ponty's formulation, "the dimension in which things or elements of things envelop each other."[42] In the case of body memory, the enveloping occurs within the lived body and its immediate ambiance. Here depth supplies a vaguely determined but firmly felt inner horizon for the remembering of habitual movements, erotic play, traumatic injuries—and all else that belongs properly to body memory.

If the lived body's movements through depth-as-distance can be described as "horizontal" in their sweeping action, its own intrinsic depth is *vertical* and is remembered as such. As upright beings we engage in an upward and downward delving into depth: an etherealizing tendency and a gravitating propensity, normally mixed in a delicate balance of aspiring and anchoring. Habitual body memories can be said to draw mainly on the downward-moving direction of bodily depth—in contrast with erotic memories, which are characteristically upward-moving ("exciting," "thrilling" are words we apply to them). Between the opposed poles of verticality thereby established, traumatic and other kinds of body memories (e.g., of health and illness) come to be situated. Actual or remembered movement toward either pole represents a mode of self-transcendence out of and into depths which the mind in contemplation or recollection can neither fathom nor abide.

In its density, body memory is therefore incurably depth-oriented and depth-affording. In this basic respect it once again differs dramatically from recollection. In recalling, I do not actively connect with the depth of the scene being called back to mind. Instead of moving into its depths, I contemplate its projected, quasi-pictorial distance from myself as a voyeur of the remembered. No such voyeurism occurs in body memory, which takes me directly *into* what is being remembered. In such remembering, I leave the heights of contemplative recollection and enter the profundity of my own bodily being. It is a matter of immersion in memorial depths beyond—or rather, beneath and before—the two-dimensional flatlands of recollected scenes.

## Co-immanence of Past and Present

We must pay close attention to the way that the past relates to the present in which body memories are actualized. On the one hand, the past can be regarded as overwhelming this present, captivating it to such an extent that the present seems to be its mere repetition. This is precisely Bergson's view of "habit memory," which so completely reinstates its own past that it ends up merely repeating it. On this view the present is the tip of a vast pyramidal past brought to bear upon it,[43] and it becomes, in effect, its own past. On the other hand, there is the complementary view that the past exists to *become present* in body memories. Now the pyramid is inverted, and the main directionality flows outward *from* the present rather than into it. Here the emphasis is not on how the past insinuates itself into the present but on how it is deployed there and carried on into the future. If habitual body memory seems to exemplify the first model, whereby the past invades the present, erotic body memory appears to illustrate the second situation, in which the past, rather than taking over the present from within, is material *for* the present (and its future).

Once more it is instructive to contrast body memory with recollection—and with verbal reminiscing as well. In these latter two activities, we peer resolutely backward toward a past that is felt to have its own independent being: hence the effect of significant distance from the present in both cases. At the most, the act of recollecting and the recollected content, the reminiscing and the reminisced-about can be said to *intersect* at certain critical points. But by and large there is precious little interfusion of past and present when we represent the past in mental images or words. Of this past Bergson said that it is "essentially *that which acts no longer*."[44] In body memory, at least in its habitual forms, we have just the opposite circumstance: here the past is fully enacted in the present. As Bergson also remarks, habit memory "no longer *represents* our past to us, it *acts* it; and if it still deserves the name of memory, it is not because it conserves bygone images, but because it prolongs their useful effect into the present moment."[45]

This suggests that in matters of body memory we should speak of *immanence* rather than of "intersection" between past and present. Instead of taking up a perspective on the past—getting a clearer "view" of it as we often attempt to do in recollection or in reminiscence—in body memories we allow the past to enter actively into the very present in which our remembering is taking place. Moreover, such immanence is a two-way affair: it is an immanence of the past in the present and of the present in the past. Carried to an extreme—an extreme which fully habituated body memories approach—the co-immanence verges on an identity of past and present. But if the two were to become strictly identical, we could no longer speak meaningfully of *memory*, which calls for the presence, however slight, of some *décalage* or differential between past and present. How are we to conceive concretely of this requirement?

The co-immanence operative in body memory can be formulated as an "effective ingredience within." This means that in body memories the past is a direct constituent of the present, a constituent mediated neither by image nor by word. By the same token, the present is effectively at work on the past's very ingression into its own realm: instead of simply repeating this past, it modifies it by extending intentional threads to ever-changing circumstances, much as a pianist extends his or her already acquired skills in playing new and more difficult pieces. In this way the past is prolonged, given a new lease on life. Yet it does not merge entirely with the present into which it is sedimented, since it is modified by this very same present. Perhaps the most apt metaphor for the two-way immanence in question is that of *enchevêtrement*, complication or entanglement by an overlapping of elements. These elements overlap in such a way as to leave a residue or remainder which maintains difference in the very context of sameness. It is a matter, in short, of a mutual com-plication of past and present in each other's fate.

This is not to deny important differences in the degree of overlap exhibited by various types of body memory. In habitual body memory we encounter a virtual coincidence with very little remainder (though it would still be mistaken to speak of "repetition" here), whereas in traumatic body memory there is much less overlap (hence the closely associated phenomena of defense and narration, both of which emphasize a greater separation of past from present). In between, we find erotic body memories, which carry the past more resolutely into the future. Despite such differences, we can say of all body memories that the *enchevêtrement* that they display acts as a cohesive internal bonding in which past and present accomplish unique and lasting forms of intimacy with each other. As the inner and outer horizons of the lived body act to draw its actions into the dense center of its own memories in depth, so the co-immanence of past-cum-present binds this body together in the realm of its self-remembrance.

## VI

"Density and depth," "co-immanence of past and present": these phrases designate respectively the spatiality and temporality of body memories. I have just discussed them as if they were neatly separable—as if they could be given the kind of precise analysis which they receive at the level of world-space and world-time (at which level they are independent variables according to a Newtonian world-view). But is this so? Are the spatial and temporal features of body memories so readily separable from each other? Consider, to begin with, that even the comparatively exact preliminary descriptions given in Part One of this book—where memorial space and time were simply juxtaposed within the "world-frame" of the mnemonic presentation—no longer obtain at this point. In the case of body memory, there is nothing like a limpid plane of presentation, much less a coherent world-frame: these are the very features that we must leave behind as we move from a model in which recollection is paradigmatic to one that allows for the peculiarities of non-recollective remembering. In the latter, spatiality and temporality cannot be held apart any more; they intertwine, realizing a version of that reversibility that has been encountered above in the touched/touching dyad of erotic body memories.

An emblematic example of this active intertwining of space and time occurs in the opening pages of Marcel Proust's *Remembrance of Things Past*. The narrator, describing his tendency to fall asleep in various postures and to awaken in a state of confusion, offers the following observation:

> When a man is asleep, he has in a circle round him the chain of the hours, the sequence of the years, the order of the heavenly host. Instinctively, when he awakes, he looks to these, and in an instant reads off his own position on the

> earth's surface and the time that has elapsed during his slumbers; but this ordered procession is apt to grow confused, and to break its ranks.[46]

The "ordered procession" is that of place and time in the waking world, where "chain," "sequence," and "order" are preserved and where position and date can be directly "read off" as from a presentation to one's lucid consciousness. But on waking from sleep—itself a species of dense bodily experience—one does not gear easily into such an ordered world of space and time. The liminal state of awakening brings with it a disarray in which space and time are not only disordered but difficult to distinguish from each other: "For it always happened that when I awoke like this, and my mind struggled in an unsuccessful attempt to discover where I was, everything revolved around me through the darkness: things, places, years."[47] Precisely as revolving around the narrator in the darkness, things, places, and years have begun to merge into a confused spatio-temporal mixture in his dawning awareness.

It is at just this moment that the narrator's body memory comes most effectively into play. Only in and through this memory, *not* through the recollections of daytime consciousness, can significant connections with past things, places, and years arise:

> My body, still too heavy with sleep to move, would endeavour to construe from the pattern of its tiredness the position of its various limbs, in order to deduce therefrom the direction of the wall, the location of the furniture, to piece together and give a name to the house in which it lay. Its memory, the composite memory of its ribs, its knees, its shoulder-blades, offered it a whole series of rooms in which it had at one time or another slept, while the unseen walls, shifting and adapting themselves to the shape of each successive room that it remembered, whirled round it in the dark. And even before my brain, lingering in cogitation over when things had happened and what they had looked like, had reassembled the circumstances sufficiently to identify the room, it, my body, would recall from each room in succession the style of the bed, the position of the doors, the angle at which the sunlight came in at the windows, whether there was a passage outside, what I had had in mind when I went to sleep and found there when I awoke.[48]

Here body memory precedes any concerted "cogitation" over ordered existence—a cogitation which results in the certain identification of things in space and time. Before such identification can occur, familiarity must obtain. Familiarization is the distinctive work of body memory, which is not concerned with the exact identities of things nor with their precise locations in time or space. It is a matter of the approximate positioning of things in experience. (And "things" are not physical only; the narrator's body recalls what he had had *in mind* when he went to sleep: here body memory encompasses memory of mind itself!) Far from such approximation being a deficiency in memory, it is for Proust the very condition of the kind of exact remembering that is aimed at in recollection. Only when the narrator's body memories of past things, places, and years have been allowed to run their course is he in a position to enter the world-frame of recollection, that is, the content of the novel itself:

> My memory had been set in motion; as a rule I did not attempt to go to sleep again at once, but used to spend the greater part of the night recalling our life in the old days at Combray with my great-aunt, at Balbec, Paris, Doncières, Venice, and the rest; remembering again all the places and people I had known, what I had actually seen of them, and what others had told me.[49]

In this citation, "memory," "recalling," and "remembering" all refer to recollecting, the more or less exact reconstitution in one's conscious mind of past scenes. Proust ingeniously inverts the usual order of proceeding from the psychical to the physical in matters of memory by showing that the richest route into recollection is through body memory. If so, the latter can no longer be considered derivative or trivial in status; nor can it even be seen as second-best (as it is for Bergson). Not only does it have its own validity and uniqueness, but it ushers in recollection itself in the most auspicious way—as we learn from the narrator's remembrances of his childhood at Combray, remembrances that begin immediately after the above passage: "At Combray, as every afternoon ended, long before the time when I should have to go to bed and lie there, unsleeping. . . ."[50]

The past that Proust's body memories brings back is at once spatial and temporal. Before the specific recollections of Combray set in—recollections that carry with them a separability of date and place[51]—the narrator's body is remembering *how it was* to lie sleepless in his bedroom at Combray: where the "how" precedes the "that" of *that it was so* as well as the "when" of *when it was so*. Notice how, in the following passage, the narrator's body memory merges place and time to the point of inseparability:

> The stiffened side on which I lay would, for instance, in trying to fix its position, imagine itself to be lying face to the wall in a big bed with a canopy; and at once I would say to myself, "Why, I must have fallen asleep before Mamma came to say good night," for I was in the country at my grandfather's [i.e., at Combray], who died years ago; and my body, the side upon which I was lying, faithful guardians of a past which my mind should never have forgotten, brought back before my eyes the glimmering flame of the night-light in its urn-shaped bowl of Bohemian glass that hung by chains from the ceiling, and the chimney-piece of Siena marble in my bedroom at Combray, in my grandparents' house, in those far distant days which at this moment I imagined to be in the present without being able to picture them exactly, and which would become plainer in a little while when I was properly awake.[52]

Not being able to picture means, in this context, not recollecting via visualized scenes; it also means not being able to affix an exact date: hence the vagueness of the text's references to "years ago" and to "those far distant days." The narrator's body, here felt through its "stiffened side," acts as guardian of a past which is not dated on any calendar and which is at once spatial and temporal. The canopied bed, the night-light suspended in an urn-shaped bowl, the marble chimney-piece: these are not simply discrete objects located in an indifferent space. Nor are they, or the narrator's original experience of them, situated in a strictly temporal interval with an exactly designatable beginning and end. Any such interval and its concrete contents, not to mention the narrator's remembered experience of these contents, are so deeply implicated with one another that their spatial and temporal dimensions have become inseparably interconnected. It is the narrator's body memory that has made this extraordinary situation possible: extraordinary precisely from the separative standpoint of recollective memory.

## VII

The present chapter is in effect an extended tribute to the importance of body memory, which has not often been singled out for detailed description of the sort that has been offered in these pages. In and through this description, I have been attempting to show just how—in which precise ways—body memory is important in human experience. But we have not yet confronted the more general question of *why* body memory is so crucial in human experience. It is only in providing a satisfactory answer to this rather sweeping question that such purely descriptive efforts will receive their full justification.

To sharpen the issue and to set the stage for this answer, let me state baldly that *there is no memory without body memory*. In claiming this I do not mean to say that whenever we remember we are in fact directly engaging in body memory as it has been discussed in this chapter. Rather, I am saying that we could not remember in any of the forms or modes described in earlier chapters without having the capacity for body memory. But it remains far from clear how this can be so. How can body memory, which is typically so reticent and so submerged, be so basic for all memory? In what does its peculiar importance consist?

A possible answer to such questions emerges when we consider once more what I have called the "marginality" of body memory. If such marginality is interpreted as *assuming a position at the margin* of any given memory, then it might seem plausible to claim that all remembering involves taking up some such stance: that is, some bodily perspective on an object, scene, or fact remembered. This would even appear to work for most recollections. Do we not recall events from a particular point of view that is, at least implicitly, defined by our bodily position at the time of the original happening? I say "at least implicitly," for it is evident that we need not explicitly call back to mind the bodily position itself—either its exact contour or even the way it felt to assume it at the time. With this proviso, we can reliably assert that all recollection—and all reminiscence as well—does include or at least imply a bodily point of view. Yet "a bodily point of view" is not necessarily equivalent to a body *memory*, much less a memory of a body. Even if we can afford to omit an express representation of our own witnessing body while still claiming its immanent-marginal presence in all recollections, this still does not prove the actual ingredience of body memory within all recollective memory. Nor, for that matter, does it begin to account for any such ingredience of body memory in other memorial phenomena such as semantic memory (i.e., the recall of sheer information in which there is no representation of a memory episode at all), reminding, recognizing, remembering-on-the-occasion-of, primary memory, dream memory,[53] etc. This list could go on almost indefinitely, so numerous are the types of memory that do not appear to include, or even to imply, a bodily stance of the rememberer at their margin.

As promising as the notion of bodily point of view is, it cannot therefore fully cash in my primary claim that there is no memory without body memory. Nor will it suffice to say that taking the body (including its own memory as an intrinsic feature of it) as a necessary condition of all human experience allows us to deduce body memory as a necessary condition of all memorial experience. Even if true as a form of transcendental deduction, this assertion rings hollow for our purposes. Its formality fails to capture the particularity of the situation; it does not tell us in just what way body memory is inherent in all memory. If point of view is too specific in its role and if condition of possibility is too general, where are we to turn?

I suggest that we turn to Whitehead's notion of causal efficacy as providing the most promising basis for understanding the deep ingrediency of body memory in memory generally. Whitehead has written that memory is "a very special instance of an antecedent act of experience becoming a datum of intuition for another act of experience."[54] The paradox is that Whitehead, while regarding memory (along with "visceral feelings") as an altogether "obvious" example of causal efficacy,[55] does not say much about memory itself, much less about the manner in which it is "a very special instance" of such efficacy. For this reason we shall have to construct from Whitehead's occasional remarks the outlines of a theory that is illuminating in the present context and yet not incompatible with his overall cosmology.

The systematic setting for the notion of causal efficacy is supplied by Whitehead's view of time. In the context of a critique of time regarded as pure succession (i.e., such as we find in Hume and Kant), he argues that "time in the concrete is the conformation of state to state, the later to the earlier; and the pure succession is an abstraction from the irreversible relationship of settled past to derivative present."[56] This means that the immediate present comes into being by conforming to the immediate past, which it reproduces as objectified in the present itself.[57] Crucial here is the notion of the past as to-be-conformed-to precisely because it is "settled and actual."[58] Such a past implodes in the present as a "stubborn fact" that refuses to go away, with the result that "the man-at-one-moment concentrates in himself the colour of his own past, and he is the issue of it."[59] Once this much is granted, causal efficacy follows forthwith. As one of the two "perceptive modes" of experience, it is definable as "the hand of the settled past in the formation of the present."[60] In contradiction to Hume and Kant, Whitehead holds that causal efficacy *precedes* "our immediate perception of the contemporary external world, appearing as an element constitutive of our own experience."[61] Where presentational immediacy (i.e., the other major perceptive mode) gives us "a world decorated by sense-data," causal efficacy shows the world as "vague, haunting, unmanageable."[62]

But what has all this to do with memory and more particularly with body memory? Thus far, we might seem to be talking at most of the mere reproduction of the past in the present, its sheer "repetition" or "reproduction" there.[63] But surely, as I have argued against Bergson, memory involves more than mere repetition of the past. What else does it involve? The Whiteheadian answer, though Whitehead himself does not put it quite so brazenly, is *body* and more particularly the body as experiencing its own organs. For the body is "our most immediate environment";[64] it is that with which we live, in contrast to the more remote environment of the physical world around us. Living with it, we conform to it: "we conform to our bodily organs and to the vague world which lies beyond them."[65] But conformation, as we have just seen, is the basic action of causal efficacy. To experience our body qua set of organs is precisely to experience the causal efficacy of these organs and, through them, that of the external world as it impinges on us.[66] Put otherwise, the actions of these organs form the settled past to which we conform in the present of perception:

> For the organic theory, the most primitive perception is 'feeling the body as functioning'. This is a feeling of the world in the past; it is the inheritance of the world as a complex of feeling; namely, it is the feeling of derived feeling.[67]

"The feeling of derived feeling": here we come to the nub of the doctrine of causal efficacy as it bears on memory. Derived feeling is feeling felt as a direct legacy from the past; it is "a feeling of the world in the past." For human beings, such derivation or inheritance could not occur except by way of the lived body, which is at once a transmitter of the inheritance of the external world and itself an inheritance for perception in the present.[68] What seems strangest in this view is just what makes it most valuable for our purposes. It is strange to think that *we feel the body feeling* its circumambient world.[69] The sense of strangeness is not altogether mitigated by Whitehead's efforts to consider the body as merely a somewhat more specialized and more intimate part of the environment: "in principle, the animal body is only the more highly organized and immediate part of the general environment for its dominant actual occasion, which is the ultimate percipient."[70] What Whitehead calls "bodily efficacy" is the unmediated feeling of the body's causal efficacy qua "withness"; given as an "objective datum," it is "feeling the body as functioning"—functioning as efficacious in its own right and not as a mere means.[71] To be efficacious in its own right is at once to be capable of producing further feelings on subsequent occasions *and* to re-enact prior feelings in memory.[72]

But if we thus feel the body feeling the world—i.e., feel the world in feeling "with" our own body—one level of feeling does not simply lead to another. Nor does one level reflect, represent, or even express another level; the first level always *includes* the second (and vice versa), whether by anticipation or by conformation. And if this is paradoxical for an act-intentional view of feeling—which has difficulty admitting a second feeling as the *content* or "object" of a first feeling—it is quite compatible with the notion of operative intentionality in terms of which (following Merleau-Ponty) we have construed bodily behavior. According to this notion, the lived body is the operative force in human projects, including the project of remembering. As such, it is the natural—and certainly the most immediate—site for causally efficacious action. Moreover, this action is *felt as such:* felt in its very bodily efficacy. It is also remembered as such—though rarely in recollection, which typically forgets it. It is remembered instead in "primary memory," the unique vehicle for knowledge of the immediate past. For the "direct knowledge" of the causal efficacy contained in the body's withness is a knowledge of something that, though actual and settled, has *just* occurred. Whitehead sometimes refers in this connection to a temporal interval of micro-seconds[73]—which would accord with Husserl's view that primary memory is sub-instantaneous.

What is most valuable in Whitehead's view of primary memory—and what serves to distinguish it from Husserl's conception—is the idea that such memory is just as bodily as it is mental in its operation. If "bodily efficacy"[74] seems at first a puzzling notion, it is the source of an insight that we cannot afford to overlook: an insight into why body memory plays such an important role in all remembering. *It does so because of the working of causal efficacy itself*. If the latter is indeed the primordial perceptive mode—is presupposed by presentational immediacy as well as by conceptual analysis—and if it is the privileged point of connection with a settled past (whether recent or remote), then its own bodily basis, i.e., the concrete feeling of bodily efficacy, will be intrinsic to *any* connection with *any* past. In other words, it will be intrinsic to *any memory of any kind*. Or to put it slightly differently: if my lived body always functions as an objective datum for the feeling that an experience has become past, then it will be an indispensable ingredient in remembering that experience *as past*—whether the experience be directly of my own body or of the external world by means of (that is, *with*) this same body. In this way recognition is bestowed upon the lived body as an internal and necessary ingredient in all remembering. This is done without having to invoke a new *kind* of memory—other than "body memory" itself. And the lived body's role, far from being merely formal, has become a *material* condition of possibility for remembering: *it is this body as actually felt in causal efficacy that gives to it its seminal importance in matters of memory*.

It is time to indicate several consequences of this importance as well as to look at some of its larger implications. There are two immediate consequences that need noting. First, if Whitehead is right, experience is *always in the process of becoming past*. What Dewey would call "an experience"[75] is something that is always already becoming settled—settled enough to be an immediate past immediately remembered. Just as there are no moments out of time, so there are no moments not settling into, or already settled in, a past to be remembered. Second, time-lapse is adventitious in memory; despite the fact that we often pride ourselves on accurately determining the exact elapsed time inherent in a given (typically recollective) memory, the lapse itself is "an abstraction from the more concrete relatedness of 'conformation' "[76]—that is, from the very relation to the past which is the work of causal efficacy and which lies at the heart of all remembering dependent thereon.

The large-scale implications are also two-fold. First, all that we call "the person," "personal identity," and the like—everything, in short, that pertains to an individual's life-history—is rooted ultimately in body memory as construed in the above manner. If it is true that "the enduring personality is the historic route of living occasions which are severally dominant in the body at successive instants,"[77] then this body's inherent memories of its own "historic route" will themselves be constituent features in the ongoing makeup of our lasting personality. The conformation realized in such memories will supply the critical connective tissue that binds together this personality and its route alike. A second implication bears on the role of mind and mentality. Although Whitehead considers it "a matter of pure convention as to which of our experiential activities we term mental and which physical,"[78] he maintains, nonetheless, that the bodily pole enjoys priority over the mental pole in a decisive way. For one thing, only the mental pole (in its intellectual phases) calls for conceptual analysis, which is itself a supervening mode of experience.[79] For another, causal efficacy in its primal form is robustly corporeal; and since bodily efficacy precedes presentational immediacy as well as conceptual analysis, bodily being has a distinct primacy. If this is so, then that form of memory indigenous to corporeality will also possess a primacy among forms of memory; and in particular, body memory will take precedence over recollection or secondary memory.[80]

Causal efficacy is said to be "a heavy, primitive experience" which occurs most saliently when we undergo "a reversion to some primitive state."[81] Furthermore, "such a reversion occurs when either some primitive functioning of the human organism is unusually heightened, or some considerable part of our habitual sense-perception is unusually enfeebled."[82] What we then experience is indeed "vague, haunting, unmanageable."[83] Suddenly we are reminded of the hapless and sleepless narrator in *Remembrance of Things Past:*

> But for me it was enough if, in my own bed, my sleep was so heavy as completely to relax my consciousness; for then I lost all sense of the place in which I had gone to sleep, and when I awoke in the middle of the night, not knowing where I was, I could not even be sure at first who I was; I had only the most rudimentary sense of existence, such as may lurk and flicker in the depths of an animal's consciousness; I was more destitute than the cave-dweller; but then the memory—not yet of the place in which I was, but of various other places where I had lived and might now very possibly be—would come like a rope let down from heaven to draw me up out of the abyss of not-being, from which I could never have escaped by myself: in a flash I would traverse centuries of civilization, and out of a blurred glimpse of oil-lamps, then of shirts with turned-down collars, would gradually piece together the original components of my ego.[84]

It is surely striking that Proust calls the experience he is describing "heavy" and that this experience, one of disorientation upon awakening in the middle of the night, is an experience of reversion: indeed, what else is sleeping and its twilight state but reversionary ("regressive" in Freud's word)? It is also telling that the very terms by which Proust's narrator comes to describe this experience—"rudimentary," "destitute," "the abyss of not-being," "blurred glimpse," etc.—express that vagueness which Whitehead ascribed precisely to causal efficacy. Striking as well as the reference to the "cave-dweller," that is, someone to whom primitivity is unhesitatingly imputed; and closely associated with this image is the sense of existing that "may lurk and flicker in the depths of an animal's consciousness," recalling Whitehead's "animal body"[85] and the general metaphorics of depth in his descriptions of causal efficacy. If Proust's narrator is indeed piecing together "the original components" of his ego, Whitehead finds in causal efficacy the original components of human experience itself. And just as the narrator's ego is linked with civilization, so presentational immediacy is held to be "the experience of only a few high-grade organisms"[86] and to be "vivid, precise, and barren"[87] in much the same way as "shirts with turned-down collars" and other accoutrements of civilized, daylight life are seen as epitomes of barrenness in Proust's nocturnal vision.

Most striking of all, however, is the way that vivid and precise memory—the recollection of particular places in detail—comes to supervene on the dimness of the bodily state from which the narrator is slowly emerging in the above passage. As presentational immediacy stands out from causal efficacy like a flare in the night, so recollective memory in its very vividness is illuminated against the vagueness of body memory. In both cases, the original components of the more primitive experience, heavy in its dense implications for all subsequent re-membering, are superseded by the pictorial precision of a secondary state—by something presentational or representational, lacking therefore the body of a primary experience with its primary memory. Body memory gives way to its recollective successor not only as causal efficacy gives rise to presentational immediacy but, still more crucially, as—*just as*—such efficacy, realized in the body, emerges into such immediacy, and is manifested in mind.

## VIII

It cannot be emphasized enough that body memories are located *in the body*—not just the objective body of sinews and fibers but much more particularly the phenomenal body. This latter is what I have been calling the "lived body" (after *Leib* in Husserl). Such a body acts as a receptacle of memories by virtue of two of its basic capacities. First of all, it is composed of manifold organs—by which I mean not physiological parts *per se* but those aspects of its being that aid in the execution of its actions—and can itself be considered as an "organ" qua totality.[88] Construed thus as organismic, the lived body possesses, in its very being, an efficacious operative intentionality animating all of its ongoing maneuvers. This intentionality is quite sufficient to account for the purposiveness of these maneuvers and does not require recourse to the act intentionality of consciousness for the completion of a given "intentional arc."[89] As a direct consequence, many body memories (above all, habitual ones) need not be accompanied by consciousness in any explicit form. Second, and closely affiliated with this first feature, is the fact that the body as a memorial container—as itself a "place" of memories—furnishes an unmediated access to the remembered past: unmediated, that is, beyond its own withness. No intercalation of representations, imagistic or verbal, is required; no mediation by mind and its machinations is called for. For such "memory can be understood only as a direct possession of the past with no interposed contents."[90] It is for this reason that so much body memory arises spontaneously and without premeditation and that it is so rarely inferential or in need of further evidence. Because it re-enacts the past, it need not represent it; its own kinesthesias link it from within to the felt movements which it is reinstating; as a way of "dilating our being in the world,"[91] body memory includes its own past by an internal osmotic intertwining with it.

The result of the locatability of memories in the body via its organismic and direct link to the past is exemplary of what I shall be discussing in chapter 11 as "thick autonomy." Although such autonomy is at work in every kind of memory—even in imagistic recollection—it is doubtless most manifest in body memories. The very density of the remembering/remembered body and the way in which it provides an original past for remembering as a whole help to make these memories a peculiarly effective expression of thick autonomy. The nimble and mercurial powers of mind—as evidenced in instantaneous "flashes" of recollection or recognition—cede place to a more stolid and stable *modus operandi* whose paradigm is the working of habitual body memory in its reliably consecutive and consistent deployment. But the same thick autonomy of the bodily is evident in alleviated forms in erotic and traumatic body memories as well. In all of these otherwise so different cases there is at work a sure sense of the thickness of the flesh, of its durable and enduring qualities, of its subdued but obdurate being.[92]

Along with the memory of places, things, and other human beings, body memory forms part of the general project in which this Part of the present book is engaged: making memory cosmic rather than strictly mental, psychological, or neurological. It is a matter, in short, of returning memory to the world. Places will take us most resolutely out into the circumambient world, since they regionalize this world and literally give it local habitations. As its most concrete denizens, material things and other people act as well to fill up the world around us. But the lived body is the truly *pivotal* member of this quaternity of cosmic terms. It is always in or from or through[93] this body that the other items are grasped or met, witnessed or transformed: *There is no getting around the body*. As Husserl said:

> In a quite unique way the living body is constantly in the perceptual field quite immediately, with a completely unique ontic meaning.[94]

Itself felt as unmediated, thanks to its self-felt bodily efficacy, the body is the mediator, the pervasive with-operator, of everything else in human experience. It is "the general medium for having a world"[95] in that only in its terms and by its intervention can anything appear at all to us. If things appear to us in constant succession, this can only be due to the fact that the kinesthesias (and synesthesias) by which they are apprehended are actively attuned to this same succession, partly reflecting it and partly constituting it.[96]

The recognition of the body's pivotal position was first explicitly acknowledged by Bergson in his descriptions of the body as a continual "center of action" and as that "ever advancing boundary between the future and the past."[97] The lived body is a center which refuses to be decentered, a central boundary that will not become peripheral, precisely because this body already encompasses the marginal within its own arena of activity: it creates its own margin even as it brings about its own modes of immanence and movement. Echoing Bruno and Pascal, we can speak of it as an entity whose center is everywhere and circumference nowhere. The lived body is the incessant center of its multifarious maneuvers—*maneuvers without any perimeters other than those which it imposes on itself as it moves in a depth of its own making*. Dense itself, the lived body is always in the thick of things; and as remembered, it continues to be concentric for the world which it has come to inhabit. What Merleau-Ponty calls the "Memory of the World"[98] is very much the memory of being bodily in the world, being a central memorial presence there.

Despite its memorious density, the lived body remains "a place of meeting and transfer."[99] Its very bulk and volume—its thickness and heft—have a borderline aspect as well. The body as lived and remembered is crucially interstitial in status. The basic borderline it occupies is traced between *mind* and *place:* it is their middle term, their *tertium quid*. On the one hand, body is contiguous with mind through the level of immediate kinesthetic experience; if my mind's intentions are to be enacted, they must achieve expression in a felt movement which itself represents the overcoming of separation between body and mind.[100] On the other hand, the lived body is conterminous with place because it is by bodily movement that I find my way in place and take up habitation there. My body not only takes me into places; it habituates me to their peculiarities and helps me to remember them vividly. It does all this in various particular ways which we must now begin to explore.

# IX

# PLACE MEMORY

> In this unique world, everything sensuous that I now originally perceive, everything that I have perceived and which I can now remember or about which others can report to me as what they have perceived or remembered, has its place.
>
> —Husserl, *Experience and Judgment*

## I

Isn't memory a matter of the past? Is it not primarily a temporal phenomenon? How can we think of it otherwise after Kant and Husserl—not to mention Aristotle, who said straightforwardly that "memory is of the past"?[1] Philosophers' propensities apart, it is certainly true that whenever we think of memory, indeed whenever we actually engage in acts of remembering, we have to do with past time: with time that in some sense has elapsed and is now being revived in some guise (whether by image or word, or by bodily movement). This is undeniable—even if it is equally undeniable that such time past is ineluctably elusive and always reappears in memory "as seen through a veil."[2] Since memory does not require exact repetition in any case, the elusiveness does not matter in the larger picture. In the larger picture, remembering seems fully preoccupied with the past. Who could possibly question such an apparently well-founded bedrock assumption as this? Would not questioning it amount to questioning the existence of memory itself?

And yet question it we must and on several grounds. Consider, to start with, the way in which the primary action of time can be said to be *dispersive*—time in Aristotle's words "disperses subsistence"[3]—whereas memory is itself mainly *collective* in its basic work (which is not to say, however, that it is mainly recollective in its basic operation). Time's dispersiveness means that, as a direct consequence, temporal phenomena tend to be conceived as grouping themselves in a monolinear pattern of sheer succession: an assumption common to Aristotle, Kant, and Husserl alike. Whitehead's trenchant critique of this conception as an effect of abstraction in the realm of presentational immediacy in no way eliminates the tenacity of the conception itself, which is only reinforced in the post-Cartesian world of "clock-time" and "public-time."[4] On a monolinear view of time, there is dispersal and disintegration as each instant arises and dies away—instantaneously. *No time is left over* in such a view: no time that might be gathered up in memory and kept therein. Thus, to say that memory is "of the past" resolves nothing; indeed, it may dissolve the effective basis for the reconnective capacity of memory itself. At the least, memory is of a non-punctiform past. But we may say more radically that memory involves something more than the purely temporal in its own makeup.

Consider the following line of thought. If remembering were a sheerly temporal phenomenon—and even allowing for a more capacious, less linear notion of time—it would remain largely disembodied. For time, even cohesive, nonpunctiform time, is something we contemplate or represent rather than something we feel "in our bones." In our bones—in our bodies—we do not experience time or its depredations directly. We experience states of corporeal existence, e.g., health or illness, ecstasy or sluggishness; but it is only when we notice discrepancies *between* such states that we begin to infer the passage of time—most notably in observing oneself "getting older." Time may be felt *by* the body (Whitehead would say "with" it) but it is not felt as such *in* it. And yet we have just learned in the last chapter that there is no memory without a bodily basis—that bodily efficacy is pervasive of all remembering, including the most purified acts of recollection. If the thesis that memory is of the past implies that memory is disembodied in its enactment, we must question the thesis itself.

But if memory is not simply or exclusively "of the past," what does it involve in addition? The very embodiment of remembering hints at an answer. To be embodied is *ipso facto* to assume a particular perspective and position; it is to have not just a point of view but a *place* in which we are situated. It is to occupy a portion of space from out of which we both undergo given experiences and remember them. To be disembodied is not only to be deprived of place, *unplaced;* it is to be denied the basic stance on which every experience and its memory depend. As embodied existence opens onto place, indeed *takes place in place* and nowhere else, so our memory of what we experience in place is likewise place-specific: it is bound to place as to its own basis. Yet it is just this importance of place for memory that has been lost sight of in philosophical and common sense concerns with the temporal dimensions of memory.

This was not always so. The ancient Greeks devised an elaborate and effective "art of memory" to which I made brief reference in the Introduction to this book. In this art, which was in fact more than a merely instrumental mnemotechnique, the role of place was altogether central: hence its classical description as a "method of *loci*." A *locus* is definable as "a place easily grasped by the memory, such as a house, an intercolumnar space, a corner, an arch, or the like."[5] A given place or set of places acts as a grid onto which images of items to be remembered are placed in a certain order. The subsequent remembering of these items occurs by revisiting the place-grid and traversing it silently step by step in one's mind. In Cicero's words:

> Persons desiring to train this faculty of memory must select places and form mental images of the things they wish to remember and store those images in the places, so that the order of the places will preserve the order of the things . . . and we shall employ the places and images respectively as a wax writing-tablet and the letters written on it.[6]

Here the model of memory as a wax-tablet returns, but this time not to be summarily dismissed as it was by Plato.[7] On the contrary: as signifying an underlying grid of places, the wax-tablet points to the reliance of the art of memory upon a stable place system. For the operative premise of this system is that "the order of the places will preserve the order of the things [to be remembered]." It is all the more impressive that such preservative power is imputed to place even when the places in question are imagined and not perceived. For the *loci* themselves can be quite fictitious in origin, and yet manage very effectively to hold in memory the images deposited on them. An extraordinary situation: the fragility of images and the silence of the memorizer[8] combine with the stability of place to bring about a mnemotechnique so efficacious that to this day it is still being recommended in popular memory manuals.

I cite the *ars memorativa* tradition as one salient piece of evidence that the relationship between memory and place is at once intimate and profound. Outside this tradition, whose subterranean vicissitudes have been traced so brilliantly by Yates and Spence, the relationship remains largely unsuspected: either taken for granted or not noticed at all. This, too, is extraordinary and calls for remedial measures of the sort which this chapter aims to provide. For it is a fact that memory of place, of *having been in a place*, is one of the most conspicuously neglected areas of philosophical or psychological inquiry into remembering. My own treatment of memory up to this point in the book has been no exception to this unspoken rule; apart from a few observations on "remembered space" and the "scene" of remembering, I have not begun to do justice to place—whereas, and very much in keeping with predominant Western proclivities, the temporal aspects of remembering have received the lion's share of attention. It is time to call this preoccupation with remembered time into question and to accord to remembered place its rightful due.

And what a due this is! Only consider how often a memory is either of a place itself (e.g., of one's childhood home) or of an event or person *in* a place; and, conversely, how unusual it is to remember a placeless person or an event *not* stationed in some specific locale. To be placeless in one's remembering is not only to be disoriented; it is to be decidedly disadvantaged with regard to what a more complete mnemonic experience might deliver. Place serves to *situate* one's memorial life, to give it "a name and a local habitation." The link between place and situation is close indeed. As Heidegger has observed:

> To situate means . . . first of all to point out the proper place or site of something. Secondly it means to heed that place or site. These two methods, placing and heeding, are both preliminaries to a topology.[9]

Where Heidegger is ultimately interested in a "topology of Being,"[10] my concern here is exclusively with a topology of the remembered. We must come to heed the proper place of the remembered—its manner not just of occupying place but of incorporating it into its own content. Situating by its very nature, place adequately heeded will help us to situate memory more fully than has been possible thus far. It is a matter of acknowledging the placement of place itself in memory; and since we become oriented in place mainly by bodily movements, we shall have to trace out the corporeal basis of remembering in ways that were barely glimpsed in the last chapter.

## II

If place is indeed so important for memory, why has it been so pervasively overlooked? One answer has already been suggested: the primacy accorded to time and to temporal phenomena generally. But there is a second reason as well.[11] This is that the significance of place, formerly unquestioned, has been forcibly undercut by a fixation on what I shall call "site," that is, place as leveled down to metrically determinate dimensions. Much has changed since the early Pythagorean Archytas declared that place is "the first of all beings, since everything that exists is in a place and cannot exist without a place."[12] Aristotle, acknowledging with Archytas that "everything is somewhere and in place,"[13] adds that "if such a thing is true, the power of place will be a remarkable one, and prior to all things."[14] In his *Physics* Aristotle attempts to spell out this power by attributing to each place in the natural world a "certain influence" and a "distinct potency."[15] Thus each place has its own distinctive dimensions such as up/down, before/behind, and right/left. These dimensions constitute "regions" which cannot be defined in terms of their occupants alone. Having thus established that place is active, independent in its being,[16] and necessary for the existence of other existents, Aristotle proceeds to define place as "*the innermost motionless boundary of what contains*."[17] It ensues that there is a tight fit between a given thing and its place; the outer surface of the thing coincides with the inner surface of the place. "Place is thought to be a kind of surface," says Aristotle, "and as it were a vessel, i.e., a container of the thing. Place is coincident with the thing, for boundaries are coincident with the bounded."[18]

Nonetheless, what is "first of all" for Archytas and Aristotle ends by being last, and it becomes so by the close of the seventeenth century—when space, and place along with it, became geometrized. For the Greeks, this development was not possible. For one thing, they did not think in terms of spatial coordinate systems, the basis for any thorough geometrization. For another, their very conception of space was resistant to being formally geometrized: space was either "something *inhomogeneous* because of its local geometric variance (as with Plato) [or] something *anisotropic* owing to directional differentiation in the substratum (Aristotle)."[19] Not even Euclidean geometry could apply without resistance to Aristotle's regionalized, direction-bound universe. It was evident that the very idea of space had to undergo a metamorphosis not just for Euclidean geometry to apply to it but more particularly for rational geometry to be able to specify it.

This metamorphosis, and with it the demotion of place (which depends on inhomogeneous and anisotropic qualities for its very vitality), was effected by the audacious speculations of Newton, Descartes, Bernoulli, and others, for all of whom space was conceived as continuous extension in length, breadth, and width and, thus, as mappable by the three-dimensional coordinate system of rational geometry. Descartes was doubtless the most unspoken on this point, and he drew the direst consequences: "We conceive a place to contain nothing but extension in length, breadth, and depth."[20] Here place is conceived as sheer spatial site. It follows that place qua site is merely a matter of relative position: "When we say an object is 'in' a place we are merely thinking of its occupying a position relatively to other objects."[21] This contention marks a turning-point in Western thinking about place. While for the Greeks the relativity of place is far less important than its inherent character ("Places do not differ merely in relative position," said Aristotle, "but also as possessing distinct potencies"),[22] for Descartes and his immediate successors place is strictly a relative matter, that is, a question of fixed positions in relation to each other within a systematic whole.

What we witness in Descartes is therefore the supersession of place by site. A site is not a container but an open area that is specified primarily by means of cartographic representations such as maps or architects' plans. It embodies a spatiality that is at once homogeneous (i.e., having no internal differentiations with respect to material constitution) and isotropic (possessing no inherent directionality such as up/down, East/West, etc.). A site is thus leveled down to the point of being definable solely in terms of distances between "positions" which are established on its surface and which exist strictly in relation to one another. As a result, a site is indifferent to what might occupy it—and to what we might remember about it.

The triumph of site over place has continued from the Cartesian epoch until the present day. This triumph has crucial consequences for the memory of place. As essentially empty (its vacuity is expressed in a phrase like "building site"), a site lacks the variegations or "obtrusions"[23] that aid in remembering unsited places. A site possesses no points of attachment onto which to hang our memories, much less to retrieve them. By denuding itself of particularity, site deprives itself of what James called "contiguous associates," i.e., the most efficacious cues for remembering.[24] Place, in contrast, characteristically presents us with a plethora of such cues. Thanks to its "distinct potencies," a place is at once internally diversified—full of protuberant features and forceful vectors—and distinct externally from other places. Both kinds of differentiation, internal and external, augment memorability. We observe this when an indifferent building lot, easily confused with other empty lots, is transformed into a memorable place by the erection of a distinctive house upon it.

It is the nature of place, in contradistinction from site, to encourage and support such distinctiveness, thereby enhancing memorability. Requisite to any full understanding of memory of place is thus a recognition of the way in which place itself aids remembering. It does so precisely as being well suited to contain memories—to hold and preserve them.

It was precisely Aristotle's contention that the primary action of place is that of *containing*. "Container" in Greek is *periechon,* literally a having or holding around. To be in a place is to be sheltered and sustained by its containing boundary; it is to be held within this boundary rather than to be dispersed by an expanding horizon of time or to be exposed indifferently in space. In fact, the most characteristic effect of place is that of maintaining or retaining rather than dividing or dispersing. This is what lies behind such idioms as "marching in place," "having a place of your own," "that's a nice place to be," "getting in place," etc. In each case the expression draws on place's peculiar power to hold in or keep in. No wonder, then, that access to place is not deeply problematic: in its abiding character, place is there to be re-entered, by memory if not by direct bodily movement. As continually available, place does not naturally lead us to become preoccupied with indirect, symbolic representations of it, or to feel that we are somehow forced to choose between these representations. The very persistence of place helps to make it accessible in a way that is rarely true of a comparable unit of time or a given site. For place tends to hold its contents steadily within its own embrace, while site and time characteristically replace their respective contents. Think of the kaleidoscopic array of items that can fill up just one hour's time as they succeed one another in a sometimes confusing alacrity, and compare this with the stability of any given place such as a house, a plaza, an office, etc. Sites are also all too easily filled up with a clutter of things or events that may appear and disappear in disconcerting rapidity.

It is the stabilizing persistence of place as a container of experiences that contributes so powerfully to its intrinsic memorability. An alert and alive memory connects spontaneously with place, finding in it features that favor and parallel its own activities. We might even say that memory is naturally place-oriented or at least place-supported. Moreover, it is itself a place wherein the past can revive and survive; it is a place for places, meeting them midway in its own preservative powers, its "reservative"[25] role. Unlike site and time, memory does not thrive on the indifferently dispersed. It thrives, rather, on the persistent particularities of what is properly *in place:* held fast there and made one's own.

## III

But let us leave history and theory aside for the moment and turn to actual cases of place memory. It is a revealing fact that five of the six examples of memory set forth in chapter 1 involved place to a significant degree. Yet in only one instance—that of my memory concerning the philosophy library—did I expressly remark on place as a relevant factor, and then just in passing. Otherwise, my analysis was oblivious to the presence of place: as oblivious as almost every treatment of memory after Aristotle. True to this forgetful tradition, I stressed either purely temporal factors (e.g., the dating of the Yosemite memory, the moment-after aspects of the tea-tasting episode) or parameters of sheer site ("we had come over to Yosemite from San Francisco": a cartographic claim). Just as contemporary cognitive psychologists are largely blind to the role of place in their experimental material despite their topographic language of "storage," "levels of processing," etc.[26]—so I was opaque to the dimension of place in my first round of examination.

But consider these early examples more closely. The Yosemite memory itself was place-saturated. It began with a look at the valley of the park as viewed on first approach: here one place was seen from another. This pristine moment was itself photographed and installed in another place I also vividly remember, my mother's dressing table. Moreover, the main memory proceeds as a virtual tour of places within Yosemite valley: Half Dome, the cabin where my family stayed, the waterfall. It is striking that the only allusion to "place" that was allowed in my analysis of this memory had to do with the indefiniteness of the cabin's exact location—that is, with an imperfectly remembered *site*. But the massive place-orientation of the memory as a whole was passed over in silence.

If less conspicuous in their neglect of place, the other examples examined in chapter 1 are nevertheless illuminating to ponder in retrospect. In the case of my *Small Change* memory, there was a marked succession of places as the setting changed from dinner at Clark's to the Lincoln Theater, with a paperback bookstore serving as an intermediate point. My family and I then found "places" in the movie theater and interchanged seats—a matter of sites set within a place. The theater building itself, however, was no mere site for me; as the scene of many memorable movies I had seen there over a period of nearly two decades, it was redolent with the past: *it held the past in place*.

Part of the power of this particular place was due to the fact that the memorable movies I had viewed there were themselves highly place-specific—as was the case with the decidedly French setting of *Small Change*.

Even the most compressed of my initial memories manifested basic place aspects. In recalling "902," the number on my office door, I was after all remembering a feature *of a place*. Although the item was remembered in a quite isolated way, it was nevertheless recollected as detached *from* the office it emptily designated. This place remained as an essential backdrop to the remembering itself. In the similar case of recalling the single word "Culligan," the backdrop (the basement of my childhood home) arose indistinctly but unmistakably into my remembrance. This penumbral quality of place—my analysis spoke of "a nebulous setting"—was also evident in the tea-tasting episode, whose scene was set by the top of my desk. At every level, then, and even in instances in which a setting was only dimly specified (and was sometimes altogether unspecified) the presence of place reveals itself on close inspection.

The same is true, *mutatis mutandis*, of every other leading example which has been employed in this book. Was it a matter of indifference that the paradigm of a habitual body memory was set in an isolated island off the coast of northern Sweden? Here the place lent poignancy and point to the circumstance of starting up a moribund automobile: remembering how to start it was especially prized in such a place, and I in turn remembered the episode as indissolubly place-bound. The same is true of my erotic and traumatic memories. In their case, however, my own body served as a pertinent place, as the immediate setting for what I came to remember. In still other cases, place continued to be deeply ingredient: whether as the postcard photograph of the Parthenon that reminded me of the glory that was Greece, the grim battlefield about which elderly veterans reminisce, or the South Bend airport in which a scene of recognition took place. The reservative role of place is evident in every instance. However unobtrusive this role may be, it serves to contain—to shelter and protect—the items or episodes on which the act of remembering comes to focus.

The paradox is that despite the undeniability of this role, it remained *terra incognita* in my own previous assessments. Not only in these, however: the place of place in human memory is enormously difficult to detect in almost any traditional model of remembering. This is as true of a Kantian account of memory as "reproductive imagination" (i.e., as imagistic recollection) as it is of a Husserlian act-intentional analysis. Indeed, it is true for Aristotle's view of memory as "the having of an image regarded as a copy of that of which it is an image."[27] As presented in his treatise *De Memoria et Reminiscentia*, this view leaves little room for Aristotle's description in the *Physics* of place as containerlike. And yet it is the latter notion that is so suggestive for a more thorough understanding of place memory, one which refuses to reduce place to site or to let the spatial aspects of memories be overwhelmed by their temporal features.

Such considerations lead us to the following two-fold observation. On the one hand, *place is selective for memories:* that is to say, a given place will invite certain memories while discouraging others. The fact is that we can't attach just *any* memories to a particular place—as can occur in the case of a site, whose featurelessness is nonselective with respect to memories, much as a blank television screen can accommodate any and all images that might flit across it. Place is always definite, and regarding a given place only some memories, indeed only certain *kinds* of memory, will be pertinent. My memory, say, of seeing *Small Change* at a particular theater calls for remembering that is limited to certain visual, auditory, and (to a lesser degree) kinesthetic modalities. It would be literally "out of place" to associate systematically with this theater memories of isolated cogitation, of jogging, of painting, etc. A movie theater is a place with local peculiarities that would not welcome such memories as these: if not disallowing them altogether, it is a most unpropitious setting for them.

On the other hand, *memories are selective for place:* they seek out particular places as their natural habitats. Why this propensity? Partly because places furnish convenient points of attachment for memories; but also because places provide situations in which remembered actions can deploy themselves. Or more precisely, places are *congealed scenes* for remembered contents; and as such they serve to situate what we remember. Here we encounter once more place's *periechon* being, its containing/surrounding function. Place is a *mise en scène* for remembered events precisely to the extent that it guards and keeps these events within its self-delimiting perimeters. Instead of filtering out (as place can do for inappropriate, ill-placed memories), place *holds in* by giving to memories an authentically local habitation: by being their place-holder.

## IV

But it is still not clear just how such an intimate relationship between memory and place is realized. Through what agency does this become possible? The answer can only be: *through the lived body*. The lived body's basic "inter-leaving"[28] activity makes it ideally suited as a means for mediating between two such seemingly different things as memory and place. As psycho-physical in status, the lived body puts us in touch with the psychical aspects of remembering and the physical features of place. As itself movable and moving, it can relate at once to the movable bodies that are the primary occupants of place and to the self-moving soul that recollects itself in place. Above all, through its active intentional arc, the lived body traces out the arena for the remembered scenes that inhere so steadfastly in particular places: the body's maneuvers and movements, imagined as well as actual, make room for remembering placed scenes in all of their complex composition. In the end, we can move into place, indeed *be* in a place at all, only through our body's own distinct potencies. And if it is the body that places us in place to start with, it will be instrumental in re-placing us in remembered places as well. As integral to the original experience of places which we come to remember, it is also central to the motion and time that depend on place.[29]

Accordingly, we must now take up the role of the body in memory of place. Doing so will carry forward the work of the last chapter. Body memory is by no means confined to matters of place. But such memory, in several of its basic aspects, can be regarded as importantly operative in memory of place. In any case, whether subject to memory or not, the lived body is indispensable to remembering places of every sort.

A full discussion of just how the body is constitutive for memory of place would have to include consideration of the ways in which it establishes directionality (e.g., right/left, North/South), spatio-temporal distance, and a sense of level in given places. As I have treated these matters elsewhere,[30] we can move immediately to a reflection on what can be called "in-habitation." By this I mean the manner in which, thanks precisely to the lived body, we find ourselves to be *familiar* with a particular place *in* which we are located. I underline "familiar" and "in" to indicate what is characteristic of places in contrast with sites. A site, for example a development lot, resists familiarization just as it resists movement into its interior. In its well-surveyed stolidity, the lot stands over against us. It seems to want to keep us *out*—unless we are prospective buyers, and even then it seems to oppose any attempt to become fully familiar with it. For familiarity to begin to set in, we must project a state of *already having inhabited it,* e.g., the dwelling we plan to build on it. Otherwise, it remains foreign, even inimical, to us. Such a site is *not* the stuff of which memories are made! Its indifference to us is answered by our commensurate indifference in remembering it. It is just one more lot to look at, and as such it is distinctly unmemorable.

Merleau-Ponty wrote that "we must . . . avoid saying that our body is *in* space or *in* time. It *inhabits* space and time."[31] When such inhabitation concerns place specifically, it is best construed under the two headings of 'in' and 'familiarity', which we must now consider at more length.

### 'IN'

In discussing eight ways in which one thing can be said to be *in* another, Aristotle cites as "the strictest sense of all, [the way] a thing is 'in' a vessel, and generally 'in' a place."[32] The vessel is not casually invoked here. It had already been introduced in Book IV of the *Physics* with the remark that "place is supposed to be something like a vessel."[33] It is like a vessel insofar as both are forms of container: "Place is thought to be a kind of surface and, as it were, a vessel, i.e., a container of the thing."[34] This is not to say that a vessel is a perfect analogue of place. Place, it will be recalled, is defined by

Aristotle as "the innermost *motionless* boundary of what contains." Therefore, whereas "the vessel is a transportable place," place itself is "a non-portable vessel."[35] But portability aside, what remains valid in the vessel analogy is the structure of close confinement, of snug fit. As water fills up a vessel into which it is poured and is protected by that vessel, so the lived body can fit snugly into a particular place and be protected by it.[36]

At play here is a two-fold movement. On the one hand, there is an active *in-sertion* into place by means of the body. In its propulsive power, its dynamic intentional arc, the body thrusts us into each successive place we inhabit, pulls us into place, puts us in the very midst of it as in a surrounding vessel. Bodily insertion into place is a matter of what Merleau-Ponty calls the "gearing" of my body into the world, becoming emmeshed in it:

> My body is geared to the world when my perception presents me with a spectacle as varied and as clearly articulated as possible, and when my motor intentions, as they unfold, receive the responses they expect from the world.[37]

This statement makes it clear that a dialectic between subject and world is operative in bodily implacement and that actions of in-sertion into the world (via "motor intentions") are matched by contributions ("responses") from the world itself. On the other hand, there is an answering activity of *in-taking* on the part of place *per se*. Such activity is responsible for my feeling fully contained in place, with no empty space left over. Here is doubtless the origin of our sensitivity to intimate places, those into which we "just fit," which seem "just right" because we sense that we are somehow perfectly coincident with what is containing us. These *lieux intimes* are especially memorable as well, suggesting a profound linkage between memorability and being bodily in a "cozy spot." The linkage is made possible by the factor of in-taking, which allows us to feel well-contained in place. Thanks to in-taking, we become convinced indeed that "our own body is *in* the world as the heart is *in* the organism."[38]

### FAMILIARITY

When taken together, the 'in' of in-sertion and the 'in' of in-taking yield the sense of familiarity that inheres in human in-habitation—in all dwelling and being-in-the-world.[39] We only inhabit that which comes bearing the familiar; and the familiar in turn entails memory in various forms. Familiar places are places we are apt to remember—to hold and keep in mind.

Familiarity of place ranges all the way from the barely recognizable ("I think I've been here before, but I can't say just when or in what circumstances") to the thoroughly known (e.g., one's office, one's domicile). Present throughout, however, is the feeling of being *chez soi*, at home, domestic. This "down home" sentiment is not only a matter of feeling at ease in a given place but of feeling at ease in a place that has become *one's own* in some especially significant way. "One's own" does not imply possession in any literal sense; it is more deeply a question of *appropriating*, with all that this connotes of *making something one's own* by *making it one with one's ongoing life*.

The appropriation of familiar places is accomplished by the lived body, which has "a knowledge bred of familiarity that does not gives us a position in objective space."[40] The kind of space that figures here is an "attuned space," a space with which one feels sympathetic at some very basic level—in contrast with the indifferent site-space of cartography or rational geometry.[41] In the presence of the latter, it is quite difficult to feel *chez soi* unless one happens to be a cartographer or a geometer.[42] In the ambiance of attuned space, it is correspondingly difficult *not* to feel at home; for this is the very space that inheres in the place one has made one's own through establishing such dimensional features as level, distance, and directionality. These features effect an attunement of in-habited space, helping it to become familiar precisely because it is largely one's own achievement.

But how are we to account for this attunement of the body in a place? How is it established and maintained? We have already encountered the source of the attunement. It lies in the customary body as conceived by Merleau-Ponty:

> Our body comprises as it were two distinct layers, that of the customary body and that of the body at this moment . . . my body must be apprehended not only in an experience which is instantaneous, peculiar to itself and complete in itself, but also in some general aspect and in light of an impersonal being.[43]

A dramatic example of the customary body existing in dissociation from the momentary body is found in experiences of phantom limbs, in which the accustomed sense of still possessing a healthy arm or leg persists even though one is forced to deny it in perceiving one's "body at this moment." The persistence can occur only because the memory of the missing member has attained a degree of generality that is not undermined by the fact that the member is perceived as absent. This generality, this "impersonal being," characterizes every aspect of the customary body, which is why it "gives to our life the form of generality, and develops our personal acts into stable dispositional tendencies."[44] Precisely as impersonal and general—as not being overwhelmed by a mass of personal recollections that take me resolutely out of the present into the past—the customary body anchors me all the more firmly in the present, even at the price of leading me to believe I possess a missing limb. Although the customary body is rooted in the past, it does not return me to the past: it engages me in present in-habitation.

It is in much the same way that familiarity of place is brought about. Proust knew this well. In a passage from the Overture to "Swann's Way" he calls upon custom in the guise of "habit." This occurs at the very point where the narrator's confused insomniacal state has acted to suspend a sense of familiarity with the room in which he finds himself:

> Habit had changed the color of the curtains, silenced the clock, brought an expression of pity to the cruel, slanting face of the glass, disguised or even completely dispelled the scent of the vetiver, and appreciably reduced the apparent loftiness of the ceiling. Habit! That skillful but slow-moving arranger who begins by letting our minds suffer for weeks on end in temporary quarters but whom our minds are none the less only too happy to discover at last, for *without it, reduced to their own devices, they would be powerless to make any room seem habitable.*[45]

As surrounding passages make clear, habit is at work here as deeply sedimented into the troubled sleeper's customary body, which has gained control over the confusion and *malaise* of his momentary body. It is this customary body that not only finds but *makes* the surrounding bedroom familiar and thus habitable; and it does so by allowing initially unfamiliar-seeming objects to find their own "right places,"[46] that is, their proper places in a fully familiarized setting. The familiarization itself does not occur by means of recollecting the room in question, much less by comparing it explicitly with other rooms of a similar sort. It arises instead from a succession of postures assumed by the semi-dormant body as it projects various possible habitats (e.g., a "Louis XVI room," "rooms in summer," "rooms in winter,"[47] etc.), inhabiting each via successive corporeal memories until it comes to attach itself securely to the actual habitat in which the narrator finds himself.

Such work of the customary body is *domesticating* in function; it forges a sense of attuned space that allows one to feel *chez soi* in an initially unfamiliar place. It does so in a manner quite analogous to the way in which the same body, through its own remembrances, feels already at home in the past places which its memories summon up. In this we observe the exceedingly close tie between body memory and memory of place—close to the point of their becoming virtually indistinguishable in many lived experiences of remembering. Body memory establishes the familiarity that is requisite to the full realization of place memory. The "things, places, years" which revolve around the Proustian narrator in the darkness and to which his mind is manifestly unequal are revolving *around his body,* a body "still too heavy with sleep to move."[48]

In-habitation, we may conclude, is at once an effectuation and a culmination of bodily being-in-place. It achieves an extremely close bonding to place by realizing the dual 'in' of in-sertion and in-taking; and it accomplishes the deep familiarity of feeling *chez soi,* thanks in turn to the sense of attuned space which the customary body brings with it. Beyond the specific contributions of human dwellings to making places more inhabitable,[49] there is, still more basically, the customary body's contribution. This contribution not only leads to enhanced memorability (above all, by helping to create places with an intensely felt intimacy) but infuses place with memory throughout. The customary body contains its own sedimented memories of place, whether these be of the particular place in which one presently finds oneself, contiguous places, places of a like kind, etc. Moving in or through a given place, the body imports its own implaced past into its present experience: its "local history" is literally a history of locales. This very importation of past places occurs simultaneously with the body's ongoing establishment of directionality, level, and distance—and indeed influences these latter in myriad ways. Orientation in place (which is what is established by these three factors) cannot be continually effected *de novo* but arises within the ever-lengthening shadow of our bodily past. As Bergson says of all "habit memory," the body's past *acts in the present:* "it is part of my present, exactly like my habit of walking or of writing; it is lived and acted, rather than represented."[50] In the actions of the customary body, then, we observe the continuance of *time in place*—a continuance that connotes not merely maintenance but active incorporation. In this way the past becomes "our true present";[51] it loses its identity as a separate past (a past of *another* time and place) through its precipitation into the present of bodily behavior, which enacts the past rather than picturing it. And this presentment of the past is nowhere more active or more evident than in bodily memory of place.

## V

Concerning the role of body in memory of place we need to make two further general remarks:

(1) This role exhibits just how decisive the distinction between place and site is. Few if any of the activities of the body that have just been sketched would be relevant, or even possible, in the kind of space determined by sites. Achieving orientation in a homogeneous, isotropic space would be at best a merely mechanical matter. It would reduce to alignment with pre-established axes and positions. Directionality would amount to convergence with, or divergence from, one of the three axes of a three-dimensional coordinate system. Level, if it existed at all, would be a matter of situatedness in relation to two of these axes, the vertical and the horizontal. Distance would be measured along the third axis, that of depth as objectively determinable in exact metric equivalents. For such factors as in-sertion or in-taking—indeed, for the sense of being bodily 'in' anything—there would be no equivalents at all.

For sites do not contain or enclose but either open out endlessly into infinity (as in a Newtonian conception of "absolute space") or are simply juxtaposed with one another (as in the case of building sites). Moreover, in the absence of a sense of place-as-container—which is, in the Aristotelian view of place that I have taken as paradigmatic, to lack a sense of lived place altogether—there can be no experience of place-as-shelter: hence, no sense of habitable place. Yet in-habitation, as we have seen, is central to a full sense of being in place, of being there in an attuned and customary way. Sites are to be built *on* but not lived *in* (it is the houses constructed on them that we dwell in), just as they are measured in space rather than savored in memory. Sites are prospective in character; they are sites *for* building, exploring, surveying, etc. Places, in contrast, are retrospectively tinged: we "build up" memories there, are moved by them in nostalgic spells, are exhilarated or get "stuck" in them. In short, it is thanks to places, not to sites, that we are inhabitants of the world. Can it be surprising to us that we find ourselves longing to get *back into place,* whether by memory or in some other way? Getting out of place, being displaced, is profoundly disorienting. As John Russell has observed:

> 'Where am I?' is, after all, one of the most poignant of human formulations. It speaks for an anxiety that is intense, recurrent, and all but unbearable. Not to know where we are is torment, and not to have a sense of place is a most sinister deprivation.[52]

No wonder, then, that we so much prize memory of place and often seek out "old haunts." Precisely as a container (not just of movable bodies but of our entire memorial lives), place acts to alleviate anxieties of disorientation and separation. Places and their memory sustain us in our everyday lives, subject as these lives are to fragmentation and rupture of so many sorts. Even persons (i.e., the very beings who are the sources of separation anxiety) are experienced and remembered primarily as persons-in-particular-places: "Crawford at Asheville," "Dan at the Handcraft Center," "Tunie in Topeka."

(2) But back to the body: unless *it* feels oriented in place, *we* as its bearers are not going to feel oriented there either. If our body does not feel at home in the world, we shall almost certainly experience *Heimatlosigkeit*. This is why I have placed such stress on the way the lived body familiarizes us with regard to place; for this familiarization, more than any other single factor, brings about the conviction of being at home in the world. We cannot even imagine what feeling *chez soi* would be like without the body's abiding presence—nor could we *remember* what it was like. It is in and by the body's polymorphic powers of situating us in place that we come to have a sense of what being-in-place can mean for human existence.

But there is a closely related matter that we must not neglect. Beyond orienting and situating us in place—in the very place in which it is located—the lived body *itself serves as a place*. It is a place not just for its internal organs but for all of its activities of presentment in place. In this respect it can be considered as a place of places—or more exactly, a *placer of places*. We could even call it, following Bergson, a "place of passage":

> [The body] is the *place of passage* of the movements received and thrown back, a hyphen, a connecting link between the things which act upon me and the things upon which I act—the seat, in a word, of sensori-motor phenomena.[53]

What kind of place is the body as a place of passage? It consists in being at once an *intra-place* and an *inter-place*.

(*a*) *Body as intra-place:* Within a given place there may be a simple unbroken expanse or else a set of subplaces (e.g., partitioned-off parts of a room). In either case the body plays a special role as an interior place: as a dynamic but stationary force that selectively organizes the spatiality of those things that surround it. Such things (material objects, other people, etc.) gain position in relation to the body-place as an organizational center. Here the body is more than an abstract point in indifferent space, more than a group of vital functions, more even than a set of habits. It is itself a place with a "distinct potency" that helps to structure the overall spatiality of the place in which it finds itself, making it into a place *within* which the body resides and *toward* which it acts in manifold ways. The body as intra-place is thus a place *through* which whatever is occurring in a given setting can take place: it is a place of passage for such occurrences, which array themselves around it (and do so even if it is only their silent witness). For this reason we almost always remember places from the point of view of our body's own intra-place within a remembered place: *there* we *were*, there and nowhere else. The body's own intra-place within place is a place of anchoring, of staying put in relation to the scene remembered; it is a mainstay of memory of place.

(*b*) *Body as inter-place:* But the lived body is at the same time a moving body. Even if it is its own place, it also moves us from *place to place*. As Erwin Straus says, "In a landscape we always get to one place from another place; each location is determined only by its relation to the neighboring place within the circle of visibility."[54] No longer is it a matter of the body as a stationary center of a to-be-remembered scene; now it is a question of the body as the basis for changing places. In changing place the body transports its whole organic mass from one stationing-point to another. The trajectory traced out by this movement describes an *inter*-place, a place *between* places that is itself a special kind of place. Inter-places arise whenever our body moves along a forest path, through a hallway, over a tennis court, etc. The body's locomotion in such cases is forward-tending, since the place-to-come-to is experienced as an aim.[55] Or more exactly, the locomotion is to be construed in terms of a dialectic between the here and the there. 'Here' is the place from which we are departing in our bodily movement; 'there' is the place we are aiming at through this same movement. The lived body creates the inter-place in which the two epicenters of the here and the there are brought into concrete connection.

## VI

The question remains: How can place, plain old place, be so powerful in matters of memory? In what does the power of place for memory consist? We have seen Aristotle driven to speak of a place's "active influence," its "distinct potencies." Similarly, the Romans posited a "*genius loci*," an indwelling spirit, for each significant place: for instance, the Lar (the "owl" of the ancestors) for the home, the Lares for more public places (typically at crossroads), and the Penates for the property and welfare of the family and the state. In English we still speak of "the spirit of a place," and ascribe to particular places attractive or repelling forces far beyond what their position in geographic space or historic time might indicate. Think of the resonance which certain place-names can possess: not only "Combray," "Balbec," "Paris," "Doncières," and "Venice" but (for many Americans) "San Francisco," "New Orleans," "Cape Cod," and (for myself) "Abilene," "Enterprise," "Asheville." The resonance stems from a distinctive power of place and, more particularly, from the way this power elicits remembering.

How are we to account for the power of place-as-remembered? I have already suggested one main line of response: namely, the orienting function of the lived body as it situates us steadily in and between places, helping to create that specific gravity by which they can exert their full power. Places are empowered by the lived bodies that occupy them; these bodies animate places, breathe new life into them by endowing them with directionality, level, and distance—all of which serve as essential anchoring points in the remembering of place.

But beyond the body's indispensable contribution, we must also look at some of the inherent features of place itself. All of these features can be considered aspects of place in its *landscape* character. "Landscape" is here taken in Straus's sense of the full correlate of bodily sensing (rather than of perceiving, which calls for an objective, universal medium): "the space of the sensory world stands to that of perception as the landscape to geography."[56] Strictly geographic or perceptual space answers to what I have been calling "site"; in such space all positions are determined in relation to each other and finally to the whole that is structured by a coordinate system. This space is "constant and invariant," "systematized and closed."[57] As mapped, it allows us to travel to points beyond the visible horizon.

In landscape, by contrast, there is always a visible (or at least a sensed) horizon. Thanks precisely to our body as basis of orientation, we find ourselves surrounded by a horizon, whatever our immediate location may be. Assuming that we know the terrain in some minimal fashion, we go from place to place within this horizon by means of our moving body, needing no map or plan with which to navigate. Moreover, the spatiality of the places between which we move in landscape is at once inconstant and variant, unsystematic and open: as anyone can attest from an afternoon's hike in the low foothills of the California Sierras. Even when there are marked trails, these follow the irregular lay of the land, converge and diverge unpredictably, vary in width and in regard to how cleared they are, and in still other ways they resist charting in strictly geographic terms. When we are in a landscape setting, in other words, we are very much in the presence of place in its most encompassing and exfoliated format, a format in which we are sensuously attuned to its intrinsic spatial properties rather than imposing on it our own site-specifying proclivities.

Landscape contributes to place's memorial evocativeness in three primary ways: by its variegation, its sustaining character, and its expressiveness.

#### VARIEGATION

It is a remarkable fact that landscape presents itself to us in continual variety—as plain and mountain, path and brook, hillside and river bed, tree and bush, not to mention such urbanscape variants as building and sidewalk, corridor and bedroom, entranceway and exit. Everywhere we encounter diversity of content, even on the barest plain or the emptiest shopping mall parking lot. The very being and structure of landscape consist in this ongoing proliferation of irregularities, of expected as well as unexpected obtrusions, all of which are thrust before us by the surrounding world. Whether facilitating or obstructing with regard to the pathways we are tracing out at the time, these obtrusions act as points of attachment: as "landmarks" by which we gauge our progress through a given part of the landscape and on which we hang lasting memories.

It is just such variegation that draws us so insistently to landscape—and if landscape itself is not available to us, then to its representation in painting or photography. Landscape of sufficient variety promises surprises at every turn; at the very least, it furnishes relief from the monotony and non-surprise of strictly sited space, in which protuberant variegation has been leveled down. What protrudes in a landscape offers us something to grasp at the most basic level of sensory awareness. Thus a rock in the midst of a mountain path arrests the body momentarily in its onward motion, *gives it pause,* that is, gives it something to fasten onto—with the result that it no longer glides through "free space" where there would be nothing to attach to, and thus nothing to remember.[58] Memory of place entails having been slowed down, stopped, or in some other way caught-in-place. Within a suitably variegated spatial scene, "the hold is held."[59]

#### SUSTAINING CHARACTER

Landscape does more than make possible various pursuits and projects of ours; it sustains them by serving as their continuing durable ground. This sustaining occurs in two forms. First, the *perimeter* of the landscape-place (perhaps best called a "placescape") acts to delimit all that lies within its compass. A perimeter can be as confined and confining as the walls of my study, or it can seem to stretch out endlessly as in sunsets at sea. Either way, it defines the outer limits of the place I find myself in. Where sites are delimited for mainly functional reasons (e.g., because a building code dictates that each construction site be precisely 1 acre), places possess perimeters in a pre-given and yet unpreplanned manner: Thus, that line of hills over there at once occludes any further vista and acts to frame the valley I am traveling through. The perimeter closes in from without; it en-closes by keeping things contained within its limits. Second, that which is thereby contained is located in a *field* upholding whatever specific action takes place in it. This field is sustaining *from below,* as it were. It stands under specific actions as a matrix of support, helping them to cohere as single events or as a concatenated set of events occurring just here and nowhere else. More extensive than a particular protuberance but less encompassing than a perimeter, the field subtends subtly but securely.[60] Taken together, perimeter and field lend to the landscape its abidingly sustaining capacity: its ability to underlie a potentially immense stock of memories and to ramify into our lives in extra-memorial ways as well (e.g., by providing us with an assured sense of ease of action). When Straus says that "in the landscape I *am somewhere,*"[61] he is invoking the sustaining power of place. The apposition of "am" with "somewhere" bears out the ancient claim of Archytas that in order to be at all, one must be *in a place:* supported and sustained there.

### EXPRESSIVENESS

Lawrence Durrell has written that "human beings are expressions of their landscapes."[62] If this is indeed so, it is only because landscapes are themselves expressive to begin with. They come to us enveloped in a "sympathetic space"[63] that favors the physiognomic over the geometric, the expressive over the merely communicative. Consider only the way that an ordinary skyscape full of clouds can spontaneously suggest human figures and faces. It is at the basic level of sensing that such expressiveness arises unbidden and unrehearsed. Sensing conveys the world's density in all of its qualitative richness: what are labeled "secondary" qualities by Locke and Descartes here become of primary importance. Only when such qualities (i.e., colors, contours, sounds, and the like) are objectified do they lose their primary expressive capacity and become items to be represented.[64]

The relationship between emotion and expression is close indeed, and it is therefore not surprising to discover that the expressiveness of landscapes is linked to their inherent emotionality. This link is especially evident in the case of "special places," which bring with them, as well as engender, an unusual emotional claim and resonance. The power of such places to act on us, to inspire (or repell) us, and thus to be remembered vividly is a function of such emotionality—but only as it finds adequate expression in the features of landscapes which have just been discussed. Instead of merely indicating or symbolizing this emotional expressiveness, these features must *embody* it.

A considerable part of the power of place to move us relates to its unique form of *visibility*, which is, along with emotionality, the other foundation of its expressiveness. By "visibility" I do not mean its literally seen configurations but something closer to luminosity—the kind of light that seems to stem *from within* an object rather than being merely refracted onto it from some external source. In this sense, places can be said to radiate out from the exact shape they possess in objective space, the space of sites. How or why they do this is not our concern here; it is only a question of observing that it occurs and that it contributes forcefully to the expressive power of places. Places possess us—in perception, as in memory—by their radiant visibility, insinuating themselves into our lives, seizing and surrounding us, even taking us over as we sink into their presence. When this happens—it is the very opposite of being in a sited situation, which we dominate by measurement, positioning, etc.—we feel ourselves merging with a place, which on this very account suddenly becomes *in*visible, dissolved in its own luminosity, disintegrated as a discriminate object. We experience this objectlessness in moments of overwhelming joy or fear or abandon. Here "landscape is invisible, because the more we absorb it, the more we lose ourselves in it. To be fully in the landscape we must sacrifice, as far as possible, all temporal, spatial, and objective precision."[65]

We also sacrifice any explicit consciousness of our own body in such a circumstance: it too becomes invisible as it merges with the very place to which it has been our main link. This is a moment of maximum expressiveness, one that is rarely achieved altogether since various modes of explicit visibility tend to remain present. But experiences of ecstasy serve to remind us of its ongoing possibility. The paradox is that the power of place is most fully manifested at the very moment when place and body fuse and lose their separate identities. At this point, the variegated and sustaining aspects of a place's power cede place to an expressiveness no longer containable by parameters of the here and the there, the without and the within, perimeter and field. Emotion itself has become e-motion, a moving out and away from the epicenters of body and place and their reciprocally realized positioning in space. Yet significance abides, and with it memorability.

The memorability of place amounts to more than what the recollection of place can yield; it is the source as well as the reinforced product of experiences of being-in-place. Perhaps the single most fateful such experience, by means of which place comes to be most deeply memorable, is that in which a given place and the lived body as its correlate dissolve as discrete source-points while uniting in a mutual invisibility. Then place becomes ours at last; but in remembering it, we remain beholden to its intrinsic power.

## VII

One of the most eloquent testimonies to place's extraordinary memorability is found in nostalgia. We are nostalgic primarily about particular places that have been emotionally significant to us and which we now miss: we are in pain *(algos)* about a return home *(nostos)* that is not presently possible. It is not accidental that "nostalgia" and "homesickness" are still regarded as synonyms in current English dictionaries and that one and the same German word, *Heimweh,* means both at once. Johannes Hofer, who coined the word "nostalgia" in his *Medical Dissertation on Nostalgia* (1688), advised that the affliction "admits no remedy other than a return to the homeland."[66] Indeed the sooner the better: "The patient," said Hofer, "should be taken [home], however weak and feeble, without delay, whether by a traveling carriage with four wheels, or by sedan chair, or by any other means."[67] Post haste in short!

It does not matter that Kant scoffed at this remedy, remarking that such a *Heimkunft* or homecoming is often "very disappointing" insofar as the home-place itself may have become "wholly transformed."[68] What does matter is that the phenomenon of nostalgia bears mainly on place; the nostalgic person is condemned, in Hofer's words, to "think continually about the Fatherland"[69]—as did the paradigmatic young Swiss conscripts who, encamped on the flatlands of Holland, longed for the valleys in which they had been brought up. In being nostalgic, we are all in the position of these dis-placed conscripts.

This is not the place to pursue the nature of nostalgia.[70] All that we need to notice is that the poignant power of the phenomenon—which can virtually paralyze those under its sway—has everything to do with memory of place. That the place in question is normally that special place called "home"—"there is no place like home," according to nostalgia's primary axiom—testifies emphatically to the strength of the internal bond between place and memory. Once more then we must ask: In what does this bond consist? Why is place so potent as a guardian of memories?

So far I have isolated three general "landscape" structures which help to answer these questions: place's variegation, its sustaining nature, and its expressiveness. These do not yet account, however, for the peculiar hauntingness of places that we experience in nostalgia—to the point where we may be quite overwhelmed by their memory, even so obsessed by them that we overlook the particular place we occupy in the present. Nostalgia leads us to invoke the following principle: *in remembering we can be thrust back, transported, into the place we recall.* We can be moved back into this place as much as, and sometimes more than, into the *time* in which the remembered event occurred. Rather than thinking of remembering as a form of re-experiencing the past *per se,* we might conceive of it as an activity of *re-implacing:* re-experiencing past places. By the same token, if it is true that all memory has a bodily component or dimension, the memory-bearing body can be considered as a *body moving back in(to) place*. Aristotelian physics remains pertinent for a phenomenology of human memory: bodies of every sort move from place to place.[71] Such is their fate—and *ours* as embodied rememberers. Our remembering/remembered bodies are ineluctably place-bound; they are bound to be in a place, whether this place be a common or a special one.[72]

In searching for a still more adequate understanding of the memorial potency of place, we need to notice the way in which the functions of memory and place are strikingly parallel. They accomplish a similar task at a quite basic level. This task is that of *congealing the disparate into a provisional unity*. To begin with, any given place serves to hold together dispersed things, animate or inanimate; it *regionalizes* them, giving to them a single shared space in which to be together. But a place can also draw together different spaces—as when a town square brings together several converging streets, each of which leads into a region of its own. As opposed to a sheer site—a space that acts to define and exclude—a place encourages the inclusion and overlap of a set of various spaces. These spaces become co-inherent in the place in which they conjoin. Thanks to place's "nearing nearness,"[73] they constitute a sense of neighborhood or vicinity.

Compare with this the way that human remembering—quite apart from memory of place as such—acts to draw together diverse moments of time: not only the remote past with the present moment (as in secondary memory) but also the immediate past with the given 'now' (as in primary memory). If it does nothing else, memory effects temporal synthesis, indeed may be the sole source of such synthesis: as Leibniz (pondering Aristotle's doctrine of motion) affirmed in his monadology, and as Kant was to proclaim still more explicitly in his doctrine of reproductive imagination, which associates items in terms of temporal succession.[74] This assertion of the importance of temporal synthesis goes hand in hand with the demise of "place" as a technical philosophical term in post-Kantian philosophy. Time is given a function parallel to that formerly ascribed to place: a congealing function (Aristotle would say "containing"). For temporal synthesis—and thus the synthesis realized by memory viewed in the modernist perspective of time—is a matter of congealing disparate moments into various forms of unity.

If congealing on the part of the lived world—i.e., that effected by place—is symmetrical in operation with congealing on the part of the temporal subject (i.e., that effected by memory), then the alliance of memory and place, as well as the peculiar power of memory *of* place, is assured, even in a post-Kantian world-view. The fact is that place has always functioned in human experience in a manner analogous to how memory was thought to operate by Leibniz and Kant. And if this is so, we have every reason to believe that to remember particular places, or to remember by means of them, will intensify our memorial powers: synthesis to the second power!

What we have been discussing as place's inherently sheltering role—its capacity to have and hold memories, to hold them *together*—can only enhance the role of remembering conceived as a power of temporal synthesis. Both roles, the one containing and the other synthesizing, are fundamentally "reservative" by dint of forming a preserve, a virtual reservation, within which disparities can co-exist. No wonder, then, that memory and place continue to reinforce each other—even in a world preoccupied by questions of time and of site.

## VIII

The place/memory parallel assumes still further forms which we can designate under the headings of "horizon," "pathway," and constituent "things." Let us take these up in succession:

### HORIZON

Horizon is essential to the reservative role of memory and place, each of which involves a sense of intrinsic delimitation. The delimitation is intrinsic because it comes from within as well as from without, resulting in a double horizonal structure. Experienced in its fullest form, a place exhibits an internal and an external horizon[75]—whereas a site, as leveled-down, possesses neither kind of horizonal structure. By "fullest form" I mean a landscape construed as a coherent collocation of intertwining places. The external horizon of a given landscape encompasses all the particular places, regions, and things within its enclosure. It is exemplified in (but is not limited to) the horizonal line formed by the meeting of earth and sky. The internal horizon of any particular entity, place, or region is its immediate inner limit. *Horos*, the root of "horizon," means boundary or limit, especially as this serves to define a material thing. Thus Aristotle's conception of place in terms of innermost boundary *(peras)* is in fact a conception of place as internal horizon.

A place as remembered will often involve both horizonal structures. When I remember, say, sweeping the porch of my grandparents' house in Abilene, I recall being contained by the internal horizon of the porch itself—a horizon constituted by the roof of the porch and the side of the house with which it was contiguous—*and* being surrounded by an entire setting composed of a yard, grape arbor, neighbors' houses, a creek, etc., all of these latter establishing the external horizon of the scene as I remember it.

It is a striking fact that Husserl, doubtless inspired by James's notion of "fringe," called the retentions of primary memory "horizons."[76] These retentions surround each fading moment like a halo or "comet's tail" (in Husserl's favorite metaphor), forming a rapidly subsiding but distinctive horizon for that moment. Moreover, this temporally internal horizon can be remembered as such—as "the past of the past"[77] which we recall in bodily, pictorial, or verbal forms. A concatenation of such horizoned moments constitutes what could be termed a "scene," the episodic-temporal equivalent of a landscape. The temporally specified limits of this scene, its duration, represent the temporal form of its external horizon. What I called "aura" in chapter 4 is nothing other than the spatio-temporal expression of the same phenomenon, echoes of which we also discerned in reminding (i.e., the outer edge of the adumbrated remindand), in recognizing (as the limits of perceptual suffusion), in reminiscing (in the beginning and ending of the reminisced-about event), and even in body memory (as the outer arc of the lived body's remembered movement from place to place). There are also equivalents of internal horizons in each case—too many to trace out here. What most merits noticing is that in every instance internal and external horizons are at once spatial and temporal (ultimately, they are spatio-temporal) and that both kinds of horizon are shared by memory and place alike.

#### PATHWAY

A second feature shared in common by memory and place is the existence of pathways in and through their midst. Such pathways are of two sorts: those that give access or egress and those that facilitate internal exploration. We witness both in our experience of place. A given place can be entered by multiple pathways through a landscape that acts as its external horizon. This place also permits exiting by the same pathways or by others that we come to discern. Once within a particular place, still more interior pathways open to us—or more exactly, to our moving bodies, which are the vehicles of path-breaking or path-following. However limited these inner paths may be, they at least allow movement in more than one direction. The resulting sense of free exploration contrasts with the planned journeys that occur within cartographic or sited space.[78]

Once more the analogy to memory is striking. A given memory possesses multiple modes of entry ("access," "retrieval"), as well as of egress (whether by moving to another memory or by simply forgetting). The structure of these routes—a structure that allows them to range from random cues to highly predictable stimulus-response situations—has been the subject of feverish and fruitful research on the part of cognitive psychologists. These same scientists have also explored the interior drama of memory in terms of its complex "associative networks."[79] Such networks exhibit ramifying pathways even in the case of a seemingly straightforward memory: to remember my childhood dog "Peggy" is at the same time to enter a microcosm of that period of my life, a mini-world in which "Peggy" links up with the other dogs my family owned, with the way they were regarded by my siblings, with the way they made that domestic space more warmly familiar, etc. Each of the themes just mentioned represents a pathway in this particular part of my past; and from each pathway still others diverge: from "Peggy" the dog to Peggy Mills, the wife of my father's law partner, to "Peg O' My Heart," or to Charles Peguy, the French writer. As the English and French associationists outlined in theory, and as Freud realized in practice, any limit on such associative pathways is a matter of arbitrary foreclosure. Exploration within memory—even within a single given memory—is potentially endless. This is something which St. Augustine knew long before the associationists, Freud, or contemporary cognitive psychologists:

> Memory . . . is like a great field or a spacious palace, a storehouse for countless images of all kinds. . . . It is a vast, immeasurable sanctuary. Who can plumb its depths?[80]

The unplumbable nature of memory has everything to do with what characterizes place as well: an openness to traversal by multiple pathways.

THINGS

Material things not only frequently constitute the specific content of places and memories alike, but by their special memorability they draw memory and place together in a quite significant way. I cannot, for example, remember my early experiences at my great-uncle Ralph's home without the reappearance, within the memory, of his house (including its interior rooms), the pond next to it, and the alley behind. Hence my sense of shock when I revisited Kansas a few years ago and discovered that his house had been razed and the pond eliminated following a major fire on the property. With the disappearance of these things, the main elements of a quite special place in my childhood, and thus the source of a treasured set of place memories, had vanished.

If things do not form necessary conditions of every memory of place—one can certainly imagine cases of remembering utterly desolate, empty places—they do enter into active alliances with particular places. Aristotle was already alert to such alliances: "Just as every body is in place, so, too, every place has a body in it."[81] Things are manifestly *of* place as well as *in* place; they are its natural occupants. If horizons and pathways serve to delimit places from without and within respectively—to give them contour and structure—things fill out places, giving to their shape a substance. And as horizons and pathways delineate movements in places, so things bring about fixation and focus there. In this regard, the role of things in places is curiously comparable to that of the lived body. The body and things both lend a distinctive density to their immediate surroundings; and as the body is central for the experiencing and remembering subject who pivots around (and with) it, so things are pivotal points in a given place, constellating it by their presence.

What we have just said of things and bodies as they figure into place is above all true of things as they form part of explicit place memories. In such memories (e.g., of my great-uncle's house), things are centers of coalescence and provide points for attentive reattachment. They augment continuing recognition of scenes we remember as well as facilitating our ability to repeat these scenes in subsequent rememberings. As the items that we recollect fill in the specific content of mnemonic presentations, so things fill out place memories by acting as their gathering-points, their main means of support. Things congeal the places we remember, just as places congeal remembered worlds—and as the present of remembering congeals the past remembered. *Things put the past in place; they are the primary source of its concrete implacement in memory.*

## IX

Despite the crucial importance of things in memories of place, it is only as positioned in relation to pathways and as situated within horizons that things assume their most fully determinative role. The interplay between all three factors is what helps to make place memories so potent a part of our memorial lives. A celebrated passage from *Remembrance of Things Past* brings out this interplay eloquently:

> As soon as I had recognized the taste of the piece of madeleine soaked in her decoction of lime-blossom which my aunt used to give me . . . immediately the old grey house upon the street, where her room was, rose up like a stage set to attach itself to the little pavilion opening on to the garden which had been built out behind it for my parents . . . and with the house the town, from morning to night and in all weathers, the Square where I used to run errands, the country roads we took when it was fine . . . in that moment all the flowers in our garden and in M. Swann's park, and the water-lilies on the Vivonne and the good folk of the village and their little dwellings and the parish church and the whole of Combray and its surroundings, taking shape and solidity, sprang into being, town and gardens alike, from my cup of tea.[82]

The "shape and solidity" of that special place called "Combray" are given to it by a diverse set of ingredients. These ingredients begin and end with things ("the taste of the piece of madeleine," "my cup of tea"); and they proceed through particular places in ever-increasing amplitude (from the pavilion giving on to the garden, and from Aunt Léonie's house to the town as it includes the Square, the local church, other houses, and the Vivonne river). Connecting all of these places within Combray are the pathways afforded by the streets of the town (Léonie's house is set "upon the street," a street eventually linking up with all other streets in the town and thus with the "country roads" leading outside of town as well). Acting as external horizon for "the whole of Combray" is the circumambient countryside, the "surroundings"; internal horizons are provided by the Square, the church tower, and Swann's estate. The concatenation of all these components contributes to making Combray a memorable place. Beyond furnishing focus and variegation, and a space in which free movement is possible, they transform what would be a sheer site—i.e., "Combray" as a mere location on a map of France—into a full-fledged place-of-provenance for memory. Horizons, pathways, and things bestow on Combray an abiding memorability for the narrator of the novel and for us as its readers.

Or recall in this connection the method of *loci* as employed in the classical "art of memory," a method in which, as we know, the establishing and revisiting of a grid of places (typically a house full of rooms or a street with many stopping points) is crucial. This technique is all the more impressive in that it may arise spontaneously—as happened in the case of "S.," the Russian mnemonist studied by Luria. S. used Gorky Street in Moscow as his underlying grid and deposited images (often in elaborate synesthetic formats) at various points along its length.[83] Quite apart from its actual utility, this mnemotechnique has the notable feature of combining the three elements which were under scrutiny in the last section. Pathways are present in the form of the routes which the memorizer takes in laying down the basic grid. Horizons are provided by factors as external as the city of Moscow or as intimate as the walls of the house whose rooms one is revisiting.[84] Things appear as the images—or rather, *in* the images—which have been devised as particular mementos of the items-to-be-remembered. These images are typically of human bodies or parts of bodies set forth in vivid, and even grotesque, poses; and as such they act to gather together, to harbor and preserve, the content to be remembered.[85]

Let us consider a final case in point, one which will allow us to observe the full panoply of traits that characterize place memories. This is the Chinese garden, about which Edwin T. Morris has written

> [it] was designed by highly cultivated individuals in such a way that a walk through the paths and arcades of its many sections would trigger reminiscences and images evoked from all aspects of the cultural tradition. Here a rock outcropping would kindle recollections of a famous mountain painting; there a few lines of calligraphy carved in stone would allude to a famous hermit who found solace in nature centuries before.[86]

Even in this cursory description of the Chinese garden, memory is very much at stake in the form of "reminiscences" and "recollections." Morris adds that "the visitor [to the Chinese garden] brought as much to the garden as he or she found there."[87] What is brought but the personal and the cultural past—and each as remembered? Remembering such pasts is elicited by the garden itself, that is, by a place whose constituent elements were designed "in memorable ways."[88]

Gardens of many kinds are conceived as intimately related to a surrounding landscape which they at once mirror and condense. This is especially true of the Chinese garden, which is designed as a microcosm of nature: "The garden is a miniature of China, transformed by the alchemy of the artistic spirit. In the garden we find represented all the great mountains, rivers and lakes, the soil, flora, and the dwellings of the people."[89] The very fact of the limited space in which Chinese gardens were set encouraged this effort at miniaturization: "A great emotional charge could be wrung from a garden that was only a few acres in physical space, but expansive in poetical space."[90] In contrast with "physical space" (i.e., sited space), "poetical space" is the space of memorable place, and it is constituted by allusions that draw specifically on memories: "Allusions were created everywhere, to stir memories already present, but dormant, in the breast of the onlooker."[91] The garden-as-microcosm, as a place within the poetical space of landscape, is thoroughly memorial. Just as a given garden would "borrow" a surrounding landscape by opening up vistas on it, so being in that garden would open up vistas of one's memory by engaging in evocations of the past.[92] Other means are used to underline the microcosmic nature of gardens: gardens within gardens, *bonsai* trees, and a sensitivity to seasons.[93] In other words, "the inclusion of all components of nature made it [into] a miniature world."[94]

The "diffused polycentrism"[95] of the Chinese garden draws on all of the factors that we have found to be essential to the memorability of place. To begin with, *expressiveness* of an explicitly emotional sort is built into a setting where the configuration of a given garden is evocative of prior experiences of being in certain landscapes (or viewing their representations in paintings). What gives to the garden experience its moving quality is not any factor of exact representation. It is the expressiveness with which it elicits memories of having been in (or seen represented) similar places. Likewise, the *sustaining character* of a garden is evident in its careful reinforcement of motifs by natural as well as by cultural means. If one is not already sustained enough by the physical entities in the garden, the written signs that are placed over doorways, inside pavilions, and on furniture afford further assurance that various pasts can be richly remembered.[96] Moreover, *variegation* was practically an obsession of the Chinese garden designer. Not only were gateways strenuously varied in name and shape—being vase-shaped, moon-shaped, fan-shaped, leaf-shaped[97]—but windows were asystematically different, both in terms of grillework and in terms of vistas offered. Staggered perspectives were employed to variegate vertical space;[98] and in the horizontal plane there was often a complex subdivision of space: the sixteenth-century Garden of the Unsuccessful Politician in Suzhou included no less than thirty-one sub-places, each with its own distinctive design.[99]

We also witness at work the three features singled out for discussion in section VIII. *Horizons* are a subdued but crucial presence in this polycentric circumstance. Given the walled-in character of most gardens, especially in urban locations, the horizons of a surrounding landscape are less perceived than adumbrated within a particular garden: e.g., through water-and-rock combinations that serve as miniature landscapes. What would otherwise remain literally external (i.e., in the space of sites) is here made interior to the internal horizons of the garden itself. These horizons are most decisively delineated by various walls, which establish north-south orientation as well as segmenting a given garden compound. "To have a garden without a wall is almost unthinkable,"[100] and the Chinese were masters of placing one wall before another in such a way as to simulate and exaggerate recession in depth. This multiplication of horizons helps to give a sense of ever-expanding space, all within an area whose actual extent may be quite modest.[101]

*Pathways* are important as well in the Chinese garden. A combination of covered arcades and open spaces maximize possibilities of movement. There is always more than one route which can be taken across a given expanse; and at any point on a given route there are striking views to be had: "While buildings frequently mark fixed vantage points for carefully composed views, the walkways and paths throughout the garden are planned for enjoying the landscape in a changing, or moving, focus."[102] In this way garden pathways become analogous to "the roads that appeared and disappeared in mountain painting."[103] Whether in a garden or in a painting imitated by that garden, pathways help to make landscape accessible from various points of view.[104]

A Chinese garden is also replete with *things* of many kinds—with buildings and plants, soil and stones. Yet these are never presented in such profusion as to confuse: there is a sense of abiding order, of clear space for rumination. Each thing in a Chinese garden counts, has its own fully accountable spot, within the perimeters provided by pavilions, terraces, and walls. This arrangement is not only aesthetically pleasing and conducive to meditation; it also gives rise to clarified remembering. Indeed, a Chinese garden is exemplary of what a well-ordered memory of place can become when brought outside the mind (where it had been confined in the art of memory)[105] and into the perceptual world. Its ingenious use of viewing-places—e.g., moon terraces or covered pavilions—invites the stroller to stop and contemplate groups of material objects as if they were items of a mnemonic presentation: which they may well become by this intense and lucid viewing. The structure of such a garden is memorial from beginning to end; memorable in itself as a privileged place to be, it also induces memories of other places one has known.

## X

I have been presenting the Chinese garden as exemplary of a place rendered acutely memorable by the employment of a number of memory-supportive factors. Their interaction results in a literal com-plication of the space of the garden, which cannot be adequately experienced in terms of what Whitehead would call "simple location." A simple location "does not require for its explanation any reference to other regions of space-time."[106] In vivid contrast with the separative aspect of simple locations is the "prehensive" character of space or time regarded as inclusive in scope, e.g., as exhibited in that bodily form of causal efficacy discussed at the end of the last chapter. In a world in which place is characterized by prehensions, one can say that

> everything is everywhere at all times. For every location involves an aspect of itself in every other location. Thus every spatio-temporal standpoint mirrors the world.[107]

Although Whitehead finds the perfect exemplification of this doctrine in the Romantic view of nature,[108] we could claim as much for the Chinese garden. In both cases the landscape world of nature is attained by a prehensive conception of place, whether this be the place of the poet or that of the solitary walker in the garden.

The implications for memory of place are crucial. Such memory cannot be based on the simple locations provided by sites; this would only lead to the very separatism in space which undermines effective remembering.[109] Instead, place memory calls for a radically inclusive notion of space in which the full landscape contexture of given places can be accounted for. As Rilke wrote to von Hulewicz, it is a matter of instating "what is *here* seen and touched within the wider, within the widest orbit."[110] Memory of place does just this by locating the particularities of place—"what is here seen"—within the "wider orbit" of a surrounding landscape.

This is not to claim that there is any exact parallelism between Chinese and Western conceptions of place in relation to memory. If we set aside Whitehead and the Romantic poets, we are left in the West with the tendency, steadily mounting since Descartes, to convert place-being into site-being. One concrete consequence of the encroachment of site on place has been the favoring of architectural space, especially architecturally modeled domestic space, as a privileged domain of memorability: Descartes meditating next to his stove is the progenitor of Proust writing in his cork-lined room. In China, by contrast, there has been a concerted search for an equilibrium between the architectural and the natural—between garden and landscape, indeed between constructed and organic elements within the garden itself. The equilibrium is sanctioned by an entire cosmology. For example, the combination of water and rocks in a garden represents the conjunction of Yin (soft, yielding, dark) with Yang (hard, resistant, bright):

> To understand how the Chinese garden works is to understand the Chinese view of the workings of the universe. According to the Chinese, the pairing of Yin and Yang concepts implies their very interdependence and interaction: their combinations and permutations guarantee infinite change as well as ultimate harmony in the universe.[111]

Such a view leads naturally to a preoccupation with microcosm/macrocosm parallels and to a special concern with varied means of representation as ways of achieving "a harmonious oneness through infinite metamorphosis."[112]

Post-Cartesian Western thinking does not seek any such ultimate harmony between microcosm and macrocosm. Instead of finding a *focus memorius* in gardens with their delicate complementarities, such thinking focuses on the house as an archetypal place for the most significant remembering. It is a revealing fact that Bachelard and Heidegger, both trenchant critics of space conceived as mere site, alike stress the space of inhabitation, of "building" and "dwelling." Heidegger's project of a "topology of Being" and Bachelard's strikingly similar notion of "topo-analysis" do not propose anything like a return to nature, nor do they intend an ideal state in which human dwelling and nature would exist in equilibrium. Heidegger's exemplary cases of things-as-locations are such decidedly artifactual objects as a jug and a bridge.[113] Bachelard defines topo-analysis as "the systematic psychological study of the sites of our intimate lives"[114]—where such "sites" are precisely houses, places of dwelling. Indeed, these manifestly non-natural locations are said to be the proper place-holders of memories:

> Thanks to the house, a great many of our memories are housed, and if the house is a bit elaborate, if it has a cellar and a garret, nooks and corridors, our memories have refuges that are all the more clearly delineated.[115]

In China the house opens onto the garden and is thus not a self-contained place of memory; being only part of a garden compound that is a microcosm of nature, its role in remembering is that of a vestibule and its memorial significance is quite literally marginal. In the Western world, where dwellings are so often closed off from nature,[116] it is therefore not surprising to be told that "the house is one of the greatest powers of integration for the thoughts, memories, and dreams of mankind."[117] In this perspective, *houses hold memories;* they are the primary exemplars of remembered places.

Precisely as self-enclosed, houses encourage memories in which intimacy is a leading value. Inhabited space brings with it what Bachelard calls "the being of within" and Frank Lloyd Wright "interior spaciousness."[118] In being remembered, each room, and each corner of each room, realizes an "intimate immensity":

> The topo-analyst starts to ask questions: Was the room a large one? Was the garret cluttered up? Was the nook warm? How was it lighted? How, too, in these fragments of space, did the human being achieve silence? How did he relish the very special silence of the various retreats of solitary day-dreaming?[119]

Here we are reminded of the silent memorizer, pursuing the ancient art of memory by introspecting the interior spaces of his remembered places—in contrast with the equally silent Chinese meditator, gazing directly onto nature from the Moon Terrace of his garden. If cosmological unity is realized spontaneously and with minimal assistance from architecture in the Chinese circumstance, it is only by a paradoxical twist that any comparable unity is achieved in the Western situation, where inhabited space is at once highly interiorized and heavily built-over. Even though such space is not attuned to landscape, it does give rise to a distinctive metaphysical unity of its own:

> It is through their [respective] 'immensity' that these two kinds of space—the space of [architectural] intimacy and world space—blend. When human solitude deepens, then the two immensities touch and become identical.[120]

This is not the place to pursue the precise ways in which Western architecture has attempted to enhance its own memorability.[121] These include a greater emphasis on perimeters and horizons than is typically found in Chinese gardens; less stress on pathways and more on various "liminal" regions such as doorways; and a more complex dialectical interplay between inside and outside. Despite such differences, one critical commonality between East and West nevertheless remains. Place memories of all kinds, however diverse they may be otherwise, require that the place remembered serve as an *enclosure* of some sort: as a reservative region. Even in the most disparate cultural settings, Aristotle's model of place-as-container remains deeply pertinent to the remembrance of place. In China the garden contains nature even as it mirrors it, and in this very capacity it is a privileged preserver of place memories. In Europe and America of the last three centuries, it is the domicile that has served as the primary container of memories of place. This is especially true of the childhood house, our first "home," itself often the subject of the most profound nostalgia. As Bachelard says in the wake of Proust:

> After we are in [a] new house, when memories of other places we have lived come back to us, we travel to the land of Motionless Childhood, motionless the way all Immemorial Things are. We live fixations, fixations of happiness. We comfort ourselves by reliving memories of [childhood] protection. *Something closed must retain our memories,* while leaving them their original value as images. Memories of the outside world will never have the same tonality as those of home.[122]

A house, especially one that has been our childhood home, is certainly not a simple location, for such a location cannot effectively contain memories. Instead, in its prehensive power, a house serves as an active enclosure for the most cherished—which is to say, the most intimate—memories of place.

## XI

Aristotle was right in another regard: "the power of place," as he said, is "a remarkable one." Even if place is not "prior to *all* things"—as Aristotle claimed, echoing Archytas—it certainly holds its own: and it holds its own (in) memories. Places are potently receptive and preservative of memories, which they hold to keep. As much as body or brain, mind or language, place is a keeper of memories—one of the main ways by which the past comes to be secured in the present, held in things before us and around us. In place, "the hold is held," for in places the presentment of memories occurs as their implacement in non-simple locations. If it is true that "what keeps us in our essential nature holds us only so long . . . as we for our part keep holding on to what holds us,"[123] then place is the primary scene in which we hold (onto) memories: we are beholden to them there, precisely to the extent that place itself is a holding power. Such is the dialectic of place memories: "They are as much in us as we are in them."[124] It is this dialectic that Straus describes as the interplay of the visible and the invisible in landscape. The same dialectic is at work in the ninth *Duino Elegy:* "Earth, isn't this what you want: an invisible re-arising in us? Is not your dream to be one day invisible? Earth! Invisible!"[125] It is in providing outward display for things and pathways as they exist within the horizons of landscape that places enable memories to become inwardly inscribed and possessed: made one with the memorial self. The visibility without becomes part of the invisibility within.

In closing this chapter, I wish to point to two concrete consequences of the foregoing analysis:

### THE INSUFFICIENCY OF RECOLLECTION

In recollection or secondary memory, place is at best a mere setting for the object or episode that is being remembered; it may not even figure in recollection's quasi-narrations, which can omit mention of place altogether. In short, recollection does not begin to do justice to the manifold ways in which place figures into human remembering. Nor does it adequately reflect the fate of body memory vis-à-vis place; just as the body moves us into place and orients us there, so body memories are often memories of body-in-place. Indeed, even such mnemonic modes as reminding and recognizing frequently imply implacement: we are reminded about doing X in situation Y, and we recognize person P in circumstance C—where "situation" and "circumstance" are both matters of place. It is evident, then, that the power of place exceeds what recollection—as well as other forms of remembering—can effectively encompass.

SPATIALITY VERSUS TEMPORALITY

Just as memory of place calls the exclusive priority of recollection into question, so it also brings us beyond a reliance on time as an exclusive medium for what we remember—that is, beyond the very thing which recollecting favors by its narratizing tendency. In particular, it reminds us of the centrality of space for much remembering. Body memory had already pointed in this direction in its position-taking capacity as well as in its kinesthetic dimension. Only in memory of place, however, are we enjoined to undertake a full-fledged topo-analysis of the spatiality of remembering. Precisely in contrast with psychoanalysis—which emphasizes diachrony and development in their interpersonal ramifications[126]—topo-analysis investigates the solitary experience of space: what it is to be, and to have been, in particular places rather than in particular times. In a great deal of remembering, this is a pervasive concern. We often remember ourselves in a given place; but how often do we remember ourselves as having been at a given date?

By its very immobility—through the stolid concreteness of things set within pathways and horizons—place acts to contain time itself. This is not to trivialize time but to make it into a dimension of space through the active influence of place. On the other hand, time *is* trivialized when it is reduced to calendrical-historical dates; and it is precisely memory of place that teaches us that

> to localize a memory in time is merely a matter for the biographer and only corresponds to a sort of external history, for external use, to be communicated to others . . . localization in the spaces of our intimacy is more urgent than determination of dates.[127]

If Bachelard is here correct about the nature of memory, not only is narratizing of secondary interest but the idea of remembering as re-experiencing the past is rendered moot, including Husserl's claim that "we can relive the present [even if] it cannot be given again."[128] Also contested is Heidegger's view in *Being and Time* that Dasein achieves authenticity only in a resolute repetition of its past. Could it be that authenticity lies instead in the very spatiality which Heidegger makes into a mere function of temporality?[129]

Throughout this chapter, we have witnessed what amounts to an elective affinity between memory and place. Not only is each suited to the other; each calls for the other. What is contained in place is on its way to being well remembered. What is remembered is well grounded if it is remembered as being in a particular place—a place that may well take precedence over the time of its occurrence. Thus it is certainly true that "memories are motionless, and the more securely they are fixed in space, the sounder they are."[130] But precisely where memory is at stake, to be fixed in space is to be fixed in place. If memories are motionless, this is the work of the places in which they come to inhere so deeply. In remembering "I can only say, *there* we have been: but I cannot say [just] where. And I cannot say, how long, for that is to place it in time."[131] To be there—to be truly *da-sein*—is to be in place, which cannot be reduced to site (the *just where*) any more than time can be shrunken to date (the *just when*). Being-in-place is a main modalization of being-in-the-world. Having been in places is therefore a natural resource for remembering our own being in the world. It is indispensable for knowing what we are (now) in terms of what we were (then).

> Footfalls echo in the memory . . .
> There rises the hidden laughter
> Of children in the foliage
> Quick, now, here, now, always—[132]

Memory of place implaces us and thus empowers us: gives us space to *be* precisely because we *have been* in so many memorable places, enjoyed such intimacy in them, known such pain there as well. If body memory moves us—is the prime mover of our memorial lives—it moves us directly into place, whose very immobility contributes to its distinct potency in matters of memory.

# X

# COMMEMORATION

> A miraculous acte, and worthie (in deede) of sempiternall remembraunce.
>
> —William Painter, *The Palace of Pleasure* (1569)

## I

> I rise early and rush to the town Green, arriving just in time to catch the beginning of the parade. With scores of other townspeople, I follow the marching bands and city officials eastward to the cemetery on Boston Street. After everyone is settled at the cemetery, prayers to the war dead are offered, a multiple gun salute explodes, and "taps" are played by a lonely bugler hidden among the gravestones. Somewhat subdued, I walk back with the crowd to the Green, pausing along the way to observe a magnificent bank of flowers that are flourishing on this late spring day. At the Green speeches are read by the First Selectman and the congressional representative from the local district. Following a benediction, the gathering disperses and the Green reverts to its usual somnolent state.

This is a description of a recent Memorial Day observance. It depicts an activity of commemoration. Commemoration? What is this? What is it doing in a book entitled *Remembering?* This last question is especially pointed in view of the fact that at no moment during the entire experience just described did I remember any single historical event—even though a number of such events were being commemorated on this occasion. Or more exactly, the occasion was designed to commemorate those who had "given their lives" in these events—all of them wars—and yet I was not remembering any of the war dead who were being honored: that is to say, I was not recollecting them in discrete scenic form. Indeed, I was not even thinking of them at all during most of the ceremony. I suspect the same mental vacuity obtained for many of my fellow citizens. But we were nevertheless commemorating and in this capacity engaging in remembering of a certain sort. What kind of remembering is this?

A crucial component of the answer to this question has to do with the role of *others*—my companions in commemoration. If I am remembering at all on such an occasion, I am remembering with them, and they with me. It is a matter of something thoroughly communal. Indeed, it is almost as if the absence of recollection on my part—and doubtless that of other individuals—was somehow being compensated for by an activity that occurred at the level of the group. We have certainly come a long way from Descartes's stove and Proust's study! Suddenly we are thrust headlong into a crowd of co-rememberers—into what Nietzsche might call disdainfully a "herd" or Heidegger "*das man*." And yet it is precisely in this unpropitious setting, in the company of others who are likely to be just as oblivious as I with regard to explicit remembrance, that remembering of a decidedly commemorative sort is going on. A strange situation perhaps, but one that arises fairly frequently in our lives, especially at crucial ceremonial moments.

In view of its recurrent importance, it is bizarre that we do not know more about the nature of commemoration. The very absence of recollective consciousness that may accompany its enactment leaves us in a vacuum—or at least a quandary. Where shall we turn for clues to the working of this "miraculous acte," in which we find ourselves unselfconsciously engaging without knowing what we are doing? Despite its importance, commemorating is among the most elusive forms of remembering, and it is surely the most recalcitrant to being understood on the model of straightforward recollecting. Even to approach it in a preliminary way is to be forced to pursue memory beyond mind—now further beyond mind than we have yet ventured in this Part. No wonder that it is rarely treated in books on memory, not even in such master works as James's *Principles of Psychology* or Husserl's *Phenomenology of Internal Time-Consciousness*. In Western philosophy and psychology alike, its fate has been to be ignored—to be as unknown as it was by me in attending an ordinary Memorial Day ceremony. Despite this neglect, commemoration remains "worthie (in deede) of sempiternall remembraunce." But how are we to comprehend its structure and operation?

## II

In this bewildering circumstance—in which we spontaneously accomplish an activity of remembering which we are not even certain we can confidently label *as* remembering—we are in desperate need of a *Leitfaden*, a guiding thread. One lies ready to hand in the fact that in its most ancient acceptation "commemoration" means an *intensified remembering*.[1] Further, two of its oldest meanings are the *deliverance of a formal euology* and *participation in a liturgical service* (wherein a "lesser feast" is observed by being included, in parts, in a "greater feast").[2] Taken together, these early senses of the word imply that in acts of commemoration remembering is intensified by taking place *through* the interposed agency of a text (the eulogy, the liturgy proper) and *in* the setting of a social ritual (delivering the eulogy, participating in the service). The remembering is intensified still further by the fact that both ritual and text become efficacious only in the presence of others, *with* whom we commemorate together in a public ceremony.

The "through," "in," and "with" that I have underlined suggest that commemoration is a highly mediated affair—that it involves a quite significant component of otherness at every turn. Neither the withness of the body nor the in-ness of place involved any comparable mediation. Body and place are things which we *are* or in which we find ourselves fully immersed: their density is not that of a medium but of an element in which we live and move and have our being.

How different is the situation in commemorating! On Memorial Day I found myself so completely with others, and so dependent on a given ritual and text, that I was taken out of my self-confinement as a body or a mind. So too I left the intimacy of my house, "my own place," to enter the public space of the ritual observance. Instead of contemplating the past in a private mental space or experiencing it "in my bones" in an almost equally private room, I attained my commemorative aim only via an interpolated ritual and text in the co-presence of others. All of these mediational factors or "*commemorabilia*" juxtaposed themselves *between* myself as commemorator and that which I was commemorating, the "*commemorandum*."

I commemorate, in short, by *remembering through* specific commemorative vehicles such as rituals or texts—or any other available *commemorabilia*. The "through" of commemorative remembering-through signifies such things as: through this very vehicle, within its dimensions, across its surface. For the past is made accessible to me by its sheer ingrediency in the *commemorabilium* itself. It is commemorated therein and not somewhere else, however distant in time or space the commemorated event or person may be from the present occasion of commemorating. For instance, one of the explicit *commemoranda* on Memorial Day is the First World War, which occurred some seventy years ago in forlorn trenches in France and was fought by soldiers whom I did not know, indeed could not have known, personally. Nevertheless, neither such distance in space and time nor such anonymity in identity detracts from the efficacy of commemoration as I and others now celebrate it on Memorial Day. The distance and the anonymity do not matter, thanks to the immanence of the *commemoranda* in the vehicles that sustain them. These vehicles make even the most alien presences available to me as a commemorator, and they do so in the only way that matters. *Through* the appropriate *commemorabilia* I overcome the effects of anonymity and spatio-temporal distance and pay homage to people and events I have never known and will never know face-to-face. The mystery of the matter—but also an insight into its inner working—resides in the way I remember the commemorated past through various commemoratively effective media in the present. It is as if this past were presenting itself to me translucently in such media—as if I were viewing the past in them, albeit darkly: as somehow set within their materiality.

Contrast this situation with that obtaining in recollection. When I succeed in retrieving the recollected past, it presents itself to me limpidly, as if through a transparent glass. No mediation, no otherness, is experienced as I seem to come back into immediate contact with what I am recollecting. Even if we have seen reason to doubt the real possibility of re-experiencing the past *per se*, it cannot be denied that it may *appear* to present itself *in propria persona* as a previously experienced scene flashes back before my memorious eyes (or ears). In secondary memory we often seem—or at least we would like it to seem—that we are holding up a looking glass to our own past. This impression (which may be, in fact, an ideal masquerading as an impression) of a transparent recapture of the past itself reflects the extraordinarily high valence which Western thinkers from Plato to Descartes and Husserl have placed on the criterion of *claritas:* especially the clarity that is achieved by the human mind in its most lucid moments, including those of recollective lucidity. Given the logocentric tendency to link *veritas* with *lux*, it is hardly surprising that recollection has been so prized as a paradigm of remembering. Nor is it surprising, by the same token, that commemorative remembering, in which the recollected past is veiled and sometimes even altogether absent, has received short shrift in prior assessments of human remembering. Insofar as commemorating is wedded to the dense translucency of remembering-through it does not bring its deliverances forward into what Husserl has revealingly described as "the brightly lit circle of perfect presentation."[3]

Not since we examined reminding in chapter 5 have we met with such mediation, such inherent indirection, such importance of the material medium. In that chapter we had to acknowledge the necessary role of an intermediary factor, i.e., the reminder itself. The latter interposes itself between the person being reminded and the remindand, that of which he or she is put in mind. It follows that both reminding and commemorating possess an essentially triadic structure. But there are two crucial differences between these forms of remembering. On the one hand, reminders, while often public in status, may be entirely private—as when I write notes to myself bearing on what I plan to do the next day. *Commemorabilia*, in contrast, are never wholly private, not even (as we shall see in detail later) when they are intrapsychic in nature: they are always trans-individual in their scope and function. On the other hand, a reminder always retains a certain instrumental bearing; it possesses the *zuhanden* structure of the 'in-order-to'.[4] If I write the letter "T" on the book mark in the novel I am reading so as to remind me to purchase tea tomorrow, this is done *in order to* motivate the future purchase. No such instrumentalism is present in a *commemorabilium,* which *embodies* the *commemorandum* rather than adumbrating it as still outstanding, still to be realized. It is precisely because what I commemorate has already entered a terminal stage that I can do nothing in the present but honor it by my commemorative activity.

This is not to deny the possibility of combining commemorating with reminding.[5] The postcard which my erstwhile student sent to me from the Acropolis had elements of both. In reminding me of "the glory that was Greece," it also commemorated this glory; the photograph of the Parthenon was at once a reminder adumbrating a vanished past and a *commemorabilium* embodying it in the materiality of the photographic medium. But even in such a hybrid case a critical distinction remains. Where the aim of reminding is fully satisfied by my mere perception of the postcard as it leads to the thought about Grecian glory, there is no comparable completeness of commemorating on the basis of this same postcard. As I stare at the photograph, I realize that something is lacking. The photographic image certainly honors the past of Athenian prowess; the mere fact of its inclusion on the postcard (and many others like it) pays homage to this past. Yet am I fully commemorating such a past as I gaze at the bare image before me? Clearly I am not. But why not? What is missing?

## III

What is missing has everything to do with remembering-through. The mute photographic image, while perfectly adequate as a reminder, is inadequate as a *commemorabilium*. It lacks throughness, that peculiar combination of a translucent medium and the power of conveying attention to the *commemorandum*. The conveyance is accomplished not despite the translucency—whose dimness is problematic only if we take the limpidity of recollection[6] as paradigmatic—but *by its very means*. While the unclarity of reminding resides in the adumbrative relation of a reminder to its remindand, the unclarity of commemorating is found in the very constitution, the actual materiality, of the commemorative vehicle itself. We could even say that the photographic image of the Parthenon, in its exact resemblance to this building, is *too clear* for commemorative purposes: it conveys this building (itself a symbol of faded Greek glory) too directly, leaving no significant unclarified remainder.

Commemorating thrives on indirection; it lives from unresolved, unimaged remainders; it is altogether a phenomenon of "restance." In being swept along by the Memorial Day parade, I was caught up in something I did not clearly grasp at all. Neither perceived images such as photographs nor the psychical images of recollections were present to me; and even had they been, they would not have been decisive in the attainment of commemoration on this occasion. Not even various body memories and place memories, important as they might be as conditions of commemorating, are sufficient by themselves in realizing the action. Once more, then, we must say: something else is called for. What can this be?

This something else, the very basis of remembering-through, is found in the mediation of ritual and text. Both of these were powerfully present in my Memorial Day experience. My movements with my fellow commemorators through a certain procession of ceremonial way-stations (i.e., Green–Boston St.–cemetery–return to Green) constituted a ritualistic action that is fixed and invariant from year to year—however seemingly casual it might appear to a non-participant. The texts that were read were equally essential; they articulated the solemn purpose of the occasion and set the honorific tone that prevailed throughout. Although I was not focusing on such ritual *as ritual* or on such texts *as texts*—nor was anyone else, save possibly the speakers—both factors served as crucial commemorative vehicles. As conjointly intensifying in effect, they added precisely what was missing in the image of the Parthenon: an image which, for all its resplendent clarity, was not a fully efficacious *commemorabilium*.[7]

Of the two main ways of realizing remembering-through—which is to say, the two primary forms of concrete *commemorabilia*—let us turn first of all to *ritual*. In contrast with place and its situating/stabilizing effect, ritual is a dynamic affair whose most determinative matrix is temporal rather than spatial. In comparison with text—which has its own, typically typographic stability, encouraging comparatively passive roles of listening and spectatorship—ritual is action-oriented and may even lack any specific form of notation. Ritual calls for direct participation by commemorators: the vicarious experience of the reader of texts cedes place to the direct involvement of the ritualist, whose commemoration is effected in the first person. The initial alienation of confronting a written text[8] gives way to an experience less dependent on a fixed medium such as print (or paint, stone, film images, etc.). Indeed, it gives way precisely to the body, which (as we have seen in its role in place memory) ties us in an intimate and non-alienating way to our immediate ambiance. For rituals are performed by bodily actions—actions that link us to our proximal environs by orienting us in them. This includes orientation with regard to fellow ritualists. While texts appeal to an indefinite and anonymous audience whose members typically do not know or even perceive each other, rituals entail bodily behavior that effects immediate interaction with (and direct perception of) other participants.

But what then is "ritual"? The word itself has expanded enormously in scope since its origin in *ritus* or "rite." It now includes such diverse phenomena as handshaking and shaving rituals, customs of many kinds, performative utterances (which, if not rituals themselves, are at least highly ritualistic: "I thee wed"), initiation rites and funeral rites, religious practices of numerous sorts, table manners and menus, Balinese cockfights and Spanish bullfights, etc.[9] The list could go on indefinitely in view of the ritualization of so much of human existence. The Chinese have long since recognized this fact in giving to all ritualistic behavior which is specifically humanizing the generic appellation "*li*."[10] Our task, however, is to delimit ritual so as to be able to grasp more perspicuously its commemorative dimensions. With this aim in mind, I shall exclude from consideration: those rituals enacted by individuals in a situation of isolation (e.g., rituals of the *toilette*, obsessive actions such as continual hand-washing, painters' rituals of preparations for painting, etc.); all those customs, habits, manners, and practices which are done unreflectively ("as a matter of course") and which cannot be said to honor an event or a person: e.g., eating rituals having to do with etiquette alone, sartorial practices (often a mere reflection of "fashion"), styles of handwriting, patterns and practices of driving a car, mowing a lawn, etc.;[11] and cyclical patterns of repetition in history—what Vico called "*ricorsi*"—whose scope exceeds not only individuals but entire collectivities as well.

What then is left which may count as rituals that are at least potentially commemorative in character? To begin with, an entire set of socially determined practices having as their minimal conditions an adequate time for reflection on the part of participants and an allusion, however indirect, to a pre-existing event or person. But such preliminary practices, even if essential, do not tell us much about rituals in their specifically commemorative aspect. Nor does the following definition offered by an anthropologist: "By 'ritual' I mean prescribed formal behavior for occasions not given over to technological routine, [but] having reference to beliefs in mystical beings or powers."[12] "Beliefs in mystical beings or powers" may well be commemorative in nature, but what matters for our purposes is the specific sedimentation of these beliefs in ritualistic actions. Consider the following example:

> It was the custom in Tanagra for the handsomest young man to walk around the city in the Hermes festival with a ram draped over his shoulders. The god himself, as the story goes, once freed the city from a pestilence by making the rounds in this way, and the ritual was established to commemorate this event.[13]

Here we certainly have "prescribed formal behavior" (the choice of the most attractive young man; the position of the sacrificial ram around his shoulders) on a non-technological occasion (what could be less technological than a Hermes festival?), along with a "reference to beliefs in mystical beings or powers" (i.e., a belief in Hermes himself and in his healing power). But the beliefs are wholly immanent in the ritualistic behavior, which honors Hermes by its enactment at the appropriate time and place. This enactment, the ceremony proper, does not simply presuppose a belief in Hermes-as-healer; it *embodies* the belief; and in so doing it affords the opportunity to reflect on Hermes in his healing capacity—a reflecting which, as enacted, is itself commemorative in character.

It is instructive to notice, however, that even when it acknowledges the mythical past of Hermes, such an act of reflection is hardly tantamount to a fully commemorative ritual. Two further fundamental factors are needed: the active role of the body and the collective character of the enterprise. Both of these elements are ingredient in the Hermetic example; the young man is forcefully ambulatory and his ritualistic walk is "around the city" at the time of a communally celebrated festival. As Otto remarks:

> The vision which the people of Tanagra saw was far from an hallucination. It was a mythic encounter which demanded that man give it concrete form by *using his own body* in ceremonial action. And with this the *community* came into contact with the sphere of the Divine.[14]

Ritual, as it contributes to commemoration, thus involves at least four formal features: an act of reflection or an occasion for such an act ("a mythic encounter" is precisely such an occasion since it gives rise to reflection); an allusion to the commemorated event or person (including a god or a mythical power) that precedes or sanctions the ritual itself (e.g., Hermes as a shepherd god who carried a ram on his shoulders); bodily action (here the perambulation of the handsome young man); and collective participation in the ritualistic action (e.g., in the form of perceiving and appreciating the significance of the young man's movements, which served as a focus for the coordinated actions of his fellow citizens).[15]

Beyond these four factors, we must consider three structurally specific features of commemorative ritual: solemnization, memorialization, and perdurance.

## Solemnization

According to the *Oxford English Dictionary*, commemorating is "a calling to remembrance, or preserving in memory, by some solemn observance, public celebration, etc.; 'solemnization of the memory of anything'."[16] "Solemnization" itself is defined as "the action of celebrating in a ceremonial manner." The first meaning of "solemnize" is "to dignify or honor by ceremonies; to celebrate or commemorate by special observances or with special formality,"[17] while the last meaning is literally "to make solemn; to render serious or grave." We may take a cue from these various definitions and say that *commemorating solemnizes by at once taking the past seriously and celebrating it in appropriate ceremonies*. Let us explore each of these subtraits separately:

### TAKING THE PAST SERIOUSLY

One can recollect, quite fully and successfully, in a spirit of insouciance or levity regarding that which one remembers. In certain situations one can even recollect *more* completely in such a spirit—that is, when one is just "going over" events in one's mind without allowing oneself to become involved, emotionally or otherwise, in this re-view. Also, a given part of the past may rise up before one's mind, unbidden and in a strictly spontaneous presentation. Contrast either of these situations with the circumstance of commemorating. In the latter, it is just because the past has been considered to be worthy-of-commemoration that we take it seriously. This taking seriously consists not in doting on the past or becoming morbidly preoccupied by it, but in acknowledging its importance to oneself or others. It is a matter of letting the past *matter*—of giving it its due weight, its full impact and import. Often this is accomplished by the way in which one rehearses past events to oneself, e.g., by carefully going over remembered content as when I ask myself, "Which summer did I go to Lindsborg with my grandmother?" Whenever I ask, "Did it really happen like that?" I am taking the past seriously, probing it, submitting it to scrutiny. But I need not actively examine it to let it matter: I can just let its content unfold before me and be its willing witness. In so doing, I do not have to be solemn in an affective sense; though I cannot be indifferent or dismissive, I can take the past seriously without having to assume a dour attitude: solemnization and humorless solemnity are by no means constantly conjoined.

### CELEBRATING IN APPROPRIATE CEREMONIES

Just as solemnizing is something more and other than acting in a dour way, so it is also more and other than rehearsing or reliving the past in one's own mind. Here commemoration moves us decisively beyond mind. In solemnizing, something distinctly extra-mental is involved: ceremonial observance. Such observance truly accomplishes solemnization, realizes it in its complete form, enacts it. It does so by bringing together these four factors:

*Repetitiveness in observance:*

There is no such thing as a ceremonial observance enacted once only; it must already have been enacted on previous occasions or allow for the possibility of future enactments, even if the form is not precisely the same throughout. Moreover, its own internal structure often includes repetitive elements: repetition-within-repetition.[18]

*Re-enactment of some former circumstance:*

This is itself a form of repetition but now in the specific sense of *reactualization,* that is, realizing again an anterior event or experience. Eliade's interpretation of myth emphasizes this aspect of ceremony. *Mythos* and ceremonial action alike are re-enactments of primordial (often cosmogonic) events posited at, or before, the beginning of human history: "Every religious festival, any liturgical time, represents the reactualization of a sacred event that took place in a mythical past, 'in the beginning'."[19] Thus a particular ceremony undertaken in concrete, worldly time (e.g., a dance), is "a repetition, and consequently a reactualization, of *illud tempus,* 'those days'."[20] We shall return to Eliade's general interpretation below. For now, we need only stress that the re-enactment is of something *significantly removed in time* (and often in space) from the scene of present observance. This very distance is crucial to commemoration, which aims at keeping a particular past event alive through ceremonial observance precisely because the increasing remoteness of this event from the here and now threatens its oblivion.

*Social sanction of the ceremony:*
Unless there is sanction of some kind by others, ritualistic action lacks a legitimation which it needs. It needs it because a private ceremonial, if possible at all, has a peculiarly deficient character vis-à-vis a more thoroughly social ritual which it reflects in truncated form. Thus, an obsessive ceremonial of continually washing one's hands is (in Freud's interpretation) only a condensed epitome of a much vaster religious ritual of collective atonement.[21] In fact "[ceremonial] performances . . . are phases in broad social processes, the span and complexity of which are roughly proportionate to the size and degree of differentiation of the groups in which they occur."[22] The "social processes" in question are not merely conditions of ceremonial observance but serve to sanction it—to legitimate what might otherwise seem to be a meaningless set of elaborate actions. The sanctioning is done by a subtle mixture of inculcated tradition ("this is the way it's always been done") and contemporary pressure ("this is how you must do it now"), with the result that the ceremonialist does not have to offer any further justification to herself or to others.

*Formality:*
This is a final feature of ceremonies. It can occur in terms of words, bodily gestures, or interactions with others—often all three. Also contributing to formality is repetition itself, which aids in making a formal structure into a coherent and well-articulated whole.[23] If social sanction provides a reason for a given ceremony, formality furnishes its rhyme. Formality is often aesthetic in its appeal to (and its hold on) the participants in a ceremony or the spectators of it, the felt perfection of the form contributing forcefully to the total experience. At the same time, formality serves to express and specify emotion while channeling any tendency to excess.[24] The formality of ritual solemnizes the expression of emotion on the occasion.

Taken together, the foregoing four features effect the ceremonialization inherent in commemoration qua solemnization: *commemorating solemnizes by communalizing in a ceremony*. Such communalizing is crucial, since taking the past seriously (the other root of solemnification) is unable by itself to achieve solemnization in any strict sense. In fact, nothing effected by oneself alone is adequate to the task of commemoration. As the "com-" of "commemorate" indicates, and as is also evident in the archaic synonym "commemorize," commemorating is an essentially *inter*personal action. It is undertaken not only in relation *to* others and *for* them but also *with* them in a common action of communalizing—as I witnessed on Memorial Day.

This situation is to be compared with that of reminiscing, which can take place in private and yet still be quite complete. In chapter 6 we saw that co-reminiscing, while paradigmatic in many ways, is not indispensable to all reminiscing. Moreover, while putting the past into words is basic to reminiscence, this verbalization does not require an explicitly interpersonal context: reminiscential discourse can occur as a "dialogue of the soul with itself." In commemorative ceremonializing, in contrast, the presence of others is explicit and (normally) experienced as such: especially in ceremonial behavior, wherein oneself and others are interinvolved in the same commemorative drama. *Commemoration comes to completeness in the co-action and compresence of ceremony.*

## Memorialization

Ceremonies are not only undertaken and enacted; they are *celebrated*. In this context "celebration" connotes not only an affirmation of there being, or one's having, such a past as is being commemorated, but above all an honoring of this past, a paying homage to it. Honoring itself consists in at least two closely co-ordinated actions:

### PAYING FITTING TRIBUTE

This is honoring in an appropriate way, not only with the right words, gestures, or other symbolic expressions, but more importantly in *the proper proportion*, that is, without either exaggeration (as in a grotesquely oversized monument) or diminution (e.g., in an implicitly demeaning eulogy). The fittingness has several parameters: language certainly ("sensitive words"), but also place (i.e., a suitable location), circumstance (the right occasion), and time (the right "timing" of the memorial's institution or expression).

### PAYING TRIBUTE IN A LASTING WAY

Honoring can be done in quite indirect and even casual forms—as when the mere mention of someone's name in a conversation amounts to honoring: "he's certainly a diligent worker all right"; "that was a brilliant article of hers," etc. But honoring in a full-bodied way requires more than passing praise. It seeks to *preserve* and *stabilize* the memory of the honoree, and to do so in a time-binding, invariant manner. The explicit aim is to maintain this memory in the face of the corrosive action that laid Ozymandias low: "Nothing beside remains, round the decay/Of that colossal wreck, boundless and bare/The lone and level sands stretch far away."[25]

In view of such a concern with lastingness, it is not at all surprising to discover that many memorials are constructed of stone, the most durable natural substance available in large quantities. The very hardness and hardiness of granite or marble concretize the wish to continue honoring into the quite indefinite future—and thus, by warding off the ravages of time, to make commemoration possible at any (at least foreseeable) time. At the same time, a memorial in stone—a tombstone, a memorial plaque, a sculpted figure, etc.—is a public presence and hence accessible to many potential viewers. *The distension in time is matched by a comparable extendedness in space*.

Such permanency need not, of course, be sought in stone alone. It can even be pursued by the use of materials which in themselves are quite perishable and subject to decay. A memorial volume, for example, will last no longer than the paper on which it is printed. Yet what this kind of memorial lacks in temporal obduracy, and even in the actual volume of space it occupies,[26] is compensated for by its considerable accessibility to the many who can own individual copies of it. One must travel to the site of the stone memorial to be in its material presence; but a mere photograph of the same memorial, or its description in words, will convey its represented presence to those who cannot visit the original site. It is as if the expanded propagating power of the image or word counterbalanced the more imposing presence of the monument itself.

Memorialization through ritualized activity shares with stolid monuments an attachment to place, being enacted in an appropriate (or at least acceptable) arena of action. But it is like a memorial volume in allowing many to participate in its commemorative function—not as isolated spectators but as conjoined participants acting together. Moreover, this "together" is strictly spatio-temporal; a given ritual brings together its enactors *during* one time as well as *at* one place, a time and place of shared assembly. Memorializing is accomplished—the past is concretely honored—by *taking action together*. Rather than paying tribute in one's mind by recollection, or in conversation by reminiscence, one creates a common object. This object, however, has neither the mute visibility of the monument nor the articulate fixity of a text—only the sun, remarks Wordsworth, reads the epitaphs on gravestones. At once perceptual in status and accessible in principle, the ritual is a strictly composite object; it is the conjoint creation of its participants.

This occurs strikingly in the case of a funeral, often revealingly labeled a "memorial service." Here textual and paratextual elements—printed programs (formerly termed "funeral broadsides"), eulogies, somber music—are encompassed within the movement of the ritual itself. Essential to this latter is the fact that those who are in attendance form a momentary community of co-mourners; they are com-memorators bound together by the common aim of honoring the deceased. However silent and unspontaneous their actions may be—to the point of seeming stultification, as if to mimic the sealed silence of death itself—these actions represent a memorialization undertaken *in concert* and in a dynamic mixture of space and time. Hence the power of a funeral service to deeply move those who are present. At the same time, it acts to ensure the continuing memory of the deceased in the minds and lives of the mourners. No less than in the case of a monument or a text, memorialization via ritual strives to effect lastingness.

## Perdurance

"Perdurance" is the concrete form assumed by the lastingness aimed at in memorialization. Perduring itself is a neglected temporal mode that has received scant attention in Western thought. The reason for this neglect doubtless lies in the fact that reflection on time has focused on the extremities of "time" and "eternity." Eternity connotes an intelligible, wholly fulfilled order of being, while time, in contrast, signifies something degenerate, fleeting, and opaque to intelligence. Indeed, time may come to be regarded as the mere "image" of eternity, its "moving likeness *(eikon)*" in Plato's phrase.[27] Beginning with such a dichotomy as this, one inevitably expends a great deal of effort trying to reconcile, or at least to relate, such disparate modes.[28]

Perdurance represents a *via media* between eternity and time. If it is something less than what the ancient Greeks (thinking of the regular epicycles of the heavenly bodies) called the "everlasting" or the Medievals (thinking of angels) the "sempiternal," it is also something more than duration as defined by Locke: "the distance between the appearance of any two ideas *in our minds*."[29] This latter view commits us to a mentalism that is the mere mirror-opposite of Greek cosmologism. Nor does mere continuancc in time—such as we find in Dilthey's idea of "the connectedness of life [in human history]"—do justice to the notion either. For sheer temporal continuity is representable only as a line connecting two datable now-points: "duration is but as it were the length of one straight line, extended *in infinitum*."[30]

In *Being and Time* Heidegger attempted to re-interpret duration by reference to Dasein's actively "stretching itself along" in history.[31] Later, he introduced the factor of "lasting," which I take to be essential to perdurance:

> To presence *(Wesen)* means to last *(Währen)*. But we are too quickly content to conceive lasting as mere duration, and to conceive duration in terms of the customary representation of time as a span of time from one now to a subsequent now. To talk of presencing *(An-wesen)*, however, requires that we perceive biding and abiding in lasting as lasting in present being *(Anwähren)*. What is present concerns us, the present, that is: what, lasting, comes toward us, us human beings.[32]

What lasts has permanence:[33] at least insofar as it "comes toward us." A cultural tradition is a case in point: it lasts, has an ongoing "effective-history," precisely insofar as it comes toward us and engages us (and we it) in that activity of mutual encounter called "interpretation." Perdurance is *enduring-through* such an encounter, and it is the most characteristic temporal form of a ritual transmitting a tradition.

Other perduring matters include natural languages and currency systems, various habits and tendencies, world-historical or metaphysical "epochs" as well as strictly local customs and mores. What all such concrete cases of perdurance share is a combination of sameness or permanence over time with a capacity to modify or evolve.[34] Between the fixity, the sheer ever-the-sameness of eternity, and the ceaseless flux of transient temporality (wherein all is ever-the-other), there is the perduring, providing sameness and difference, motion and rest, *at the same time* and not just in succession.

It is hardly surprising to discover that ritual—itself such a decisive *tertium quid* in human affairs[35]—exhibits perdurance as its own main temporal mode. This is evident, for example, in Confucius's summation of the ancient *Odes* as teaching us the lesson of "not swerving from the right path."[36] Where Lucretius makes swerving or *clinamen* the very principle of creativity in the otherwise unproductive universe of atoms moving in straight lines,[37] swerving from the straight lines of *li*—from the human universe of ritual—is unproductive inasmuch as it undermines the perduringness of ceremonies enacted and re-enacted over generations. Not swerving from a tradition is what allows it to *last*—not just to come *down to* the present but, as Heidegger suggests, to come *toward* it actively.

Nevertheless, just as perduring does not require simple continuance of the self-identical (which would amount to the stasis of eternity—or to death), so the non-swerving of a tradition-based ritual is compatible with modification and innovation within its formal structures.[38] Here, as elsewhere, it is a matter of what Confucius calls "the spirit of the rites."[39] For what matters in the performance of rites is the manner in which they are conducted.[40] Conduct makes manifest the spirit of ritualized activity which, without this spirit, falls into the emptiness of bare repetition. It also helps to make ritual genuinely perduring, and therewith more readily rememberable and more lastingly memorable.

Perdurance, thus construed, can be considered the main means by which the temporality of memoralization is achieved. What in the individual is divisive and diasporadic (thanks to the effects of succession in time) becomes, in and through the perdurance realized by ritual, consolidating (in oneself) and conterminous (with others). In fact, the commemorating that is accomplished by a memorializing ritual is an especially efficacious remedy against time's dispersive power.

Furthermore, it is through perdurance that the past, present, and future dimensions of commemorative ritual are at once affirmed and made compatible with each other. In the lastingness achieved by such ritual the past to which tribute is being paid is allowed to perdure—to last as coming toward us—through the present of the commemorative act and onward into the future as well. Or more exactly:

(1) The *past* figures as the primary temporal locus of the *commemorandum*. Whatever its precise position in world-time, and whether it is dated as such, the pastness is indispensable: we do not memorialize *in* the present what is happening *at* present. A time-lapse of some significant sort is needed if we are truly to pay tribute by memorialization. Moreover, part of what we honor by memorializing the past is the sheer fact of the survival of its memory in the present. The memorial action seeks to enshrine and to perpetuate this same survival.

(2) The *present* forms part of memorialization in two ways. First, it is always and only in the present that we pay homage to the past; there is *no other time* for the ritualistic enactment of memorializing. Second, the ritual is itself devised to command our attention and bodily activity. Not unlike the grimly admonishing skulls on early New England gravestones—which are literal *memento mori*[41]—commemorative rituals draw in their participants by salient features dramatically displayed in the present: an open casket, a ram carried on a young man's shoulder, a moving melody.

(3) The *future* is also implicated in a dual capacity. On the one hand, it is emblematic of the very survival which the ritual seeks to encourage in the present: by its sheer recurrence it points to a future that may well postdate the demise of present participants. On the other hand, a genuinely commemorative ritual is exhortatory in nature; it calls to us from a certain indefinite future as if to say: "I will be constant in my own permanency; will you, in ritualistic recognition of this, be constant in your commemoration of what I honor?" It also calls to others, yet unborn, who will hopefully draw inspiration from the same ritual as it comes to be re-enacted.

That all three temporal *modi* of perdurance are operative in memorialization is evident in the text inscribed on a Civil War monument located on the same Green that figured in my opening example in this chapter:

IN MEMORY OF
THE MEN OF GUILFORD
WHO FELL
AND IN HONOR OF THOSE WHO SERVED
IN THE WAR OF THE UNION
THE GRATEFUL TOWN ERECTS THIS MONUMENT
THAT THEIR EXAMPLE MAY SPEAK TO COMING GENERATIONS

Here the tenses or aspects say it all: "fell/served" (past); "erects" (present); "may speak to" (subjunctive in allusion to the future). But they say it *in a text*, not a ritual. What kind of difference does this make? What is the role of texts in commemorative actions?

## IV

That full commemoration occurs by ritual alone might seem to follow from Eliade's view that the point of commemorative ceremonies is to achieve "reactualization" of an act of cosmic creation.[42] In this view, such ceremonies aim at "collective regeneration through repetition of the cosmogonic act."[43] Insofar as the cosmogonic act itself is not textual, its repetition in ritual would not have to be textual either: the wordless Ur-act of creation would seem to call for an after-act, a re-enactment, that is equally wordless. Yet Eliade himself avers that any ritualistic reactualization of "the atemporal instant of primordial plenitude" is always a "symbolic return."[44] A symbolic return must include the possibility of a return through language and not through bodily action alone. Indeed, one of Eliade's own leading examples of a repetition of a cosmogonic event in *The Myth of the Eternal Return* involves words centrally. Io, a supreme god among the early Polynesians, creates the world by *saying* "Ye waters of Tai-Kama, be separate. Heavens, be formed!"[45] As a consequence:

> The words by which Io caused light to shine in the darkness are used in the rituals for cheering a gloomy and despondent heart, the feeble aged, the decrepit; for shedding light into secret places and matters. . . . For all such the ritual includes the words (used by Io) to overcome and dispell darkness.[46]

But we need not have recourse to such an exotic source as this to appreciate the role of texts in acts of commemoration. In one form or another, a text figures even in the most quotidian cases of commemoration. My Memorial Day experience included speeches, invocations, and a benediction. Funeral services make use of eulogies, prayers, and sometimes printed programs—not to mention reminiscences shared among the mourners. One of the most complete commemorative events still extant is the celebration of the Eucharist, which provides a subtle and elaborate blending of written and spoken liturgy ("Take this in remembrance of me") with bodily action (e.g., the ingestion of wine and bread). Even the granite Civil War Memorial on the Guilford Green is far from mute: its inscribed stony surface still speaks to us today. Indeed, everywhere we look we find ritualistic acts—and stolid monuments—intimately conjoined with words.

The presence of a textual element in so much commemorative activity does not mean that it is unproblematic in status. Is it simply subordinate to ritual, as occurs when words serve only to introduce or conclude a commemorative ceremony? Does it displace or replace the ritualistic factor—as seems to happen when a commemorative ceremony becomes largely or entirely formulaic, e.g., the singing of "The Star-Spangled Banner" in rote fashion at the beginning of sporting events? Does it complement ritual, matching word with action—as occurs so saliently in the finely balanced performance of the Eucharist? Does it supplement ritual, either in the straightforward sense of adding on something that is otherwise missing (e.g., the precise naming of otherwise anonymous soldiers fallen in war) or in Derrida's more radical sense of being the very condition for that which it is supplementing?[47] In differing degrees and on different occasions, *all of these alternatives obtain*. This is true even of the last, most extreme alternative. One way of construing a funeral service, for instance, is to view it as the radical supplementation of death itself by words proffered in honor (and in place) of the deceased. Commemorative language not merely replaces the loss effected by death; it is a substitute for death that allows death to come forward *as* death—as when a moving eulogy brings home to mourners the full impact of the loss they must now sustain. Much the same situation obtains in the chanting of mantras in Tantrism: "mantra" has the same root as "memory" and is itself a commemorative act. Not only does the chanting of a given mantra take over from bodily action—an action reduced to a non-moving position of meditation—but in its scope and significance this chanting conditions bodily action of any kind, including that which is explicitly ritualistic.

Extreme as such cases might seem—and apart from any vindication of Derrida's grammatological theses—they point to a central issue in any consideration of commemoration. This is the indispensability of language or "text" in the broadest sense.[48] It is striking that the very first definition of commemoration in the *Oxford English Dictionary* is "the action of calling to the remembrance of a hearer or reader." This implies that there is no commemoration without calling, which occurs in and through language.

Recall the leading features of ritual as I discussed it in the last section. How could there be such a thing as "an allusion to the commemorated event or person" without the mediation of language? How would "collective participation" arise if not by means of a language shared by all participants and a text that prescribed their conjoint actions (e.g., *The Book of Common Prayer*, which sets forth the appropriate actions of commemorators in the Eucharist)? Indeed, how could there be solemnization without a solemnizing formula or text that not merely sets the tone of a celebrative ceremony but furnishes both point and purpose to such a ceremony? Can we adequately memorialize without a text of some sort? What would it mean to "pay tribute" without the tribute itself being stateable in language? Is not even perdurance most effectively achieved in and by a text?

What I am suggesting is that the remembering-through that lies at the basis of commemorating is always a remembering through a text. The text itself may be merely implied or tacit on a given occasion, for example, when the melody of "The Star-Spangled Banner" is played. But at whatever remove the text exists and in whatever guise it is found, when we do commemorate we do so through a verbal medium. Language is intrinsic to the otherness that is part and parcel of all commemorating; it is uneliminable from its mediational nature. It is also at one with its irredeemably social aspect: the "com-" of com-memoration is inseparable from what I called the "communal-discursive" factor in my discussion of reminiscing. In being inescapably communal, commemoration is at the same time discursive: that is to say, a matter of language, dependent upon language, taking place *through* language.

It follows that there is no purely ritualistic commemorating if by "ritualistic" is meant occurring by bodily movements alone. Although I considered the ritualistic element of commemoration in isolation from any verbal factor in section III, this was at best a provisional move in which I prescinded from the role of language. "Ritual" henceforth must include text as well as bodily action if it is to be adequate to the complex tasks of commemoration.

A more radical line of questioning opens up here. Could it be that in its communal-discursive aspect commemorating forms part of *all* remembering? If so, this would imply that *there is no remembering of any kind that is not in some sense verbal or verbally-based:* if not occurring expressly *in* language, then arising *through its agency*. Just as commemoration is a calling to remembrance through language—through ritual-cum-text, ritual *as* text—so memory is indeed a matter of "re-call." Might it even be that recollection, seemingly dependent upon images alone, occurs as re-collection through language? Can there be such a thing as a purely renascent image that counts as a memory—or a purely bodily action that counts as a commemoration—without the intervention of words at some significant stage?

Whatever the answers to such questions may be, it is evident that certain kinds of commemorating are more text-bound than others. This is due to the fact that they employ texts more centrally in their enactment and show vividly the effects of these texts in their result. The effects include a greater specificity of reference (i.e., a more exact articulation of the *commemorandum*), a larger audience of co-commemorators in principle (thanks to the virtually unlimited range of a text's potential dissemination), and a greater freedom from a given material medium. This last property is especially noteworthy. Whereas the strictly ceremonial aspects of commemoration require bodily movements of a certain sort and could not take place without them, the textual aspects can be conveyed in any of several ways: by printing or speaking out loud, by words on a tape, or even by skywriting. But some particular material vehicle remains requisite in every case; the articulateness of the wording on a given occasion, including its elegance of style, in no way transcends the concreteness of the *commemorabilium* in which the wording is embodied. While alleviating what might otherwise be an almost complete opacity of a commemorative medium such as unsculpted and uninscribed stone, a text never succeeds in making this medium fully transparent: it remains translucent at best. For instance, the addition of the proper names beneath the gigantic heads of American presidents at Mt. Rushmore might make the commemoration effected by these megaliths less likely to be misidentified by unknowledgeable spectators. But it would not overcome the obdurate density of the sculpted images themselves, which commemorate efficaciously in the eloquent silence of their stony stares.[49]

At the opposite extreme from such petroglyphic muteness are cases of commemoration that can be considered entirely textual. In addition to the mantras alluded to above, there are whole texts that are commemorative in character. These include autobiographies, biographies, and historical memoirs. Poetry can also be quite fully commemorative, whether directly (e.g., Stevens's "To an Old Philosopher in Rome") or indirectly (e.g., Eliot's "The Wasteland"). One of the most striking examples of sheerly textual commemoration is found in the *Analects*, which at first does not appear to be commemorative at all. Supposedly by Confucius, this text was in fact written by his disciples in an act of collective commemoration. Practically all of its passages, even those that are not engaged in directly quoting "the Master," can be said to be commemorative of Confucius. Of Confucius in what respect? Not of him as a historical personage but as someone possessing an unrivaled practical wisdom. His sagacity is the true subject of the commemoration, and it is specified as a *commemorandum* by citing appropriate aphorisms:

> The Master said, "In his errors a man is true to type.
> Observe the errors and you will know the man."[50]

As in the case of Socrates, the commemorative vehicle is constituted by the Master's originally spoken words, words which in their condensed written transcription embody the very wisdom they recommend.

A second kind of *commemorandum* is also present in the *Analects*. This is an entire *tradition*—that is, something massively collective. For Confucius conceived himself not as an original thinker but as a "transmitter" of the tradition begun in the Chou dynasty and disintegrating in his own time. In particular, he wished to preserve the insights contained in the "Six Classics," which stemmed from that earlier period. He is thus *cited citing* from these revered books:

> The Master said, "The *Odes* are three hundred in number.
> They can be summed up in one phrase,
> Swerving not from the right path."[51]

As Fung Yu-lan says in this connection: "Confucius was 'a transmitter and not a creator, a believer in and lover of antiquity' (*Analects* VII, 1). What he transmitted was the Chou civilization."[52] Where Socrates set out to dispute existing traditions, Confucius sought to honor the Chou tradition, offering exemplary actions and sayings as vehicles *through which* it could be remembered. These actions and sayings are therefore *commemorabilia* in their own right, since they commemorate the Chou tradition even as they convey it. This outcome is not incompatible with the fact that most readers of the *Analects* take the text to be only secondarily a celebration of Chou wisdom or the Six Classics. Primarily the book is taken as setting forth the wisdom of Confucius himself. In being commemorated by Confucius, the Chou tradition is less *represented* in the text than *embodied* there, becoming so fully immanent in the cited words of the Master as virtually to dissolve as a separate entity. This tradition is thereby commemorated in a curiously indirect or submerged way: through the very words through which, in turn, we as readers commemorate Confucius. Commemoration is redoubled by means of this adroit textual remembering-through.[53]

Most cases of commemoration lie somewhere between the taciturnity of Mt. Rushmore and the articulateness of the *Analects*. They are frankly hybrid in status. Sometimes they mix images with text: e.g., in painted icons bearing an attached text and in quilts that depict an object while also describing it in words. More often, however, the hybridization is composed of ritualistic bodily actions combined with texts: as in funeral services, the celebration of the Eucharist, and Memorial Day parades. In fact, almost every public ceremony that is commemorative in character brings together the impelling corporeal movements of the participants with the equally urgent authority of a text. This becomes evident when we think of the observance of a public holiday, which carries with it a factor of proclamation and a feature of festivity. The 4th of July is routinely celebrated with official pronouncements on the one hand (e.g., a "special message" by the president) and with picnics and fireworks on the other. Each signifies "Independence Day"; or more exactly, the two together embody the Day: in the one case, by an apposite text, in the other, by ritualistic forms of action. In this composite way, American independence from Britain is remembered through two *commemorabilia* that are at once concretely instantiated and conjointly realized. (By "conjointly realized" I mean both the co-ordinate action of text-*cum*-ritual and the thoroughly public character of the occasion.) On this occasion and many others like it, the sociality of the observance is rendered all the more effective by occurring in two registers, ritualistic and textual—registers that together act to extend the scope (and hopefully to improve the quality) of the commemoration thereby effected.[54]

## V

We have been encountering the deeply communal and communalizing character of commemoration at every turn: most overtly on public holidays but just as importantly at private funerals, in the celebration of the Eucharist, and in the words of Confucius. Whenever commemorating occurs, a community arises. Not only is something communal being honored, but the honoring itself is a communal event, a collective engagement. What are the roots of this common enterprise? On what is it based?

A clue is furnished in Van Gennep's idea that there are three phases in every significant rite of transition: separation, margin, and aggregation.[55] Each of these phases is found in the Eucharist. "Separation" involves purification, which we observe in the placement of the "Confession of Sin" *before* the act of communion: the worshipper needs to be properly penitent before receiving the sacraments. From the separation which such penitence implies one can move to a "marginal" state—as in that state of readiness for communion which is expressed concretely by the communicants' movement together to the edge or threshold of the altar, where one spatial margin (that of the domain of the celebrants) becomes contiguous with another (that of the communicants). "Aggregation" follows as the formation of an ongoing community of worshippers who will continue to practice the Eucharist when together (or even, remembering each other, when apart).

Looking at the eucharistic ceremony in this three-stage manner has the effect, however, of keeping the phase of marginality apart from community: as if the latter were to be achieved only after the attainment of the former. In fact, there is reason to believe that the two are much more closely conjoined than this peremptory application of Van Gennep's phase analysis suggests. If we consider more closely the constituent features of the marginal period as this occurs in rituals of many kinds, we begin to suspect that, far from being precommunitarian, it possesses its own form of community. The anthropologist Victor Turner supports this line of thought by his research into the relationship between the marginal phase or "liminality" and community. As something "essentially unstructured (which is at once destructured and prestructured),"[56] liminality in Turner's view resists facile unifications by virtue of its paradoxical combination of the no-longer and the not-yet, the living and the dead. People who are in liminal states such as those undergone by initiates

> are at once no longer classified and not yet classified. In so far as they are no longer classified, the symbols that represent them are, in many societies, drawn from the biology of death, decomposition, catabolism. . . . The other aspect, that they are not yet classified, is often expressed in symbols modeled on processes of gestation and parturition. . . . The essential feature of these symbolizations is that the neophytes are neither living nor dead from one aspect, and both living and dead from another. Their condition is one of ambiguity and paradox, a confusion of all the customary categories.[57]

Further contributing to the ambiguity and paradox is a characteristic role reversal. The chieftain-to-be in the Ndembu tribe is reviled and humiliated during the liminal period before he assumes office: "Be silent! You are a mean and selfish fool, one who is bad-tempered! You do not love your fellows, you are only angry with them! Meanness and theft are all you have!"[58] In the pre-installation ceremony, the chief-elect wears only a worn-out waist-cloth and must sit with one of his wives in a posture of shame and servility. Given this circumstance, it is evident that liminal persons "have no status, property, insignia, secular clothing indicating rank or role, position in a kinship system."[59] They are in a limbo of non-being and non-distinction; they are dispossessed and disoriented.[60]

What makes otherwise painful and senseless liminal experiences sustainable are two closely related functions which they serve: commemoration and the creation of community. The commemoration is effected via the tradition that prescribes the forms of liminality itself. The submissiveness that is exacted of the initiate is finally submissiveness to this tradition conceived as a "total community."[61] In following the injunctions of the ceremony, the initiate is in effect commemorating all those who, anonymous as they may be, have been responsible for giving to these injunctions their present shape and sequence. The purified state of the neophyte—which is analogous to the confessed mind of the communicant—is maximally receptive of tradition and ready to commemorate it.[62] Sometimes, indeed, the commemoration is explicit—as occurs in the same Ndembu ceremony cited above. When the chastened chief-to-be emerges from his confined state, a subchief offers the following prayer:

> Listen, all you people. Kanongesha [the new chieftain] has come to be born into the chieftainship today. This white clay [*mpemba*], with which the chief, the ancestral shrines, and the officiants will be annointed, is for you, all the Kanongesha of old gathered together here. [Then the ancient chiefs are mentioned by name.] And, therefore, all you who have died, look upon your friend who has succeeded [to the chiefly stool], that he may be strong. He must continue to pray well to you. . . . The chieftainship has appeared.[63]

Here the theme of rebirth from the commemorated person(s) is as expressly stated as in the Eucharist, wherein the communicants are spiritually reborn through their incorporation into Christ. Still more generally, we can say that both ceremonies illustrate the principle that *commemoration, in honoring the past, revivifies the present,* giving it a new birth—whether of a political or of a spiritual nature.

But such renascence of the individual participant in commemorative rituals can only occur in the presence of others who form with him or her a special form of community. One of the primary meanings of the Ndembu liminal ceremony of enforced abstemiousness is the setting aside of "private and privative wishes"[64] so as to join together with others in the formation of what Turner calls "*communitas*." In the case of the Ndembu ceremony, such *communitas* is implicit in these words spoken by "Kafwana" to the expectant chieftain:

> We have granted you chieftainship. You must eat with your fellow men, you must live well with them. . . . Do not be selfish, do not keep the chieftainship to yourself: You must laugh with the people. . . . You must not be ungenerous to people![65]

It is striking that the most concrete activity here recommended is to "eat with your fellow man"—which is just what happens in the ingestion of eucharistic sacraments. In such shared activity of incorporation, the injunction to "live well with [others]" is most concretely realized. Moreover, the common partaking of food and drink acts to suspend rigid distinctions of rank and status that obtain in society at large. In a *communitas,* where unity is less important than fellowship, all who come are welcome. This is the situation in the eucharistic ceremony, to which all are welcome whatever differences of class or education obtain otherwise. As much as the Ndembu ceremony so tellingly described by Turner, the rite of the Eucharist offers a blend of "lowliness and sacredness, of homogenity and comradeship."[66]

It is the liminality of both ceremonies that fosters *communitas*. In a marginal or threshold state, which brings with it the suspension of constraints and differentiations that hold people apart in civil society, there can occur the kind of commingling—laughing with others, sharing food with them, welcoming them—that overcomes separation while not yet becoming organized into determinate aggregations. It is evident that rituals of the sort we have been considering are enacted in sacred spaces and effect perduring times. Thanks to the notion of liminality, we can also understand how such rituals in their intermediary being (the "liminal period," says Turner, is "betwixt and between")[67] make possible confluences of sacred and profane, and of past, present, and future. In so doing, they favor, and often themselves realize, commemoration.

The remembering-through which represents the core action of commemorating finds one of its most fortuitous occasions in ritualistic enactments containing a marked liminal phase. For in that phase the various *commemorabilia*—whether these be words and sacraments as in the Eucharist or words alone as in the Ndembu chieftain's initiation ceremony—most effectively conjoin the disparate spatial and temporal factors of which commemorating is composed. By the same token the liminality of these occasions helps to create the kind of community that is essential to the collective character of commemorating. The *communitas* thereby realized is comparatively free from those established social and political distinctions that prevent commemorating from being an activity in which all who wish to honor a given past person or event can freely participate. Just such distinctions are held in abeyance when people commemorate together. This is most manifest on festive public holidays. But the distinctions in question are at least muted at other commemorative moments, especially in rituals of the kind that have been analyzed in the pages of this section. The liminality of these rituals—

expressed in manifold ways—encourages *communitas,* itself the most propitious setting for commemoration in its collective dimension.

## VI

Can there be commemoration without *communitas?* Is action on the part of a closely co-ordinated community required for commemorating? Need this action always be fully concrete in a material-visible mode, and must it represent the express concerns and interests of the participants? Could we eliminate both bodily rituals and written or spoken texts and still speak of genuine commemorating? In short, can we commemorate without recourse either to an active community of co-present commemorators or to concrete *commemorabilia?* In fact we can—and we do so much more frequently than we consciously realize. How does this occur?

It occurs by means of a process that I shall term "intrapsychic memorialization." The primary operative factor within such memorialization is *identification* understood in Freud's sense of the term. The process of identification suggested itself to Freud as he pondered the nature of the totem meal in his highly speculative essay *Totem and Taboo*. The totem meal—which may well be the progenitor of the eucharistic meal[68]—represented in his view the ritualistic re-enactment of an ancient parricide. As such, it is "a repetition and a commemoration of this memorable and criminal deed."[69] But something more than symbolic repetition is involved in the totem meal—something more than the sacrifice of a "surrogate victim" that stands in for the sacrifice of the primal father.[70] This extra factor is identification. Speaking of the parricidal group of brothers, Freud reflected that in institutionalizing the totem meal, they "satisfied their hatred and . . . put into effect their *wish to identify themselves with [the father]*."[71]

The identification in question has three main distinguishing marks. First, it is an entirely *psychical* process. Even if concretely enacted by a totem meal, it is not itself a material matter since it involves identifying part of one's psyche with the character or person of another. Second, the identification itself occurs by way of a psychical *incorporation* that is analogous to the ingestion of a meal but decisively different in its history and consequences. Third, the identification typically occurs *between oneself and one other person:* the critical "cohort" has two members only. Despite being psychical in status and limited to a dyadic format, such identification with another is more tenacious in its effects than is the totem meal. Whereas the sacrificial meal must be continually re-enacted, psychical identification, once established, needs no further repetition; unlike the meal, *it commemorates without repeating*.

Freud found reinforcement for the idea of psychical identification in the phenomenon of mourning. In "Mourning and Melancholia," he reflected on how slow and drawn out is the "work of severance" from a mourned-for object. Since detachment from such an object is not done willfully, it has to be effected little by little. But the very process of giving up memories of a loved one only acts to intensify these same memories: will I not cling desperately to them if they are the main means of access to the person I have lost? How can I give them up so that the experience of mourning will not become indefinitely prolonged? Identification provides the answer: it "makes it easier for the object to be given up."[72] Thanks to the incorporative action of identification, I interiorize the other, set him or her up *within me* as an abiding presence. More than narcissistic assimilation of self and other is involved in such deep-going identification. As I take the other in, I am essentially altered, aggrandized. I gain increased psychic structure by means of greater internal differentiation. As Hans Loewald has put it:

> Identification is a way-station to internalization, but in internalization, if carried to completion, a redifferentiation has taken place by which both subject and object have been reconstituted, each on a new level of organization.[73]

How then is identification a matter of commemoration? It cannot just be that, as Roy Schafer says, "introjects are made out of memories."[74] Introjects or internalized presences are not simply composed of (mainly unconscious) memories; *they are themselves memorializing* in their effects. Mourning itself is to be construed as a way of establishing an internal memorial to (and of) the lost other, and in this very activity it commemorates that other. Freud, concerned with the issue of detachment from hypercathected recollections, omits this crucial point, even though his entire treatment of the mourning process calls for it. When he says, for example, that "mourning impels the ego to give up the object [as recollected] by declaring the object to be dead and offering the ego the inducement of continuing to live,"[75] we need to add that this inducement is bolstered by the establishment of the lost object within as a commemorated presence. This presence is "redifferentiated" (in Loewald's term) precisely when it attains a genuinely commemorative status in the mind via intrapsychic memorialization. And if it is true that "internalization as a completed process implies an emancipation from the [lost] object,"[76] it also implies this object's continuing presence as commemorated within the psyche.

Even if Freud did not elect to interpret his own idea of psychical identification as a form of commemoration, he was extremely alert to its pervasive consequences. Let us consider the most critical of these in brief succession:

SUPER-EGO

The super-ego is the product of two stages of identification: first, a "primary" identification with both parents that occurs very early in life;[77]

second, an identification with the child's main parent-rival after the "dissolution" of the Oedipus complex. As the "heir" of this nuclear complex, the super-ego is "the representative of our relation with our parents."[78] Precisely in this capacity it commemorates these parents, especially the parent of the same sex. The latter is said, revealingly, to be "*erected* . . . within oneself,"[79] just as a memorializing marker might be. In fact, the super-ego is expressly designated by Freud as "a memorial of the former weakness and dependence of the ego"[80] and therefore also a memorial of the corresponding strength of one's parents as primal authorities. Such memorials give "permanent expression" to the persons thus memorialized and "perpetuate [their] existence."[81] The super-ego's values, indeed its very voice (typically the voice of the conscience), memorializes these persons in a perduring way thanks to the power of multiple identifications with them.[82] The term "überich" (literally, "over-ego") eloquently expresses this memorializing function: as if to suggest that one's parents are remembered in (and as) a magisterial monument erected *over* one's ego, much as a gravestone stands over the body of the very person it memorializes.

CHARACTER

Freud remarks that "the character of the ego is a precipitate of abandoned object-cathexes and . . . contains the history of these object-choices."[83] The precipitation is the work of incorporation, and the containment stems from the ego's identification with the abandoned object-choices. What is unusual in Freud's statement is the explicit acknowledgment of the *history* of these choices. What could such an internalized history be other than an intrapsychic memorialization—effected not in static, monumental terms but in terms of diachronic retelling, as if it were the biography of others recounted wholly within oneself?

TRANSFERENCE

One of the main operative factors at work in transference is the revival of parental *imagoes* through varying degrees of identification with the analyst. These *imagoes* are in turn distillations of primary identifications with parents and become the prototype for all later relationships with figures who stand (like the analyst) *in loco parentis*. As stable internalized entities, these *imagoes* serve as intrapsychic *commemorabilia* of parents as *commemoranda*. Thanks to their perduring presence, a "transference" of libidual energy can be made onto the figure of the analyst, who comes increasingly to resemble one or both parents as the analysis proceeds.

PRIMAL PHANTASIES

These were posited by Freud to designate schematic, universal psychic structures that organize one's phantasy life in an *a priori* fashion: e.g., viewing the primal scene, seduction by a parent, castration threat, etc. Since Freud holds that such *Urphantasien* are inherited, they are in effect memorializations of phylogenetically acquired experiences: they are the genically-transmitted memories of such experiences. Similarly, the overwhelming sense of individual guilt to which Freud increasingly directed his attention is held to have a phylogenetic basis: to be the continuation in memorial terms of the very guilt which the parricidal sons incurred in primeval times: "what began in relation to the father is completed in relation to the group."[84]

With the allusion to primeval parricide, we have come full cycle. According to the bold hypothesis of *Totem and Taboo*, this parricide gave rise—thanks to ambivalent feelings of remorse and guilt—to its ritualistic repetition and commemoration in totem meals. But it was still bolder of Freud to suggest that commemorating could take place within the psyche—without the support of concrete *commemorabilia*, much less of a surrounding community of co-commemorators. As such purely psychical commemorating is without a text, so it is also without a ritual. No external vehicle is required to bear or express the identifications of which it is composed. Nevertheless, intrapsychic memorialization shares the following features with overt ritualistic commemoration:

(1) Both proceed by a form of incorporation, whether as actual ingestion (e.g., of the totem animal) or as interiorization of the absent other. It is striking that such incorporating precedes other phases of the commemoration as if it were a necessary condition for them. The logic seems to be: unless the other has been brought within, in-corporated, I cannot fully commemorate it.

(2) Ongoing, steady remembering is accomplished in an at least quasi-permanent way (i.e., over many generations; or at least over the lifetime of a given psyche) without any dependence on recollective remembering. Something like a law of inverse ratio—which Freud might call a "complemental series"[85]—seems to obtain in the two instances: the less recollection is active or needed (or even pertinent), the more efficacious and valuable is commemoration. Already in *Totem and Taboo* Freud wrote that "the less [the original parricide] was recollected the more numerous must have been the substitutes to which it gave rise."[86] So too we have seen how the decathexis of recollective memories in the mourning process exists in inverse ratio to identifications that prove indispensable to the fully internalized presence of the other.[87]

(3) A *focus memorius* is at work throughout. In the case of ritualized commemoration, this focus is provided by a spatio-temporally specified set of particulars (whether objects or actions), whereas in intrapsychic memorialization it is given in the form of the other as introject: as inward memorial. Despite such a focus, however, in both instances there is a continual trespassing of established boundaries, whether these be generational-social (e.g., totemic) or personal-psychological (e.g., egological). This means that both sorts of commemorating can be considered liminal in status, occurring at the edges of psyche and of society alike.

(4) Despite this very liminality—this playing at the borderlines of our experience—commemoration by ritualistic action and commemoration via indentification accomplish for their respective objects an "immortality,"[88] or at least an abiding perdurance. If it is indeed true that "the memory of the first act of sacrifice thus proved indestructible, in spite of every effort to forget it"[89]—the memory surviving as ritualized commemoration—the memory of others we once loved also proves indestructible: in spite of every effort to forget them, we commemorate them within our psyche by means of intrapsychic memorialization.

But wait! Are we not "pursuing memory *beyond* mind" in this Part of the book? How can we be moving beyond mind with all this talk of the "intrapsychic" and the "internalized"? Isn't "identification" a strictly psychological conception—thus belonging exclusively to mind or psyche? Granting that we have moved beyond representationalism, have we moved beyond mentalism?

In drawing on Freudian psychoanalysis for a coherent model of nonritualistic commemoration, we have indeed moved beyond mind: beyond mind conceived in that determinate way which has come to dominate our thinking about it. I refer to the Cartesian-Lockian notion that the mind is an exclusively private arena. In this view, mind is always and only *my* mind, self-enclosed within its own epistemological space. It follows that any and all memories—considered as denizens of such a mind—are *my* memories only. In other words, memories of every kind are at once:

*Individuated:*
This reflects the fact that memories are affairs of the solitary individual, the *solus ipse* who recalls his or her past in hermetic isolation. Thus we speak of "possessing" our memories and of "storing" them as if they were privately acquired commodities, stamped somehow with our own proper names. No wonder that we speak of "jealously guarded" memories, as if sharing them were to threaten their very being!

*Individuating:*
This is Locke's twist on the paradigm; precisely as existing within the ambiance of the self alone, memories become self-definitive. More than any other factor, they determine our personal identity: to be a self at all is to be the self that we can remember.[90] Memories, our own possession, come to possess us; instead of expanding our experience, they serve to limit it.

Psychoanalysis proposes a model of mind that challenges the Cartesian-Lockean prototype. It challenges it not just by recognizing an unconscious dimension of fantasy and memory, but also by specifying that mind is ***ineluctably intersubjective in origin and import***. Such is the implication of the idea of identification itself. It needs to be stressed that identification is always identification *with an other*, whether this other be parent, sibling, lover, friend, an ideal, or even one's own mirror image.[91] When Freud spoke of "a new psychical action"[92] by which every ego is formed, he meant the action of identification (mainly identification with one's parents); and we have seen how the super-ego is entirely a product of identifications. Even the id "inherits" identifications in the form of *imagoes* and repressed memories, mixing these in with instinctual representatives. At every level, the human psyche is constituted by identifications. And if this is so, the mind is radically non-solipsistic; it is something shared and non-solitary from the start. Likewise with regard to the memories attached to this mind: these will be neither strictly individuated (or will be this only at a pathological extreme that is named precisely "isolation") nor wholly individuating. The self that we remember is a composition of many selves—all the selves with which we identify in the course of a life. There is no such thing as strict self-identity; or rather, such identity is thoroughly inter-subjective from the beginning: "le je est un autre."[93] If the self is indeed an other, its memories will be at once othered and othering:

*Othered:*

Memories are formed from the first *in the image of* the other, primarily the caretaking parent; also *in view of* the other, though not just the literal view. It is a matter of keeping the other in mind. In all this, the other(s) act as a template for further development thanks precisely to identification, which establishes these other (s) within as active internalized presences.

*Othering:*

Once such presences are in place, they become the basis of still further identifications, as occurs most manifestly in the case of transference or in relation to mentors. Older identifications, essential to the formation of the self in the first place, enable new identifications, which alter the self once again, i.e., make it still other than what it was.

If this double othering obtains—if Freud and his followers (most notably the British School of object-relations) have set forth a plausible alternative model of mind according to which memories are intrinsically non-private—we have indeed moved memory beyond mind considered as a solipsistic snare. By the same stroke we have preserved the commemorative status of the intrapsychic sphere as a whole. On the psychoanalytic paradigm, to be mental or psychical at all is to arise from identifications with others. However unconscious they may be, memories of these identifications will be commemorative of these same others by furnishing inward memorials of them and of the acts by which identifications were first formed. Far from being exceptional, such memories come to provide the memorial infrastructure of mind itself; taken together, they at once reflect and further mind's own inherent alterity. The commemoration they effect from within, instead of keeping us within, expresses the fact that mind is fashioned from without—known from without via identifications with others. *The intrapsychic is ineluctably interpsychic:* this is the operative principle. Just as memory of place has mainly to do with containment (despite being ostensibly preoccupied with externality), psychic commemoration, seemingly so self-contained, breaks out of self-enclosure through its enduring identifications with others.

## VII

What are the role of body and place in commemoration? Here brief indications will have to suffice in the face of the considerable complexity of the topic.

### BODY

The body's role in ritualistic commemoration is altogether central. It serves as the primary bearer of the concrete *commemorabilia* through which such commemorating is effected. The body moves the commemorator into the appropriate ritualistic space, in which it proceeds to perform the gestures by which the commemorative act is accomplished. Thus, in the Eucharist, it brings the worshipper into the vicinity of the officiants, and it guides the movements of all parties in the ceremony. Moreover, the body of the worshipper is an analogue of the body of Christ; and the incorporation of the bread and the wine is an assimilation of Christ's symbolic body into the worshipper's physical body. In other circumstances, the body itself may become a *commemorabilium:* as happens in the case of the young man from Tanagra whose body, bearing a sacrificial ram, becomes Hermetic. Either way, the body does more than represent the commemoration; it serves as an *expressive sign* of that which is commemorated: hence the importance of nuanced differences in the exact form of ritualistic re-enactment. At the same time, the body assumes a quite liminal role in many commemorative ceremonies, being the borderline between actual and virtual movement, present and past, sacred and profane.[94]

The body is also active in textually focused commemoration. This becomes evident when we consider the intoning of the liturgical formula, "Take this in remembrance of me," as the worshippers are ingesting the sacraments: the sonorous physicality of the heard text intimately rejoins the kinesthetic-tactile physicality of the giving/receiving body. The bodily production of sounds by actual pronunciation is no less important in the Ndembu ceremony, where the invocations of Kafwana and other figures are chanted out loud. Even when the text is written and not spoken—as in its inscription on war memorials—the body is solicited: e.g., in circumambulating the memorial so as to take in its message from several points of view.[95]

But what of the psychic sphere? Does not my claim in chapter 8 that body memory is indispensable to *all* human memory find its limit just here?

It does—if "body" means visibly moving, phenomenally perceived body only. But body can mean much else besides; quite apart from claims as to the existence of an "astral" or "sublime" body, there is a straightforward, unmysterious bodily component of psychical identification. To identify with someone in Freud's rich sense of the term is to merge not only with that person's mental or psychic being. It is also to assimilate his or her corporeality in its full emotional resonance. This is above all true of those early identifications on which Freud in fact centered his attention. The infant identifies with the mother's felt flesh, especially with particular parts of it such as breast, lips, and hands. These "part-objects," once introjected into the infant's psyche in the form of fantasies and memories, become veritable *commemorabilia* of the mother's body qua *commemorandum*. In this way, endopsychic memory contains an unmistakable bodily component; it is bodily in its being—and bodily precisely in being commemorative in character.

PLACE

Commemoration is no less implaced than it is embodied. Once more, this is most evident in ritualistic commemorating:

> Time and place are essential features of ritual action, and both mark a specific orientation or setting for ritual. . . . The shape, spatial orientation, and location of the ritual setting are essential features of the semantics of ritual action.[96]

Consider only that the setting of the Eucharist in a church, and more particularly at the altar, is hardly an indifferent feature of the ceremony; this setting provides internal and external horizons, prescribed pathways (e.g., aisles), and, in general, a sanctified ambiance in which the ritual can be carried out. Funeral services also require a properly solemn setting. In both of these cases the place is variable within certain limits. In the Hermes festival at Tanagra, however, only that one city (indeed, only a certain street of that city) is permitted as a place of enactment. Whatever the exact circumstances, place is primordial in ritualized commemorating—as we might expect in view of the prominence of overt, expressive bodily movements in the performance of ritual. Bodies, after all, move us into places and keep us there.

Commemorative texts possess a dimension of placement as well. Not only are they read or presented in an apposite public space—say, in a cemetery at a Memorial Day ceremony—but they exhibit spatial or quasi-spatial qualities of their own. By these latter I have in mind all that Derrida has discussed under the general heading of a text's *espacement:* e.g., its framing effects, especially those of its margins.[97] Indeed, the importance of margins in commemorative texts—the edges of epitaphs, the pauses before and after a eulogy, etc.—remind us of the critical role of liminality in the constitution of so much commemorating. Such margins signify the very state of transition that characterizes the *commemorandum* as an absent or vanishing existent.

Even intrapsychic memorialization is not without its own mode of implacement. It is not accidental that Freud was concerned to devise a convincing topographic model of the mind in *The Interpretation of Dreams*, his first treatment (after the abortive "Project for a Scientific Psychology") of the mind in its full scope. In fact, the very idea of "*in*-corporation" presumes a psychic space into which the other-to-be-identified-with is drawn. Moreover, the internalized presences which are the precipitates of incorporation not only *occupy* psychic space but also help to *create* it. Each of these presences brings about a new place in the psyche—a new memorial location that, far from freezing the past into fixity, opens ever more expansively into the future.

## VIII

We have yet to confront what might be termed the "functional essence" of commemoration. This is *participation*. Commemorating, by its very structure, encourages and enhances participation on the part of those who engage in it. The primary participation is in the *commemorandum*, the commemorated object, person, or event. This participation occurs via the mediating presence of various *commemorabilia*, material or psychical; we remember *through* these translucent media; but we could just as well say that we participate *with* them in honoring a common *commemorandum*. In ceremonial commemoration, we also participate with other persons, forming with them a "horizontal," participatory *communitas* that lies perpendicular to the "vertical" community which the commemorator (or group of commemorators) establishes with the *commemorandum* proper.[98] On certain occasions, the two communities—the two kinds of participation—coincide. In mourning, for example, the dyadic community of myself-as-griever and the other-as-grieved is at once horizontal and vertical. Here, participation is unusually intense: not only is there incorporation of the other into myself (as also occurs in the Eucharist and in totem meals) but a con-fusion of self and other thanks to identification, itself a form of inter-psychic participation.

I borrow the term "participation" from Lucien Lévy-Bruhl, whose writings on the subject of "primitive mentality" first developed the idea of a "law of participation." This law is "the first and most general"[99] feature of such mentality in its collective character. The participation is between

> beings and objects linked in a collective representation. This is why, for want of a better term, I shall call the appropriate principle of the 'primitive' mentality which governs the connexions and the preconnexions of these representations, the *law of participation*.[100]

For a Western philosophical mind, the single most striking aspect of participation is its freedom from the constraints of contradiction. Thanks to participation, things can be simultaneously themselves and *not* themselves, here and also there, past as well as present.[101] The metaphysical basis for participation is "a mystical community of essence between beings," beings which enjoy an "essential identity."[102] Thus, identity of the members of one's clan "results from participation in the invisible and timeless essence of the group."[103] The totem of such a clan *is* its essence. As a consequence, there is "a similar identity between the individuals of a totemic group and their totem."[104]

Participation is not, however, limited to horizontal and vertical communities as these relate to a totem. Lévy-Bruhl was struck by the sheer multiplicity of types of participation. For the primitive, there is a profound participation between himself and his "appurtenances," that is, any part of himself or his life with which he could be said to be identical: e.g., clothes, fingernails, excreta, footprints. These appurtenances do not merely represent or simply "belong to" a particular person. They *are* him: hence the respect with which they must be treated. There is also participation between humans and non-totemic animals; between an individual and his or her ancestors (mythical and real); between a person and what he or she eats.[105] In the end, everything is swept up into participation: "All objects and beings are involved in a network of mystical participations and exclusions."[106]

The law of participation gives rise to three working principles, each of which is highly suggestive for a study of commemoration:

BI-PRESENCE

This refers to being present in two different places at the same time. Lévy-Bruhl cites an example from a missionary named Grubb: an Indian dreamed that he [Grubb] was stealing pumpkins from the garden, even though Grubb was able to prove that he was 150 miles away at the time. The Indian, unimpressed, maintained that *both* claims were true and did not conflict.[107]

DUALITY-UNITY

A being can become two beings and still stay *one* being nonetheless. The most common instance of this is found in the relation between a corpse and the ghost which has arisen from it. Whereas a Westerner might distinguish these carefully, for many primitive peoples the two entities remain one: "the ghost and the corpse constitute together a duality-unity, in short they participate in one another."[108]

CONSUBSTANTIALITY

Participation at once presupposes and confirms an abiding consubstantiality between participating items. Thus, parts of the body cannot be considered as separate from each other or the body but as strictly con-substantial. As a result, in many primitive languages "the organs are never [named] without possessive pronouns";[109] "foot" is always "*my* foot."

We need only call to mind the Eucharist to realize that such principles of participation are by no means restricted to the practices of pre-literate peoples. In the eucharistic rite, Christ's bi-presence is at work: he is at once in the communion taking place in the present *and* in the Last Supper honored by this communion. Duality-unity is also felt: there is at once Jesus, the finite and historical man, and Christ, who transcends death and history.[110] And consubstantiality is actively present: in and through the sacraments the communicants become con-substantial with Christ, their bread and wine become identical with his body and blood.

Participation is prominently present in many other commemorative practices as well. Ancestor worship in early Chinese civilization, for example, attempts to strengthen continuity with forebears by reminding a person of his or her participation in the same family line. What Lévy-Bruhl says of the initiation ceremonies of the Arunta could also be said of Chinese ancestor worship: "By imitating what, in certain circumstances, the mythical ancestors have done, and by reproducing their gestures and actions, one has communion with them and truly shares in their essences."[111] For the Arunta as for the Chinese there is consubstantiality between one's ancestors and oneself.

In the same vein we could say that the Tanagran ritualist has become identical with Hermes through participation in a common essence: Hermes and the young man have become two-in-one, and bi-presence is realized. Even in the less dramatic instance of modern funerals, the departed soul is invoked in the eulogy as if asked to linger near his or her own corpse in an ambiguous state which, if not duality-unity in any strict sense, is an emotionally effective analogue of it. In funerals, ritual and text combine in an effort to promote participation, enabling the mourners to feel at one with the deceased person. Even texts isolated from any expressly ritual component call upon commemorators to identify themselves with the object or event they commemorate: "in memory of the men of Guilford . . . that their example may speak to coming generations." What *The Book of Common Prayer* calls "continual remembrance," or what still earlier in the English language was designated as "sempiternall remembraunce,"[112] points to the temporal character of an ongoing sense of identity between commemorators and *commemoranda*. Indeed, "perdurance" can be construed as a mode of continuing participation. It is perduring participation which the Eucharist as well as the *Analects*, funeral services along with many commemorative texts, strive to foster in commemorators.

Intrapsychic memorialization also exhibits aspects of participation. Perdurance in the form of a lasting super-ego, character, and active internalized presences is accomplished by a deepgoing participation between one person and another. I have already suggested that *inter*psychic identification is a form of participation. Now we can add that it occurs in each of the three forms recognized by Lévy-Bruhl: bi-presence is at play in identification, whereby one is at once oneself *and* another, even though continuing to inhabit a separate body; duality-unity is experienced inasmuch as the other comes to be so fully interiorized within my psyche as to become *one* with me, an added layer of my being; and consubstantiality is effected by the entire process—as the other becomes more fully incorporated, I become more *like* him or her, psychic flesh of his or her introjected flesh. Thus, even in something as unconscious and unritualized as is identification we can observe the truth of Lévy-Bruhl's dictum: "what is given *in the first place* is participation."[113] Our very being as independent individuals, as well as our existence as effective commemorators, is formed in the crucible of participation with others.

## IX

The preceding considerations give rise to some still more encompassing concluding reflections. If commemoration has everything to do with participation—if its functional essence is to solicit and sustain participation between commemorators and that to which they pay homage, often by means of *co*-participation in special communities and just as often by sharing in *commemorabilia* through which the *commemorandum* is made present—then by the same token commemoration has to do with overcoming the separation from which otherwise unaffiliated individuals suffer. Still more radically, commemoration suggests that such separation is a sham. If it is true that "*to be is to participate*,"[114] the beings who participate cannot be atomic entities who are merely gathering to commemorate out of a motive of repetition, guilt, piety, or fellow feeling. The commemorators are *already* deeply conjoined, bonded at the most profound level:

> The representation of a separate individual, which seems to us so simple and so natural, is nevertheless not a primitive one. It occurs only secondarily and never alone. . . . [Let us] show how much this mental attitude differs from ours. . . .[115]

But *does* it differ so greatly from ours as Lévy-Bruhl here avers? Doubtlessly it does so at an explicitly conscious level, especially in the post-Cartesian and post-industrialist West. It is, indeed, our conscious conviction that minds are discrete entities and that remembering is an individual affair alone. But at a preconscious or unconscious level we know how shallow (and how vicious) such separatism can be. Separatism itself presupposes collective roots of various kinds: from language to class, from gender identity to personal identity, from shared history to shared tradition. And it is just because of the reality of such deeply interpersonal roots that commemoration assumes unusual importance in our culture—and doubtless in *every* culture. For *commemoration promotes participation even as it thrives on it*. Commemorating calls upon us not as separate beings but as always already intertwined; it calls on us in our strictly social being.

But more than this is at stake. Commemorating also creates new forms of sociality, new modes of interconnection: between past and present, self and other, one group and another, one form of thinking or acting or speaking and another, one sex and another, one art form and another. In these ways commemorating brings about "a mystical community of essence between beings,"[116] constituting a shared identity more lasting and more significant than would be possible in an uncommemorated existence. Commemorating does more than pay tribute to honorable actions undertaken in the past and at another place. It constructs the space, and continues the time, in which the commendably inter-human will be perduringly appreciated. Rather than looking back only, commemoration concerns itself with "what, lasting, comes toward us."

From this view of commemoration as a thoroughly conjoint participation in a project of continuing connection with the *commemorandum*—whether this be effected by ritual or text or by psychic identification—we may derive three corollary insights:

(1) Commemoration cannot be accomplished by representations alone, however accurate or adept or dramatic these may be. It is noteworthy that Lévy-Bruhl claims that the participation ingredient in primitive rites does not yield to a representationalist model:

> [Participation is falsified when] we connect it, in whole or in part, with mental activity in so far as this is representational or cognitive; because, in doing this, we inevitably apply to it the general scheme of representation and knowledge as established by ancient philosophy, and by modern psychological thought or attempts at a theory of knowledge. Now, to try to apply this scheme to participation is to do it violence and to distort it.[117]

The fact is that representationalism in philosophy and psychology goes hand in hand with that very individualism which the experience of commemorative participation contests: as we can see most clearly in the case of John Locke, for whom representations are private possessions and for whom specifically memorial representations are the exclusive constituents of personal identity.[118] The Lockian paradigm is antithetical to understanding commemoration, which cannot be effected adequately by means of set and static representations belonging to an isolated human subject. The contrary is the case. As any ritual must allow for, and as we have observed most tellingly in the case of intrapsychic memorialization, whatever representations are at play must be capable of changing and deepening over time: as in the transition from the mere imitation of the other (an activity whose products resemble Lockian "ideas" or representations in their isomorphic character) to the internalized presence of that other. In short, whenever we become engaged in commemorative activity—whether this occurs in a dyadic or a polyadic context—*representation cedes place to participation*.

(2) The participatory element in commemoration is so extensive that it includes not only minds or psyches but aspects of body and place as well. In a circumstance of commemoration, body, place, and psyche become more fully participatory. They commingle with one another intimately, and they invite other factors to join in. A revealing instance of such mutually enhanced participation, especially as it involves body memory, is found in another passage from the episode of the "petite madeleine":

> And suddenly the memory revealed itself. The taste was that of the little piece of madeleine which on Sunday mornings at Combray (because on these mornings I did not go out before mass), when I went to say good morning to her in her bedroom, my aunt Léonie used to give me, dipping it first in her own cup of tea or tissane.[119]

This brief but critical scene shows body, place, and psyche not merely as juxtaposed but as dynamic co-participants. Just as the taste of the madeleine penetrates Marcel's remembering/remembered body and as the latter moves through the bedroom of Aunt Léonie, so the room itself and the larger setting of Combray are inseparable from the body memory awakened by the tea taste: this memory *imbibes* place as surely as Marcel's young body imbibed the fateful tea. Body memory and place memory alike fill out the recollection, "the memory" of the entire event as this is recaptured in the psyche of the adult Marcel, who is recollecting the petite madeleine episode from a point in time many years later. But thanks to the embodied and implaced character of this episode, what would otherwise be a purely psychical act of recollection exfoliates fully into the past it is remembering, participating concretely in it. The passing mention of a "mass" on Sunday morning reinforces the participatory power of the scene as we are suddenly made aware that Marcel and his aunt, who together form a dyadic *communitas,* are experiencing their own communion in advance of the official ceremony. The petite madeleine and the tea become the sacraments in an informal ritual that is no less commemorative than the Eucharist itself, since it exhibits elements of solemnification and memorialization. Perdurance is present as well: the remembrance of this particular scene unlocks an entire past which will be continually recaptured in the course of the novel, and it encourages the reader to perpetuate this same past in his or her memory—to honor it by future readings or rememberings. From this moment on, the past of Combray will be lastingly coming toward us.

It is telling that the opening onto this past is provided by a sensation of *taste,* surely the most thoroughly participatory form of body memory and contrasting, in this very respect, with visual memory. Remarking that it could not have been the visual shape of the petite madeleine that would evoke the world of Combray—having seen so many similar shapes that it had lost its "power of expansion"[120]—Marcel muses:

> But when from a long-distant past nothing subsists, after the people are dead, after the things are broken and scattered, taste and smell alone, more fragile but more enduring, more unsubstantial, more persistent, more faithful, remain poised a long time, like souls, remembering, waiting, hoping, amid the ruins of all the rest; and bear unflinchingly in the tiny and almost impalpable drop of their essence, the vast structure of recollection.[121]

Memory of taste (and of smell, closely associated with it) perdures because of its capacity to permeate one's entire sensibility and thus to be an invaluable sacrament, a worthy *commemorabilium* able to "bear unflinchingly" the weight of the *commemorandum* (here, Combray-in-the-past). Precisely as so deeply interfusing—as a profoundly participatory element—such memory is also able to bear "the vast structure of recollection": which is to say, the episodic past as conveyed by successive mental representations. In comparison with body memory in its most highly participatory mode—and in a significantly commemorative setting—recollection presents itself as a secondary formation, as a superstructure of memory. This suggests that just as representation supervenes upon and presupposes participation, so recollection is parasitic on body memory and the commemoration which it helps to realize.

(3) Commemoration is not separable in the end from body memory—or from place memory either. Each is an essential component, an equiprimordial part, in remembering that goes beyond—perhaps we should also say *under*—mind. Moreover, far from being a momentary affair, something restricted to particular ceremonial occasions, commemorating is continually occurring. We can even say that *all remembering has a commemorative component*. How can this be?

The factor of participation is once again of critical importance: "participation enters into the very constitution of these things. Without participation, they would not be *given* in experience. They would not exist."[122] We have seen how commemoration brings together such seemingly disconnected things as past and present, self and other, body and mind. In doing so, it draws on powers of participation that are at play in every act of remembering, however concealed these powers may be. This is especially evident in the case of past and present, whose merging in commemoration can be viewed in the light of Lévy-Bruhl's three modes of participation and with continuing reference to Proust's text:

(*a*) *Bi-presence* of past and present is realized in commemoration as a matter of course: for the reader, the time of narration (i.e., the present of Marcel's narrative discourse, which effects the commemorating) becomes co-present with the time narrated (i.e., the past of the tisane-taking with Aunt Léonie, a past which is the effective *commemorandum* in the circumstance).[123]

(*b*) *Duality-unity* is at work in commemorative participation as it fuses present with past. We can say of Marcel-the-narrator and of Marcel-the-child-at-Combray precisely what Lévy-Bruhl says of the corpse and its ghost in primitive cultures: they "constitute together a duality-unity, in short, they participate in one another."[124] And the same thing obtains for Marcel qua narrator-and-subject of this novel: they are the same "Marcel" in being two very different bearers of this name.

(*c*) *Consubstantiality* is also operative in commemorating, which makes past and present substantial with one another. Such consubstantiality is achieved in the madeleine episode by a body memory of taste, which merges a past tasting of tea in the presence of Marcel's mother with a still more removed episode of tea-tasting with his aunt. It is striking that this taste is said to function in "the tiny and almost impalpable drop of [its] *essence*"[125]—reminding us that the entire point of participation according to Lévy-Bruhl is to realize "a mystical community of essence between beings."[126]

The remarkable capacity of participation to connect even the most disparate entities and events is what lies behind commemoration's own quite remarkable connectiveness, which is unrivaled in the realm of memory. Consider, for example, the fact that the universe for Plato would be hopelessly bifurcated between Forms and particulars unless the latter somehow participated in the former, that is, managed to share in their constancy and reiterability. Material particulars would otherwise be so wholly contingent as to be parts of Becoming only; they would be strictly *in*constant, indeed would never really *be* at all. By the same token, Forms need the participation of particulars if they are not to be entirely abstract and otiose.[127] In other words, the participation is quite reciprocal: what the particular gains by way of definiteness, the Form gains as realization in the empirical world.

Even in the most ordinary forms of commemorating we discover just such a mutual conditioning of primary terms—terms that thereby participate in each other in ways that strikingly resemble the operation of Platonic *methexis* or metaphysical participation. As the *commemorandum* gives specificity of focus and stability of reference to the *commemorabilium*, so the commemorative vehicle in its material or psychical concreteness allows the commemorated object or event to be regained in memory—to be realized there. What I have called "remembering-through" is itself an expression of this reciprocal participation: the commemorative medium can be traversed in two directions. Moreover, just as the result of *methexis* is the creation of continuity where before there had been only the prospect of an unredeemed dualism, so commemorating likewise links terms otherwise belligerently opposed (e.g., body/mind, self/other) or indifferently juxtaposed (i.e., past/present). The effect is one of interpenetration from within, an effect which resonates throughout remembering of every major kind. *If body memory anchors human existence and if place memory locates it, commemoration connects it*.

That the participation ingredient in the operation of commemoration and the participation at work in Platonic metaphysics are more than merely formally similar is suggested by Plato's own doctrine of *anamnesis*, "recollection" in his strictly non-representational use of the term. In grounding a finite awareness of one's immediate world in an absolute knowing of the Forms, *anamnesis* at the same time connects the individual soul with its own past existence. Attainment of eidetic knowledge occurs only in and through re-connection with a former state of being. Further, this re-connection is commemorative in character: not just because tribute is being paid to previous experiences of knowing or because there is a ritualistic element involved (i.e., moving through preordained stages of philosophical dialectic) but more importantly because a process of intrapsychic memorialization is at play in *anamnesis*. As in mourning, there is a sedimentation of earlier experiences into the soul such that they require being drawn out in acts of *maieusis* ("mid-wifery") which are reminiscent of acts of psychoanalytic transference. As consolidated within, these proto-experiences[128] constitute psychical memorials of a primal knowing which it is the object of *anamnesis* to recover. Such inward coming-to-know-again is as deeply commemorative as is the equally interior retaining of other persons as internalized presences in mourning. If "knowledge is recollection,"[129] knowledge is also commemoration; it re-connects us with a past life via internalized sedimentations of an Ur-knowing originally obtained in that life.[130]

## X

But, surely, commemoration has as much to do with ends as with origins! For one thing, we cannot fully commemorate something unless it has come to an end in some significant sense: if it were still going on, still acting or living, we would be enjoying or celebrating it (or suffering from or execrating it) rather than commemorating it. For another, the very ending of something may induce regret or nostalgia—a feeling of loss—which in turn encourages commemoration as a way of coping with the fact of ending itself. Commemoration can even be viewed as a way of coming to terms with the absence or distance effected by ending. This is the gist of Freud's treatment of the commemoration accomplished by mourning, itself a response to "object loss." Couldn't we say that much of the motivation for commemoration derives from having to confront "separation anxiety"—for which death merely provides the most acute occasion? Could we not even say that commemoration of origins themselves is somehow about ends—about events (or persons or ideas) that, precisely as origins, have come to an end,[131] or that are still engaged in a process of ending?

This last-named possibility is an important one. Even when commemoration bears straightforwardly on something that is ending—e.g., "the end of an era"—it still may not be directed at anything simply terminal. On the contrary, the commemorating may itself serve to *prolong* the ending, giving to it (and to its origin) a species of after-life. If "what has been brings about futural approaching,"[132] this is all the more true in the case of commemorating, which is capable of transforming something "frozen in the finality of *rigor mortis*"[133] into a re-living presence, alive in the minds and bodies of its commemorators. In mourning, the dead or absent other is transmogrified into an active internal presence; thus something that has come to an end in terms of world-time acquires an ongoing end*ing* in and through commemoration. Insofar as such ending is not yet concluded, it will be going on in the future. Commemorating here exhibits its Janusian ability to look at once forward and backward: or more exactly, to look ahead in looking back.

Freud would have described such a situation as one of "deferred action" *(Nachträglichkeit):* by being commemorated, what might otherwise end altogether, come to a definite close, is granted a delayed efficacy. In this respect commemorating enables the past not just to evanesce in the present[134] but, more crucially, to traverse the present on its way to becoming future. It is as if the very delay in discovery or recognition—or in simple appreciation—empowers the past to gain an increased futurity. As Freud remarks of deferred happenings generally, the effect seems to exceed the cause, contravening the Aristotelian-Cartesian assumption that there must be at least as much reality in a cause as in its effect.[135] Such is the force of commemoration when it is fully and freely enacted.

If commemoration is indeed a way of coming to terms with ending and if it succeeds to the extent that it refuses to succumb to the sheer pastness of the past—its facticity, its "frozen finality," its severe "It was"[136]—then it must consist in an action of carrying the past forward through the present so as to perdure in the future. But the past can be carried forward in this fashion only if it has attained a certain consistent selfsameness in the wake of the perishing of the particulars by which it had once presented itself. This selfsameness is what Whitehead calls "objective immortality": "actual entities 'perpetually perish' subjectively, but are immortal objectively."[137] Commemoration not only looks forward in looking back, thereby transmitting deferred effects of the past, it affirms the past's selfsameness in the present by means of a consolidated re-enactment, thus assuring a continuation of remembering into the future. Whether this re-enactment is by text or ritual, or whether it occurs within the psyche, it connects past with present in a genuinely perduring way. And if commemoration brings about a circumstance in which "what has been offers future to itself,"[138] it does so less *from* the future—as Heidegger holds—than from the present. In this present, where commemorating is bound to occur, a memorialization of the past is brought forth which, as ritualistic, textual, or intrapsychic, allows for the past to be borne forward rememoratively into the future. Ultimately, we remember *through* such a memorialization, which defies reduction to the separatist categories of 'matter' or 'psyche'—indeed, to 'self' and 'other', or even to 'past' and 'present'. In this memorialization all such metaphysically determined dyads begin to dissolve, and the inner connection of their respective members—their intimate participation in each other—becomes apparent.

It is usual to regard commemoration (when commemoration is considered at all) as a merely derivative mode of memory. But I have been suggesting that, on the contrary, commemorating is an "intensified remembering" and that it is integral to remembering, as inherent in it as are body memory and place memory. Memory is always memorializing—however fleetingly, inconsistently, or inadequately on a given occasion. To remember is to commemorate the past. It is to redeem the perishing of particulars in a selfsameness that conspires in the present to persist into the future.

Whitehead cites a Latin inscription on ancient sundials: *Pereunt et imputantur,* "the hours perish and are laid to account."[139] Commemoration can be considered the laying to account of perishings, the consolidating and continuing of endings. It is the creating of memorializations in the media of ritual, text, and psyche; it enables us to honor the past by carrying it intact into new and lasting forms of alliance and participation.

# CODA

The purpose of this Part has been to pursue memory beyond mind—or more exactly, to show that it is already beyond it. "Beyond" does not mean simply external to, much less triumphant over. Mind remains essential to human remembering; it continues to exhibit its importance in memorial matters—as we have just witnessed in the case of intrapsychic memorialization. And precisely because an activity like commemorating puts the body/mind dichotomy into suspension, it suggests that mentation continues to be deeply ingredient in memory even when a given act of remembering is not explicitly cogitative in character. Indeed, the rooting of the word "memory" in *memor-* (mindful)—and ultimately of "remembering," "reminding," and "reminiscing" in *mens* (mind)—bespeaks the same ingrediency, as does the striking fact that *gemynd* in Old English means equally "memory" or "mind." If we are to move beyond mind in memory in the ways that have been explored in the preceding six chapters, we must not forget that mind always lies close behind memory. However withdrawn it may be as an origin, and however skeptical we may be as to its role in modern theories of memory, it is never altogether absent from the memorial life.

It is of considerable interest, however, to notice that memory is also cognate with "Minerva," goddess of wisdom, and with "mania," madness in the express sense of being "out of one's mind." Minerva would doubtless advise us to move beyond constricted conceptions of mind so as to be closer to the heart: *minna* (love) is yet another etymon of memory.[1] The way of wisdom is not to become caught in encapsulated, self-limiting notions of what is to have (or to be) a mind—notions which are all too prominent in the post-Cartesian era of representationalism. To follow the lead of Minerva in this matter may well take us out of our minds; it may even require a measure of mania, a certain *démesuré* boldness that contrasts with the sobriety of many accounts of memory, including that given in Part One of this book. But *mania* is in turn closely related to *mantis* (seer), and to *mantra* (counsel, prayer, hymn).[2] To go out of one's mind is to see beyond what there is to see within the confines of the sheerly mental, where everything is nested within a hierarchy of representations. It is to obtain counsel, a special seeing, which might not otherwise be obtainable: excess may be the only means of access.

So it has been in the present case. In Parts Two and Three intensive and extensive treatments have been devoted to aspects of memory that move us beyond mind construed in any narrowly epistemological sense. This has been possible only because the mind that is genuinely immanent in memory was already beyond itself when it was construed as solipsistic self-enclosure. *The mind of memory is already in the world:* it is in reminders and in reminiscences, in acts of recognition and in the lived body, in places and in the company of others. In each of these six circumstances, mind, interpreted as a *cogito* thinking a *cogitatum,* is exceeded; each case is extra-cogitational. Yet, except as refracted in the mental mirror of a Cartesian consciousness, these circumstances have not been accorded their rightful due in modern epistemologies. They are either systematically neglected—as happens with reminders and reminiscences, and with body and place—or considered irresolvably problematic (as in the history of lucubrations on the nature of recognition or "the problem of other minds"). But precisely in their outcast status they merit our attention: they deserve being remembered in their own right.

In a common movement beyond mentalism, the three topics treated in Part Three—body memory, place memory, commemoration—are of special significance. Each offers an adverbial twist to human memory:

WITHNESS

Whitehead remarks that "we see the contemporary chair, but we see it *with* our eyes"[3] and that, overall, "we feel *with the body*."[4] This bodily withness, though elusive, is ever-present: "It is the withness that makes the body the starting point for our knowledge of the circumambient world."[5] Body memory can be said to bear and build on this very withness: to be concerned with it in a basic sense even if it is often only tacitly experienced. What else is habitual body memory but memory of an ongoing, reliable withness of the body in its customary actions? Other kinds of body memory—e.g., erotic or traumatic—bring out other aspects of corporeal withness.

AROUNDNESS

To be implaced in memory is to know our way *around:* to know the world around us. In memories of place we remember things, pathways, horizons as these concern and encompass us. Together, they constitute a structure of containment, an environment for remembering of many kinds and with many interests: "interest, *interesse,* means to be among and in the midst of things."[6] As we are among and amidst things in the world, so we are enclosed by the places we inhabit and remember.

THROUGHNESS

The remembering-through of commemoration occurs in many possible modalities—most conspicuously in textual and ritualistic ones. Quite apart from explicit ritual actions, what I have called "vertical" and "horizontal" communities exhibit an interpersonal throughness, which in commemorative ceremonies occurs in close conjunction with the withness of the body and the aroundness of place. Even in intrapsychic memorialization, however, there is a distinct through-factor, that of identification with the other as sedimented into internalized presence.

Withness, aroundness, and throughness are notably missing from the substantive, unadverbial Cartesian model of mind. As mirroring, this mind is essentially empty; in Locke's version, it is an entirely empty slate unless and until it is filled with representations. Adverbial variegation of the sorts introduced by the three kinds of memory treated in this Part is lacking in a view of mind as strictly self-identified, as egologically self-confined, and as transparent to itself. Hence the concern of the Cartesian conception of mind with accuracy of representation in recollection and reconstruction; hence too its tendency to center, to be centered and central, wherever possible. By contrast, the effect of structures of aroundness, throughness, and withness is to suspend a preoccupation with exactitude and thus to de-center: as we have seen in the polyvalence operative in body memory, the unsuspected complexity of a Chinese garden, and the intricate movements of participants in commemorative ceremonies. In all such cases, there is a noticeable outward-directedness, a moving beyond egological boundaries, a moving beyond oneself—beyond one's self-contained mind in a connective re-membering that is at once manic and mantic, ecstatic and encompassing, outgoing and ongoing.

# *Part Four*
# *Remembering Re-membered*

# XI

# THE THICK AUTONOMY OF MEMORY

> As those mysterious beings in ancient tales rise from the ocean's bed invested with seaweed, so [your innermost thought] now rises from the sea of remembrance, interwoven with memories.
>
> —Kierkegaard, *Either/Or,* Vol. I

## I

At this late point in an increasingly demanding project we need to perform our own act of anamnesis lest amnesia set in. We have come a long way from the moment of departure in chapter 1—when brief, straightforward analyses of a few first-hand experiences of remembering sufficed to get things underway. We have come a long way, too, from the self-assurance that accompanied the application of an intentionalist model of mind to memory, not to mention the comparative ease of picking out conspicuous eidetic traits of remembering. Since then, matters have become considerably more complex. We have had to confront the many ways in which we remember *in media vita,* in the very thick of things. This is why we undertook a trajectory in Part Two that drew us not just into the past world of the remembered but decisively into the life-world of the rememberer. To take such memorial phenomena as reminding or recognizing seriously is to be thrust into the particularities of the perceptual world—just as reflection on the nature of reminiscing lands us squarely in the domain of the communal and the discursive. Still more dramatically, we found ourselves caught up in Part Three in circumstances of growing difficulty and diversity as we explored the roles of body and place in remembering, reaching a climax in a consideration of commemorating that had to account for such disparate factors as text, ritual, and intrapsychic identification. By the end of chapter 10, a situation had been reached in which any pretense of providing a merely formal treatment, especially as measured in the classical phenomenological terms with which the book commenced, had to be given up. At that point, "ecstasy" (i.e., literally "standing outside" oneself) had become just as constitutive as anything "encompassing" (i.e., being surrounded in a comfortably comprehensive way).

As it stands, the situation edges on the entropic. Excess and unbalance seem to have replaced the equipoise attained by the end of Part One. Before things get out of hand altogether, we need to re-member remembering; we must put the pieces back together again. These pieces have become not merely numerous—so far, at least twelve major forms of remembering have been identified,[1] along with many minor modes—but difficult to assimilate to each other. The danger is only partly that of ending with a static *tableau*, a mere listing, of prominent features. This is a danger that inheres in any descriptive enterprise, including the present one. Of graver consequence is the danger of incoherence itself—that the forms and structures discussed in the course of our investigations do not cohere with each other, that the pieces do not fit together. What does reminding share with body memory? How does recognition relate to commemoration? Where do place memory and reminiscing become contiguous?

In asking such questions, I am *not* seeking for a new set of universal traits held in common by the variety of phenomena scrutinized in this book. To seek such traits would be to attempt yet another eidetic analysis, this time with respect to the results of the book as a whole. Nor is it a question of pursuing in detail the intricate interrelations between particular forms of remembering. Fascinating as these interrelations might prove to be—think only of the subtle interplay that arises between recognition and habitual body memory—they are beyond the scope of the present project. Let me attempt instead to remember where we have been. By this I mean a literal re-membering of the course we have taken, viewing it in terms of what an Aristotelian might label a "unity by analogy."[2] By such unity is not meant a strict synthesis, but a way in which the various parts of the analysis may be seen to cohere with one another in the end.

We may take as a clue—a crucial *Leitfaden*—the observation that as this book has progressed from Part to Part, and even from chapter to chapter, there has been a noticeably deepening rooting of remembering in what could be called the "native soil" of its own enactment. But this rooting has not meant—as we might expect it to mean—an engulfment of memory, its dissolution in particular contents or contexts. Even in the most engaged moments—say, in the very midst of an Ndembu initiation ceremony—remembering retains its identity as a recognizably memorial event. Such self-persistence is one aspect of what I shall designate as memory's "autonomy." But more than autonomy is involved in the distinctive self-identity possessed by remembering in its various forms. These forms exhibit in differing degrees a trait which can be called "thickness." It is this trait, above all, that offers a guiding thread at this concluding point.

Already, in the opening paragraph just above, I said that in the course of this book we had been thrust into "the very thick of things." This phrase points to the single most inclusive movement in which earlier chapters have been engaged. This is a movement of progressive *thickening*. The progress of this movement has its own immanent logic. What may have seemed naive or disingenuous about the first steps undertaken in Part One resulted less from an attempt at simplification than from an effort to consider those features of remembering that are diaphanous by nature—transparently given, as only mind can be to itself. As a consequence, the picture of remembering that emerged, based as it was on an intentionalist paradigm, shared much in common with the quite mentalistic portrait of imagination which I have presented elsewhere. Remembering, like imagining, can be depicted as a lambent, evanescent mode of mentation. At once fragile and pellucid, self-aware and self-transcending, memory seen in this light is modeled on a representationalist view of mind—a view controlled by a concern with clarity of insight and with detachment from the surrounding world.

It is just such clarity and detachment that come into question when remembering is considered apart from the prismatic looking-glass furnished by mentalism. As soon as we look beyond the glass—and in the actual experience of remembering we always do, even when we think we are still confined within it—we encounter an entire circumambient world, filled with such concreta as instruments and words, perceived objects and other people. In Part Two, I began to take account of such critical "intermediaries" by considering ways in which remembering links up concretely with the world of specific tasks, perceptual configurations, and forms of social life. The role of adumbrative signs in reminding, for example, was seen to tie us to instrumental complexes wherein basic actions are accomplished. So too the communal-discursive aspect of reminiscing serves to mediate between the privacy of auto-reminiscence and full-scale reminiscing in public. And the suffusion that is operative in recognition is characteristic not just of our own remembering minds but of the obdurate objects we confront routinely in the everyday world of work and leisure. In singling out these phenomena, we were acknowledging the interpenetration of remembering into the world around us and of this world itself into our remembering. Thanks to this mutual contamination, each could be said to "thicken" the other in the process.

The thickening deepened in Part Three. There, we looked carefully into forms of remembering that draw directly, and not just through intermediaries, on our immersion in the life-world. What could be more intimately connected with the life-world than our own body as it remembers itself? Thanks to its powers of habituation and orientation, this same body moves us resolutely into the places that make up the familiar landscape of our lives. The body-place *Gestaltkreis* is itself a basic unit—perhaps *the* basic unit—of human being-in-the-world. Through the stabilized implacement it makes possible, we truly enter into the thick of things, and thus into their enriched memory as well. When still other modes of thickening are in play—thickenings via text, or ritual, or the psychical incorporation of others—we find a dense situation indeed: thickening on thickening, thickening *of* thickening. This is precisely what we discover in commemoration, which represents an extreme in this very respect. In its multi-layered translucency, it stands as an antipode of recollection's self-transparency and monoscenic dimensionality.

Other indications of the thickening of memory include the adverbial structures of throughness, aroundness, and withness that were delineated in the Coda to Part Three. Each of these structures represents a special manner of memory's insertion into a particular life-world. We realize some of our most significant remembering by means of these structures: e.g., enacting bodily skills, or remembering having been in certain places. Perhaps most strikingly, the inherent solipsism of recollecting, that is, recalling the past to myself and by myself, gives way to the collectivism of commemoration, in which the density of group awareness and interaction figures prominently. Furthermore, the participation whose prototype is found in commemoration is also at work in body memory and place memory, and in all three cases the divisive dualisms of body/mind, self/other, and past/present are suspended—in contradistinction to recollection, which thrives on these very dualisms. The suspension itself is a matter of thickening, of allowing for increased coalescence of otherwise disjunctive terms.

Although I have been drawing thus far mainly on the metaphorical resonances of the word "thick" in the phrase "thick autonomy"—as is most evident in my talk of memorial "thickening" of several kinds—the word has a determinate semantic content. For "thick" as it applies to matters of memory means centrally: possessing a depth not easily penetrable by the direct light of consciousness (most obviously in the case of obdurate body memories but also in circumstances of reminding and recognizing, reminiscing and commemorating); resistant to conceptual understanding (for example, when I cannot understand why a given memory obsesses me so much); sedimented in layers (as occurs when an entire set of memories clusters around a particular place); and having "historical depth" (i.e., when my memories bear on the same thing as those of a preceding generation through our sharing the same symbolic nexus). Also invoked in calling memories "thick" are such things as a specific temporal density (e.g., "perdurance" as this was discussed in chapter 10); a concentrated emotional significance, ranging from feelings of regret or nostalgia to the sheer pleasure of recognizing a long-absent friend; a coarsely textured surface (i.e., as a result of the overlay of successive rememberings); a closely packed or "thickset" format (e.g., filled up with detail); an intimate familiarity in content (as is connoted in the phrase "as thick as thieves"); a compression of objects or events which Freud would label "condensation" in the instance of dreams; and an indistinct presentation (as is true of almost all except "eidetic" memories). As this group of primary and secondary meanings suggests, the semantic scope of "thick" is practically co-extensive with the range of remembering itself. It follows that to remember at all is to connect up with the past in a manner that can be described as thick in one or more of the senses just mentioned. It is to become enmeshed in the thicket of the past—a past which yields itself to remembering only across densely presented (and often multiply mediated) modes of display.

In the very midst of these diverse modes of memorial thickening we can detect an autonomous action of remembering at work. In fact, I am more, not less, autonomous when I remember in place and about place, in and with my body, in and through others. The range as well as the subtlety of my remembering is enhanced as I enter more fully into my memorial *in-der-Welt-Sein*. The same is true of the mnemonic modes studied in Part Two. By reminding myself and others, I am a more autonomous agent in the world, less dependent on the whims of others or on the vagaries of circumstance. Indeed, I would scarcely be an autonomous being if I could not recognize others in the first place; and my reminiscing with them consolidates social bonds that empower me in various ways. At every step, an increased density goes hand in hand with an undiminished autonomy. Without this autonomy, the density might be suffocating. But we do not yet know in what such autonomy consists.

## II

The thick autonomy of memory exists in relation to what we might call the factor of the "unresolved remainder." Certain human activities are essentially remainderless. They merely take place—and exhaust themselves in their occurrence without leaving any significant residue. Imagining is often a case in point, especially when it arises gratuitously and disappears without leaving a trace. Given imagination's proclivity for the purely possible, it is not surprising that many acts of imagining—e.g., those that we would describe as mere "passing" reveries—do not precipitate themselves into our subsequent life in any lasting way. They "go their own way." What I have called their "thin autonomy" is an expression of this etherealizing, evaporating tendency. It is hardly surprising, either, that one would tend to conceive such thin autonomy in resolutely mentalistic terms. And it is also not surprising that my own eidetic-*cum*-intentional analysis of imagination could claim completeness, if not exhaustiveness.[3] In the domain of imagining, the question of the unresolved remainder, the *restance* in Derrida's term, is not of pressing concern. When imagining does move into matters of weight and force (as happens in "active imagination" in Jungian analysis), it moves with more import and yields a more lasting sedimentation. Remembering, in contrast, abides in these same matters as if they constituted its original habitat: it dwells like a native in the realm of remainders. If imaginative autonomy possesses the gossamerlike quality of the wings of Icarus, rising sunward in dry cerulean freedom, any autonomy to which memory may aspire must, like Antaeus, make continued contact with the dense earth of recalcitrant experience.

This does not mean, however, that remembering is anything like a uniform phenomenon. The forms of remembering considered in Part One exhibited minimal density in their operation and so tended to leave very little by way of residue. Such structures as the "mnemonic presentation," the "memory-frame," even the "aura" encircling an enframed presentation: all of these imply that remembering consists in a play of surfaces or that it is merely epiphenomenal, having little depth and leaving no important remainder. Similarly, such neatly paired eidetic traits as were explored in chapter 2—i.e., search/display, encapsulment/expansion, and persistence/pastness—suggest that memory can be categorized and condensed into formal patterns without significant residua. The intentionalist account given in chapters 3 and 4 revealed much the same commitment (or more exactly, *pre*-commitment) to a binary structuring of the phenomenon—as if it could be exhaustively examined in terms of its act and object phases. The combined results of Part One, constituting only a first approach, need not be questioned at their own level. But we cannot help but wonder whether there was not already in play an uncaptured remainder to which a formalistic analysis is not fully sensitive.

It was, of course, much this same kind of concern that led Heidegger to depart from Husserl's noetico-noematic conception of mind with its stress on act-intentionality and to turn to being-in-the-world as a realm in which phenomenology could deal more adequately with all that fell outside the lucidity of pure consciousness—all that *remained over* after an intentional analysis of such consciousness had been accomplished. Inspired in part by Heidegger's example, Part Two of this book turned to the unexamined residues which Part One, in its Husserlian zeal, had left out of consideration. Whether in the form of the perceptual particulars that provide the context for recognizing, the semiotic dimensions of reminding, or the role of concrete discourse in reminiscing, we confronted things that would no longer submit to the austerely formal treatment that had been possible in the opening chapters of this book. With this move beyond the eidetic and the intentional, we moved not so much beyond phenomenology as into some of its deeper reaches.

In Part Three we entered into still deeper domains. Much as Merleau-Ponty, in the wake of Heidegger, taught us to immerse ourselves in a single aspect of being-in-the-world—in his case, that of the lived body—so we took up three ways in which mnemonic remainders exist in depth. One of these is body memory itself, and its decidedly ingrained character was seen to exhibit a *restance* resistant to classical or modern categorizations. But we also discovered comparable resistances in the case of place memory and commemoration. Neither unsited landscape features, such as meandering pathways, nor the unplanned movements of rituals can be absorbed without remainder into maps or prescriptions for ceremonial order; and yet precisely as resistant to such modes of organization, these features and movements are crucial for the remembrance of place and of events of collective significance. Not only is there a close affinity between remembering and remaindering in these cases; the thick texture of memory itself is seen in bas-relief.

Freud liked to cite Virgil's oracular pronouncement: *Flectere si nequeo superos, Acheronta movebo,* "if I cannot bend the Higher Powers, I will move the Lower Regions."[4] Not altogether unlike Freud, we have turned away from the Higher Powers of mind so as to move into the Lower Regions of body, place, and commemoration—regions where the waters of Acheron, winding circuitously within the memorial underworld of unredeemed remainders, run as thick as they run deep.

## III

Let us grant the remarkable and ever-growing density of memorial phenomena as we descend into the lower depths of remembering. In these depths much has remained unexplored, indeed often unsuspected, in previous accounts. But to acknowledge the thickening of memory, its dark underside, is not the same thing as to affirm its autonomy. In fact, it might seem that autonomy is less and less likely to be found as we move into the full density of the phenomenon. At least this would be so in any classical conception of autonomy as self-controlled and self-regulated action.[5] The more we discover how immersed memory is in our lives—and our lives in it—the less we may be inclined to consider it as either a creature or a creator of autonomous action.

If autonomy appears to be an inappropriate designation at this darkened end of the memorial spectrum, it seems just as inapt at the other end, where luminosity prevails. I am thinking specifically of secondary memory in its canonical form as the visualized representation of an episode or scene. Here all is, or should be, clarity and light: the better the memory, i.e., the more "accurate" it is, the more it ought to resemble the original scene as first experienced. The ideal of what Husserl calls "clarification" *(Klärung)* is pertinent and frequently invoked: "let's get clear about this memory" we say in this context.[6] With the language of illumination goes the idea of transparency; the most completely clarified secondary memory would represent the past so diaphanously that it would rise before us without any of the distorting effects of an interposed medium such as a text or a bodily action. The absence of any such medium is what allows for the unburdened, the self-illumined character of the situation. We rejoin Kundera at this point: "The absolute absence of a burden causes man to be lighter than air, to soar into the heights, take leave of the earth and his earthly being."[7]

Unbearable as the lightness of being may be when regarded from a metaphysical standpoint, it is highly prized in the realm of mind—especially when the mind is considered capable of reproducing the past by recollecting it in secondary memory. Given the criteria of accuracy and transparency, the aim of such remembering can only be to *picture* the past as exactly as possible. What does the "secondary" of secondary memory—and its German analogue, the *wieder* ("again") of *Wiedererinnerung*—mean except precisely to offer a reprise, a repetition, a second presentation, a re-presentation, of a past event that has elapsed in its first form of appearance? The more we press in this direction, the closer we come to an ideal of pictoriality that deserves to be called "photographic." The photograph suggests itself all too naturally as a paradigm of what recollective remembering ought to be in its fullest realization. "Picture your memories" is a standard statement in Kodak advertising. We are also reminded of the high value placed in our culture on a "photographic memory," as rare as it is impressive. The ancient *ars memorativa*, as we have seen, called for the use of explicit and detailed visual imagery. Even in ordinary procedures of memorizing the exact picturing of items is consistently prized and encouraged.

The photographic paradigm as applied to memory is a revealing instance of what I called the "passivist" tradition in the Introduction. Passivism, it will be recalled, is the view that all memories of necessity repeat the past in a strictly replicative manner. The contribution of the remembering subject, according to this view, is nugatory—if it is not outright distortive or destructive. From here it is but a short step to the claim that memories are (or should be) copies of past events and objects. Memories should take the form of images that are isomorphic with what they are images *of*. Aristotle, as we know, was the first to formulate explicitly the claim that remembering is "the having of an image regarded as a copy of that of which it is an image."[8] The claim persists in Russell's insistence on the pictographic status of "visual memory-images," which have an "analogy of structure" with their origins.[9] Indeed, the hold of passivism is as widespread as it is tenacious, as is evident in a continuing adherence to the idea that memory traces are "structural analogues" of remembered experiences.[10]

The photographic ideal of a purely pictorial memory brings the tradition of passivism to an extreme point. For it suggests that the reproduction of the past at work in secondary memory or recollection is sheerly mechanical in operation. This is an even more extreme conception than is found in the neurophysiological view of engrams—a view which at least maintains the idea of an organic basis of replication. The crucial point for our purposes is that *to the extent that pictoriality of a quasi-photographic sort becomes a paradigm for recollection, no significant sense of autonomy can attach to such memory*. For a photograph is nothing other than the determinate effect of a particular efficient cause: such is its fate as a merely mechanical process. As a purely physical product, it has zero autonomy even when "autonomy" is understood in the most constricted sense. A photograph cannot control or regulate itself; it is entirely dependent on external conditions (i.e., the scene to be photographed, the photographer, the physical camera itself). If recollection is indeed a matter of depicting the past in a crisp, visualized format, a format modeled on that of photographic likeness, it will be deprived of any effective autonomy of its own.

In fact, it will lack even the thin autonomy that can be attributed to imagination in its freest movements. In its "verticalizing" capacity, imaginative autonomy is guided by the pursuit of pure possibilities.[11] No such pursuit, and therefore no such autonomy, is possible in a circumstance in which nothing but the strict replication of settled actualities is at stake. For when recollection takes place in the form of an exact image—that is, with a pictoriality that is isomorphic with the scene remembered—the image employed is wholly dependent on the scene it depicts. No autonomous play, much less any free play, is possible in such a closely conditioned setting.[12]

It must be emphasized, however, that any such situation of zero autonomy is itself a limiting case. It conveys what *would* obtain *if* recollection were indeed strictly modeled on the prototype of the photograph. The paradox it presents—the fact that its being disburdened of a distorting medium brings with it the burden of having no autonomy of its own—need not detain us if, in fact, the enactment of recollection rarely attains anything like the photographic ideal but only, at most, a lame approximation to it. And this latter is indeed often the case. Was my memory of vacationing at Yosemite painstakingly pictographic in character? Far from it. Not only were many crucial details lacking—details bearing on such principal matters as time, place, even the sequence of events—but large parts of my recollection were altogether indistinct (e.g., as to where my family ate, the spot we stayed in overnight, the route to the falls). So pictorially imperfect was the memory as a whole that I even called on an actual photograph as an *aide-mémoire*. My secondary memory itself invoked this photograph as a valuable supplementary object, yet this invocation did not mean that my own act of remembering was quasi-photographic in status.

The truth of the matter is that recollective memory, however much it may strain after an ideal of purely pictorial replication, only rarely achieves this ideal in practice and, still more tellingly, just as rarely considers the actualization of this ideal to be required for successful remembering. My recollection of the Yosemite visit, for all its obvious shortcomings, was perfectly satisfactory for my purposes—for my personal purposes in remembering it spontaneously and even for my didactic purposes in presenting it as an initial example in this book. What complicates matters is not the experience of recollecting itself but the charged expectations that are laid on it—expectations that arise from a tendentious theoretical ideal of clarity and exactitude.

We can be still more positive in our assessment of secondary memory. Not only is most recollecting not purely passive—as it comes to be considered when it is analogized to engrams and especially to photographs—but it contains important elements of activism. These elements include retrospective interpolations, self-interpretations, factors of search-within-memory (as when I ask myself "what must have happened next?"), the heuristic use of imagery or words (i.e., so as to elicit a spontaneous recollection), and even the deliberate use of another quite different recollection to illuminate a currently obscure recollection. In all of these ways I am being anything but passive, much less mechanical. I am not merely picturing my memories; I am bringing them forth in a concerted, and often a quite constructive, manner. Even reproduction, therefore, has a productive aspect. Collection is at work in recollection, and there is something "primary" in secondary memory—something attributable to my own efforts.

This is not to say that such an analysis of recollection would confirm Piaget's position of extreme activism, whereby the schematizing activity of the recollector is given the lion's share of the credit for what is recollected.[13] But it would certainly rule out the opposite extreme of abject passivism as it is found in Aristotle or Russell—and in many kindred empiricists. In fact, it would suggest that the situation is a mixed one, in which active and passive elements vie with one another in the generation of any given recollection. In this situation, passivism serves to remind us that memory is indeed "*of* the past";[14] it bears on it and borrows from it. This means that memory must be *true to the past* in certain basic respects. (These will be examined below in section VI.) But mimicry of the past is not required for remembering to occur: to remember is not to pantomime (literally, to "imitate all"), much less to copy something pre-existent. For one can very well have in mind—or enact in the lived body—a *simulacrum* of the past without remembering that past at all: as in highly repetitive behavior (e.g., a phobia whose origin we have forgotten), or in a memory image so isolated from an appropriate identifying context as to lose its memorial power (as when an unidentified tune haunts us). Just here passivism reaches the limit of its own truth.

In contrast, activism is right to remind us of the positive contributions of the rememberer. The mind of this person—quite apart from his or her bodily actions, implacement, and interpersonal relations—makes a very real difference, not only in *how* things are remembered but even in precisely *what* is remembered on a given occasion. Here we observe a formative structuring of the remembered in its cognitive, affective, social, and still other aspects. Think merely of all the circumstances in which "believing makes it so": as often occurs in the notoriously dubious testimony of witnesses to automobile accidents. But this is not to say that memories literally *create* the past by bringing it into being.[15] That thesis lies at the limit of activism, and we need to avoid it as decisively as the corresponding extremity of passivism, while preserving what is permanently insightful in both positions.

What has all this invocation of activism and passivism to do with the issue of autonomy? A great deal indeed. Despite our propensity for subjecting recollection to the passivist paradigm of the photograph, recollecting itself is hardly an unactive affair. It models the past rather than merely remodeling it, and to be able to do this is to be autonomous in a way that is not just "thin," tempting as it may be to apply this term to it. Recollecting no more pursues pure possibilities than does the most engaged body memory. It deals with past actualities, which it transforms rather than simply transmits. The transformative work of recollection belongs to a complex circumstance in which effort and resistance, recasting and re-viewing, are all in play. The existence of such complexity means that any criterion of immediate transparency, when not rejected altogether, will need to be questioned. So too will any notion of sheer passivity. It would be better to speak with Husserl of a "passivity in activity" that brings with it its own complexity of operation.[16]

The autonomy of recollection is nevertheless much less dense than that displayed in many other forms of remembering. In such forms there is a more considerable thickening to be observed, one that takes place in the very midst of autonomous actions. No longer is the thickness merely a function of interventions on the part of the rememberer. The medium of remembering comes into prominence as the seeming transparency of recollecting gives way to translucency. The role of context, which is often kept at a decided distance in recollection, becomes indispensable and is acknowledged as such—above all, when attention is given to the factor of place. Perception and language loom large—rendering the mnemonic presentation anything but purely pictorial—as do entire communities of co-rememberers. As the world of the rememberer is brought bodily into his or her remembering, this remembering itself is thickened with all that has remained over, and was unaccounted for, on the regulative ideal of a purely pictorial recollection.

Remembering, rendered ever thicker in these ways and others, is no less autonomous for becoming so intertwined with the circumambient world. In addition to passivism, the other threat to memorial autonomy is memory's own increasing thickness, its immersion in the remembering/remembered world. Nevertheless, remembering stays autonomous in the thick of things. Not only is its autonomy uncompromised by its immersion: it is even enhanced and strengthened. How can this be?

## IV

Let us consider certain indications laid down in the history of language. There we find that the very etymology of the word "memory" already points toward its thick autonomy. As this etymology is extraordinarily diverse and rich—it merits one of the most detailed entries in Eric Partridge's *Origins*—I shall restrict consideration to three particularly pertinent cases in point.

### MOURNING

*Memor,* Latin for "mindful," and the Old English *murnan,* "to grieve," are both traceable to the Sanskrit *smárati,* "he remembers."[17] This is not entirely surprising, since we realized in the last chapter that mourning, as a process of intrapsychic memorialization, is itself a form of commemoration. "Commemoration," as we also learned, originally meant an *intensified* remembering.[18] One way to intensify something is to give it a thicker consistency so as to help it to last or remain more substantively. Such thickening is surely the point of any memorialization, whether it be ceremonial, sculptural, scriptural, or psychical. Every kind of commemoration can be considered an effort to create a lasting "remanence" for what we wish to honor in memory—where "remanence" signifies a perduring remainder or residuum (as in the literally thick stone of war memorials or grave markers). Mourning effects such remanence within the psychical sphere; and it is notable that it is accomplished slowly. In the context of mourning, we are especially prone to say that "the old dies hard," implying the thickness of time and history. Mourning is also concerned with endings—with deaths or absences that linger like ghosts or *revenants* to haunt us. These ghostly endings are "remanents," that which is "left behind, remaining, when the rest is removed, used, done, etc."[19] But it is precisely because mourning is a slowly enacted process of working-through that it manages to transform such remanents/revenants into genuine *remnants:* exorcizing the ghosts of their external haunting power and aiding us in identifying with what is left. In this way, internal presences are moulded from the thick memorial magma of the mourning process. The moment of transfiguration is the moment of autonomy, since it lends new (psychical) life to the departed persons. It is an autonomy that is achieved not despite, or beyond, the memorial magma but in and through this thickened matter itself. Hence, the prolonged grieving, often extending over many years; hence also, a frequent failure to see the process through to its full ending.

### CARING

Closely related to mourning is caring: how could I mourn for what is indifferent to me? Caring also implies remembering, that is to say, keeping the other person (or thing) in mind. Thus, it comes as a confirming fact to learn that "memory" is also cognate with the Greek *mērimna,* "care," "solicitude," "anxiety," "sorrow."[20] Remembering *is* caring for what we remember—intensified, once more, in commemorating. Indeed, it can be loving as well, via *minna:* this way lies the heart-memory link. Moreover, both caring and loving *take time;* neither can occur instantaneously; both require the fullness of time. Yet neither, when fully enacted, becomes time's fool: each represents a triumph *within time,* not a subordination to it. And in this "sweet victory" each is autonomous in its memorial action, realizing itself through the density of its immersions.

Care, anxiety, solicitude: these are strikingly Heideggerian terms, bespeaking enmeshment in being-in-the-world. Whereas imagining characteristically glides above and beyond such enmeshment—its thin autonomy signifying freedom from concern and solicitude[21]—remembering cannot help but engage us in *Angst* and *Sorge* along with their many affiliated states of mind. This is how the thick autonomy of remembering is experienced at the level of emotion and mood: as *mermeros,* "solicitous," "caring," "anxious."[22] Brooding is not far afield here, as we are reminded by *mimeren,* "to muse," "brood" in Middle Dutch. In its pensive slowness, brooding is the cognitive counterpart of care and solicitude: to brood is to be painfully care-ful in thought. Brooding also belongs to the Heideggerian *Weltbild,* in which "the burdensome character of Dasein"[23] is so prominent. In all of these closely related ways, the caring aspect of memory's thick autonomy manifests its tethering action, its tendency to tie things down tenaciously rather than to release them.

### DELAY

Delay is implicit in mourning and caring alike, both of which act in a patient and slow fashion. *Mora* is Latin for delay: stopping and pausing; hence *moratorium* and such words as Old Irish *maraim,* "I remain," and Gaelic *mair,* "to last," and *mairneal,* "dilatoriness." All of these moratorial matters are deeply memorial in character, reflecting not merely the fact that remembering always *takes place* "after the fact" but more importantly that it is an essentially time-taking operation (whether the time at stake be the micro-seconds of primary memory or the epochal durability of Egyptian monuments). Indeed, many kinds of memory involve massive delaying tactics, that is, concerted efforts to delay time's erosive force.[24]

The factor of delay is also found in one of memory's most distinctive capacities: its "deferred action" or *Nachträglichkeit.* Freud introduced this notion in a letter to Fliess written in 1896:

> I am working on the assumption that our psychical mechanism has come into being by a process of stratification: the material present in the form of memory-traces being subjected from time to time to a *re-arrangement* in accordance with fresh circumstances—to a *re-transcription (Umschrift).*[25]

In other words, memories may gain a new psychical efficacy as a result of modifications introduced by evolving circumstances over time. Delay in time, instead of diminishing the force of a given memory, serves to increase this force—to give the memory "a new lease on life." We encounter here the unsuspected power of *belatedness:* "the memory-trace is revised belatedly so as to adjust either to new experience or to a new vision of experience."[26] It is not just that new vision calls for re-vision but that the later vision is inherently stronger—more lasting, more forceful—than the first vision. Pausing strengthens; and the remainder of events, their true remanence, may become more powerful than the original events themselves.[27]

Memory's delaying power constitutes in effect another critique of passivism, for which the power resides in the initial impressions and not in the memorial outcome. But it also calls into question any pure activism that would invite us to conceive the past as a manipulable, neutral matter without any form or life of its own. The delaying power points instead to a model in which the past provides the very depth of memory, yet is continually reshaped in the present. Rather than being a simple stockpile of dead actualities—an instance of what Heidegger would term "standing-reserve"[28]—the past "begins now and is always becoming."[29] In short, *the past develops*, thanks to the delaying action of remembering. Such development is abundantly apparent in the role of narration as re-shaping what we have experienced. As Janet makes clear in his notion of *la conduite du récit*, a narrative account reilluminates and reformulates the past in multiple ways.[30] Any such *après coup* action in memory gestures toward a middle ground lying between the poles of activism and passivism: an in-between of past and present in which the brunt of the past, its very thickness, is supported and carried forward (often heavily re-vised) by an autonomous remembering in the present that is not the mere proxy of its own origins.

The slowness inherent in delay—and prominently present as well in mourning and caring—evokes what I called "ruminescence" earlier in this book. The fast action of imagination and alert thought gives way to a regime of slow digestion: of considerate ingestion and accrued assimilation. This is not only a temporal affair. The autonomy of remembering is all the thicker for having to deal as well with the spatial densities that populate body and place memories, where the slowness exhibits itself in *ritardando* movements through space. There, too, ruminescence is solicited as an emotional correlate of memory's thick autonomy.

## V

Thus far does language speak on the matter. The very etymons of "memory," in their crisscrossing histories and slow growth, attest eloquently to the thick autonomy of remembering. Etymological dictionaries, after all, are themselves forms of public memory; "digests" of the genealogy of words and their meanings, they constitute a diachronic map of the memory of natural languages.[31] But we are by no means restricted to the history of language in witnessing the work of memorial autonomy. Our lives are pervaded by this work, which refuses confinement to any single area of human experience. *Nothing human is unmemorial*—even if very little is immemorial! And if this is so, it will also be the case that everything human will be touched by the three aspects of memory's thick autonomy which have just been identified: mourning, caring, and delaying.

To appreciate the pervasiveness of such autonomy, consider a seemingly unpromising instance: a modern wedding ceremony. Such a ceremony certainly has far more to do with beginnings than with endings, and in this respect contrasts graphically with the Eucharist or with funeral rites. Nevertheless, a closer look reveals other dimensions than merely "beginning a new life together." To start with, any such beginning entails a leaving—hence an ending—whether this be in relation to one's parents, a former marriage, friends, a part of the country, or one's previous status as single. For this reason, mourning is by no means absent from weddings, even though it is typically suppressed or delimited; the ceremony itself, by its very formality, acts to forestall excessive displays of grief—e.g., on the part of the father who "gives away his daughter" in a public and pre-established manner. Any contemporary mourning tends to be left to the future—as is fitting, not only for reasons of propriety but in view of the prolonged process of mourning. The ceremony conspires with the process. Notice, further, that a wedding expressly celebrates caring, especially in the forms of cherishing and loving. Indeed, marriage is the very institutionalization of caring over time: "till death do us part." The ceremony can even be considered the admonitory inculcation of *Fürsorge* or caringness of the marriage partners for each other. As a performative action, it calls for caring in a committing way that, it is hoped, will last indefinitely. In the face of such commitment, it is only to be expected that anxiety—closely related to care if language does not mislead us—will also arise and will even be quasi-institutionalized ("the nervous groom"). Just as marriage is a leave-taking and a matter of mourning, so it is equally an engagement in *Mitsein,* in a new being-together-in-the-world, and as such it involves anxious care.

Even beyond what has already been suggested, the role of delay is strikingly present. Rather than a mere instantaneous acknowledgment of affection between two people, a wedding ceremony acts to underscore the fact that the value of a given marriage will only be known in and through a considerable period of time. Its very gravity and solemnity point in this direction and set the tone. At the same time, the ceremony and the occasion themselves serve to *lay down memories* whose importance can be savored only in a *nachträglich* manner: they will be most effective precisely in their deferred action. The role of wedding gifts, and especially of wedding photographs, illustrates the power of deferred appreciation. Often barely noticed or considered banal at the time, such gifts and photographs can come to be increasingly cherished as time goes by. Photographs in particular seem to be conventionally taken largely with an eye to possibilities of future enjoyment. The memorability of the occasion is, as it were, displaced onto subsequent moments of ruminescent savoring. Through the medium of the formal photograph, the ceremonial moment becomes belated in respect to itself; it becomes what it *will be seen to be;* it becomes something which will lastingly come toward us.[32] The exchange of rings and vows works in much the same manner. Binding by its very enactment, this ritual will nevertheless gain force only with time—that is, when lived out in new and often trying circumstances. It is evident that delay here links up closely with "perdurance." A ceremony such as a wedding establishes memories that are meant to perdure—not just because they are encased in photographs or crystalized in gems, but because only as perduring will they gain that deferred efficacy that will render them sustaining and inspiring in the future to come.

It is only as thickly autonomous that remembering can figure in such an unlikely format as this, in which the emphasis falls upon the future. Or more exactly, upon a past on its way to becoming future in a certain present. Remembrance is not only now, but then . . . and then . . . and then. . . . The sequence of then's indicates that it is not a question of achieving permanence—only memorials and monuments pretend to this—but of attaining a reliable and ongoing remanence. Or we could say that, thanks to its thick autonomy, remembering here *remainders itself*. The remainders do not consist in depositions laid down—as is assumed in theories preoccupied with leaving marks and traces in an unchanging material base—but in pathways that branch off ever more diversely into a multiple futurity. The belatedness, in other words, is not that of deferred events which *have* happened, but of expanding eventualities that *might* happen. As in marriage itself, the issue is less one of actuality (the actual ceremony, the actual guests, the actual vows, the actual gifts and photographs) than of virtuality: what all this will have become in the unchartable course of time (and in the vagaries of space).[33]

When the past is viewed as something simply actualized or settled, it is reduced to being an inert sedimentation, a mere residuum. It is just such a past that is regarded as acting upon the present by efficient causality, pushing this present into existence by its pre-formed and unchanging actuality. The notion of *Nachträglichkeit* has forewarned us of the insufficiency of this model, since the present (and the future!) can outdo its own causal origins in terms of effective force. But memorial autonomy is more than a matter of deferred effects: this is still to speak the language of *causa efficiens* even if by reversal of order. As Heidegger reminds us, the issue is that of human beings' own distinctive way of putting this autonomy into practice: one "historizes out of [the] future on each occasion."[34] Such historizing happens not just once in a while (e.g., in moments of decision or resolve) but "on each occasion"—not only at weddings but in divorce proceedings, not only in buying clothes but in wearing them daily, not only in setting out to write a book like this one but in finishing it a decade later.

Here the thickness of memory's autonomy consists in the way in which the past is carried continually forward in being remembered at different moments—indeed, even when it is momentarily forgotten or repressed. But if there were only such conveying actions, we might indeed be overwhelmed by the past in our present and succumb to the efficient causalism of the passivist model; for we could easily become stuck in the past, mired in its repetition. Yet we are not so mired—or need not be—if the carrying forward is anticipatory of a future toward which we are actively tending. To historize *out of* such a future is to realize a genuinely autonomous action, one that requires us to come to terms with the virtuality of the past itself. Rather than awaiting the future—e.g., by "expectation," through which we make the future determinate beforehand, a form of inauthenticity[35]—we *make it possible*.

We make the future possible precisely by envisaging it in terms of the past we bear in the viscosity of the present, allowing its remanence to arise in an act of foreshadowing *what might be*. In contrast with the purely possible that is projected in imagining, however, "what might be" is here a function of *what has been* and thus of the thickness of the past as it comes to bear on the present and on the future. Hence we must modify Eliot's formula: "What might have been and what has been point to one end, which is always present."[36] Rather: what might be and what has been point to one end, which is the future as enlivened in the present. Only an activity capable of a remarkably compressed density could possess such an intimately interwoven temporality as this. As Lacan states:

> What is realized in my history is not the past definite of what was, since it is no more, nor even the present perfect of what has been in what I am, but the future anterior of what I shall have been for what I am in the process of becoming.[37]

It is precisely because the remembered past is neither "definite" nor "perfect"—is not to be forced onto the Procrustean bed of date and bare event—that a future of open fulfillment (and not of mere projection) becomes possible. And vice versa: an open future helps to keep the remembered past alive. Even "what I shall have been" is not to be confined to the future perfect tense in which it is formulated; as reflecting "what I am in the process of becoming," it is anterior to its own perfection. At every point—"now" and "then" and "then" (where the "then" can be future as well as past in status)—the thick autonomy of remembering dismantles, by its own massive action, the temporal determinacy of the past.

Since the same deconstructive process is at work in matters of space—as we have observed in chapter 9, where "site" gave way to "place" in being remembered—we begin to discover the larger implications of memorial autonomy. This autonomy acts to undo the stranglehold of the determinate wherever this arises in time or space. The determinate is a perfectly appropriate object of thought—e.g., in the guise of the necessary—but it cannot be regarded as having supreme value even in perceiving, where internal and external horizons introduce an essential indeterminacy. In imagining and remembering it is of distinctly dubious value. Whereas to imagine is to engage in the indeterminate as such—indeterminacy is the close counterpart of pure possibility[38]—to remember is to commit oneself to an ever-thickening admixture of the determinate (i.e., as actual) and the indeterminate (as virtual). Remembering cannot do without reference to the actual—whether straightforwardly in allusion to the past, or indirectly via perception—but it always manages to exceed any simple actualism of experience. Thanks to the bivalent orientation of its own autonomous action, it is always on the move: *away* from what was and has been and *toward* what is now becoming via-à-vis a still-to-be determined futurity. Memory moves us as surely into the realm of what shall be as it moves us back to what has been; by extracting what is indeterminately lasting from the latter, it allows the former to come to us.

## VI

To acknowledge the active element in remembering is already to point toward its possible autonomy, at least its negative autonomy. For a major consequence of the findings of thinkers as diverse as Piaget and Freud is that memories are not strictly tied down to their own origins; in varying degrees, they may become free from these origins by virtue of the transforming effects of displacement, projection, sublimation, or schematization. In being negatively autonomous, remembering is not restricted to a sheer replication of the past, as is demanded by the model of passivism. Particular and pertinent origins—e.g., perceptual, historical, linguistic—are certainly incorporated into eventual memories and are often represented in or alluded to by such memories; but they need not provide the sole source of their content, much less their total structure. In gaining this independence of causal/factual origins, memories exhibit a negative autonomy, a capacity *not* to be determined by the past.

But this leaves unanswered the more difficult question: what *positive* autonomy, if any, does remembering exhibit? By "positive autonomy" I mean not merely free *from* (origins, sources, causes regarded as exclusive and sufficient conditions) but free *for*—for a development, an expressive exfoliation, which moves beyond the heteronomous power of past particularities. Such autonomy is comparatively easy to demonstrate in the case of imagining, which exhibits an indigenous freedom of mind. But the price to be paid for this freedom, which consists largely in the indefinite variability of imagined content, is an equally indigenous ethereality that reflects a dramatic distance from particular origins. The positive autonomy of remembering, in contrast, is enmeshed in its origins even when it seems to be functioning independently of them. The result is an autonomy so dense as often to obscure its own recognition and description—indeed, precisely dense enough to tempt many to view memory as an utterly passive process.

We must acknowledge that there is nothing in remembering that is comparable to imaginative freedom of mind; there is nothing like an open ranging among freely projected variants that have no assignment to instantiate (or even to represent) the actual. Whatever its ability to broach the virtual, the commitment of memory to the already actualized cannot be rescinded. Nor does remembering possess any exact equivalent of two features of imagining that support its inherent freedom of mind: ease of access and assured success of enactment. Precisely because of remembering's engagement in the actual—its duty to stand in for it faithfully to some significant extent—we are not always able to come up with the particular memory we seek. As everyone knows to his or her frustration—sometimes excrutiatingly so in a tip-of-the-tongue experience—many memories slip away and evade our most earnest efforts to retrieve them. In David Krell's phrase, they are "on the verge."[39] At the same time, even when a quite crystalline mnemonic presentation does emerge as a possibility, we are by no means assured, by its appearance alone, that its specific content is the content we are looking for: there is no inbuilt guarantee that our intention and its fulfillment will coincide in that seamless *Deckung* that Husserl posited as an epistemological ideal.[40] Quite apart from amnesia (i.e., the inability to remember anything), paramnesia (remembering the wrong thing) threatens us throughout.

The thick autonomy of remembering is therefore a more difficult autonomy to accomplish than is the thin autonomy of imagining. More of "the patient labor of the negative" is required in its realization. As the Sisyphean labors of psychoanalysis painfully attest, it is not uncommon to engage in quite strenuous efforts to bring back certain memories—efforts that include disentangling these memories from the morass of contiguous or similar memories to which they stand closely related. Moreover, internal clarifications of a given memory are also often needed. It is evident, then, that the autonomy of remembering is hard-won; it does not fall into our laps in the way in which autonomous imagining characteristically does. Despite these difficulties, however, autonomous remembering does occur; and the autonomy therein achieved is of a distinctly positive sort.[41]

I shall restrict consideration of such positive autonomy to a single instance, that of the truth we attain in remembering. The issue of truth arises not just from the ever-present possibility of erroneous memories or from moments of forgetting. It also arises from the fact that the past we recall has a certain definiteness of form, spatial and temporal and qualitative, to which we somehow try to do justice. In other words, we try to be true *to* it, to speak the truth *about* it—where both "to" and "about" express an action of positive approximation. Such approximation to the past certainly does not mean producing a duplicate of it, something that would correspond to it point by point. In Platonic language, an *eikon* does not convey the *eidos*. Iconicity is neither necessary nor sufficient for remembering, which can be true to its own subject matter in a non-isomorphic fashion. But in what does such truth consist, and how does it embody a positive autonomy of remembering?

The truth in question possesses two basic forms: truth to the "how" and truth to the "that."

### TRUTH TO THE HOW

This is a matter of being true to our own experienc*ing*, to how we experienced a given situation. Included under "experiencing" are emotional responses, stray thoughts we had at the time, interpretations we may have made of the original experience, fantasies arising from it, etc. In addition, there is the body's mode of experiencing—how we assimilated the event corporeally, how it felt "in our bones." Given the complexity and multi-layeredness of how we experienced the situation, it is clear that we cannot do justice to all such factors as those just mentioned; nor need we do so in order to attain adequate or even accurate remembering. We can be highly selective and still retain the special subjective savor of our experiencing: the selectivity may be the most effective way of preserving the savor. Indeed, even where there is no explicit representation whatsoever of the original experience—as occurs in many body memories—we can be true to how it felt to have been present in that experience by summoning up pertinent feelings or related thoughts.

### TRUTH TO THE THAT

This is the truth to the factuality of the event experienced—to the fact of its occurrence. By "event" is usually meant a publicly ascertainable happening; but events may also include my own feelings, perceptions, and thoughts, which I may remember as facts in separation from their experiential content *per se*. Thus I can recall *that* I was feeling acute remorse three weeks ago without now engaging in an analogous emotional state or a representation of any such state and its specific content. The evidence for the truth of such a claim will most likely be found within my own experience. Of course, I can consult others who were with me at the time and who may have noticed my remorse; but since I may have been deceiving them by pretending to be happy, their testimony cannot be regarded as requisite, much less definitive, for the truth of what I claim about my own state of mind. Such a situation contrasts with that of remembering a public fact. In that case, corroboration by other people *is* essential for bearing out the truth of memory claims, which can be definitively disproven by others: as when I claim to recall seeing Joan at noon downtown, whereas she was having lunch in her home with persons who now testify to this fact. Here the factual component of remembering belongs to a public domain in which my own subjective states can no longer count as evidentially decisive. But in neither instance—whether it is a case of a public event or a state of mind—does the memory of a factual occurrence demand detailed representation. Even in the case of public remembering-that, the sketchiest of descriptions may suffice: e.g., "yesterday, sometime in the late afternoon, I remember that the ferry pulled into the dock."[42]

Taken together, truth to the "how" and truth to the "that" constitute a distinctive positive autonomy of remembering. Our being true to the past in these two ways does not mean merely that we are *not* beholden to it—that we are not bound to repeat it. In entering into the domain of truth, something other than negative autonomy—i.e., independence *from* the past—is at stake. Nor is it just a matter of degrees of latitude allowed with regard to determinate origins. For it is now a question of being able to affirm that the past *was* thus-and-so as a fact, or was *experienced* in such-and-such a way. In this circumstance, memories are not reducible to mere evidential sources, mere pre-texts to truth: affirmation cannot be reduced to confirmation. And the affirmation itself is not to be confused with assertion, i.e., its articulation in words. Truth emerges in and through the act of remembering itself. This is what we mean when we say that a given memory is "true to an experience," or that we are "truly remembering" something. In such cases the truth resides not in statements that may accompany the remembering, or in items of evidence, but *in the remembering itself*—in its relation to the past with which it is reconnecting, whatever the precise evidence or expression in words may be.

It follows that for such an immanent truth-in-memory to arise no explicit representations of the past, whether in the form of words or images, need to be involved. Memorial truth is attainable without employing representations of any kind. Although we see this most clearly in the case of body memories, it also occurs whenever I think rememoratively and yet non-imagistically and non-verbally of the past—as happens in meditative musings on previous experiences. In fact, I can even remember the past truthfully through a *mis*representation of it, as we observe not only in the instance of screen memories (when I remember something through a false facade) but when a certain figure is misidentified, a detail is omitted, or a false substitution of one thing for another arises. Despite the manifest inaccuracy of such rememberings, they can still manage to convey the "how" of the remembered situation and perhaps also its "that" as well: the gist of the situation. For I can achieve a significant level of truthful remembering even as I frankly fail at the level of documentation or proof. I can regain the past in truth even if I cannot regain it in exactitude, much less in totality. I can regain it as a partial and even distorted presence—as part of my own past as I now reclaim it, or as part of a collective past as an entire group might commemorate it. To be able to do such things—to fly in the face of the ideal of verisimilitude in remembering—is a forceful sign of memory's positive autonomy.

Such autonomy is not a matter of transcending perceptual or historical or linguistic origins, whether personal or social. Its action occurs in their very midst. Memorial truth is discovered *within* the various matters of memory, not outside them or beyond them. Because of this immersion, the autonomy of remembering remains thick. Implicit in all remembering is a commitment to truth concerning the past, a truth that reflects the specificity of this past even if it need not offer an exact likeness of it. Once I enter into remembering, there can be no backing out of this commitment, which creates a special bond to the past in its "how" and its "that." This bond links us to the past in a relation of "certification":[43] to remember is to certify, to oneself or to others, the truth of what one remembers. It is to engage in a claim to truth and a responsibility for it. It is thus to thicken the experience of remembering past a point that is found in experiences of imagining or thinking, neither of which entails a commitment to relations of the truth-to variety.[44]

Not only is truthful remembering not accountable for each and every detail in its rendering of a given past scene, it can modify in a far-reaching way those details which it does select for purposes of presentation. This is not merely to say that we remember what we want to remember, though this is often the case. We may not know precisely what we want to remember, and still attain to truth, recapturing the brute being of an original scene even though we had no intention of doing so and even though we grasp this scene in a format considerably altered from its original configuration. The recapture, undertaken without conscious motive or aim, is exemplary of the thick autonomy of memory in its unrehearsed operation. Far from being antithetical to the achievement of truth, such unwitting transformation of the remembered may be a quite effective means of attaining truth. Instead of a mechanical rehashing of what has happened in its pointillistic detail, this transformative remembering presents us with the brunt, the force or thrust, of what occurred—*what truly happened in what actually happened*. We remember the significant thing that occurred. Hence our tendency in many kinds of remembering, consciously pursued or not, to valorize conspicuous but condensed features in what we recall; to make them bearers of the burden of truth. These features are incomplete from the standpoint of an ideal of pictorial representation, but they may be essential from the standpoint of truth. For the truth of which we are capable in remembering is not just a truth *about* what we remember—an "about" that calls for completeness as well as accuracy—but an actively engaged truth *in* what we remember.

## VII

Precisely in its thickness, memory's positive autonomy cannot help but reflect its tie to past actualities, whether this tie occurs as rootedness in perception, origination in the past, or involvement in the quest for truth about the past itself. Perception, the past, and truth all act as anchors for remembering, settling it into the dense *impasto* of human experiencing. This anchoring gives to memory its very materiality, along with a grounding in something at once recalcitrant and substantial. From such grounding, remembering gains not only its ultimate validity—its being well-founded as well as well-funded—but also its value in everyday life. Just because memory is so massively grounded in the past, it can be of inestimable importance in the present, illuminating it with a light not otherwise available, proferring insight that cannot be acquired in any other way—insight "from within," from within our own experience-as-remembered.

The result of memory's multiple ties to sources such as perception, language, or thought, over which it does not exert complete control, is its enrichment from these same sources. It imbibes from them what it cannot bring forth from itself alone—a process to which a model of pure activism fails to do justice. Yet it imbibes not in the interest of imitation and transmission—as models of passivism so often propose—but in order to gain sustenance from what exceeds it, from what is outside its own immediate reach in the present. Such sustenance is not taken in dumbly or unappreciatively; it is incorporated selectively and sensitively. As a consequence, memory finds itself continually aggrandized—not simply by the accretion of specific contents remembered but more importantly by the incorporation of new directions and new orders of orientation, new ways of proceeding and new styles. What "remains over"—not to be confused with any bare residuum—becomes embedded in memory as an "abiding possession"[45] and is transmuted in the process. In this way memory grows—grows beyond what any preestablished receptacle of experience could absorb or contain.

Rather than a mere repository *of* experience, remembering becomes thereby a continually growing fund *for* experience: a source itself, indeed a resource, on which not only future acts of remembering but many other experiential modes can draw as well. This funding function provides more than a storehouse of ready-to-hand information and knowledge (though it certainly does this too, and indispensably so). It also supplies a supportive *Hintergrund* for ongoing experience: a backdrop which at once unifies and specifies what comes to appear in the foreground. Any experiential scene, even one with a quite minimal unity, possesses such a background, which contributes depth to an otherwise shallow setting. The depth is both temporal, insofar as it leads us back into the past, and spatial, insofar as it furnishes other scenes to the place in which we are presently situated.

This memorial depth is a primary instance of the virtual dimension of remembering. Although such depth is also tied to the actual by numerous historical and perceptual threads, the actual qua actual—the strictly determinate—is superseded in the end. For the impingement of discrete actualities is not what is at stake here; indeed, their too finely detailed recollection can even induce that state of clutter and confusion which Luria's subject "S" reported as a living nightmare.[46] What *is* at stake is the presence of something much more diffuse—something virtual that has been held in readiness for many eventualities. It is this virtuality which keeps open and proliferates the ways by which unfolding experiences of various kinds can be funded from their abiding memorial background.

Memory thus regarded establishes a *basso continuo* for much of human experience—a "figured bass" that provides meaning and value. Remembering keeps this experience together, keeps it coherent and continuous, by virtue of its re-membering action from below. Even in this profoundly bass position, it remains positively autonomous, and still more thickly so than ever before. For here it realizes an identity, and achieves a force, of its own. No longer the mere agglomeration of the actualities which it nevertheless presupposes and which on occasion it singles out as such, remembering at this level is a dimension of our experience not reducible to any other—not even to its own ingredients of perception, pastness, and truth. Linked irrevocably to these latter, and made thicker still by its own diffuse virtuality, remembering regarded as "a diverse organized mass"[47] funds experience in the life-world from within its own unending resources.

## VIII

One central conclusion can be drawn without hesitation from the fact of memory's thick autonomy as it has been described in this chapter. This is that whenever we remember and in whatever way we remember *we get a different past every time*. If memory is not a matter of pictographic transparency—if it is an active affair of dense interinvolvement with a massive past—it will not bring any particular past experience back again in a pristine format. Or more exactly, if and when it does so, e.g., in "photographic memory," this will be exceptional, something to wonder at rather than to take for granted. Otherwise—which is to say, most of the time—we keep getting the past back differently. That we do so says something important both about the past and about memory. (*a*) *About the past* it says unmistakably that what has become past in relation to the present is in no way comparable to an essence. In other words, Hegel was wrong to claim dogmatically that "*Wesen ist was gewesen ist*" (essence is what has been).[48] As Husserl insisted, an essence or *Wesen* is precisely what is indefinitely repeatable in acts of cognition, above all those involving eidetic insight.

Indeed, as Derrida adds, an essence *depends on* this repeatability.[49] But the presence of thick autonomy means that the clarity of eidetic insight is notably lacking in the case of memory. What memory, including secondary memory, brings back is not the ever-the-sameness of an essence. It retrieves a past that is ever-different—different not just because of the erosion effected by time or because of the different act-form of remembering it corresponds to, but *intrinsically* different thanks to the action of thick autonomy.

(*b*) *About memory,* therefore, something important is also being said. This is that remembering makes a very considerable difference in how we relate to the past. Indeed, through its action of uncovering the past as ever-different, it *makes all the difference*. In remembering we do not repeat the past as self-identical, as strictly unchanging and invariant. We regain the past as different each time. Or more exactly, we regain it as different in its very sameness. Sameness, as Heidegger (commenting on Hegel) has pointed out, is not to be confused with strict self-identity. Where the self-identical excludes the different altogether, the same allows for the different—even fosters it on occasion.[50] One of these occasions, I would suggest, is that of remembering itself. And it is precisely memory's thick autonomy that makes this possible. In and through the dense operations of autonomous remembering, I recall the *same* past *differently* on successive occasions: now as I recapture it in reminiscence, now in body memory, now commemoratively, now even in recognition. Indeed, I regain the same past anew even as I return to it continually in the same act-form of remembering. No wonder we keep coming back to the past in memory—whether in ordinary life or in history or in psychoanalysis—without finding it in the least boring! As autonomous rememberers, we are generating our own ever-differing versions of the same past. No wonder, either, that what had seemed cause for despair when measured against exact recall (wherein we recollect the self-identical past *per se*) becomes reason for hope. For we *are* getting the past back as self-same, if not as self-identical. We are remembering this past and not merely spinning off variant versions of it. Each time we remember truly we are refinding the past, our past; however radical the differences between successive rememberings may be, they remain differences that accrue to the same past which we are attempting to recapture. In recognizing and in reminding, in place memory and in commemorating—and in all the other ways in which the thick autonomy of memory expresses itself—we are refashioning the same past differently, making it to be different in its very self-sameness.

This is even true in recollection, which also makes the past in its image, and precisely *as an image*. For images have their own thickness. As forming part of memory of any kind, they are less than fully diaphanous. Whatever personal or theoretical expectations we may place on them, and however much we might wish or demand that they live up to the highest standards of *claritas*, they do not render recollecting luminous. Despite my animadversions against recollection regarded as a paradigm for all remembering, it cannot be denied that recollecting itself shares, however sparingly, in the same thickness that we have observed to characterize other forms of remembering in more patent ways. And precisely in having its own thick autonomy, it conveys and transfigures the past in its own distinctive manner.

We may go still further. Even the past as photographed has a unique memorial value. That which serves so readily as a norm for recollection itself possesses its own density as a material medium through which we remember the past differently. Why else would we so assiduously document our travels with multiple photographic images—and savor these images afterwards so much—unless they displayed a peculiar power to re-present (and not just to represent) the past effectively? Hence, the importance of that photograph of myself and my sister standing eagerly and expectantly near the entrance to Yosemite. This photograph has its own dense mode of insertion into the past, which it retrieves and recreates as distinctively as my own flawed secondary memory. Hence, too, the importance of the wedding photographs discussed in section V above. They also reconnect with a poignant moment, forming a bond with it that cannot be described as thin or unsubstantial. Through such photographs we remember the past differently but not less effectively than if we recollected it or reminisced about it.[51] At the same time, by this same image—mechanical as it is in its production, and precise as it is in the accuracy of its depiction—we inculcate a funded future of remembering, thereby thickening the matrix of our memorial participation.

If what I have just said is true of recollection as well as of the photograph, then we need not depend exclusively on Lower Regions in gaining an appreciation of the thick autonomy of remembering. This appreciation can be acquired as well among the Higher Powers. In the enactment of thick autonomy the mind itself may play an essential part—and so may recollection and recollection's own putative prototype, the photograph. Just as remembering reaches out to every aspect of the past as different-in-its-sameness, so every kind of remembering, including the most mentalistic (and this latter as mechanically aided), has pertinence and validity in the effort to recapture the past and to let it flourish in the present and in the future.

# XII

# FREEDOM IN REMEMBERING

Memory is a kind of accomplishment a sort
of renewal even an initiation

—William Carlos Williams, *Paterson*

This is the use of memory: for liberation—
not less of love but expanding of love
beyond desire, and so liberation from the
future as well as the past.

—T. S. Eliot, "Little Gidding" *(Four Quartets)*

## I

In the course of this book we have seen an eidetic and intentional analysis of remembering—in which recollection played a privileged role—give way to a concern with the outreach of memories into the surrounding world of the remembering subject. This outreach led us to explore reminding, reminiscing, and recognizing as three ways in which the mentalistic model of act-intentionality proved to be inadequate. The transcending of mind as a container of memories was even more strikingly evident in our investigations of body memories, place memories, and various forms of commemoration. As we pursued memory beyond mind we continually found a centrifugal movement outward from the rememberer's mind into his or her world—a world filled with perceptual objects and historical events, signs and texts, rituals and other people. So engaging is this world that the insertion of memories into it, their manifold modes of connection with it, came to be described as a matter of "thick autonomy"—a density of involvement that, as we saw at the end of the last chapter, inheres in recollection itself.

But even if the validity of this book's exterocentric direction is granted—especially in the light of theories of memory that have been dominated by mentalistic prejudices—the reader may be moved to ask a final set of questions. Has justice been done to the remembering subject in all this? Won't this subject come forth to say that in some inalienable sense memories are "mine"—not mine as mere minions of my mind, or as something that I simply possess, but as part and parcel of my personal being? When I remember, after all, do I not engage in an activity that is undeniably *my own?* However much this activity may be shared with others in ceremonial moments, does it not remain identifiably mine insofar as *I* enact it and have continuing access to it—where "I" signifies myself-as-rememberer? Moreover, does not the content of a given memory inevitably include perspectives which can only be called "personal" and which reflect my unique position as a rememberer? And will not the same memory become integral to my ongoing life history, not just because it can be re-remembered but because it may alter my personal identity in the process? Indeed, if it is true in general that my existence is "mine to be in one way or another,"[1] then are not my memories mine to live out, as intimately as any other aspect of me? In other words, is not the incursion of memories into my life as massive and unavoidable as the rooting of these memories themselves in the world? Isn't "the world" finally *my world* in some significant sense?

Even if they cannot be completely answered at this late point, these questions cannot be evaded. This book's commitment to showing the efficacy and scope of memory beyond mind has been purchased at the risk of neglecting the remembering subject as such. Only this subject's lived body has been accorded concerted attention. But our headlong *hegira* from the entrapment of mind into the embrace of the world has meant passing over many personal features of remembering—features that belong intrinsically to my *Jemeinigkeit*.[2] It is about time, therefore, that the rememberer himself or herself reclaim our attention. This book began by setting out an informal grouping of its author's own, i.e., *my* memories, and it is only fitting that we come full cycle and return at the end to the personal self of the rememberer.

In the trajectory we have undertaken, this self has been in effect *depersonalized*. What remained of the self from the externalizing movements of Parts Two and Three was effectively submerged in the treatment of thick autonomy with which the present Part opened. Even in its positive, truth-generating mode, this autonomy expresses the immersion of the rememberer in an anonymous pre-personal level of experience—a level that resists specification in terms of the individual self. Its most characteristic dimension is that of depth, and its description as a layer of the "Lower Regions" reinforces the sense in which thickly autonomous remembering *underlies* the remembering subject. The very terms by which I have designated its enactment—e.g., "funding," "background," "*basso continuo*," etc.—only serve to underscore the impersonality of memory's thick autonomy. In depicting memory as autonomous in this immersionist mode, we court the danger of losing ourselves in our own description; our sense of intact self-identity may dissolve.

## II

Precisely in this circumstance of submergence in the depths of thick autonomy, it is not surprising that the remembering subject might wish to reclaim responsibility for his or her own actions. To own up to this responsibility is another way of saying "these memories are *mine*," mine to experience and mine to dispose of as I see fit. But to reclaim mineness in the guise of responsibility is at the same time to claim *freedom in remembering*, a freedom with which we must now come to terms. To understand this freedom is to gain an understanding of memory's thick autonomy as it is enacted "in person"—as it is based in the actions of the rememberer as well as in his or her world. Such freedom assumes two main forms, freedom to be oneself and freedom of in-gathering.

### Freedom to Be Oneself

It is an inescapable fact about human existence that we are made of our memories: *we are what we remember ourselves to be*. We cannot dissociate the remembering of our personal past from our present self-identity. Indeed, such remembering brings about this identity. The theme is familiar to readers of John Locke:

> For as far as any intelligent being can repeat [i.e., in memory] the idea of any past action with the same consciousness it had of it at first, and with the same consciousness it has of any present action; so far it is the same personal self. For it is by the consciousness it has of its present thoughts and actions, that it is self to itself now, and so will be the same self, as far as the same consciousness can extend to actions past or to come . . . the same consciousness uniting these distinct actions into the same person.[3]

As we have seen, remembering thrives in the constitution of the same (in contrast with the self-identical), and it is not at all surprising to find Locke claiming that sameness of consciousness is established by remembering. This sameness is the basis for a continuous personal identity, which requires that my consciousness now be the same as my consciousness then—where "the same" allows room for the significantly different as well. Thus, where Locke says that it is "the same consciousness" that unites past, present, and future selves "into the same person," we can just as well say that it is the same memories that unite our temporally disparate selves into one self: *my* self.

The failure of memory to integrate experiences into a single personal identity can be dire, resulting in the pathological condition of "multiple personality." In this predicament someone who is historically and physically continuous at the level of gross description is radically splintered at the level of personal identity. Even when there is a central, "official" self, the various separate selves fail to connect with each other, whether directly or through the core self. The critical dysfunction is that of memory: the multiple selves cannot remember one another (if and when they do, it is in a merely superficial fashion, that is, without any sense of belonging to the same self-system).[4] The causative mechanism in multiple personality is usually designated as "dissociation."[5] But the dissociation itself reflects a failure of memory to link the multiple selves of the same person into "the same consciousness," that is to say, the same continuously felt personhood. In still other instances, we may detect an analogous if less severe, failure: e.g., the lack of connection between the true and false selves of the "schizoid" personality. Indeed, whenever I cannot "get my life together" and feel it to be divisively fragmentary, the reconnective powers of memory have failed me.

Short of such situations of dispersion, I find myself able to connect temporally diverse aspects of myself and put them into meaningful communication with each other. Even more importantly, I can consolidate the self I have been and shape the self I am coming to be. As Locke intimates, both my past self and my future self are involved in my personal identity, since "the same consciousness can extend to actions past or to come." My freedom in remembering is accordingly bi-directional. It bears on prior as well as subsequent aspects of my life. (*a*) Concerning what has already taken place, it acts to organize what might otherwise be a mere assemblage of contingently connected events. It does this by selecting, emphasizing, collocating—sometimes condensing and sometimes expanding—and in general regrouping and reconfigurating what I have experienced so as to allow a more coherent sense of self to emerge. I am free to reconstruct and reconstrue what I have experienced: there is no set script for my life as I elect to remember it. This does not mean that there are no limits to such backward-looking modes of re-membering my experiences. We confront limits in the empirical and historical actuality in which the thick autonomy of memory immerses us—and even more so in the concern of this autonomy (in its positive form) to be true to the past so far as is possible. Yet these limits do not undercut memorial freedom of the specific sorts just mentioned. They may even collaborate with such freedom, as when an effort to be true to a particular part of my past allows me to recall its detailed infrastructure more freely.

(*b*) At the same time, I am free in establishing my ongoing and future personal identity by means of my own remembering. This remembering determines (in Lacan's formula) "what I shall have been for what I am in the process of becoming." What I shall have been, my eventual personal identity, is very much a function of what I shall remember myself to be—which is in turn a function of what I now remember myself to have been. And what I now remember myself to have been is by no means a fixed affair. It is once more a matter of freedom, specifically the freedom to decide which features of my previous life to honor or reject, celebrate or revile, in the future. This freedom is expressly evaluative; it is a freedom realized through assessing my own past as a prologue for my own future—an assessment carried out on the basis of values I am maintaining in the present.

At play in both phases (*a*) and (*b*) of the constitution of personal identity is the noticing of differences between past and present selves. The sameness of personal identity not only incorporates these differences; it may even thrive on them. Thus, just because I grasp my tolerance for sexism on my part and others noticeably decreasing with age, I gain an ever more secure sense of who I am in the present—and very likely will be in the future. Operative here is a peculiar capacity of memorial freedom to consider myself both same and other in one and the same apprehension: the same self precisely *in* and *as* differing from itself. Husserl has named such self-differing self-apprehension "de-presentation."[6] By remembering myself in this self-differentiating way, I de-present myself to myself. The forging of my personal identity calls continually for such de-presentational activity. Through this activity, I come to know myself, indeed, to be myself.

Therefore, it is clear that, thanks to memory, we have a quite considerable part to play in our own self-begetting as persons—where "person" connotes not just the biological or legal entity but the very self which we know to be an indispensable basis for being-in-the world. It is not a decisive objection to claim (as did Butler in his critique of Locke) that the self that thereby constitutes itself from memories must be presupposed in the process of constitution.[7] This must be conceded: there is never a selfless moment—at least not after the earliest phases of an individual's development—and each successive self is built on its own selective stock of memories. But by the same token, each successive self can re-orient itself by altering its hold on old memories and weaving in new ones; it can reinterpret its history in a different manner; it can even represent itself to itself in a variant manner. Everywhere there is the production of personal identity, a production proceeding by the free remembering of the self by itself.

## Freedom of In-Gathering

If it is now evident that personal identity is dependent upon the free activity of remembering, we still do not know how this activity actually works. A clue is contained in a statement of Heidegger's: "Memory is the gathering of thought."[8] In its free action, memory gathers much else besides thought; it also gathers emotions, perceptions, bits of discourse—ultimately, all the parts of our life history. "Gathering" connotes assembling, drawing together of items into a provisional unity. When gathering is memorial in character, the unity is no longer merely provisional—it is a unity that we retain, guard, keep. "Keeping," says Heidegger, "is the fundamental nature and essence of memory."[9] The freedom at work in such gathering-as-keeping is more than merely selective in its operation. It is a freedom of amalgamation, of creating synthetic wholes, and not just of selecting parts. At the same time, this freedom involves the decision to preserve the wholes thus drawn together: to validate them as memorable, as worthy of being retained in memory.

It is striking that the word "recollection," understood in terms of its origins rather than in terms of the use to which it has been put in Western thought, captures these same two aspects of memorial gathering. "Collection" derives from the Latin *collecta*, a "gathering together," and, still more primordially, from *colligere*, literally a "binding together" (as is signified in the English verb "to colligate"); whereas "re-" signifies "back" or "again." In a primary act of re-collection, I bind things together, keep them in a gathered unity, so that I can return to them again and again. Such re-collecting contrasts strikingly with recollection qua secondary memory, wherein the basic action is that of reflecting (as in a mirror or photograph) whatever is presented to it. The result of this basic action is a re-presentation that, in claiming to possess likeness to an original presentation, offers no unification of its own, no gathering together that is binding on its own terms. In other words, recollection fails to be genuine re-collection. Or more exactly, it fails to manifest the way in which, despite its derivative status as iconic, it gathers the past together and guards it in its own unique manner.

But the gathering action of free remembering involves still more than a twofold movement of collecting and keeping. The gathering of memory is a gathering *in*, as is testified in such phrases as "keeping *in* memory" or "bearing the past *in* mind." It is not sufficient for remembering to draw together and retain its content so as to exhibit it—that is, to *display* it as might a computer screen. The language of "display," to which I was tempted in chapter 2, all too easily becomes just another expression of the predominance of the visual mode that is already evident in the constrictive interpretation of recollection as iconic re-presentation.[10] Beyond the presentational immediacy of display, memory seeks to preserve its content within.

Within what? *Within the remembering subject*. I say "subject" and not "mind"—despite the force of the idiom, "keeping the past in mind."[11] To keep the past in the mind alone is to keep it within something that fancies itself to be transparent to itself and its objects—indeed, to be the very image of the objects it encounters and knows. Once again we must suspend a dogmatic adherence to "the nobility of sight" in order to uncover layers of our personal being that are not valued for their strictly visual display. The lived body represents one such layer, and it is crucial that we have been able to locate memories *in* this body: body memories, as we saw in chapter 8, are not just about the body but sedimented into it and at one with it. Yet in its free action remembering gathers itself into *every* aspect of the human subject—not only into the body and mind of this subject but into his or her emotional life, circle of thoughts, set of social relations, and capacity to speak and listen. It is a matter, in short, of in-gathering memory into the person as a whole. Nothing less than this will do if freedom in remembering is to attain its full range in human existence. As Plato himself put it, remembering of the most significant sort—and this means recollection of forms, *anamnesis*—takes place "within oneself" *(ex hautou)*.[12]

It is just here that we reach the inwardmost point of our journey in this book. To be within the remembering subject—Plato would say the remembering soul[13]—is to be at a point considerably more interior than mind itself is. In fact mind, as it has come to be conceived since Descartes, is, for all of its self-encapsulation (and precisely in flight from such self-enclosure), turned resolutely *outward* in its eagerness to absorb and reflect—to "represent"—the determinate outer world. In its ec-centricity, it lacks the inwardness that remembering requires in the most complete expression of its freedom. How are we to conceive such distinctively memorial interiority if it cannot be conveyed by a mentalistic model and if we hesitate to revert to the language of the soul—if we decide to follow neither Descartes nor Plato?

My suggestion is that the 'in' of memory's in-gathering freedom be conceived as *a matrix of matrices*. "Matrix" has the curious property of signifying something that is at once material and formal. From its root in *mater*, "mother," it stands for a material region of origin and development.[14] In the present context, the materiality of a matrix is detectable in the depth of the remembering subject and more particularly in the thick autonomy through which this subject realizes its freedom. As a matrix in depth, the subject who remembers inwardizes experiences, incorporating them into the density of his or her inner being instead of merely refracting these experiences back onto the world. But "matrix" also means formal framework, a topologically defined network in which items can be allotted locations. In this capacity, the notion of matrix points to another aspect of memory's in-gathering activity, namely, its proclivity for arranging its contents in ordered groupings and for finding a location, a specific *topos*, for these groupings within the vast keep that we denote by the mass noun "memory." The density of memory's material inherence in the subject is here matched by the elegance and economy of its formal arrangements. When we take into account this dual dimensionality, we are led to conceive the in-gathering action of remembering as a material matrix (in depth) of formal matrices (located within this same depth).

In-gathering is a concrete process of drawing in memories from various states of forgetfulness, marginality, virtuality, and indirectness. These memories are grouped or "filed"—put into a formal matrix—in terms of their thematic content: e.g., visits with a close friend to a certain place, traumatic experiences of a given type, my childhood during a particular stretch of time, etc. In relation to these special groupings (each of which represents a discrete domain of my existence), my personal identity can be considered a guiding matrix, that which gives coherence and consistency to all the others, allowing them to articulate with each other. The identity of my person (itself a product as well as a repository of remembering) enables me to identify these formal aggregates as "*my* memories," and it lends to them a peculiar depth they would not otherwise possess. As a matrix of matrices, my personal being is a being-in-depth, a *moi profond,* in and through which my thematically distinct memories come to be connected from below. In this Lower Region memories fuse and become owned as mine; here the autonomy of memory is as thick as the self is deep; and here, too, my freedom in remembering is most fully gathered in upon itself.

## III

We need to explore the freedom of in-gathering more fully. Such freedom has three main components: collecting; keeping; and inwardizing by means of material and formal matrices. Taken together, these components serve to distinguish such freedom from any mere process of selection or what is traditionally termed "freedom of choice." Or more precisely, the components incorporate freedom of choice into a more encompassing sphere of free action. Take, for example, that part of personal identity which we are accustomed to call "character." We tend to consider a person's character as a group of settled dispositions to act in certain ways, and we may think in this connection of the dictum "a man's character is his fate."[15] This is to presume that character is somehow unchangeable or a matter of external compulsion. In fact, as both Aristotle and Freud point out, character is very much a matter of freedom—freedom of choice. Aristotle specifies that the reliable "habits" *(hēxeis)* on which character is based depend on particular choices made during the time when the habits were being formed.[16] Freud, as we have seen, explicitly defines character as "a precipitate of abandoned object-cathexes [which] contains the history of these object-choices."[17] What is left unacknowledged by both thinkers is the role of remembering in the transformation of mere "object-choices" into that "precipitate" or massive habituality we call personal character. This role is epitomized in the freedom of in-gathering, all of whose component parts are operative in the formation of character. There is, first of all, an activity of drawing together inasmuch as character condenses all of the determinate choices which have preceded it: it is, as it were, their summary statement. Precisely as it is unifying these choices, the gathering action of remembering also preserves them, keeps and guards them, as the ground of character. As specifically *in*-gathering, remembering takes prior choices (collected together as an amalgamated mass) into the self, where they are grouped by thematic content into formal matrices and connected in depth by the material matrix of one's personal identity. Thanks to this complex assimilative process, we are able to say that "my character" has many facets (reflecting the many kinds of choices on which it is founded) and yet is fully consolidated (and thus is a constituent feature of my personal identity). Far from being fated, then, my character is altogether an expression of my free remembering in its in-gathering power.

Tempting as they may be to employ, models of subsumption (of matter under form, content under category) do not adequately delineate the basic activity of in-gathering. Whether these models are set forth in a Kantian or a Piagetian format—i.e., in terms of categories or schemes—they fail to capture the intricate, side-long, non-hierarchical movements that both allow and express freedom in remembering. The in-gathering of memory contests the presumption that there is some single concept (or scheme, thought, idea) *under* which remembered content must be subsumed. In their laterality, memorial matrices resist any such hierarchical ordering. As a particular matrix is itself always evolving and is never fully settled, nothing can be definitively subsumed under it, nor can it be simply subsumed under something else. Instead of such coming-*under* in a pre-established, top-down (or bottom-up) situation, there is a coming-*in* of memorial material, which radiates laterally and non-subsumptively within the remembering subject. As we have seen, there is a loose grouping into formal matrices; but the thematic content of these latter is not rigidly defined: "my college years," "the times when I worked on the book," "last year in Marienbad," "that trip to Yosemite." The members of each such aggregate may overlap one another; in any case they are not arranged in a vertical hierarchy of subsumption. They are not even subsumed under the material matrix of personal identity: I have termed this critical matrix "material" in order to indicate that it is ingredient *within* the formal matrices with which it is allied. Mineness is thus not an abstract universal but a concrete notion immanent within every memory I can rightfully claim as "mine."

Just as we must resist the seductions of subsumption in any thorough consideration of in-gathering, so we must also resist the temptations of containment. The very word "in" arouses these temptations: recall Aristotle's discussion of this word and its implications for a strict containership view of *topos*.[18] Where the snug fit of the vessel could serve as an appropriate image for our discussion of the role of place in remembering, this fit is not applicable to all forms of memory. Nevertheless, the idea of strict containment dies hard. It is an *idée fixe* in contemporary information processing models of human memory. So as to fit the closely confining containers represented by parts of computers, incoming experiences must be tidily presented to begin with: hence their designation as "input" that is divisible into "bits" of information. Moreover, one form of determinacy begets another. For memory to be efficient, bits of information need to be "chunked" into mathematically determinable sets and then given "encoding specificity."[19] The language of "input," "bit," "chunk," "encoding" bespeaks a situation in which to be *in* memory is necessarily to be snugly ensconced within predetermined limits and exact boundaries. No wonder that there is so much talk of "packaging" information in this self-contained machine model. Not to mention repackaging! As a leading psychological theorist states, "Our language is tremendously useful for repackaging material into a few chunks rich in information."[20] Useful this language may be—and it is increasingly tempting to employ it as computers become indispensable parts of our lives—yet we have to ask whether it does justice to the indirections of the 'in' of in-gathering. *This* 'in' resists being containerized—and thus quantified—as fiercely as it resists being subsumed under a category or a scheme. The same resistance applies to any effort to assimilate it to a neurological model of containment within brain cells.

The crucial question for our purposes is: what if memories are *not* neatly packageable and repackageable—at least not without losing what is essential to their very nature within the in-gathering person? And what if the inward movement they undergo in being in-gathered into the remembering subject is not comparable to entering a storage vault or "memory bank"? What if the interior of human memory is more like a laterally exfoliating labyrinth with numerous intentional threads connecting the in-gathered memories belonging to one formal matrix with memories in other formal matrices? And what if the same labyrinthine structure has, instead of a single "output," many exits, many issuing avenues that give upon the same being-in-the-world from which the memories were initially gathered? If answers to these questions are affirmative, then not only container models of memory but the dualisms of self/other, self/site, and mind/body that subtend these models also fall under suspicion. The gathering-in is an active trespassing of, and a collecting across, the boundaries that separate the members of such dyads. As an expression of the freedom of the remembering subject, in-gathering cannot be understood as generating input for an internal archive of the mind, brain, or computer. Rather than being brought like captives into any such archive, memories are drawn into the many matrices of already funded experiences: into the ambience, indeed the circum-ambience, of other memories, co-existing with which they come to constitute a delicate web of relations not reducible to containerlike structures.

I am not proposing that we simply avert our gaze from models of memory based on computers. Much is to be learned from these models—much that is suggestive for a phenomenological approach such as I have been developing in this book. Just above I drew spontaneously on the idea of "files" as a way of understanding a formal matrix of in-gathering. More substantively, the notion of "information flow" evokes an inherent dynamism that is also at work in my concept of thick autonomy. I suspect that a more extensive treatment of the metaphorics of information processing would reveal other illuminating features of its models of human memory—much as we found the photograph as a prototype for recollection to possess its own positive potential.

It remains, however, that the computer, like the photograph, pushes human memory out of its natural shape. If the photograph (like the wax tablet of the *Theatetus*) leads remembering too far in the direction of sheer passivism (i.e., by privileging passively received impressions), the computer (akin to Plato's metaphor of the aviary) conducts it to the opposite pole of activism. What else does "processing" connote but a continual reshaping of memories? Much the same is true of "rehearsal" and the incessant cycle of encoding, decoding, and recoding to which memories are said to be submitted. Moreover, just as the photograph offers a parody of the legitimate passivism that is an intrinsic feature of human remembering—namely, its embroilment in thick autonomy—so the computer caricatures the valid activism that belongs to the freedom we realize in remembering: above all, the freedom of in-gathering. In the end, both the photograph and the information processing machine fail to capture any significant sense of the freedom to be oneself. Each is utterly impersonal in operation—if not in origin or effect. Thus neither is capable of conveying what it is like to build up from fragmentary memories a truly *personal* identity, a quality of perduring mineness. Any identity they possess is imputed to them by the photographer or the programmer; it is not generated from within, *ex hautou*. A photograph or an item stored in a computer may certainly be regarded as strikingly memorylike. But I cannot coherently say of either that it *is*—that it counts legitimately as—"my memory."

In-gathering is the basic action of a fully realized memorial freedom. It includes phases of fore-gathering—i.e., in anticipatory and exploratory movements—as well as after-gathering (e.g., consolidation and reflection). We remain at liberty during the circuitous process of in-gathering to change its course and content. At one pole of possibilities, we may yield to instreaming memories as they arrange themselves into convergent groupings without any concerted intervention from us: just this pole dominates the efforts of those who make exact reduplication an ideal (e.g., in the form of an eidetic or photographic memory). We have already found reasons—discussed in the last chapter—for questioning this ideal. At another pole, in-gathering becomes a willful, and even a forceful, effort to reshape a given matrix: this pole holds sway in the cult of computers, a cult which pretends that there are no abiding constraints on memorial freedom. These constraints—evident in such diverse phenomena as habitual body memories, a tenacious character structure, the length of time required for adequate working-through—preclude us from embracing an overzealous activism. They also warn us against any meliorism or progressivism in matters of memory. Despite the fact that the word "gather" has its Greek origin in *agathon* (good),[21] the gathering of in-gathering need not accomplish any particular good, any manifestly beneficial aim or end. It can amount to amassment for its own sake, and on occasion it can breed trouble (as when in-gathered memories of emotions serve to detonate a buried anger). All that one can say for certain is that in the realm of remembering, in-gathering is continually going on.

Memory is indeed "the gathering of thought." It is also the gathering of much else—of our personal history, our personal identity, ultimately of our lives themselves. If this is so, it is thanks very much to the intricate activities at work in the in-gathering by which we finally become ourselves. These activities weave veritable inseams into our lives—inseams that not only serve to connect disparate parts (some of which would never become contiguous save for the intermediation of memories) but that create together a fabric which is at once distinctive in format and expressive of many experiences. It is due to such interweaving that remembering becomes genuine re-membering, a re-gathering of these experiences in and through in-gathering.

## IV

It is one thing to point to the general structure of freedom in remembering. It is quite another to detect this structure in actual operation. In this section I shall take a look at memorial freedom *in concreto* in three distinct regions of human experience.[22] Despite their diversity, and setting aside many nuances of detail, these regions manifest the two main forms of free remembering in an instructively specific manner.

### Depth Psychology

Here I shall restrict consideration to the depth psychology of Freud and Jung and more especially to their conception of psychotherapy. Precisely as concerned with the depth of the psyche, they provide what information processing views of memory refuse to offer—a treatment of personal identity that is neither quantified nor containerized and that respects memorial freedom at every turn. To begin with, both psychologists attempt to promote on the part of their patients a distinctive freedom to be themselves. This is achieved, paradoxically, by encouraging them to get in touch with a *pre-*personal part of themselves, whether this be conceived as the repressed unconscious (Freud) or the collective unconscious (Jung). In both instances remembering leads the way, either in the form of the abreaction of a repressed trauma or as introverted libido. As do dreams, vividly experienced memories offer a *via regia* into the unconscious. Thanks to their sinuous subterranean status—their thick autonomy—they are able to guide patients downward beneath their encrusted ego defenses and their social *personae* to a realm where a re-enlivened sense of personhood becomes possible. In Freud's language, it is a matter of delving beneath the reality-dominated demands of "secondary process" to make contact with the "primary process" of the unconscious. For Jung, it is a question of getting in touch with the archetypal basis of one's personality: with one's "paleopsyche." Either way, one emerges from this *nekyia* or journey into the underworld with an enriched and strengthened self; and at every stage along the route, remembering is essential to the emergence. In being continually elicited and valorized in the course of therapy, this remembering restores otherwise forgotten or dissociated content to one's personal identity, while at the same time it acts as a liberating force in its own right. "This is the use of memory: for liberation"—if Eliot's line applies anywhere, it applies just here. Memory not only supports the freedom to be oneself; in depth-oriented psychotherapy it is the privileged means of attaining this freedom.

Memorial freedom in its other dominant form, that of in-gathering, is also prominently present in such psychotherapy. Consider merely the fact that in undergoing psychoanalysis of either sort a nuanced grasp of one's life as a whole—its main directions and covert intentionalities—is a *desideratum*. In attaining this grasp, depth-therapeutic in-gathering is indispensable, for it enables the unification (or re-unification) of disparate memories: memories previously disunified by psychopathology, which has as one of its most acute effects the dispersal of the patient's memorial life. As collected together in therapy—and as aided by conjoint efforts at reconstruction of the past on the part of analyst and patient alike—these memories are retrieved and retained as an invaluable "stock" on which subsequent therapeutic moves can draw. Not only discovering lost memories (or revaluing familiar ones) but *keeping them continually available* for further insight is basic to the therapeutic process. Even more crucial is the inwardizing that completes the cycle of in-gathering. After being rescued from the nether realm of the unconscious, therapeutically efficacious memories must be grafted back onto the conscious life of the afflicted self if this self is to be liberated from their oppressive spell as un-remembered. As with all inwardizing, there is a collocation of the regained memories in open-ended formal matrices and a rooting of them in the material matrix of personal identity. In the course of depth-psychological therapy one can observe at first-hand the ramiform matrix of memories as they extend through one's life-history. "Free association" for Freud and "active imagination" for Jung rely expressly on this spontaneously non-subsumptive, non-vertical character of free remembering in its actively in-gathering action.

In quite direct and graphic ways, therefore, depth psychology in its very practice exhibits freedom in remembering. Or more exactly, it persistently inculcates this freedom in its subjects as an integral part of its therapeutic task. In a moment of candor, Freud once said that the aim of psychoanalysis is to restore to patients their "freedom to decide one way or the other."[23] But this freedom of choice is in turn made possible by the memorial freedom at work in the psychoanalytic process itself.

## Art

Goethe wrote that "closely scrutinized, the productions of [artistic] genius are for the most part reminiscences."[24] If so, they embody that freedom in remembering which we have been tracing out. Leaving aside the place of memory for the spectator or critic of works of art—a momentous place indeed, considering that there could be no continuous perceiving of works of art, much less reflecting on them, without their accessibility in the memory of appreciators—let us focus on the artist, and more particularly on his or her creation of a style. When we say that the artist "struggles to find his style," we are speaking of the very situation I have designated as eliciting the freedom to be oneself. Just as an individual realizes this freedom by attaining a coherent personal identity, so the artist actualizes the same freedom by creating an achieved style. But in so doing the artist must be prepared to go outside established ego boundaries, indeed to lose himself or herself in the non-personal or extra-personal. No less than in psychotherapy, the way to the self lies outside the self. The artist has to touch base with the unconscious—as both Freud and Jung liked to emphasize—but he or she must, in additon, connect with other artists, especially with those most admired figures in a given tradition. Thus Cézanne routinely copied revered predecessors in the Louvre, and Picasso's works allude continually to classical Greek art and to Spanish Baroque painting. Each painter was extraordinarily inventive in attaining a style (in Picasso's case, several of them), and yet each came to this achievement only through a profound immersion in the work of others. The immersion is evident even in their most "original" works—so that we remark the presence of Chardin and Poussin in Cézanne's still lifes and figure studies, and of Velasquez in Picasso's later paintings. As concerted and prolonged remembering leads to a more consolidated self-identity, so these two artists' active remembering of their predecessors came to fruition in their mature styles: styles that established their lasting identity as painters.

Memorial in-gathering is at work in such instances as well. The creation of a style involves a deep-going collocation of all that one has seen and learned—and now remembers in a synoptic manner. Memory's contractive power, first observed early in this book, is drawn upon in the constitution of a style, which condenses a vast array of an artist's experiences over time, much as an emblem or monogram is a compressed expression of a larger totality. For this very reason, an artist's style is able to bear memories—to hold them formally and materially in its own preserve. In its "stamp" and allure, style exhibits what I have called memory's "reservative" capacity, its ability to hold its content within its own keeping.

What is perhaps most remarkable about artistic style is its combination of collective-*cum*-preservative power with the singularity that marks it as an artist's *own* style, allowing him or her to say: "This is *my* style." The evolution of a style's mineness, the artist's most demanding struggle, is at one with the process of inwardizing. For the artist must bring *in*—bring into himself or herself—what he or she has absorbed from others, not to reflect it back (this would be mere "imitation") but to enable it to become his or her own creation. In this way something personal and unique is created, and the artist feels redeemed via-à-vis other artists, whatever may be the "anxiety" of their influence.[25] This accomplishment—which may end up taking a lifetime—involves the creative juxtaposition of material and formal matrices of memories in an evolving network that is truly labyrinthine in its complexity: hence the difficulty of tracing the precise evolution of a particular style. But the result is there for all to see. It is manifest in that recognizable *Gestalt* that we call Cézanne's "proto-Cubism" or Picasso's "analytic Cubism," each of which is nevertheless quite distinct from the other. "Le style, c'est l'homme même" goes the French adage. Exactly. *In finding his or her style, the artist finds himself or herself.* In this convergence of findings, remembering in its two forms of freedom plays an indispensable role. No wonder that Mnemosyne was said by the Greeks to be the Mother of the Muses: she brings forth the style of works of art as surely as she ushers in the personal style of the human beings who create these works.

## Philosophy

The alliance between memory and philosophy is intimate and long-standing. As Nietzsche remarks:

> The most diverse philosophers keep filling in a definite fundamental scheme of possible philosophies. . . . Their thinking is, in fact, a return and a homecoming to a remote, primordial, and inclusive household of the soul, out of which [philosophical] concepts grew originally: philosophy is to this extent a kind of atavism of the highest order.[26]

Let us narrow our attention to the role of memory in philosophical method. My invocation of Plato's doctrine of recollection has already introduced the topic. This doctrine shows considerable affinity with Freud's view of memory. Much as abreactive recollection becomes possible only through dialogical confrontation in psychotherapy, philosophical recollection or *anamnesis* arises after a process of dialectical cross-examination *(elenchus)*. And just as we reconnect in therapy with the pre-personal sphere of the unconscious, so in Platonic recollection we rediscover those sources of our knowledge that originate in a pre-existent state. Moreover, as in both depth psychology and art, here too we realize our memorial freedom to be ourselves most effectively by going out of ourselves in an essential detour. For Plato, this recapture of the self outside itself is sanctioned not only by his official theory of the soul's pre-existence, but by the very grammar of the crucial phrase "*ex hautou*," which we have seen to be central to his theory of recollection. Although the phrase is usually translated as "within oneself," its literal meaning is "from out of *(ex)*/oneself *('autou)*." The activity of recollection, in which the method of dialectic culminates, occurs—as an *activity*—within ("from") one's current mortal self, and yet it aims at something transcendent to ("out of") this same finite self: i.e., the Forms of Knowledge. Only insofar as transcendent and immanent directions coincide in the inquiring subject—arise "from out of" this subject—can we speak of the inquirer as gaining his or her identity as a knower. As with the personal identity of any given individual, such noetic identity is dependent on appropriate acts of remembrance.

In-gathering, the other form of memorial freedom, is also important in the pursuit of philosophical method. "Recollection," traced from its root in *recolligere* and ultimately in *legein,* means to assemble and lay out an articulate account: hence Plato's claim that learning qua recollection is a matter of assembling pertinent examples and picking out essential defining features. At play here is that component of in-gathering which we have already termed "collecting." This component is also thematized by Husserl, who insists that his method of "free variation in imagination" has to include a survey of relevant and variant examples so that one can notice the "congruences" or overlaps between them. Husserl further stresses that these examples must be "retained in grasp"[27]—much as the interlocutors in a Platonic dialogue are enjoined by Socrates to keep in mind the course of their discussions. In both cases, eidetic insight is the ultimate objective, and such insight becomes possible only in and through the collective-*cum*-retentive powers of memory.[28]

It is quite striking that Husserl classifies the objects of eidetic inquiry into "formal" and "material" essences. Such essences occupy corresponding formal and material regions, which are suggestively akin to the formal and material matrices that structure the activity of inwardizing in memory. As inhering in the depth of the personal subject, these matrices occupy a domain that Husserl would name "the transcendental ego" and Plato simply "the soul." For both thinkers the purpose of philosophical method is to suspend the baneful effects of unexamined belief so as to make insight into essences possible. Whether the basic act conveying this insight is called "recollection" (as by Plato) or "reactivation" (Husserl),[29] it arises through an intensive inwardizing, a soul-searching, "a return and a homecoming to a remote, primordial, and inclusive household of the soul."

In depth psychology, art, and philosophy we can thus observe a concurrence as to the concrete importance of freedom in remembering. Whether in the form of the freedom to be oneself—oneself as eidetic inquirer, or as depth-psychological self-knower, or as artist who creates a style—or by virtue of the freedom of in-gathering, the patient, the artist, and the philosopher alike come to a more sensitive self-awareness, a deepened sense of the thick autonomy of memory, thanks to the subtle workings and reworkings of their own free remembering.

## V

Let us grant that the freedom we realize in remembering is considerable—or at least much more considerable than mechanistic or physiological models, including those that take information-processing as a paradigm, might permit. Does this mean that the more remembering we can do—the more items we recall—the freer we are? Not at all. Recall the poignant plight of "S," whose life was enormously overburdened by the mere fact that he remembered *too many* things. In any event, the two forms of freedom under discussion in this chapter have little if anything to do with the sheer amount, or even the accuracy, of information retained by the remembering subject. (This realization suggests that the ideals of flawless retention and unlimited storage—both of which guide the design of computers—are misleading as applied in any rigorous way to human memory.)

If memorial freedom is not to be assessed quantitatively, is it the case that remembering is (in Aristotle's phrase) "up to us when we wish"?[30] It is not clear that this is true even of imagining—which is what Aristotle is characterizing in this phrase—and it is certainly not true of remembering. As we witness so dramatically in the instance of Proustian "involuntary memory" as well as in many quotidian cases of obsessively returning memories, much remembering arises without our wishing or willing it. And, by the same token, much remembering fails to arise precisely when we want it to: "what *is* her name?" we ask ourselves in stupefaction as we encounter someone we know very well, racking our brain to discover the name. The mere existence of amnesias of many sorts, with or without an organic basis, forbids us to assert that remembering is an activity whose course we can confidently control, or even predict. But if remembering is by no means entirely within our control, it is also not wholly outside our control either—something merely mechanical, a sheer process of biological determinism. We, individual rememberers and co-rememberers, are part of the process, contributing to it vitally albeit often in a tacit manner. *What remains in memory remains up to us*—if not precisely when we wish or as we wish, nevertheless as belonging to the realm of our own freedom to remember.

But now we must confront remembering's *un*freedom, which is just as pressing a matter as its freedom. The idea of thick autonomy developed in the last chapter already pointed in this direction. In its positive modes, thick autonomy conveys the concrete freedom of the rememberer, the critical difference that free remembering can make in his or her memorial life. But just as "thick," as a matter of thorough immersion, such autonomy also reminds us that most remembering is *not* up to the remembering subject when he or she wishes. So much does remembering embroil us in experiences and structures over which we do not retain effective control that it would be more accurate in many instances to say merely that "remembering is going on" rather than that "I choose to remember." The going-on is the primary phenomenon, not the willed actions of the rememberer; and this ongoing remembering is happening, always, in the thick of things—sometimes most of all when it seems most irrelevant (e.g., when a spontaneously appearing memory image reveals a seemingly senseless preoccupation with its specific content).

Another way of stating this is to say that memories *impose themselves* upon us. They demand respect. They demand respect not only as stemming from the past but as clarifying and influencing the present, and as shadowing forth a possible future. We are certainly free to in-gather them in various ways and to interrelate them with differing degrees of intensity and involvement. But this freedom does not alter the fundamental fact that we are not—and should not expect to be—masters of the memory game. Only in mnemonics, thanks to its formal and manipulative aspects, is anything like mastery approached; but our ambivalence toward even the most remarkable mnemonists is reflected in the epithet "memory freak." It is as if their manifest mastery of remembering were freakish or monstrous: too much of a monstration, too little of substance.[31] We are thereby admonished to admit to the inherent limitations of our memorial powers. The sheer ability to recall facts and figures, even whole experiences, is not a fair gauge of the genuine prowess of remembering and fails altogether to capture the density of its autonomy. Once more, accuracy and quantity regarded as ideal parameters fall short of the mark; they do not give the true dimensions of the phenomenon.

But unfreedom connotes more than lack of control or mastery. It also signifies sheer repetition—blind, meaningless reinstatement of the selfsame. "Those who do not remember history are condemned to repeat it." This familiar proverb distills the essence of the situation. Failure to remember involves unfreedom in the precise form of being "condemned to repeat" a given circumstance rather than understanding it or creatively varying it. It is therefore not surprising to learn that Freud contrasts remembering and repeating in his description of the unfree, symptomatic "acting out" of the psychoanalytic patient: "The patient does not *remember* anything of what he has forgotten and repressed, but *acts* it out. He reproduces it not as a memory but as an action; he *repeats* it, without, of course, knowing that he repeats it."[32] If the therapeutic goal of psychoanalysis is "to fill in gaps in memory,"[33] this goal is adopted in order to overcome the unfreedom of impulsively or compulsively repetitive actions. And if Freud himself came to abandon the explicit aim of abreactive recollecting—which is a matter of replay ultimately modeled on visual re-enactment—and to replace it with the much more diffuse co-remembering effected in transference, it was because he realized that such recollection is itself merely repetitive in its operation. The true *telos* of remembering, of a remembering that liberates us from the future as well as from the past, cannot be achieved by any form of strictly "secondary" memory, not even that which embodies exact replication.[34]

Freud's position on this matter brings with it another crucial lesson: *we come to the freedom of remembering only from the unfreedom of repetition*. For everyone, and not only the patient, is in the same predicament when it comes to early childhood memories. Not remembering these self-formative memories (thanks to "infantile amnesia"),[35] we act them out as adolescents and adults, repeating their inherent patterns endlessly and thoughtlessly. Only as finally remembering them—which is *not* tantamount to recollecting them—do we become free from them and thus free for the future as well: free for what we shall have been for what we are in the process of becoming.

Such a liberating movement from unfreedom to freedom by means of the right remembering is by no means confined to what happens in psychoanalysis. The same movement is at play in the domain of artistic creation. The artist, too, must free himself from merely repeating others (and even himself) if he is to forge a style that is genuinely his own; his task is no less one of liberating himself from the burden of an inadequately remembered past so as not simply to repeat it. The accomplishment of this task is not guaranteed by recourse to the exact recollections of art history: repainting the relevant past, experiencing it in body memory and commemorating it as Cézanne and Picasso did, is a much more veridical way of remembering it, of being true to it, than recollecting dates or revisualizing forms. In philosophy as well, we can trace out much the same trajectory from unfreedom in repeating to freedom in remembering. What Plato would term *doxa* or "everyday belief" and Husserl the "natural attitude" refers to the situation in which we merely repeat the opinions of others instead of thinking things out for ourselves. To move beyond this situation—which is as universal as infantile amnesia—requires the right kind of remembering, one which cannot be reduced to secondary memory. Doxic repetition gives way to noetic or eidetic insight when the free thinking necessary for such insight is made possible by free remembering.

The burden of repetition does not, however, pass easily from our shoulders—as Freud and Jung, Cézanne and Picasso, Plato and Husserl would all hasten to remind us. Even after we have made the liberating movements just outlined, this burden remains in our lives. It does so in the form of *forgetting*, which is at once the most pervasive and the most insidious kind of memorial unfreedom. Not only can many modes of repetitive behavior themselves be understood as types of forgetting—of "amnesia" in its literal meaning of "not-remembering," the privation of memory[36]—but our ordinary lives are riddled with the vacuities, the pockets as well as the long stretches, of oblivion. Perhaps such oblivion is, in Kundera's phrase, "the heaviest of burdens." But, as is suggested by the conception of forgetting as a matter of "*gaps* in memory," it may also betoken "the lightness of being." How can this be? How are we to understand a paradoxical situation in which forgetting is at once light and heavy, a blessing and a curse?

To resolve the paradox, it is not sufficient to recall the blissfully oblivious state of the bovine being with whose description by Nietzsche the Introduction to this book opened. The beast who forgets to answer that he always forgets what he was going to say—who is thus locked into double oblivion—may be quite happy in his own manner. But he singularly lacks the possibility of gaining that happiness which stems from free remembering, a remembering that triumphs over oblivion itself. The answer to the paradox is not to recommend forgetfulness, much less narcotization. Nevertheless, Nietzsche may be right when he comments that "life in any true sense is absolutely impossible *without forgetfulness*."[37] Indeed, as we know, Nietzsche advocates an active forgetfulness to be set over against an overactive remembering: hypomnesia rather than hypermnesia. If forgetting results in the lightening of the burden of our existence, then it may certainly be a good thing: the lightness of being may be (again in Kundera's word) "unbearable," but it can disburden this existence in important ways. From this point of view, it would be remembering that is the heavy matter, the activity that "crushes us."[38] By the same token, however, this heaviest activity is "simultaneously an image of life's most intense fulfillment"[39]—a fulfillment to which the beast cannot even begin to aspire.

A response to the paradox I have posed thus emerges. Perhaps forgetting and remembering are *equiprimordial in human experience;* both are valuable, both are required. If so, the unfreedom of forgetting is not to be regretted vis-à-vis the freedom of remembering. Each is essential to human existence.

To value forgetting instead of vilifying it is to recognize that the forgetting of many details of daily life is not only practically useful—in order to become less distracted or preoccupied—but, in fact, necessary to our well-being, a basis for being-in-the-world. Far from being a matter for regret or something merely to overcome, forgetting may be salutary in itself. Indeed, it can be a condition for remembering:

> It is this 'mass of the forgotten', it is the forgotten [itself] which seems to be the first intuition of the past, to constitute the essential basic material upon which memory comes to embroider the remembrances of isolated events. Forgetting is thus not simply memory failure. It appears to us now in its positive value. . . . From this point of view, the vision that everything is destined to be forgotten seems much more natural, much more appeasing, than the fact that it can be reproduced again as an isolated event.[40]

If these claims of Minkowski's are true, we might even be tempted to speak of a *freedom to forget* that is the analogue of the freedom to remember. However possible or desirable such a freedom to forget may be, it is nonetheless severely curtailed at critical points. No more than we can remember everything—except precisely in a freakish condition such as that from which "S" so acutely suffered—are we able to forget everything. Unless we are subject to the extreme amnesia of amentia, Korsakoff syndrome, or chronic temporal lobe epilepsy,[41] we *cannot forget* certain devastating experiences such as the death of a parent or a friend, or battle scenes in Vietnam. The same is true of exhilarating experiences: the first moment of falling in love, the birth of a child, the publication of a book impose themselves upon our remembrance.

On the other hand, the incursion of unwilled and uncontrolled forgetting into remembering serves to delimit the latter in drastic ways. Whether it assumes the comparatively benign (but highly frustrating) form of our being unable to remember a proper name or the much more momentous form of losing contact with whole tracts of our remembered past as a result of a stroke (which can lead to the undermining of our personal identity), such involuntary forgetting—especially in its more monstrous displays—acts to remind us of our contingency and frailty as rememberers. No wonder that so many models of remembering attempt to underwrite its efficiency and reliability by demonstrating the rigor of the stages through which the formation of a single memory must presumably pass. Indeed, the recourse of many memory theorists to notions such as cognitive "levels of processing" or neural memory-traces can be seen as part of a determined effort to shore up (and to defend against) the faulty workings of memory, its liability to error and breakdown, the ever-present possibility of falling into temporary or even permanent oblivion. Considered in this light, forgetting is indeed a condition of remembering: its constant specter inspires the neurologist (as well as the idealist) to a vision of perfect retention. As Minkowski admonishes, however, it is far from certain that we should ever wish to achieve an error-free memorial life. Not only is erring always likely to occur; it is itself something actively to be desired. Physiological models—abetted by computer paradigms—project a state which it is doubtful we would wish to attain once we consider the consequences of having an infallible memory: for "S" it was a continual curse.

Despite its intrinsic importance and its undeniably salutary effects, the fact of forgetting underscores the inherent imperfection of our operative memory. From the standpoint of this memory, forgetting is indeed a matter of unfreedom. To be forgetful beyond the reach of any available act of remembering—and beyond the aid of any serviceable technological device—is to come up against a foreclosure upon our freedom as rememberers. This freedom cannot be assimilated to the limitless freedom of a Kantian noumenal self—or to the ethereal freedom of imagining, which is limitless in a quite different sense. Nor can it be reduced to the "secondary autonomy" of the ego as conceived in post-Freudian ego psychology. As memory moves us beyond mind, it also moves us beyond any such ego and its techniques of adaptation-to and control-of the immediate environment. The massive presence of forgetting in our lives shows decisively that we are not egological masters in our own memorial houses, much less in the many mansions that memory enables us to inhabit. If in imagining there is considerable assurance of self-incurred success, in remembering there is no comparable assurance: the titular author of such success, the ego, here becomes buried in the thick mass of the forgotten as well as surpassed in the realm of the remembered. In both respects, the ego is itself mastered, out-remembered.

Where does this leave us as rememberers? Not altogether in submission to the unfreedom introduced by forgetting, and thus merely cast adrift in the vicissitudes of the memorial life. If we cannot be said to make our own memories—if we cannot remember endlessly or flawlessly any more than we can remember pointlessly—this does not make us into mere pawns in a vast and indifferent memory game. Let us say instead that we are made *of our memories:* that our psyche, our body, our life with others, our place in the world, is memorial through and through. To be made of memories is to be made of something that mind alone cannot fabricate nor its representations contain. It is also to be composed in a way that machine design, however ingenious, is unlikely ever to match—especially when the machines are themselves dependent upon our own unconditionally necessary neurons, and upon our equally necessary conscious intentions, for their conception, design, and use.

## VI

But now, after reclaiming remembering for the individual human subject—after showing memories to be genuinely *mine*, whatever threats are posed by forgetting—we must return memory to the world. The need to undertake such a return first became evident in Parts Two and Three of this book. It re-emerged in the present chapter when we discovered that the freedom to be ourselves as rememberers requires that we leave ourselves—ourselves as egological, self-centered subjects—in order to find ourselves. Another way of putting this is to say that, in being made of our memories (rather than being their makers), we are also *beyond ourselves in our own memories*. Instead of sucking us into a tight container of the mind or the brain, memories take us continually outside ourselves; and they do so in the very midst of the enactment of their own distinctive in-gathering action.

How is this possible? We may take a final clue from Heidegger. In *Being and Time* he discusses "being-in" *(In-Sein)* as a mode of existing in the world that cannot be construed as being situated within mind or brain and their representational contents. Just as the circumambient world cannot be adequately mirrored in such contents, so we do not have to climb out of them in order to reach the world:

> When Dasein directs itself towards something and grasps it, it does not somehow first get out of an inner sphere in which it has been proximally encapsulated, but its primary kind of Being is such that it is always 'outside' alongside entities which it encounters and which belong to a world already discovered . . . even in perceiving, retaining, and preserving, the Dasein which knows *remains outside*.[42]

The remembered past also remains outside—outside the confinement of "the 'cabinet' of consciousness."[43] Memories, making us, refuse to be cabined, cribbed, and confined in the manner described by most theories of memory from Cartesianism to cognitive psychology, where "progress" in the latter consists mainly in introducing one type of containment (that offered by the computer) in place of another (that provided by the mind or brain). And making us as they do, these same memories take us out of ourselves and into the world; or more exactly, they show us that we have always already been there—and precisely in and through remembering itself.

Think of it: memory not in brain or mind but *in the world*, and thus in the things that belong to the world such as lived bodies, places, and other people. Indeed, there is no reason not to suppose that even mute material things, inanimate as well as animate, can be thoroughly memorial in status: they, too, can embody memories and are not limited to evoking them. So can machines, not excluding information processing machines once they are divested of their pretension to model human memory itself. *Any thing*—anything in the world, even the frailest footprint—can become memorial: can become a bearer of memories with as much right as a monument built to stand forever. The fact is that memory is more a colander than a container, more porous than enframing. Its final freedom of in-gathering is a freedom of letting the world *in* through its many subtle pores (and this in many fashions) only in order to allow us to realize how richly we already in-habit the world *without*. Ramifying through such being-in-the-world, tying together its diverse facets in incomparably multiple ways, remembering deflates the ambitions of sheer activism just as it undermines the purposes of a resigned passivism. For the world that memory makes known to us in terms of the world's own "things"—its constituents or elements conceived as forms of "subdued being, non-thetic being"[44]—serves to undercut any such divisive dualism as the active/passive dyad itself exemplifies. As memory moves us beyond mind, it moves us *before* the dualisms that mind itself begets in its incessant cogitations, whether these dualisms be those of the active and the passive, mind and body, mind and brain, self and other, ego and reality . . . or of memory and perception, memory and imagination, memory and thought. The thick autonomy of remembering ensures that the mutual emeshment of these otherwise disparate items is thorough and deep—as thorough and deep as our involvement in our own being-in-the-world.

Remembering goes on and we go on with it; we could not go on without it even if we do not make it or control it; crucial contributors to it and continuing collaborators in its company, we act to return remembering to the world. For it is in the world that memories are begotten, and it is in the world that they find their natural destiny. To acknowledge this is to de-center and de-individuate remembering as we usually think of it—namely, as the possession of individual selves—and it is to consider that things, not just representations of things, may be thoroughly steeped in memory.

We can only conclude that memory is co-extensive with world. "Everything," as Piaget says, "participates in memory."[45] Nothing is not memorial in some manner; everything belongs to some matrix of memory, even if it is a matrix which is remote from human concerns and interests. It might even be that *things can remember us* as much as we remember them. Perhaps they even remember themselves: "I did not have to remember these things; they have remembered themselves all these years."[46] Black Elk's words resonate with the possible cosmological implications of a more capacious view of memory, a view which refuses constriction to the human sphere. Could it be that "the hold is held" by things as much as by minds—and by places as much as by brains or machines? Is it possible that remembering goes on, in some fashion, in things and places as well as among human beings? If so, it goes on in such intricate and indirect ways that we hesitate even to think of it as a matter of memory. But how else are we to understand the way in which trees in a grove reflect each other's presence in their patterns of growing, or the way that marks left on boulders indicate receding glaciers? It requires a semiologically attuned observer to interpret such patterns or marks as express memorials of earlier events. Human beings are adept at just such discernment, though perhaps not as uniquely capable of it as was once thought. Yet neither the fact of such sensitivity to memorially suggestive signs, nor the fact that humankind continually engages in remembering, gives to human beings any ultimately privileged position in the realm of memory. Privileged as articulate participants in the process of their own remembering and as acute explorers of its structure, they are nonetheless not entitled to assume that their own remembering conveys the essence of every kind of remembering. If memory in some significant sense is truly to be found in things and their implacement in the world, we cannot presume that an exclusive—or even the most inclusive—paradigm of all memory is provided by the remembering which is characteristic for the human species alone.

One must nonetheless begin somewhere—and best of all with what one knows most intimately. Thus the present study began without embarrassment by scrutinizing a miscellaneous set of casual memories experienced by the author. These all-too-human memories were themselves remembered as a starting point. Their immediate analysis into eidetic traits and intentional structures exemplified yet another finitude—not just that of authorial subjectivity but that of the constraints of phenomenological method. The extension of this analysis into mnemonic modes that do not fit the pattern of intentionality with the exactitude achievable in the traditionally favored case of recollection represented a step away from the inherent limitations of mentalism as this has been practised from Descartes through Husserl. When such decidedly extra-mental phenomena as body and place memories, along with forms of commemoration, were taken up in what Plato might term a "third wave"[47] of consideration the compass of memory was broadened still more: neither the human mind, nor even the individual rememberer in his or her self-identical being, could any longer claim to be the unique vehicle of memories. Instead, remembering can be said to be going on *between* the embodied human rememberer and the place he or she is *in* as well as *with* the others he or she is in the presence *of*.

Thanks to our ruminations on thick autonomy, we should be prepared to take a final step in this de-subjectification of memory. That which has been regarded since the seventeenth century as unambiguously outside the human subject—and consequently as capturable only in the mind regarded as the "mirror of nature," including memory as a main mirror of the external world—is to be understood as altogether continuous with this subject. As immersed in the world, human beings are as much 'outside' as 'inside'. If this is so, the world and its elemental things are themselves matters of memory: not simply there to be entrapped and pictured in recollections, but there as distinctively memorable on their own and from the beginning. What had seemed to be ineluctably dependent on human mentation—and, by extension, on human brains and human-designed machines—turns out to have its own autonomy, densely enacted and yet diaphanously exhibited. Memorial power resides as much in the things of the world as in ourselves or our inventions. The autonomy of remembering goes on not only inside human beings, nor even only between such beings and the world's things, but outside in the midst of things themselves—those very *Sachen selbst* that Husserl had posited as the ultimate objects of phenomenological method.

"To be is to participate": this formula of Lévy-Bruhl's[48] is to be remembered a last time. If to be is to participate, and if everything participates in memory—inanimate things as well as their human percipients—this can only mean that everything is memorial through and through. As in the case of commemoration (that most encompassing form of human remembering), the key is provided by the notion of participation. Memory not only registers modes of participation between animate and inanimate things, minds and bodies, selves and others, persons and places; it also contributes its own re-enlivening capacities to the festival of cosmic participation. Its very porousness, its open-endedness and ongoingness, its ability to bond deeply across remotenesses of time and space, its own virtual dimension—all of these help to make memory a powerful participatory force in the world. Or more exactly: *as* the world. Just as everything participates in memory, so memory participates in everything: every last thing. In so doing, it draws the world together, re-membering it and endowing it with a connectiveness and a significance it would otherwise lack—or rather, without which it would not be what it is or as it is.

# NOTES

## Preface

1. Paul Rozin, "The Psychobiological Approach to Human Memory" in M. R. Rosenzweig and E. L. Bennett, eds., *Neural Mechanisms of Learning and Memory* (Cambridge: MIT Press, 1976), p. 6. Rozin is summarizing the case of M. K. as originally reported in A. Starr and L. Phillips, "Verbal and Motor Memory in the Amnesic Syndrome," *Neuropsychologica* 8 (1970):75–88.

2. A. R. Luria, *The Mind of a Mnemonist*, trans. L. Solotaroff (Chicago: Regnery, 1976), p. 11; his italics. The Dante example is reported on p. 45.

3. Ibid., p. 65.

4. See R. N. Haber and R. B. Haber, "Eidetic Imagery: I. Frequency," *Perceptual and Motor Skills* 19 (1964):131–38.

5. On hypermnesia, see M. Erdelyi, "The Recovery of Unconscious (Inaccessible) Memories: Laboratory Studies of Hypermnesia" in G. Bower, ed., *The Psychology of Learning and Motivation: Advances in Research and Theory* (New York: Academic Press, 1984).

6. Edward S. Casey *Imagining: A Phenomenological Study* (Bloomington: Indiana University Press, 1976).

7. On this neologism, see Jacques Derrida, *Dissemination*, trans. Barbara Johnson (Chicago: University of Chicago Press, 1981), pp. 8, 9, 11, 15–16, 45.

8. For a related sense of the inadequacy of intentionality as a basis for understanding memory, see Maurice Merleau-Ponty, *The Visible and the Invisible*, trans. A. Lingis (Evanston, IL: Northwestern University Press, 1968), pp. 243–44.

9. An important exception is Marcia K. Johnson's essay, "The Origins of Memories," *Advances in Cognitive-Behavioral Research and Therapy* 4 (1985): 1–27.

10. George Steiner, *After Babel* (Oxford: Oxford University Press, 1975), p. 134.

11. "Tantum scimus, quantum memoria tenemus": cited as an epigram in Johann Grafen Mailath, *Mnemonils oder Kunst, das Gedächtnis nach Regeln zu stärken* (Vienna, 1842).

## Introduction

1. Friedrich Nietzsche, "On the Uses and Disadvantages of History for Life," in *Untimely Meditations*, trans. R. J. Hollingdale (Cambridge: Cambridge University Press, 1983), pp. 60–61.

2. On the survival of an oral epic tradition in certain regions of Yugoslavia, see Albert B. Lord, *The Singer of Tales*, Harvard Studies in Comparative Literature, 24 (Cambridge: Harvard University Press, 1960), *passim*.

3. Nietzsche, "On the Uses and Disadvantages of History for Life," p. 62. I here follow the translation of A. Collins in Friedrich Nietzsche, *The Use and Abuse of History* (Indianapolis: Bobbs-Merrill, 1957), p. 7.

4. Milan Kundera, *The Unbearable Lightness of Being*, trans. M. H. Heim (New York: Harper & Row, 1985), p. 5.

5. Ibid.
6. Ibid.
7. Nietzsche, "On the Uses and Disadvantages of History for Life," p. 61 (Hollingdale translation).
8. Kundera, *The Unbearable Lightness of Being*, p. 5.
9. For an elaborate and ingenious effort to conceive memory on the model of a specific computer program, see J. Anderson and G. H. Bower, *Human Associative Memory* (Washington, D.C.: Winston, 1973). See also G. R. Loftus and E. F. Loftus, *Human Memory: The Processing of Information* (Hillsdale, NJ: Erlbaum, 1976).
10. Sigmund Freud, "Fragment of an Analysis of a Case of Hysteria" in *The Standard Edition of the Complete Psychological Works of Sigmund Freud* (London: Hogarth, 1953–74), 7:24; his italics. (Hereafter cited as *Standard Edition*.) Compare Neisser's remark: "Until we know more about memory in the natural contexts where it develops and is normally used, theorizing is premature" (Ulric Neisser, *Cognition and Reality* [San Francisco: Freeman, 1976], p. 142). Here psychoanalyst and cognitive psychologist join hands in a common suspicion of artificial models of human memory.
11. I have drawn this list of words, itself only a partial sampling, from the *Oxford English Dictionary*, abbreviating the definitions given therein.
12. "Certainly, then, ordinary language is *not* the last word. In principle it can everywhere be supplemented and improved upon and superseded. Only remember, it *is* the *first* word" (J. L. Austin, "A Plea for Excuses," in Austin's *Philosophical Papers* [Oxford: Oxford University Press, 1961], p. 133; his italics).
13. On the significance of the transition from a primarily oral culture to one in which chirography and typography predominate, see Walter J. Ong, *Orality and Literacy: The Technologizing of the Word* (London: Methuen, 1982), pp. 5–15, 93–103, and *passim*.
14. In American education, the main method of memorizing used to be that of rote repetition, which, since William James's critique, has become recognized as the least efficient method. See William James, *Principles of Psychology* (New York: Dover, 1950), 1:663–68.
15. A recent report of the United States Office of Educational Research and Improvement states that memorizing such things as historical dates and passages of literature can "help students absorb and retain the factual information on which understanding and critical thought are based" (cited in *New York Times*, March 1, 1986, p. 12).
16. Harry Lorayne and Jerry Lucas, *The Memory Book* (New York: Ballantine, 1974).
17. William Stokes, *Memory* (London: Houlston & Wright, 1888), p. 37. Cited by Lucas & Lorayne, *The Memory Book*, pp. 3–4.
18. Frances Yates, *The Art of Memory* (London: Routledge & Kegan Paul, 1966), p. 3; my italics. For a fascinating attempt to trace the fate of the *ars memorativa* tradition during its introduction to China in the sixteenth century by Matteo Ricci, see Jonathan D. Spence, *The Memory Palace of Matteo Ricci* (New York: Viking, 1984).
19. See Friedrich Nietzsche, " 'Guilt', 'Bad Conscience', and Related Matters," in *The Genealogy of Morals*, trans. Francis Golfing (New York: Doubleday, 1956), pp. 189–94, especially sections 1–3.
20. Nietzsche, "On the Uses and Disadvantages of History for Life," p. 61.
21. "It may indeed be questioned whether we have any memories at all *from* our childhood; memories *relating to* our childhood may be all that we possess" (Freud, "Screen Memories," in *Standard Edition*, 3:322; his italics).
22. On childhood amnesia, see Freud, *Three Essays on the Theory of Psy-*

*chosexuality*, in *Standard Edition*, 7:174–76, 189. See also the still earlier statement that "forgetting is often intentional and desired" (ibid., 4:111).

23. Ibid., 12:147–48: "The aim of [psychoanalytic] technique has remained the same. Descriptively speaking, it is to fill in the gaps in memory; dynamically speaking, it is to overcome resistances due to repression."

24. Ibid., 10:243. (This is taken from the case history of the "Rat Man.")

25. Ibid., 2:117 n.

26. Martin Heidegger, *Being and Time*, trans. J. Macquarrie & C. Robinson (New York: Harper and Row, 1962), p. 21. The words in italics represent the title of the first section of the Introduction. The sentence that follows is the first statement in the section.

27. Ibid., pp. 398–99; his italics.

28. See Martin Heidegger, *What Is Called Thinking?* trans. J. Glenn Gray (New York: Harper and Row, 1968), pp. 4, 11, 143, 146–47, 150–51, and 244. See also J. Glenn Gray, "Heidegger on Remembering and Remembering Heidegger," *Man and World* 10 (1977):62–78.

29. Hermann Ebbinghaus, *Memory: A Contribution to Experimental Psychology*, trans. H. A. Ruger & C. E. Bussenius (New York: Dover, 1964).

30. For a candid assessment of such self-enclosure and an admirable attempt to suggest how experimental psychology might reconnect with the concerns of everyday remembering, see Ulric Neisser, "Memory: What Are the Important Questions?" in Ulric Neisser, ed., *Memory Observed: Remembering in Natural Contexts* (San Francisco: Freeman, 1982), pp. 3–19.

31. Freud, *Standard Edition*, 12:153: "For [the psychoanalyst], remembering in the old manner—reproduction in the psychical field—is the aim to which he adheres."

32. A. R. Luria, *The Mind of a Mnemonist*, trans. Lynn Solotaroff (Chicago: Regnery, 1976).

33. Walter J. Ong, *Orality and Literacy*, p. 169.

34. Plato, *Phaedrus* 275 a (Hackforth translation). "Recipe" translates *pharmakon*, drug or remedy. On writing as *pharmakon*, see J. Derrida, "Plato's Pharmacy" in *Dissemination*, trans. B. Johnson (Chicago: University of Chicago Press, 1981), pp. 95–116.

35. "In the ancient world, devoid of printing, without paper for note-taking or on which to type lectures, the trained memory was of vital importance. And the ancient memories were trained by an art . . . which could depend on faculties of intense visual memorization which we have lost. The word 'mnemotechnics', though not actually wrong as a description of the classical art of memory, makes this very mysterious subject seem simpler than it is" (Yates, *The Art of Memory*, p. 4.) On the oral aspects of early Greek memorizing, see the now-classical work of Milman Parry, *The Making of Homeric Verse*, ed. A. Parry (Oxford: Clarendon Press, 1971), esp. pp. 325–42; as well as Ong, *Orality and Literacy*, pp. 16–30, 57–67.

36. See the account by Robert Graves, *The Greek Myths* (Baltimore: Penguin, 1955), 2:292 (as based on Tzetzes and Plutarch).

37. Jean Pierre Vernant, "Aspects Mythiques de la mémoire et du temps," in Vernant's *Mythe et pensée chez les Grecs* (Paris: Maspero, 1965), p. 85. In what follows, I am indebted to Vernant's account of the place of memory in ancient Greek culture.

38. Poets in particular were credited with the ability to intuit the past directly and without any mediation other than their own inspired words. These words not merely depict the past but transport us into it: they make us contemporaries of the events described, and their order is the order of these events. As Socrates says to Ion, the rhapsode:

> When you chant these [verses of Homer], are you in your senses? Or are you carried out of yourself, and does not your soul in an ecstasy conceive herself *to be engaged in the actions you relate,* whether they are in Ithaca, or Troy, or wherever the story puts them? (Plato, *Ion* 535 b–c; my italics.)

39. Vernant, *Mythe et Pensée,* p. 87.

40. See Karl Kerenyi, "Mnemosyne-Lesmosyne. On the Springs of 'Memory' and 'Forgetting' " *Spring,* (1977):120–30, esp. 129–30.

41. Ibid., pp. 129–30; his italics.

42. Plato, *Ion* 533e.

43. Ibid., 536b: "One poet is suspended from one Muse, another from another; we call it being 'possessed' but the fact is much the same, since he is *held*" (emphasis in the translation of Lane Cooper). Ong reminds us that "rhapsodize" derives from *rhapsóidein,* "to stitch songs together" (Ong, *Orality and Literacy,* p. 13).

44. Plato, *Ion* 536a. On Mnemosyne as loadstone, see ibid., 533d-e, 535e-536b.

45. Hesoid, *Theogony,* 32 and 38. Note that the Muses have such knowledge of past, present, and future too: see *Larousse Encyclopedia of Mythology* (New York: Prometheus Press, 1960), pp. 127–29.

46. Heidegger, *What Is Called Thinking?*, p. 11. Heidegger adds that "this is why poesy is the water that at times flows backwards toward the source, toward thinking-back" (ibid.). ("Thinking-back" translates *An-denken,* commemorative thought.)

47. On this point, see Vernant, *Mythe et Pensée,* pp. 80–81. In further tribute to their perception of memory's invaluable role in the lives of men, the Greeks accorded to Mnemosyne a critical position in the scheme of things. Mnemosyne is one of only twelve Titans, the offspring of Gaea (Earth) and Uranus (Heaven, Sky); along with their siblings, the 100-headed giants and the Cyclops, the Titans represent the tumultuous forces of Nature, headstrong beings who overthrew Uranus. Cronus, the castrator of Uranus, was the brother of Mnemosyne; the latter became in turn the lover of Zeus, Cronus' youngest son and the chief of the Olympian gods. It was said that nine nights of love between Zeus and Mnemosyne led forthwith to the birth of the nine muses. Since at least three of these latter are directly, and three others indirectly, concerned with poetry, the close tie between memory and poetry is recognized and preserved in this mythical form—just as the liaison between Mnemosyne and Zeus ensures Mnemosyne's intrinsic power: her capacity to seize poets, rhapsodes, and listeners alike with "the Bacchic transport." (Plato, *Ion* 534a).

48. In Plato's view, previous lives are *presupposed* as the basis for present recollection; but they are not themselves remembered, thanks to the forgetfulness induced by the river Ameles (i.e., "mindlessness"). See Plato, *Republic* 621a–d.

49. Thus the invocation of divine inspiration at the end of the *Meno* offers only a pseudo-solution, an aporetic conclusion, to an inquiry into the nature of virtue: see Plato, *Meno* 99 c–e.

50. Vernant, *Mythe et Pensée,* p. 103.

51. See Aristotle, *De Memoria et Reminiscentia,* trans. Richard Sorabji, in *Aristotle On Memory* (London: Duckworth, 1972).

52. Aristotle, *De Memoria et Reminiscentia,* 499 a 15 (Sorabji translation).

53. See ibid., 452 b 7–453 a 3.

54. Ibid., 451 a 15–16.

55. Plato, *Timaeus* 37 d (Cornford translation).

56. See Plato, *Meno* 81 a ("searching and learning are, as a whole, recollection") and Aristotle, *De Memoria et Reminiscentia,* 453 a 15–16 ("recollection is a search in something bodily for an image").

57. See Pierre Janet, *L'évolution de la mémoire et de la notion du temps* (Paris: Chahine, 1928), esp. vol. 1; Sigmund Freud, "Constructions in Analysis," in *Standard Edition* 23:257–69; F. C. Bartlett, *Remembering: A Study in Experimental and*

*Social Psychology* (Cambridge: Cambridge University Press, 1964), pp. 197–214; Jean Piaget and Bärbel Inhelder, *Memory and Intelligence,* trans. A. J. Pomerans (New York: Basic Books, 1975), pp. 1–26.

58. Cf. Plato, *Theatetus* 197d–199b; Freud, "Repeating, Remembering, and Working-Through," in *Standard Edition,* 12:147–56.

59. "I have chosen to end my history with Leibniz . . . because it may be that here ends the influence of the art of memory as a factor in basic European developments" (Yates, *The Art of Memory,* p. 389).

60. Descartes, *Meditations On First Philosophy,* trans. L. J. Lafleur (Indianapolis: Bobbs-Merrill, 1960), p. 23. Since this statement epitomizes modern skepticism toward memory—especially in contrast with Greek veneration toward the same power—I have used it as an epigraph to this Introduction.

61. See ibid., pp. 70, 71, 84—where it is simply *assumed* that memory is not altogether deceitful insofar as it is able to "join together present information with what is past" (p. 84).

62. Spinoza, *The Ethics,* bk. 2, prop. 18, note, in the translation of R. H. M. Elwes (New York: Dover, 1951), 2:100; my italics. Cf. the commentary of H. A. Wolfson, *The Philosophy of Spinoza* (New York: Meridian, 1950), 2:80–90, where the rooting of Spinoza's conception of memory in Aristotle's *De Memoria et Reminiscentia* is stressed. The close link between memory and imagination which all of these compound terms imply is forcefully expressed by Hobbes: "*Imagination* and *Memory* are but one thing, which for divers considerations hath divers names" (*Leviathan,* ed. C. B. Macpherson [London: Pelican, 1968], p. 89; his italics).

63. Hume, *A Treatise of Human Nature,* ed. L. A. Selby-Bigge (Oxford: Oxford University Press, 1967), p. 9. But see p. 85 for Hume's own questioning of the criterion of order.

64. Hume also speaks of "order and form" at ibid., p. 9.

65. "When we remember any past event, the idea of it flows in upon the mind in a forcible manner" (ibid., p. 9). This is to be compared with what Hume calls the "gentle force" of imagination (p. 10).

66. For Hume's explicit espousal of a copy model of memory, see ibid., p. 8.

67. I am thinking here of such figures as de Condillac and Taine in France and the two Mills in England: all continue to conceive of remembering as copying.

68. See Kant, *The Critique of Pure Reason,* trans. N. K. Smith (New York: St. Martin's Press, 1965), pp. 132–33, 143–44, 146, 165, 183. Wolfson demonstrates that the very distinction between "reproductive" and "productive" imagination has its origins in medieval Arabic and Hebrew texts that distinguished "retentive" from "compositive" imagination. See Wolfson, *The Philosophy of Spinoza,* 2:82.

69. On "productive imagination" see Kant, *Critique of Pure Reason,* pp. 142–43, 145, 165. Only productive imagination has a transcendental status. This is why Kant's only direct discussion of memory (in his *Anthropologie in Pragmatischer Hinsicht* [Könisberg: Nicolovius, 1798], sect. 34) treats it as a merely empirical faculty of human beings.

70. Norman Malcolm, *Memory and Mind* (Ithaca, NY: Cornell University Press, 1977).

## Part One

### 1. First Forays

1. Kant's analogy of "the light dove, cleaving the air in her free flight" occurs in *The Critique of Pure Reason* trans. N. K. Smith (New York: St. Martin's Press, 1965),

A5–B9. The contrast between "random groping" and "the secure path of a science" is found at ibid., B xiv and B xxxi.

2. R. E. Nisbett and T. D. Wilson, "Telling More than We Can Know: Verbal Reports on Mental Processes," *Psychological Review* 84 (1977):232.

3. Edward S. Casey, "Imagination and Phenomenological Method" in *Husserl: Expositions and Appraisals,* eds. F. Elliston and P. McCormick (South Bend: University of Notre Dame Press, 1977), pp. 70–83; Casey, *Imagining: A Phenomenological Study* (Bloomington: Indiana University Press, 1976), pp. 25–26.

4. Freud argues that this inalienable but puzzling presence of the self in one's memories is a proof that they cannot be purely reproductive, for at the time we were not at all aware of ourselves as sheer spectators. See his early essay, "Screen Memories," in *Standard Edition,* 3:321.

5. I refer to the moments in the film when the young protagonists are seen in a movie theater, and we are shown part of the movie which *they* are watching.

6. This experience thus puts into question Freud's strict division between "word-presentations" and "thing-presentations" (*Standard Edition,* 14:202–4, 209–15). The presentation here, though manifesting itself explicitly as a word, is equally (though more implicitly) a presentation of the thing denoted by the word. Is this perhaps always true of memories of proper names? One is also struck by the fact that it is often proper names that return most suddenly in memory (and that, conversely, are just as suddenly lost, especially as we get older). Is this because phonological encoding occurs first and is most easily decoded as well as because encoding of proper names has a privileged position?

7. The word, however, was not *only* visible, but appeared to have an ambiguous status in my memory as visual and verbal at once and as a whole.

8. Contexts, even quite loose ones, always put constraints on what we experience, leading us to take the experienced item in one way or another, to disambiguate it in a certain fashion, etc. The more specific the context, however, the more delimiting and restrictive the constraints.

9. William James, *Principles of Psychology* (1890; reprint, New York: Dover, 1950), 1:643–52.

10. See Robert Crowder, *Principles of Learning and Memory* (Hillsdale, NJ: Erlbaum, 1976), chap. 6.

11. The nature of place memory is treated at considerable length in chapter 9 herein.

12. As Freud describes himself in *The Interpretation of Dreams (Standard Edition,* 4:105).

## 2. Eidetic Features

1. Aristotle, *De Memoria et Reminiscentia* 453 a 15–16. Here and elsewhere in this book I employ Richard Sorabji's translation in his *Aristotle on Memory* (London: Duckworth, 1972).

2. A variation on this circumstance is described by Freud: "Something is 're-membered' which could never have been 'forgotten' because it was never at any time noticed—was never conscious" (*Standard Edition,* 13:149). Freud restricts this to "purely internal acts" (ibid.) such as fantasies and emotions, but there seems to be no reason for excluding sensory perceptions from this process.

3. See chapter 4 under "The Mnemonic Presentation."

4. At least *apparently* disconnected: on further reflection (e.g., in psychoanalysis) one may well discover initially unsuspected connections after all. Thus my claim must be restricted to ostensibly disconnected memories.

5. Yet what is expansion from one perspective is encapsulment from another: to remember the tea-tasting *now*, some time after it has occurred, is also to condense and encompass the original moment of the experience within the present moment. This holds even less ambiguously in the other examples, where entire stretches of previous experience are at once extended and encapsulated in the act of remembering them—thereby exhibiting the co-ordinate and even conterminous character of these two basic actions of remembering.

6. William James, *Principles of Psychology* (1890; reprint, New York: Dover, 1950), 1:463.

7. Of course, we need not be *explicitly* reminded; much of our past experience persists in a more insidious and subtle manner, as in the largely unacknowledged role of memories of my former movie-goings in the Lincoln Theater: these memories persisted under the cloak of the consciously entertained memory of viewing *Small Change* at this theater a short time ago. I return to the phenomenon of reminding in chapter 5.

8. It should be underscored that the actualities we remember are for the most part *datable* even if not necessarily dated. Indeed, it is comparatively rare that we remember the date as such; "1492," "1066," one's birthdate, our anniversary: such contents of memory are few in number. In many cases, an approximate indication of the date is given with the memory: "a few weeks ago" (example #2), "several summers ago" (example #6). In other cases, not even this much of an indication is given, and we must institute a search to specify the date, as in example #1. In the cases of remembering "902" and "Culligan," however, we encounter a limit of datability itself. Although these memories no doubt derive from datable events, they are not datable as such. This is not to say that they are out of time or timeless; they are perfectly well *in* time, but in such a manner as to resist being dated.

9. Edmund Husserl, *The Phenomenology of Internal Time-Consciousness*, trans. J. S. Churchill (Bloomington: Indiana University Press, 1964), p. 75.

10. "We have *an* experience when the material experienced runs its course to fulfillment . . . such an experience is a whole and carries with it its own individualizing quality and self-sufficiency. It is *an* experience." (John Dewey, *Art as Experience* [New York: Capricorn Books, 1958], p. 35; his italics.) In what I have said just above I do not mean to deny that we can (and often do) have fragmentary memories. However incomplete such memories may be, they nonetheless count *as memories*—i.e., can be identified as memorial in status—only if they manifest sufficient determinateness ("finishedness") to be considered as conveying, in whole or in part, what Dewey calls "*an* experience."

11. James, *Principles of Psychology*, 1:650; my italics. See also p. 652, where "reality" corresponds to what I have been calling "actuality": "The sense of a peculiar active relation in [an object] to ourselves is what gives to [this] object the characteristic quality of reality, and a merely imagined past event differs from a recollected one only in the absence of this peculiar feeling relation."

12. Once more I must make exception of the "902" and "Culligan" memories. In such memories—which are generic rather than episodic in status—no significant sense of self-presence is operative. Put otherwise: no part of their manifest content includes myself-as-witness.

13. See Roman Ingarden, *The Literary Work of Art*, trans. G. Grabowicz (Evanston, IL: Northwestern University Press, 1973), pp. 265–67, 330–39.

14. Even the hazy recollection of Aunt Leone can be construed as the unfocused ground for the name "Aunt Leone" as the focused figure. Such figure/ground analysis is applicable in all the other cases too.

15. Henri Bergson, *Matter and Memory*, trans. N. M. Paul and W. S. Palmer (1896; reprint, New York: Doubleday, 1959), p. 18.

16. By this I mean that although the tasting itself is an episode and rememorable as such in recollection or "secondary memory," I remembered it non-episodically as lingering in primary memory and thus as non-narratized.

17. This is not to deny that the description *per se* of any given experience of remembering is always implicitly narrative in form insofar as it makes mention of relevant antecedents, surroundings, and consequences of the experience. All of my written descriptions above would count as narrations in this broad sense. But the same cannot be claimed of the specific *content* of the experiences thus described.

18. Gilbert Ryle, *The Concept of Mind* (New York: Barnes & Noble, 1949), p. 279. The full statement is: "Being good at recalling is not being good at investigating, but being good at preserving. It is a narrative skill, if 'narrative' be allowed to cover non-prosaic as well as prosaic representations." The issue of narration will be taken up again in chapter 6, where I shall also further explore the matter of self-recounting.

19. This is the Piagetian view. See Jean Piaget and Bärbel Inhelder, *Memory and Intelligence,* trans. A. J. Pomerans (New York: Basic Books, 1973).

20. "Forsan et haec olim meminisse juvabit" (Virgil, *Aeneid,* I, p. 203).

21. From the essay "Screen Memories," in *Standard Edition,* 3:317. Freud goes on to cite the quotation from Virgil given just above.

22. I want to stress that these events, qua remembered *content,* may be intrinsically unpleasurable (e.g., disgusting, despairing, etc.). But as *remembered* at the present remove of time, they can take on a bittersweet quality that represents a compromise between their inherent painfulness and the equally inherent pleasure of ruminescence. This is not to deny situations in which the painfulness is such as to overwhelm any subsequent recollective pleasure.

## 3. Remembering as Intentional: Act Phase

1. Importantly different is Freud's use of "diphasic" as referring to sequential periods of development. See S. Freud, *Three Essays on the Theory of Sexuality,* in *Standard Edition,* 7:66, 100.

2. For further discussion of the basic notions of act and object phases as component features of intentionality construed in a phenomenological sense, see Edward S. Casey, *Imagining: A Phenomenological Study* (Bloomington: Indiana University Press, 1976), p. 38ff.

3. The capacity to remember is our innate or acquired ability to do so; the disposition to remember is the tendency to do so on certain occasions. For further discussion of this distinction, see Richard Sorabji, *Aristotle on Memory* (London: Duckworth, 1972), pp. 1–2; and Gilbert Ryle, *The Concept of Mind* (New York: Barnes & Noble, 1949), p. 131ff.

4. On short-term storage, see Robert G. Crowder, *Principles of Learning and Memory* (Hillsdale, NJ: Lawrence Erlbaum, 1976), chaps. 6, 7. On long-term storage, see ibid., chaps. 8–10.

5. For a discussion of these cases, see Brian Smith, *Memory* (London: Allen & Unwin, 1966), p. 48: "There may be some memories which are constantly, as people say, at the back of their minds . . . in such cases we could equally well regard the memory as occurrent or as dispositional." This is meant as a critique of Ryle's original distinction between dispositional and occurrent senses of memory in *The Concept of Mind,* pp. 272–73.

6. Systematic amnesia such as is found in Korsakoff patients, for example, illuminates the distinction between short-term and long-term memory, both being aspects of memory capacity. See G. A. Talland, *Disorders of Memory and Learning* (New York: Penguin, 1968), esp. p. 126ff.

7. See *inter alia* C. B. Martin and Max Deutscher, "Remembering," reprinted in R. M. Chisholm and R. J. Swartz, eds., *Empirical Knowledge* (Englewood Cliffs, NJ: Prentice-Hall, 1973), p. 306.

8. On this notion, see Casey, *Imagining,* pp. 19, 60, 178, 200, 233.

9. William James was the first to distinguish primary from secondary memory. He did so in his *Principles of Psychology* (1890; reprint, New York: Dover, 1950), I, pp. 606, 609–10, 613, 643–53. Bergson hints at primary memory in his notion of "a perception of the immediate past" (Henri Bergson, *Matter and Memory,* trans. N. M. Paul and W. S. Palmer [1896; reprint, New York: Doubleday, 1959], p. 130). Influenced by James, Husserl discussed primary memory in his 1904–1905 lectures: *The Phenomenology of Internal Time-Consciousness,* trans. J. S. Churchill (Bloomington: Indiana University Press, 1964), esp. secs. 8–13 and app. I. For treatments of primary memory in experimental settings, see Crowder, *Principles of Learning and Memory,* ch. 6.

10. Hence it is misleading to refer to primary remembering as involving an "echo box" phenomenon, even if this term is accepted or suggested by subjects who are questioned on the point. See N. C. Waugh and D. A. Norman, "Primary Memory," *Psychological Review* 72(1965):89–104. Any effects of reverberation or resounding are better considered under the designation of "iconic" or "echoic" memory, a special form of transient storage of strictly sensory aspects of experiences. Since we are not aware of such memory—it arises and vanishes extremely rapidly—I do not consider it as essential to a phenomenological study of memory. The classical source here is G. Sperling, "The Information Available in Brief Visual Presentations," *Psychological Monographs,* 1960, no. 11.

11. "Retention" and "sinking away" are Husserl's terms for this process. See *Phenomenology of Internal Time-Consciousness,* secs. 8–13.

12. James, *Principles of Psychology,* 1:613. James also posits a "forward fringe" (ibid.)—as does Husserl in his notion of "protention" (see *Phenomenology of Internal Time-Consciousness,* sec. 24).

13. James posited 12 seconds as the normal nucleus of primary memory. See *Principles of Psychology,* I: 611ff. On more recent estimates and measurements, see Crowder, *Principles of Learning and Memory,* p. 146ff., esp. the conclusion on p. 173: "The stability of primary memory capacity across measurement techniques . . . argues that it is quite a fundamental structural feature of human information processing."

14. See Husserl, *Phenomenology of Internal Time-Consciousness,* p. 52.

15. On the specious present, see James, *Principles of Psychology,* 1:609ff., 647. For Husserl's discussion of the living present, see Klaus Held, *Lebendige Gegenwart* (The Hague: Nijhof, 1966). That the same phenomenon could be termed at once "living" and "specious" attests eloquently to its ephemeral and vanishing character. It also attests to its ready deconstructibility, as is brilliantly demonstrated by Jacques Derrida in *Speech and Phenomena,* trans. D. Allison (Evanston, IL: Northwestern University Press, 1973), p. 60ff. I leave Derrida's efforts out of consideration here, however, since they bear on the metaphysical premises at play in Husserl's descriptions of primary memory rather than on these descriptions themselves.

16. James, *Principles of Psychology,* 1:646.

17. See Crowder, *Principles of Learning and Memory,* chaps. 7–8; Henry C. Ellis, *Fundamentals of Human Learning, Memory, and Cognition* (Dubuque, IA: Brown, 1978), chaps. 4–5.

18. This distinction is made by E. Tulving and Z. Pearlstone in their essay, "Availability versus Accessibility of Information in Memory for Words," *Journal of Verbal Learning and Verbal Behavior* 5 (1966):381–91. A thorough discussion of stage analysis is found in Crowder, *Principles of Learning and Memory,* pp. 4–12.

Crowder differentiates between stage analysis, coding analysis, and task analysis as the three most fruitful means of approaching memory as a total phenomenon.

19. This phrase, originally from Shakespeare (*Sonnet* XXX, line 6), is used by James without quotation marks in *Principles of Psychology,* 1:662.

20. This is entailed in information-processing and computer simulation models of memory. See, for example, John R. Anderson, *Language, Memory, and Thought* (Hillsdale, NJ: Lawrence Erlbaum, 1976).

21. For Husserl's use of *Re-präsentation* see *Phenomenology of Internal Time-Consciousness,* sec. 17.

22. James, *Principles of Psychology,* 1:647–48.

23. Husserl, *Phenomenology of Internal Time-Consciousness,* p. 66; my italics, where "it" refers not only to the pristine present but to its retention in primary memory as well.

24. E.g., "World War II," "the Guilford Green," "my house," "the Star-Spangled Banner," etc.

25. Thus remembering *simpliciter* is to be distinguished from imaging, which is *always* sensuous. See Casey, *Imagining,* pp. 41–42.

26. In fact, a formula or group of words is more likely to be given a sensuous form in memory than to be designated by abstract symbols, presumably as an *aide-mémoire*. Imagery allows for what psychologists call "parallel processing," that is, the representation of a plurality of items simultaneously and together. Hence its value in recalling multi-element bits of information.

27. On the predicational crease, see Robert Sokolowski, *Presence and Absence* (Bloomington: Indiana University Press, 1978), pp. 104–5.

28. Such is Norman Malcolm's term for the entire class of such memories. Cf. his "Three Kinds of Memory" in *Knowledge and Certainty* (Englewood Cliffs, NJ: Prentice-Hall, 1963), p. 204ff. See also Endel Tulving, "Episodic and Semantic Memory" in E. Tulving and W. Donaldson, eds., *Organization of Memory* (New York: Academic Press, 1972), pp. 381–403.

29. I may remember seeing paintings or photographs of some of the facts mentioned, and these may well furnish pictorial details. But the details still do not pertain to situations at which I was present: I can remember that I saw such representations, I can import details from them into my remembering of the situations in question (e.g., as decoration or support), and I can even delude myself into believing that I *was* present by confusing the representations with the situations they depict. Yet I cannot non-delusively *remember that* these situations took place with the sensuous features provided by the representations: such situations, which have the status of learned but unwitnessed facts, are consigned to non-sensuousness as contents of my acts of remembering-that.

30. Martin and Deutscher restrict their otherwise illuminating discussion of non-sensuous remembering-that to this single kind. Neither of the two types of remembering-that which they discuss adequately reflects the second kind of non-sensuous remembering which I am about to describe. See "Remembering," in *Empirical Knowledge,* pp. 303–5.

31. See Gilbert Ryle, *The Concept of Mind,* chap. 2.

32. Cf. Casey, *Imagining,* pp. 42–48.

33. As Bergson implies in contrasting all recollective, visualized memory with "habit" or "motor" memory—the former being regarded as a matter of "spontaneity," the latter of "repetition." See *Matter and Memory,* pp. 69–77. I discuss Bergson's conception of habit memory in my essay "Habitual Body and Memory in Merleau-Ponty," *Man and World* 17 (1984):279–82.

34. By "do" I mean not only practical actions but actions of feeling and thinking as well.

35. Of course, cues of various sorts are employed at later stages of any learning process such as this one: but if the learning has been thorough, they are not then *consciously needed* as they must be at the stage of habituation. It is of interest to note here that New York City taxi drivers report that one of their critical cues is the sense of rapidity with which they pass through a given part of the town: i.e., the rate at which buildings or other landmarks "whiz by"; such cues are strictly kinematic. (I am indebted to Ray McDermott for this observation.)
36. For a detailed discussion of habitual body memories, see chapter 8, secs. II and III herein; Casey, "Habitual Body and Memory in Merleau-Ponty," p. 282ff.
37. In Heideggerian language, it is a matter of the structure of the "in-order-to" *(um-zu)* in human experience. This structure is in turn part of an "equipmental totality" which provides its essential context. See Martin Heidegger, *Being and Time*, trans. J. Macquarrie and C. Robinson (New York: Harper & Row, 1962), sec. 15.
38. Richard Sorabji is an exception. See his list of kinds of remembering in his *Aristotle on Memory*, pp. 1, 8, 13. But he only mentions remembering-to in passing and without giving any further discussion.
39. This is an especially characteristic example, since many cases of remembering-to involve the performance of a duty or task.
40. A notable exception is remembering-how to do. This, too, may be directed toward the present or the future, but in unequal measure. Its primary *nisus* is toward the future, i.e., toward a time when our action or movement will have realized its aim. Only secondarily is it directed toward the present alone; but an exception occurs when I remember how to swim for the sake of the activity of swimming itself (*not* to become a better swimmer or to impress others, etc.). Another exception will be treated below under "Subsidiary Types of Remembering" ("Remembering the Future").
41. As in Roy Schafer's theory of human behavior: see his *A New Language for Psychoanalysis* (New Haven: Yale University Press, 1976), esp. Part III.
42. My claim is not that this is always so—we do have distinct recollections on the occasions in question—but that there is a pronounced tendency in the direction of the amorphously recalled.
43. Commemoration is treated separately in chapter 10.
44. I say "happen" because we can also remember future events in which we are not personally engaged: e.g., in remembering an upcoming religious holiday that we do not ourselves observe.
45. For further treatment of memory and the future, see chapter 5, section II.
46. James and Husserl belong together in their adherence to primary versus secondary memory, while Bergson allies himself with habitual versus recollective memory. M. I. Posner posits "verbal," "imaginative," and "enactive" remembering in his *Cognition* (Glenview, IL: Scott, Foresman, 1973).
47. Bergson acknowledges recollective imagery to be of value in the very acquisition of habit memory: "We make use of the fugitive image [of habit memory] to construct a stable mechanism which takes its place" (*Matter and Memory*, p. 74).

## 4. Remembering as Intentional: Object Phase

1. Brian Smith, *Memory* (London: Allen & Unwin, 1966), p. 45.
2. Thus William James says quite justifiably that "what memory goes with is . . . a very complex representation, that of the fact to be recalled *plus* its associates, the whole forming one 'object' " (*Principles of Psychology* [1890; reprint, New York:

Dover, 1950], 1:650–51.) But I cannot agree with him that "there is nothing unique in the object of memory" (ibid., p. 652). This is true insofar as we do tend to remember the same *sorts* of things we perceive, ponder, etc.; but as remembered, the structure of their objecthood is modified significantly.

3. So, too, are the act phase and the object phase themselves, which may not be distinguished in fact in many cases of remembering but which remain distinguishable upon reflection and by means of a nuanced description. For this reason, Merleau-Ponty's objection to an "intentional analysis" of memory (namely, that "consciousness of" is an inadequate model for the recapture of a massive, "vertical" past) fails to be decisive. What counts in a descriptive analysis is not necessarily what one is immediately conscious of in an experience. (See M. Merleau-Ponty, *The Visible and the Invisible*, trans. A. Lingis [Evanston, IL: Northwestern University Press, 1968], pp. 243–44.) Later, however, when remembering will be considered as something other than mental in status, Merleau-Ponty's critique will become apposite: see Parts two and three below, especially chapter 8.

4. Aristotle, *De Memoria et Reminiscentia*, 449 b, 21–23; my italics.

5. I say "specifiable" and not "specified," for the specific content of a given act of remembering may not yet be specified verbally. But it must always be possible to do so eventually. Thus I cannot agree with Sorabji's critique that the passage just cited invokes only a contingent criterion of remembering. See Richard Sorabji, *Aristotle On Memory* (London: Duckworth, 1972), pp. 9–10.

6. As James says, "Wherever, in fact, the recalled event does appear without a definite setting, it is hard to distinguish it from a mere creation of fancy. But in proportion as its image lingers and recalls associates which gradually become more definite, it grows more and more distinctly into a remembered thing" (*Principles of Psychology*, 1:657–58). I should make it clear that the case of oneiric memory is atypical insofar as the sense of a setting may occur independently of the dream-content itself—whereas in the other cases we shall be examining, the memory-frame forms part of the mnemonic presentation.

7. Even here exceptions occur. To remember a particular date may evoke an entire ambiance. This is especially true of anniversary dates and other commemorative occasions; this also holds for historical facts whose recollection evokes an entire life-world for us.

8. The ephemerality of these mini-worlds precludes their functioning as "fields" in any strict sense. See Edward S. Casey, *Imagining: A Phenomenological Study* (Bloomington: Indiana University Press, 1976), p. 50.

9. This term is Heidegger's, although he intends it in a quite different way than that in which I am using it here. See *Being and Time*, trans. J. Macquarrie and E. Robinson (New York: Harper and Row, 1962), sec. 70.

10. I am using "place" and "locus" here in a purely descriptive or formal sense, not in the much richer sense which will be the focus of attention in chapter 9.

11. See James, *Principles of Psychology*, 1:650–51, 654–55, 657–58. James also refers to these as "concomitants" on p. 655.

12. It is not that they could *not* be thematized by a subtle shift of attention on our part. Think, for example, of the vaguely delineated but not wholly indefinite figures who surrounded me in the theater during the viewing of *Small Change*. Although I could not give anything like a full description of these figures, I could certainly say more than I did in my actual description of them. In particular, I could indicate the way in which they helped to situate me within the interior space of the theater by their manner of surrounding me. Nevertheless, precisely as *un*thematized, such surroundings contribute all the more powerfully to the worldhood of a given memory-frame.

13. James, *Principles of Psychology*, 1:239, 331, 333.

14. As a result, self-presence is not discussed as a basic element in the imaginative presentation in Casey, *Imagining,* pp. 50–51. Indeed, the comparative infrequency of imagined self-presence is what led me to use the term "world-frame" for what I am here calling the "memory-frame" and to give to the former a somewhat more subordinate position within the imaginative presentation than I here assign to the latter within the mnemonic presentation.

15. See Bertrand Russell, *Analysis of Mind* (London: Allen & Unwin, 1921), p. 161.

16. It is true, however, that a sense of familiarity may cling to the remembered facts or skilled actions here in question. But such familiarity derives exclusively from their repetition (in mind or in practical action), not from self-presence as such. It is to be noticed that the subtypes of remembering-that and remembering-how cited here also normally lack any factor of worldhood in their respective memory-frames.

17. Birth-dates are an exception to this rule; but necessarily so, since it is expressly a question of the *day* of birth and this day needs to be specified as such in any explicit reference to it. In relation to ourselves, then, each of us is an historian *faute de mieux*.

18. This is ultimately due to the symbolic status of a date. Any symbol, whether logical, mathematical, or verbal, has the same dual property: "2" includes a considerable (and still to be specified) range of phenomena having to do uniquely with the number 2, while it excludes its neighbors "3" and "1" definitively and without need of further specification.

19. As James says, "If we wish to think of a particular past epoch, we must think of a name or other symbol, or else certain concrete events, associated therewithal. *Both must be thought of, to think the past epoch adequately*" (*Principles of Psychology,* 1:650; my italics). "Other symbol" here includes date.

20. James, *Principles of Psychology,* 1:650.

21. James, from whom I borrow the term "contiguous associates," uses it more broadly to apply to spatial *or* temporal adjacency. But this is to presume a perfect parallelism between remembered time and space—a parallelism which I do not think exists.

22. Note that the first two examples also exhibit sameness of place in addition to similarity of time. Such a dual classification has a strong reinforcing effect, increasing the meaningfulness and unity of the memories belonging to such a group. On the grouping of memories, see Henri Bergson, *Matter and Memory,* trans. N. M. Paul and W. S. Palmer (1896; reprint, New York: Doubleday, 1959), pp. 155ff, 238.

23. The indefiniteness of these times themselves contributes further to their conjointly massing effects.

24. Edmund Husserl, *Phenomenology of Internal Time-Consciousness,* trans. J. S. Churchill (Bloomington: Indiana University Press, 1964), p. 66.

25. Hence our feeling that such a place is somehow "haunted" by its past character; the place abides and as such solicits what formerly occupied it to return once more.

26. Except by distortion, imposition, or misconstrual. On this point, see my paper "Imagining and Remembering" *Review of Metaphysics* 31 (1977): esp. 200–204.

27. Bergson, *Matter and Memory,* pp. 21, 24.

28. Eugene Minkowski, *Lived Time,* trans. N. Metzel (Evanston, IL: Northwestern University Press, 1970), pp. 155–56.

29. See Casey, *Imagining,* pp. 53–55, 108–9, 120–21, 171.

30. Minkowski, *Lived Time,* p. 163. This phrase is applied to "the past as forgotten," but it pertains as well to the aura of the remembered past.

31. In all such cases, the dissolving is equivalent to the fading that occurs in primary memory—that is, to what Husserl calls the "sinking away phenom-

enon" *(Ablaufs-phänomen)* in *Phenomenology of Internal Time-Consciousness,* sec. 10.

32. See Casey, *Imagining,* pp. 194–95.

33. On pure possibility, see Casey, *Imagining,* chap. 5. Strictly speaking, occurring in *any* particular spatial or temporal form is excluded from this notion. See especially ibid., pp. 117–19.

34. What I here call "atmosphere" is closely akin to what Walter Benjamin, commenting on Baudelaire, has called "aura" *tout court*. But Benjamin restricts aural phenomena to a special relationship between people and natural objects. See "On Some Motifs in Baudelaire" in *Illuminations,* trans. H. Zohn (London: Fontana, 1973), p. 189ff.

35. This involvement of the self in the atmosphere also distinguishes remembering from imagining: as actively projecting what we imagine, we are much less prone to be drawn into its atmospheric embrace.

36. See Plato, *Philebus* 33b–36b.

37. Indeed, the *very activity of remembering* often serves to induce emotions of the sort that specify the atmosphere pervading the mnemonic presentation. Perhaps the primary such emotion thereby induced is nostalgia, which as a mood is especially pervasive. As we have seen, nostalgia is an important ingredient in "ruminescence," the most distinctive state of mind that occurs when we remember.

38. "Monogram" is Kant's term for the pure image. See *Critique of Pure Reason,* trans. N. K. Smith (New York: St. Martin's, 1965), A570–B598 (p. 487).

39. Husserl, *The Phenomenology of Internal Time-Consciousness,* p. 71.

40. See ibid., p. 65 and sec. 20. For a treatment of the freedom of remembering, see chapter 12, herein.

41. Husserl attributes this non-contingent diminishing to the very constitution of the "absolute flux" that is the ultimate level of all time-consciousness. The "running-off" of this flux, its gradual fading in continua of retentions, is in his view an "*a priori* temporal law." Cf. *The Phenomenology of Internal Time-Consciousness,* secs. 10–13, 21, 34–36.

42. On the notion of an unavoidable veiling in secondary memory, see ibid., p. 72.

43. A single memory may harbor within itself a number of different texturalities, held together by participating in a common aura. At the same time, the aura can possess its own felt texture.

44. Gaston Bachelard, *The Poetics of Space,* trans. Maria Jolas (New York: Orion Press, 1964), p. xi.

45. Franz Brentano, *Psychology from an Empirical Point of View,* trans. L. A. McAlister (New York: Humanities Press, 1973), pp. 78–91.

## Part Two

### Prologue

1. See Gilbert Ryle, *The Concept of Mind* (New York: Barnes & Noble, 1949), esp. chap. 1 ("Descartes' Myth"); and Richard Rorty, *Philosophy and the Mirror of Nature* (Princeton: Princeton University Press, 1979), esp. chap. 1 ("The Invention of the Mind") and Part two ("Mirroring").

2. Ludwig Wittgenstein, *Philosophical Grammar,* ed. R. Rhees, trans. A. Kenny (Oxford: Blackwell, 1974), p. 79.

## 5. Reminding

1. See Martin Heidegger, *Being and Time,* trans. J. Macquarrie and E. Robinson (New York: Harper and Row, 1962), pp. 95–121.

2. Notice that I can also be reminded of a non-action: e.g., "don't plug in here!" Refraining from action is nevertheless a genuine action, as is any form of intentional inaction or non-action. On this point, see Roy Schafer, "Claimed and Disclaimed Action," in *A New Language for Psychoanalysis* (New Haven: Yale University Press, 1976), pp. 127–54.

3. Thus it is misleading to say that "a reminder is that which *evokes memory*" (Norman Malcolm, *Memory and Mind* [Ithaca: Cornell University Press, 1977], p. 105; my italics). Reminding, especially in the form of thinking of the past, does not simply evoke memories; *it is itself a form of memory*.

4. I often purchase postcards at museums to serve precisely as pictographic reminders of memorable experiences or objects.

5. Aristotle, *De Memoria et Reminiscentia* 450 b 21–451 a 1.

6. Edmund Husserl, *Logical Investigations,* trans. J. N. Findlay (New York: Humanities Press, 1970), 1:270.

7. Ibid; my italics.

8. Ibid; Husserl italicizes much of this passage.

9. See ibid., pp. 269–75 for these examples and others.

10. By "remindand proper" I designate that of which we are consciously or explicitly reminded—in contrast with the implicit content of remembering-that as discussed above. The latter *is* genuinely real; but it cannot count as the *indicatum* in Husserl's sense of the "objective correlate" of an indicative sign (ibid., p. 170).

11. On *schēma* as appearance, see Plato, *Timaeus* 61 d.

12. It is to be noted that "figure" translates (via the Latin *figura) schēma*. Moreover, the *fig-* root of "figure" is equally the origin of "feign" via *fingere,* which means to form, mould, conceive, or contrive and which is itself the etymon for "fiction" and "figment."

13. In chapter 2 I detected a comparable schematical quality in many ordinary recollective memories. But where this quality is a secondary trait of these latter, it is a distinctly primary trait of reminders.

14. In Husserl's terminology, the perceptually adumbrated constitutes a perceived object's "internal and external horizons"; in Gurwitsch's language, it makes up this object's "perceptual implications." (See E. Husserl, *Experience and Judgment,* trans. J. S. Churchill and K. Ameriks [Evanston, IL: Northwestern University Press, 1973], p. 150ff.; and Aron Gurwitsch, "The Phenomenology of Perception: Perceptual Implications" in J. Edie, ed., *An Invitation to Phenomenology* [Chicago: Quadrangle, 1965], pp. 17–29).

15. Thus I must disagree with Paul Weiss when he claims that "strictly speaking, adumbration occurs only in perception" (*Modes of Being* [Carbondale: University of Southern Illinois Press, 1958], p. 521).

16. Moreover, such obliqueness points as well to the often quite tacit relation between reminder and remindand. The former conveys the mind to the latter not so much by expressly referring to it (though it may do this at the level of verbal discourse) but more typically by a spontaneous allusion in which we are aware of what is evoked rather than of the activity of allusion itself.

17. E. Husserl, *Experience and Judgment,* p. 162; my italics.

18. We here confront a situation in which memories become reminders, even though reminders themselves constitute a subset of remembering itself. It is as if Mnemosyne were devoured by one of her own muses: I shall return at the end of the next chapter to the issue of memory's remarkable recursiveness.

19. A systematic and pre-established usage of images employed as reminders can also be completely conventional; say, the American flag as a reminder of certain specific patriotic virtues. Whether this usage is itself ultimately parasitic on verbal language is a question which we must leave open here.

20. Thus I would resist imposing on reminders Peirce's trichotomy of signs: indices, icons, and (verbal) symbols. See Charles S. Peirce, *Collected Papers*, eds. C. Hartshorne and P. Weiss (Cambridge: Harvard University Press, 1960), vol. 2. Peirce himself seems to have regarded reminders as indexical signs: see ibid., vol. 2, 2.285, 2.288. Indeed, it appears that *all* memories are indicative in Peirce's view: see ibid., vol. 1, 1.305.

21. Plato, *Phaedo* 73b–73d.

22. Thus Plato speaks of the first moment of reminding as "the exercise of one's senses upon sensible objects" (ibid., 75e).

23. Ibid., 74c, 76a.

24. Plato, *Meno* 85d; my italics. On this theme, see also *Phaedo* 75e; *Theatetus* 198c; and *Philebus* 346a.

## 6. Reminiscing

1. William Faulkner, *Absalom, Absalom!* (New York: Vintage, 1972), p. 9. In italics in the text.

2. Thus the first definition of "recount" in the *Oxford English Dictionary* is: "to relate or narrate; to tell in detail; to give a full or detailed account of (some fact, event, etc.)."

3. "Every good story must have a beginning that arouses interest, a succession of events that is orderly and complete, a climax that forms the story's point, and an end that leaves the mind at rest" (E. P. St.-John, *Stories and Story-Telling* [New York: Pilgrim Press, 1910], p. 13).

4. A further difference between reminiscing and story-telling involves the factor of *audience*. It is a singular fact that one almost never tells a story to oneself. To tell a story without any audience, actual or potential, is for story-telling to lose all point and purpose. In this respect story-telling is even more thoroughly social than is reminiscing. As we shall observe in some detail below, one can reminisce to oneself quite effectively. Further, when others *are* present, they are typically present as themselves participating: as co-reminiscers. The role of others in story-telling is, in contrast, solely that of listening: taking the story in. Hence the focus on the story-teller himself or herself as an indispensable preserver and purveyor of the story itself.

5. E. Husserl, *Experience and Judgment*, trans. J. S. Churchill and K. Ameriks (Evanston, IL: Northwestern University Press, 1973), p. 178: "Through associative linkage, the no longer living worlds of memory also get a kind of being, despite their no longer being actual."

6. I say "*per se*," for we normally do re-enter the affective ambiance of the reminisced-about world, that is, its pervasive mood, its "*Gestimmtheit*" as Heidegger might say. This ambiance remains distinguishable both from a particular past emotion and from the present emotion generated in the reminiscing itself.

7. C. B. Martin and Max Deutscher, "Remembering" in *Empirical Knowledge*, ed. R. M. Chisholm and R. J. Swartz (Englewood Cliffs, NJ: Prentice-Hall, 1973), p. 306.

8. See Nietzsche, *On the Uses and Disadvantages of History for Life*, trans. R. J. Hollingdale (Cambridge: Cambridge University Press, 1983), p. 67ff.

9. Gadamer's notion of "horizon-fusing" *(Horizontsverschmelzung)* provides a

paradigm for the way in which one's present consciousness is transformed by reconnecting with the past imaginatively. See Hans-Georg Gadamer, *Truth and Method* (New York: Seabury Press, 1975), p. 270ff.

10. But they can be regarded as constitutive of that which they serve to supplement. For this view, see Jacques Derrida, *Speech and Phenomena,* trans. D. Allison (Evanston, IL: Northwestern University Press, 1973), p. 89ff.

11. Vladimir Nabokov, *Speak, Memory* (New York: Putnam's, 1966), pp. 49–50. Nabokov is here writing of his mother, Elena Ivanovna Nabokov.

12. E. Husserl, *The Phenomenology of Internal Time-Consciousness,* trans. J. S. Churchill (Bloomington: Indiana University Press, 1964), p. 66.

13. This statement is attributed to George Haines by *Webster's Third International Dictionary*.

14. All from the entry "wistful" in ibid.

15. Faulkner, *Absalom, Absalom!,* p. 66.

16. Virgil, *Aeneid,* I, 203. Even Virgil might have to admit limits: e.g., the memory of overwhelmingly traumatic events. I return to this issue in chapter 8.

17. I have treated this point in an unpublished essay "The World of Nostalgia."

18. "Discourse is existentially equiprimodial with state-of-mind and understanding" (M. Heidegger, *Being and Time,* trans. J. Macquarrie and E. Robinson [New York: Harper and Row, 1962), p. 208; the entire passage is in italics).

19. Ibid., p. 205; Heidegger's italics.

20. On this point, see Ferdinand de Saussure, *Course in General Linguistics,* trans. W. Baskin (New York: McGraw-Hill, 1966), p. 12ff.; and Jacques Derrida, *Of Grammatology,* trans. G. Spivak (Baltimore: Johns Hopkins University Press, 1974), p. 62ff.

21. Heidegger, *Being and Time,* p. 204. He adds: "But word-things do not get supplied with significations" (ibid.).

22. "Discourse is the articulation of intelligibility" (ibid., pp. 203–4).

23. A. N. Whitehead, *Process and Reality,* ed. D. R. Griffin and D. W. Sherburne (New York: Free Press, 1978), p. 129.

24. Plato, *Sophist,* 263e.

25. It overlooks, for example, the blatant fact that we understand nonverbal works of art. On this point, consult especially Susanne Langer's theory of art as a form of non-discursive symbolism: *Feeling and Form* (New York: Scribner's, 1953).

26. Arthur Rimbaud, letter to Paul Demeny, May 15, 1871.

27. Plato, *Sophist,* 263d.

28. J. Derrida, *Of Grammatology,* p. 68; *Speech and Phenomena,* pp. 129–30, 136–37.

29. This tendency may be pushed further by resorting to encrypted writing, as in the two notable cases of Leonardo da Vinci and Edmund Husserl.

30. *Linotte: The Early Diary of Anaïs Nin—1914–1920* (New York: Harcourt Brace, 1978), pp. 432–34 (entry of Jan. 28, 1920).

31. As in the case of Anaïs Nin herself. See also William Earle, *Imaginary Memoirs* (Evanston, IL: Great Expectations, 1986), Vols. I-III.

32. For details, see Vladimir Nabokov, *Speak, Memory,* Foreword—esp. p. 14: "When after twenty years of absence I sailed back to Europe, I renewed ties. . . . At these family reunions, *Speak, Memory* was judged. Details of date and circumstance were checked and it was found that in many cases I had erred, or had not examined deeply enough an obscure but fathomable recollection. Certain matters were dismissed by my advisors as legends or rumors or, if genuine, were proven to be related to events or periods other than those to which frail memory had attached them." We witness in such verifying activity yet another intersubjective aspect of reminiscence.

33. See especially chapter 10 herein.

34. Thomas Mann, *Joseph and His Brothers,* trans. R. Mannheim (New York: Knoph, 1948), 1:3.

## 7. Recognizing

1. See E. Husserl, *Phenomenology of Internal Time-Consciousness,* trans. J. S. Churchill (Bloomington: Indiana University Press, 1964), secs. 24, 26. On the existential-hermeneutical-as-structure, see M. Heidegger, *Being and Time,* trans. J. Macquarrie and E. Robinson (New York: Harper and Row, 1962), pp. 201–203.

2. This is Heidegger's term in "Time and Being" for a basic activity of Dasein's spatiality. See *On Time and Being,* trans. J. Stambaugh (New York: Harper and Row, 1972), p. 15ff.

3. See L. Wittgenstein, *Philosophical Investigations,* trans. G. E. M. Anscombe (Oxford: Blackwell, 1967), p. 193ff. On the notion of the "determinable x," see Edmund Husserl, *Ideas: A General Introduction to Pure Phenomenology,* trans. W. R. Boyce Gibson (New York: Macmillan, 1975), secs. 131–33.

4. On the role of imagination in seeing-as, see Edward S. Casey, *Imagining* (Bloomington: Indiana University Press, 1976) chap. 6, where I argue that imagining is involved in the experience of multiple-aspect seeing-as.

5. J.-P. Sartre, *Being and Nothingness,* trans. Hazel Barnes (New York: Washington Square Press, 1966), p. 130.

6. William James, *Principles of Psychology* (1890; reprint, New York: Dover, 1950), 1:674n; his italics.

7. Ibid., 1:675n.

8. For a treatment of this point, see Husserl, *Logical Investigations,* trans. J. Findlay (New York: Humanities Press, 1970), vol. 1, secs. 1–10.

9. For penetrating remarks on the nudity of the face *(le visage),* see Emmanuel Levinas, *Totality and Infinity,* trans. A. Lingis (Pittsburgh: Duquesne University Press, 1969), pp. 194–204.

10. On auto-iconicity, see my essay "Communication and Expression in Art," *Journal of Aesthetics and Art Criticism* 30 (1971):197–207.

11. Husserl, *Ideas,* sec. 69, p. 181: "scharf erhellten Kreis der vollkommenen Gegebenheit."

12. Ibid., p. 180; his italics. Compare the comment of William James: "It is, in short, the re-instatement of the vague to its proper place in our mental life which I am so anxious to press on the attention" (*Principles of Psychology,* 1:254).

13. Merleau-Ponty, *The Visible and the Invisible*, trans. A. Lingis (Evanston, IL: Northwestern University Press, 1968), p. 220: "Say that the things are structures, frameworks, the stars of our life."

14. For a highly literate—and quite entertaining—account of prosopagnosia, see Oliver Sacks, *The Man Who Mistook His Wife For A Hat* (New York: Summit Books, 1985), pp. 7–21.

15. As James says, "We make search in our memory for a forgotten idea, just as we rummage our house for a lost object. In both cases, we visit what seems to us the probable *neighborhood* of that which we miss" (*Principles of Psychology,* 1:654).

16. See Husserl, *Cartesian Meditations,* trans. D. Cairns (The Hague: Nijhof, 1960), esp. secs. 50–54.

17. It will be noticed that this is also the case with *déja vu* experiences, with this difference only: that one simultaneously doubts the truthfulness of one's conviction. In the *déja vu* situation one asks oneself, "but did it really take place before?"

18. I use the word "enactment" to indicate that the action in question need not be overt bodily action, but could be as well an act of thinking, feeling, calculating, or whatever.

19. By the same token, it is not a matter of perceptual illusion, in which we actually take, e.g., the abstract form in the painting, to *be* that of a leering face.

20. It is idealized to the extent that the mirror-image omits the inward travail and sense of gross awkwardness which accompany the infant's first efforts to walk and to perform other skilled movements. See J. Lacan, "The Mirror Stage as Formative of the Function of the I as Revealed in Psychoanalytic Experience," in *Ecrits,* trans. A. Sheridan (New York: Norton, 1977), pp. 1–7.

21. Perhaps this offers a clue as to why the only area of our lives in which self-recognition remains problematic is to be found is *dreaming,* that incessant activity of the nighttime self. In contrast with states of strict unconsciousness, for which self-recognition becomes an issue only after the termination of the state itself, we are confronted in dreams with a problem of self-recognition *in medias res*. During dreaming we may ask ourselves implicitly or explicitly: is this really *me* dreaming this? Am *I* really here? The identity of the dream-ego is a complex matter which cannot be fully addressed here; suffice it to say that one basis for the complexity is precisely the confusing character of self-recognition in relation to any such ego. Does this ego in recognizing itself recognize the dreamer's actual self, or only a disguised version of the latter? And yet, despite such complications, self-recognition of some sort appears essential to dreaming as an analogue of daytime self-recognition; without it, it would be difficult to speak of one's *own* dreams, much less to analyze and interpret them as meaningful self-expressions. For a discerning discussion of the dream-ego in its various roles, see James Hillman. *The Dream and the Underworld* (New York: Harper and Row, 1979), pp. 94–97, 107f., 156–58.

22. James even speaks of the "mysterious emotional power" of recognizing and of its "psychosis" (*Principles of Psychology,* 1:252).

23. Tempting as this reduction is, it does no more than rename the mystery, since "recognizable" simply entails "familiar." As James remarks: "Strong and characteristic as [recognizing] is . . . the only name we have for all its shadings is 'sense of familiarity' " (ibid., 1:252).

24. As is evident in the otherwise excellent collection of essays entitled *Recall and Recognition,* ed. J. Brown (New York: Wiley, 1976).

25. Between recognition and evocative memory comes "reconstruction." See Jean Piaget and Bärbel Inhelder, *The Psychology of the Child,* trans. H. Weaver (New York: Basic Books, 1969), pp. 80–84. On recognition memory in children, see also Robert Kail, *The Development of Memory in Children* (San Francisco: W. H. Freeman, 1979), pp. 61–80.

26. Jean Piaget and Bärbel Inhelder, *Memory and Intelligence,* trans. A. J. Pomerans (New York: Basic Books, 1973), pp. 4–5. The premise of the "presence of the object" is actively at work in "signal detection" theories of recognition; see W. P. Banks, "Signal Detection Theory and Human Memory," *Psychological Bulletin* 74 (1970):81–99.

27. S. Freud, "Remembering, Repeating, and Working-Through," in *Standard Edition,* 12:153.

28. Ibid.

29. A. N. Whitehead, *Process and Reality,* ed. D. R. Griffin and D. W. Sherburne (New York: Free Press, 1978), pp. 45, 108, 239–40, 248, 308, 316. There is a corresponding "physical pole" as well.

30. On this notion, see Piaget and Inhelder, *Memory and Intelligence,* p. 11, where such indices are said to be "the most elementary signifiers."

## Part Two—Coda

1. On this notion, see Jean-Paul Sartre, *Being and Nothingness,* trans. Hazel Barnes (New York: Washington Square Press, 1966), pp. 244–49. Sartre is here drawing upon Heidegger's idea of an "equipmental totality" in *Being and Time,* trans. J. Macquarrie and E. Robinson (New York: Harper and Row, 1962), pp. 109–13.

## Part Three

## Prologue

1. See Martin Heidegger, *Being and Time,* trans. J. Macquarrie and E. Robinson (New York: Harper and Row, 1962), pp. 91–95.
2. Ibid., pp. 95–107.
3. Maurice Merleau-Ponty, *Phenomenology of Perception,* trans. C. Smith (New York: Humanities Press, 1962), pp. xviii, 418, 426, 429.

## 8. Body Memory

1. Martin Heidegger, *Being and Time,* trans. J. Macquarrie and E. Robinson (New York: Harper and Row, 1962), pp. 102–5.
2. I am referring to the case of "H. M." as first reported by W. B. Scoville and B. Milner in "Loss of Recent Memory After Bilateral Hippocampal Lesion," *Journal of Neurology, Neurosurgery, and Psychiatry* 20 (1957):11–21.
3. Hans Jonas, "The Nobility of Sight: A Study in the Phenomenology of the Senses" in *The Phenomenon of Life: Toward A Philosophical Biology* (Chicago: University of Chicago Press, 1966), pp. 135–56.
4. On habit memory as treated by Bergson, see his *Matter and Memory,* trans. N. M. Paul & W. S. Palmer (1896; reprint, New York: Doubleday, 1959), pp. 67–78.
5. See Maurice Merleau-Ponty, *Phenomenology of Perception,* trans. C. Smith (New York: Humanities Press, 1962), pp. 142–47.
6. Ibid., p. 206, p. 178 respectively.
7. This is not to deny that such recollections can be *sufficient*. Pertinent recollections of learning or relearning may sometimes be employed in the service of habitual body memory. In the vocabulary adopted earlier in this book, remembering-that can be placed in the service of remembering-how, yet *need not be*.
8. But it may serve as a *reminder* of such remembering, and precisely in the sense discussed in chapter 5, namely as *adumbrating* in function. For a devastating critique of the mentalistic interpretation of habitual bodily actions as an "intellectualist legend," see Gilbert Ryle, *The Concept of Mind* (New York: Barnes & Noble, 1949), pp. 25–40.
9. In chapter 3, I distinguish between "habitual" and "habituating/habituated" remembering-how as a way of marking the difference between a routinized body memory (i.e., a strictly "habitual" memory) from one that is more exploratory or provisional (i.e., "habituated," "habituating"). In the present chapter, the term "habitual body memory" denotes the full phenomenon under discussion. As such, it includes *both* types of remembering-how, and is not reducible to one or the other.

The proper vehicle for habitual body memories is what Merleau-Ponty technically terms the "customary body." In contrast with the "momentary body," which is the lived body as it operates to meet the particular demands of a given moment, the customary body acts in terms of continuing and general features of the surrounding world. The customary body is thus not importantly different from what Merleau-Ponty calls the "habitual body," which serves to guarantee the actions of the momentary body. When an amputee continues to act as if his or her limb were not missing or a typist is able to master a new typewriter with only a few hours of practice, it is the customary or habitual body that makes possible such diverse things—one radically misguided, the other remarkably adaptive. The habituality enacted in both cases is "a power of dilating our being in the world" (*Phenomenology of Perception*, p. 143). Neither would be operative without habitual body memories, which are the means by which all bodily actions—whether innovative or routine, adaptive or maladaptive—gain their momentum and pattern of deployment. (For further discussion of these matters, see ibid., pp. 81–82, 142–47 as well as my essay, "Habitual Body and Memory in Merleau-Ponty," *Man and World* 17 [1984]: 279–97.)

10. "Though we control the beginning of our states of character the gradual progress is not obvious, any more than it is in illness; because it was in our power, however, to act in this way or not in this way [to start with], therefore the states are voluntary" (Aristotle, *Nicomachean Ethics* 1114b–1115a; W. D. Ross translation). See also ibid. 1103b: "states of character arise out of like activities."

11. "Moral virtue comes about as a result of habit" (ibid., 1103a).

12. On the primacy effect in free recall experiments, see Robert G. Crowder, *Principles of Learning and Memory*, (Hillsdale, NJ: Lawrence Erlbaum, 1976), pp. 136, 140–41, 146–50, 452–56.

13. *Hēxis* itself derives from *ekhein*, to have or to be conditioned in a certain way. See C. T. Onions, ed. *The Oxford Dictionary of English Etymology* (Oxford: Oxford University Press, 1966), article on "habit."

14. "Habitude" has the dictionary meanings of: customary manner of acting; mental constitution or disposition; bodily condition or constitution. (These are the only non-obsolete definitions given in *The Oxford English Dictionary*.)

15. The oldest meaning of "habitual," now obsolete, is "belonging to the inward disposition [of something]" *(The Oxford English Dictionary)*.

16. On this question, see "The History of the Human Body," in *The Dallas Institute Newsletter* (Summer, 1985) with contributions by Illich, Sardello, Jager, Thomas *et al*.

17. On tradition and effective-history, see Hans-Georg Gadamer, *Truth and Method* (New York: Seabury Press, 1975), esp. pp. 267–74. Moreover, habitual body memories intersect with cultural traditions and are sometimes deeply influenced by such traditions in a complex dialectical interplay.

18. John Russell, "How Art Makes Us Feel At Home in the World," *New York Times*, April 12, 1981.

19. Merleau-Ponty, *Phenomenology of Perception*, p. 82.

20. The example is Merleau-Ponty's; see ibid., pp. 145–46: the organist "settles into the organ as one settles into a house" and comes to "create a space of expressiveness."

21. In this particular respect—i.e., its all-at-once character—the revival of habitual body memories is to be compared to many cases of recognition. Both forms of memory are also typically involuntary, arising more as circumstance suggests than as sought for. When we "*search* our memory," on the other hand, we are usually searching among our recollections—not among our habitual body memories or resources of recognition.

22. Igor Stravinsky, *The Poetics of Music* (New York: Random House, 1960), p. 68.

23. See Kant, *The Critique of Pure Reason,* trans. N. K. Smith (New York: St. Martin's, 1965) A189 B233 ff. (Second Analogy). Such succession structures all causal sequence.

24. See Jacques Lacan, "The Mirror Stage as Formative of the Function of the I" in *Écrits,* trans. A. Sheridan (New York: Norton, 1977), pp. 1–7.

25. In fact, the body memory of the trauma leads not only into the past in which the trauma was situated but also into the future when one fears action will be inhibited or lost. This phenomenon is closely related to the anticipatory aspect of signal anxiety.

26. Still another form of taming occurs when we transform genuine childhood memories into screen memories by substituting for the representation of a traumatic event a more idyllic scene, mistakenly taking this latter to have been the true state of affairs. In this case we play a ruse upon ourselves for the sake of transforming the memory of a painful event into the memory of a pleasant one. On screen memories, see Freud, "Screen Memories," in *Standard Edition,* 3:303–22.

27. Thus Freud speaks of a memory of sexual assault as "a repetition [of the original trauma] in a mitigated form" (*Standard Edition,* 20:166).

28. On this notion, see Maurice Merleau-Ponty, *The Visible and the Invisible,* trans. A. Lingis (Evanston, IL: Northwestern University Press, 1968), pp. 133–35, 137–38, 143.

29. Cf. Bergson's similar stress on the future-orientedness of "habit memories": such memories are "always bent upon action, seated in the present and looking only to the future" (Henri Bergson, *Matter and Memory,* trans. N. M. Paul and W. S. Palmer [1896; reprint, New York: Doubleday, 1959], p. 70).

30. See Heidegger, *Being and Time,* pp. 108–9.

31. "The ownmost possibility, which is non-relational, not to be outstripped, and certain, is *indefinite* as regards its certainty" (ibid., p. 310; his italics). Heidegger is here speaking of death as anticipated by an individual human existent. On repeatable possibilities, see ibid., p. 438ff.

32. "Anticipation makes Dasein *authentically* futural, and in such a way that the anticipation itself is possible only insofar as Dasein, *as being,* is always coming toward itself" (ibid., p. 373; his italics).

33. Any such division between recent and remote memories is notably lacking in the case of habitual body memories, for which the very distinction between recent and remote in origin is normally meaningless. As I have emphasized in the foregoing, it rarely matters at all to us exactly *when* we first learned a given habit or picked up a certain propensity. What matters is only that we *now have* the habit or propensity and can employ it in pursuing some particular project: it is the service-ability that counts here, not the comparative distance of the origin from the present moment. This distance *does,* however, count in the instance of traumatic memories—since the phenomenon of "after-glow" inheres in long-term samples only, while recent such memories are all too vivid and need no such assistance.

34. Recent research by A. Baddeley indicates that primary memory may itself be largely bodily in character. Such memory is analyzable into an "executive system" and several sensory-specific "slave systems" which "recruit" particular bodily organs or parts. The result is a quasi-autonomous operation; the functioning of primary or "working" memory goes on automatic pilot unless it is interfered with by an activity that competes directly with the slave system. See A. Baddeley, "Domains of Recollection," *Psychological Review* (1981); and D. Riesberg, I. Rappaport, and M. O'Shaughnessy, "The Limits of Working Memory: The Digit Digit-span," *Journal of Experimental Psychology: Learning, Memory, and Cognition* (1984).

35. Most notably in Alzheimer's disease. For a detailed descriptive account, see Marion Roach, *Another Name for Madness* (Boston: Houghton Mifflin, 1985).

36. Merleau-Ponty, *Phenomenology of Perception,* p. 419 and p. 147 respectively.

37. For Dewey's view, see *Human Nature and Conduct* (New York: Random House, 1950), pp. 14–88, esp. 42, 66, 172–80.

38. Such marginalizing may be usefully contrasted with Breuer and Freud's notion of "abreacting" memories, i.e., re-engaging them so as to allow the affect strangulated beneath them to re-emerge. As a technique for "filling in the gaps in memory," psychoanalysis tries to reverse our natural propensity for making the most painful memories marginal. It is not accidental that it began with an effort to abreact traumatic memories—as Breuer and Freud make clear in their "Preliminary Communication" of 1893. (See *Standard Edition,* 2:3–17.) To this beginning should be added the later notion of "undoing the defenses," including the very denial, isolation, projecting, etc. which are so massively involved in keeping traumatic body memories at bay. We witness here, incidentally, the surprisingly parallel courses of psychical and physical traumatic memories: indeed, the very difficulty of drawing a hard and fast line between the two. (In the same "Preliminary Communication," the authors move unhesitatingly from one to the other.)

39. On erotic desire as insatiable—as a form of "fury mocking the abyss"—see Jacques Lacan, *Ecrits,* pp. 154–55, 301–2.

40. A characteristic statement of Berkeley's is that "Looking at an object, I perceive a certain visible figure and color . . . which from what I have formerly observed, determine me to think that if I [were to] advance forward so many paces or miles, I shall be affected with such and such ideas of touch." (George Berkeley, *An Essay Towards a New Theory of Vision* [London: Dent, 1934], pp. 32–33.)

41. Erwin Straus, *The Primary World of Senses,* trans. J. Needleman (Glencoe, IL: Free Press, 1963), p. 384.

42. Merleau-Ponty, *Phenomenology of Perception,* pp. 264–65.

43. See Bergson, *Matter and Memory,* p. 70ff. On the metaphor of the past-as-pyramid, see Merleau-Ponty, *Phenomenology of Perception,* p. 393: "We are, as Proust declared, perched on a pyramid of past life."

44. Bergson, *Matter and Memory,* p. 55; his italics.

45. Ibid., p. 70; his italics.

46. Marcel Proust, *Remembrance of Things Past,* trans. C. K. Scott Moncrieff and T. Kilmartin (New York: Random House, 1981), I, 5.

47. Ibid., p. 6.

48. Ibid.

49. Ibid., p. 9.

50. Ibid.

51. Bergson makes "place" and "date" the two distinguishing marks of recollection. See Bergson, *Matter and Memory,* pp. 68–72. It is also striking that Bergson calls recollection "picture memory" (ibid.): pictures are eminently datable and placeable.

52. Proust, *Remembrance of Things Past,* pp. 6–7.

53. The case of dream memory, which I have almost completely neglected in this book, is highly ambiguous. Is the "dream ego" (itself often quite marginal in a given dream) embodied and, if so, in which specific forms (e.g., as solely visual, or auditory, etc., in its mode of apprehension)?

54. Alfred North Whitehead, *Process and Reality: An Essay in Cosmology,* Corrected Edition, ed. D. R. Griffin and D. W. Sherburne (New York: The Free Press, 1978), p. 142.

55. See ibid., pp. 121–22.

56. Alfred North Whitehead, *Symbolism: Its Meaning and Effect* (New York: Macmillan, 1959), p. 35.

57. "The immediate present has to conform to what the past is for it [i.e., through objectification], and the mere lapse of time is an abstraction from the more concrete relatedness of 'conformation' " (ibid., p. 36). The basic action of conformation to the past does not preclude the capacity of the present to compose something new.

58. Ibid.

59. Whitehead, *Symbolism,* p. 37, p. 27 respectively.

60. Ibid., p. 50.

61. Ibid., p. 21.

62. Ibid., p. 14 and pp. 43–44 respectively.

63. Nevertheless, repetition is crucial; it is precisely what Hume overlooks. On memory as repetition, see Whitehead, *Process and Reality,* pp. 135–37; as reproduction, ibid., pp. 237–39.

64. Whitehead, *Symbolism,* p. 18. More completely: "Our most immediate environment is constituted by the various organs of our own bodies, our more remote environment is the physical world in the neighborhood" (ibid., pp. 17–18).

65. Ibid., p. 43.

66. Thus "our primitive perception is that of 'conformation' vaguely, and of the yet vaguer relata 'oneself' and 'another' in the undiscriminated background" (ibid., p. 43). Thus we can say that "our bodily efficacy is primarily an experience of the dependence of presentational immediacy upon causal efficacy" (Whitehead, *Process and Reality,* p. 176).

67. Whitehead, *Process and Reality,* p. 81.

68. See ibid., p. 119: "The crude aboriginal character of direct perception is inheritance. What is inherited is feeling-tone with evidence of its origin." This is not to deny the importance of "conceptual feelings" or of the "mental pole" generally: cf. pp. 239–40. But it remains the case that physical feelings are "the *basis* for conceptual origination" and that "the intellectual feelings must all be initially supplied with the content of the conformal physical feelings" (Nancy Frankenberry, "The Power of the Past," *Process Studies,* vol. 13, no. 2 [1983], p. 135; her italics.)

69. "From this point of view, the body, or its organ of sensation, becomes the objective datum of a component feeling [i.e., bodily efficacy]; and this feeling has its own subjective form" (Whitehead, *Process and Reality,* p. 312). In other words, the body is itself the objective datum for the very feeling of bodily efficacy by which we come to conform to the world beyond the body.

70. Ibid., p. 119. See also: "The body, however, is only a peculiarly intimate bit of the world. Just as Descartes said, 'this body is mine'; so he should have said, 'this actual world is mine' " (ibid., p. 81). Nor does Whitehead's stress on the "withness" of the perceiving body alleviate the paradoxicality of a two-tiered feeling situation. It is one thing to say that "we see the contemporary chair, but we see it *with* our eyes; and we touch the contemporary chair, but we touch it *with* our hands" (ibid., p. 62; his italics). "With" suggests transmission, means of conveyance—a suitable description for bodily organs in general. But it is quite another thing to claim that this withness is itself directly felt as causally efficacious: "we find here our direct knowledge of 'causal efficacy' " (ibid., p. 81).

71. On the "withness" of the body, see ibid., p. 62. On "objective datum," cf. ibid., pp. 164, 237, 240.

72. In the formula of a recent commentator, each actual occasion is "other-caused, self-caused, and other-causing" (Jorge Luis Nobo, "Transition in Whitehead: A Creative Process Distinct from Consciousness," *International Philosophical Quarterly,* 19 [1979]:273).

73. "Our immediate past is constituted by that occasion, or that group of fused occasions, which enters into experience devoid of any perceptible medium intervening between it and the present immediate fact. Roughly speaking, it is that portion of our past lying between a tenth of a second and half a second ago" (Alfred North Whitehead, *Adventures of Ideas* [New York: Mentor, 1955], p. 181).
74. On bodily efficacy, see Whitehead, *Process and Reality*, pp. 312, 316.
75. See John Dewey, *Art as Experience* (New York: Putnam's, 1934), pp. 35–57.
76. Whitehead, *Symbolism*, p. 36.
77. Whitehead, *Process and Reality*, p. 119.
78. Whitehead, *Symbolism*, p. 20. Cf. also Whitehead, *Process and Reality*, p. 317: "mental and physical operations are incurably intertwined."
79. Cf. Whitehead, *Symbolism*, pp. 18–20.
80. Just such precedence seems to be unequivocally endorsed in the following passage: "The direct relevence of this remote past [i.e., remote in comparison with the immediate past], relevant by reason of its direct objectification in the immediate subject, is practically negligible, so far as concerns prehensions of a strictly physical type" (Whitehead, *Process and Reality*, p. 63). I take "direct objectification in the immediate subject" to be an act of recollection, a term which Whitehead rarely uses in *Process and Reality* and then mainly in reference to Hume (cf. ibid., pp. 242, 249, 271). Insofar as the relevance of the immediate past in instances of causal efficacy is direct, indeed massive, the importance of the body memory associated with it is commensurately intensified in comparison with any form of memory lacking such a relevance and such a basis.
81. Whitehead, *Symbolism*, p. 44.
82. Ibid.
83. See ibid., pp. 43, 55, 57.
84. Proust, *Remembrance of Things Past*, I, pp. 5–6.
85. Whitehead, *Process and Reality*, p. 119.
86. Whitehead, *Symbolism*, p. 23.
87. Ibid.
88. For this view, see Edmund Husserl, *Crisis of European Sciences and Transcendental Phenomenology*, trans. D. Carr (Evanston, IL: Northwestern University Press, 1970), p. 107, and esp. p. 217: my living body is "given to me originally and meaningfully as 'organ' and as articulated into particular organs."
89. Cf. Merleau-Ponty, *Phenomenology of Perception*, pp. 136, 157.
90. Ibid., p. 265. For difficulties with Merleau-Ponty's own conception of direct access to the past, however, see my essay "Habitual Body and Memory in Merleau-Ponty," pp. 292–95.
91. Merleau-Ponty, *Phenomenology of Perception*, p. 129.
92. On the notion of "subdued being" as this derives from Bachelard, see Merleau-Ponty, *The Visible and the Invisible*, p. 267.
93. "In," "from," and "through" can be regarded as the three primary modes of Whitehead's "withness" of the body.
94. Husserl, *Crisis of European Sciences*, p. 107. Husserl goes on to say that the meaning in question is precisely that "indicated by the word 'organ' (here used in its most primitive sense)" (ibid.).
95. Merleau-Ponty, *Phenomenology of Perception*, p. 146.
96. On this point, see Husserl, *Crisis of European Sciences*, p. 106: "Clearly the aspect-exhibitions of whatever body is appearing in perception, and the kinestheses, are not processes [simply running] alongside each other; rather, they work together in such a way that the aspects have the ontic meaning of, or the validity of, aspects of the body only through the fact that they are those aspects continually required by the kinestheses."

97. Bergson, *Matter and Memory*, p. 131 and p. 66 respectively.
98. Merleau-Ponty, *The Visible and the Invisible*, p. 194.
99. Bergson, *Matter and Memory*, p. 168.
100. We can go still further and claim with Bergson that the body is itself already *like* mind or consciousness: "Concrete movement, capable, like consciousness, of prolonging its past into its present, capable, by repeating itself, of engendering sensible qualities, already possesses something akin to consciousness" (ibid., p. 243).

## 9. Place Memory

1. Aristotle, *De Memoria et Reminiscentia*, 449a 15 (Sorabji translation).
2. E. Husserl, *Phenomenology of Internal Time-Consciousness*, trans. J. S. Churchill (Bloomington: Indiana University Press, 1964), p. 72. See also p. 47: "As the temporal object moves into the past, it is drawn together on itself and thereby also becomes obscure *(dunkel)*."
3. Aristotle, *Physics* 221b 2. I am indebted to Peter Manchester for this translation.
4. See Martin Heidegger, *Being and Time*, trans. J. Macquarrie and E. Robinson (New York: Harper and Row, 1962), secs. 81–82.
5. Frances A. Yates, *The Art of Memory* (London: Routledge and Kegan Paul, 1966), p. 6.
6. Cicero, *De oratore*, II, lxxxvi, 251–4 (cited by Yates at ibid., p. 2).
7. Plato, *Theatetus* 196d–200d.
8. "Who is that man moving slowly in the lonely building, stopping at intervals with an intent face? He is a rhetoric student forming a set of memory *loci*" (Yates, *The Art of Memory*, p. 8).
9. Cited by Reiner Schürmann in his essay, "Situating René Char: Hölderlin, Heidegger, Char and the 'there is,' " in *Heidegger and the Question of Literature*, ed. W. V. Spanos (Bloomington: Indiana University Press, 1979), p. 173.
10. "Das denkende Dichten ist in der Wahrheit die Topologie des Seyns" (Martin Heidegger, *Aus der Erfahrung des Denkens* [Pfullingen: Neske, 1965], p. 23). See also O. Pöggeler, "Heidegger's Topology of Being" in *On Heidegger and Language*, ed. J. Kockelmans (Evanston, IL: Northwestern University Press, 1972), pp. 107–33.
11. A much more complete treatment is set forth in a monograph (tentatively entitled "Placing: Getting and Being Placed") I am in the process of writing on the nature of place in human experience.
12. Cited by Simplicius, *Commentary on Aristotle's Categories*, as quoted in Max Jammer, "The Concept of Space in Antiquity" in J. J. C. Smart, ed. *Problems of Space and Time* (New York: Macmillan, 1964), p. 28.
13. Aristotle, *Physics* 208 b 33 (Hussey translation).
14. Ibid., 208 b 34–36 (Hussey translation).
15. Ibid., 208 b 10, 208b 24 (Hardie & Gaye translation).
16. "In nature each [place] is distinct" (ibid., 208 b 18; Hardie & Gaye translation).
17. Ibid., 212 a 20–1; translators' italics. Hussey translates: "The first unchangeable limit of that which surrounds."
18. Ibid., 212 a 28–31 (Ross translation).
19. Jammer, "The Concept of Space in Antiquity," p. 40; my italics.
20. Réné Descartes, *Principles of Philosophy*, sec. V, trans. G. E. Anscombe and P. Geach in *Descartes' Philosophical Writings* (Edinburgh & London: Nelson, 1959).

21. Ibid., sec. XIV.

22. Aristotle, *Physics* 208 b 23–5 (Hardie & Gaye translation). Unless specified otherwise, I shall cite this translation of the *Physics* from here on.

23. Husserl posits these as existing at the lowest level of sensory perception: See E. Husserl, *Experience and Judgment*, trans. J. S. Churchill & K. Ameriks (Evanston, IL: Northwestern University Press, 1973), sec. 17.

24. William James, *Principles of Psychology* (1890; reprint, New York: Dover, 1950), 1:654ff.

25. In devising this term, I am drawing on connotations of "preservation," "reservation," "holding in reserve," "being reserved," etc.

26. With the notable exception of Marcia K. Johnson, who has begun a systematic exploration of place parameters in her recent research on a "reality monitoring" model of memory. See her "A Multiple-Entry, Modular Memory System," *Psychology of Learning and Motivation* 17 (1983):81–123.

27. Aristotle, *De Memoria et Reminiscentia* 451 a 15–16.

28. I adapt this term from Maurice Merleau-Ponty, *The Visible and the Invisible*, trans. A. Lingis (Evanston, IL: Northwestern University Press, 1968), p. 264.

29. For an examination of this two-fold dependency, see my essay "Getting Placed: Soul in Space," *Spring: An Annual of Archetypal Psychology* (1982): 17–19.

30. In my unpublished manuscript, "Placing: Getting and Being Placed," chaps. 4 and 5.

31. Maurice Merleau-Ponty, *Phenomenology of Perception*, trans. C. Smith (New York: Humanities Press, 1962), p. 139; his italics.

32. Aristotle, *Physics*, 210 a 24–5.

33. Ibid., 209 b 28.

34. Ibid., 212 a 28–9. Note that a vessel is the sort of container that is separable from what it contains and that the inner surface of a vessel is exactly coincident with the outer limit of what is contained within it.

35. Ibid., 212 a 13–14.

36. For a fascinating study of snugly fitting containers, see William C. Ketchum, Jr., *Boxes* (Washington: Cooper-Hewitt Museum, 1982).

37. Merleau-Ponty, *The Phenomenology of Perception*, p. 250.

38. Merleau-Ponty, *Phenomenology of Perception*, p. 203; my italics.

39. I here allude to familiar Heideggerian themes. On the *In-Sein* of *In-der-Welt-Sein*, see *Being and Time*, sec. 12. On dwelling, see "Building Dwelling Thinking," trans. A. Hofstadter in *Poetry, Language, Thought* (New York: Harper and Row, 1971), pp. 143–62.

40. Merleau-Ponty, *Phenomenology of Perception*, p. 144.

41. See Erwin Straus, *The Primary World of Senses*, trans. J. Needleman (Glencoe, IL: Free Press, 1963), pp. 388–90, for a treatment of indifferent space in contrast with attuned space. On landscape versus geography, see ibid., pp. 318–23.

42. Even a good a geometer as Pascal could nonetheless say that "ces espaces infinis m'effrayent" (*Pensées*, ed. L. Lafuma [Paris: Delmas, 1960], p. 114).

43. Merleau-Ponty, *The Phenomenology of Perception*, p. 82.

44. Ibid., p. 146. Merleau-Ponty alerts us in the very next sentence that he is not thinking of "customary" in the sense of "long-established custom," which implies a passivity foreign to any basic bodily action.

45. Marcel Proust, *Remembrance of Things Past*, trans. C. K. Scott Moncrieff and T. Kilmartin (New York: Random House, 1981), I, 8–9; my italics. I have analyzed this same passage at greater length in "The Memorability of Inhabited Place" (forthcoming).

46. "The good angel of certainty . . . had fixed approximately in their right places

in the uncertain light, my chest of drawers, my writing-table, my fireplace . . ." (*Remembrance of Things Past*, I, 9).

47. Ibid., pp. 7–8.

48. Both citations are from ibid., p. 6. Cf. also ibid.: "My mind struggles in an unsuccessful attempt to discover where I was."

49. On this contribution, see Kent Bloomer and Charles Moore, *Body, Memory, and Architecture* (New Haven: Yale University Press, 1977), and Christian Norberg-Schulz, *The Concept of Dwelling* (New York: Rizzoli, 1985).

50. Henri Bergson, *Matter and Memory*, trans. N. M. Paul and W. S. Palmer (1896; reprint, New York: Doubleday, 1959), p. 69. It is distressing that Bergson consigns place entirely to recollection, which "leaves to each fact, to each gesture, its place and date" (ibid.).

51. Cf. Merleau-Ponty, *Phenomenology of Perception*, p. 83: "This past, which remains our true present, does not leave us but remains constantly hidden behind our gaze instead of being displayed before it [i.e., as in recollection]."

52. John Russell, "How Art Makes Us Feel at Home in the World," *New York Times*, April 12, 1981. I have cited part of this same passage early in the last chapter.

53. Bergson, *Matter and Memory*, p. 145; his italics.

54. Straus, *The Primary World of Senses*, p. 319.

55. The aim, however, need not be entirely explicit: "Every animate movement demands direction and goal. Whether the goal be a well-defined place lying before us, or a vaguely indeterminate 'somewhere,' it is still a goal and thus an Other, and thus a There toward which we are directed" (ibid., p. 391).

56. Ibid., p. 317.

57. The first phrase comes from ibid., p. 325; the second, from ibid., p. 319.

58. On the experience of gliding, see ibid., pp. 362–67.

59. Merleau-Ponty, *The Visible and the Invisible*, p. 266.

60. Landscape painters once more bear witness to this: as in Constable's rural scenes, where an entire countryside acts as such a field factor.

61. Straus, *The Primary World of Senses*, p. 321. My italics.

62. Lawrence Durrell, *Spirit of Place: Letters and Essays on Travel* (New York: Dutton, 1969), p. 157.

63. On the idea of sympathetic (versus indifferent) space, see Straus, *The Primary World of Senses*, pp. 317ff, 388ff.

64. On this last point, see ibid., p. 317.

65. Ibid., p. 322.

66. Johannes Hofer, "Medical Dissertation on Nostalgia," trans. C. K. Anspach in the *Bulletin of the History of Medicine* 2 (1934):382.

67. Ibid., pp. 389–90.

68. Immanuel Kant, *Anthropologie in Pragmatischer Hinsicht* (Könisberg: Nicolovius, 1798), sec. 32. Kant finds the source of nostalgia in an afflicted imagination, *not* in memory.

69. Hofer, "Medical Dissertation," p. 385.

70. For a detailed account, see my forthcoming essay "The World of Nostalgia."

71. " 'Motion' in its most general and primary sense is change of place, which we call 'locomotion' " (Aristotle, *Physics*, 208a 31–32).

72. The distinction between "common" and "special" places is found in the *Physics*: cf. 209a 32–209b 6.

73. Martin Heidegger, "On Time and Being" in *Time and Being*, trans. J. Stambaugh (New York: Harper and Row, 1972) p. 15ff.

74. Of course, the body is itself a forceful synthesizing power, foreshadowing (and doubtless underlying) the synthesizing properties of memory and place themselves: "It is not this epistemological subject [i.e., as in Kant] who brings about the

synthesis, but the body, when it escapes from dispersion, pulls itself together and tends by all means in its power toward one single goal of its activity" (Merleau-Ponty, *Phenomenology of Perception*, p. 232).

75. This distinction is made by Husserl in *Experience and Judgment*, sec. 33. I have elaborated on it in *Imagining* (Bloomington: Indiana University Press, 1976), pp. 153–64.

76. See Husserl, *The Phenomenology of Internal Time-Consciousness*, sec. 10.

77. Husserl, *Experience and Judgment*, p. 107.

78. See Straus, *The Primary World of Senses*, p. 320: "As a rule, our journeys are planned and an itinerary mapped out." Straus prefers to speak of "geographic space" where I talk of "sited space"; there is no fundamental difference between the two terms, which also resemble Merleau-Ponty's notion of a "spatialized space" (*Phenomenology of Perception*, p. 244).

79. On the intricacies of association in memory, see John P. Anderson and Gordon Bower, *Human Associative Memory* (Washington, D.C.: Winston, 1973).

80. St. Augustine, *Confessions*, Book X, chap. 8 (Pine-Coffin translation). For St. Augustine, memory is precisely place-like in its capacity—as is attested by an entire metaphorics of "cave," "den," "cavern," "treasurehouse," etc. In this view, memory is a super-place of storage.

81. Aristotle, *Physics*, 209 a 28–9. Recall as well Proust's description of his narrator's experience: "Everything revolved around me through the darkness: *things, places*, years . . ." *Remembrance of Things Past*, I, 6; my italics.

82. Proust, *Remembrance of Things Past*, I, 51.

83. See A. R. Luria, *The Mind of a Mnemonist*, trans. L. Solotaroff (Chicago: Reginery, 1968), esp. p. 41ff.

84. In the classical form, several such memory-houses are clustered together on a single street: see the reproduction in R. Sorabji, *Aristotle on Memory* (London: Duckworth, 1972), p. viii.

85. On the disposition of images in the art of memory, see Yates, *The Art of Memory*, pp. 9–12.

86. Edwin T. Morris, *The Gardens of China: History, Art, and Meanings* (New York: Scribner's, 1983), p. xi.

87. Ibid.

88. Ibid., p. 96.

89. Ibid., p. 3.

90. Ibid., p. 47.

91. Ibid.

92. On the concept of borrowing, see ibid., p. 75f. Lakes were especially effective in this role.

93. On these means respectively, see ibid., p. 112, p. 90, p. 91.

94. Ibid., p. 91. By the same token, we can say that "all nature [is] a garden" (ibid., p. 55). It is important to realize, however, that this is not a matter of any simple, straightforward resemblance. If *shan-shui*, the Chinese word for landscape, means literally "mountains and water," the plants, rocks, and ponds of a Chinese garden allude to a more encompassing landscape only as mediated by painting and poetry. At work here is a subtle blend of nature and culture. For example, a configuration of three stones in a garden may refer at one and the same time to the artificial "lion" peaks in the Lion Grove Garden in Suzhou; to the painting by Dao Ji entitled "Three Peaks of the Heavenly Realm"; and to the calligraphic sign for mountain, *shan*, which is the schematic representation of just such an arrangement of mountain peaks. In this case, therefore, the *rememberata* include another garden, a particular painting, and a written character—but no actual mountains. (On the relation between memory and literature, see Stephen Owen, *Remembrances: The*

*Experience of the Past in Classical Chinese Literature* [Cambridge, Mass.: Harvard University Press, 1986].)

95. Morris, *The Gardens of China,* p. 57.

96. The use of the covered arcade also aided in this process of sustenance: here in the specific form of protection from the elements.

97. Morris, *The Gardens of China,* p. 77.

98. "Staggered perspectives also helped create distinct divisions. . . . One terrace rising above another tended to carry the imagination away into the empyrean; one roof visible in the distance beyond another suggested that the space went on ad infinitum" (ibid., p. 78). Once more, what Morris claims for imagination is valid for memory as well.

99. See Alfreda Murck & Wen Fong, *A Chinese Garden Court: The Astor Court of The Metropolitan Museum of Art* (New York: n.d.), p. 29.

100. Ibid. p. 42. Thus, if one looks through the Moon Gate at the Astor Court Garden, the outside wall is seen to give way to the inner wall of the vestibule, which opens further onto the perforated wall of the Ming Room—which in turn displays grilled windows giving onto a plant-and-rock grouping enclosed within yet another wall. See the photography of the Moon Gate at ibid., p. 31.

101. In larger gardens similar effects are achieved with water; a pond or lake establishes "a horizontal plane that contrasts with [the vertical space] of rock mountains and pavilions: (Morris, *The Gardens of China,* p. 87). One particular way of achieving depth or horizon was to bring about the impression that the water that disappeared under a bridge or a bank continued on indefinitely in unperceived parts. On the role of water, see Murck and Fong, *A Chinese Garden Court,* p. 13.

102. Murck and Fong, *A Chinese Garden Court,* p. 29.

103. Morris, *The Gardens of China,* p. 85.

104. See also ibid., p. 199, for further discussion of this point.

105. I should say "largely confined," for there have been efforts to construct physical models of the method of *loci,* most notably that undertaken by Guilio Camillo in the sixteenth century. On this model, see Yates, *The Art of Memory,* pp. 129–72.

106. A. N. Whitehead, *Science and the Modern World* (New York: Macmillan, 1953), p. 49.

107. Ibid., p. 91.

108. See ibid., p. 92ff.

109. The same point holds for time: if "there is nothing in the present fact which inherently refers either to the past or to the future" (ibid., p. 51), there can be no meaningful remembering.

110. Rainer Maria Rilke, Letter of Nov. 13, 1925, reprinted in R. M. Rilke, *Duino Elegies,* trans. J. B. Leishman and S. Spender (New York: Norton, 1963), p. 128. His italics.

111. Murck and Fong, *A Chinese Garden Court,* p. 40.

112. Ibid.

113. See Heidegger, "Building Dwelling Thinking," pp. 152–61 (on the bridge), and "The Thing," pp. 167–77, trans. A. Hofstadter in *Poetry, Language, and Thought*.

114. Gaston Bachelard, *The Poetics of Space,* trans. M. Jolas (New York: Orion Press, 1964), p. 8.

115. Ibid.

116. Frank Lloyd Wright sought to reverse this tendency: "I fought for outswinging windows . . . [which] gave free openings outward" (F. L. Wright, *The Natural House* [New York: Horizon, 1954], p. 38).

117. Bachelard, *The Poetics of Space,* p. 6.

118. Wright, *The Natural House*, p. 40; Bachelard, *The Poetics of Space*, p. 7.
119. Bachelard, *The Poetics of Space*, p. 9. On intimate immensity, see ibid., chap. 8.
120. Ibid., p. 203.
121. On this question, see my unpublished essay, "The Memorability of Inhabited Place," and especially, Kent Bloomer and Charles Moore, *Body, Memory, and Architecture*, passim.
122. Bachelard, *The Poetics of Space*, pp. 6–7; my italics.
123. Martin Heidegger, *What is Called Thinking?*, trans. J. Glenn Gray (New York: Harper, 1972), p. 3.
124. Bachelard, *Poetics of Space*, p. xxxiii.
125. In the Leishman and Spender translation cited in n. 110 above.
126. On this point, see Bachelard, *The Poetics of Space*, p. 9.
127. Ibid., p. 9. A corollary is that "space is everything, for time ceases to quicken memory."
128. Husserl, *The Phenomenology of Internal Time-Consciousness*, p. 66.
129. See Heidegger, *Being and Time*, sec. 70.
130. Bachelard, *The Poetics of Space*, p. 9.
131. T. S. Eliot, "Burnt Norton" *(The Four Quartets)*, stanza II; his italics. (From T. S. Eliot, *Collected Poems 1909–1962* [New York: Harcourt, Brace & World, 1963], p. 177.)
132. Ibid., stanza I, V.

## 10. Commemoration

1. See the entry under "commemorate" in C. T. Onions, ed. *The Oxford Dictionary of English Etymology* (Oxford: Oxford University Press, 1966), p. 194.
2. I draw here on the *Oxford English Dictionary*, entry under "commemoration."
3. Edmund Husserl, *Ideas*, trans. W. R. Boyce Gibson (New York: Collier, 1962), p. 181.
4. On the "in-order-to," see Martin Heidegger, *Being and Time*, trans. J. Macquarrie and E. Robinson (New York: Harper and Row, 1962), secs. 14, 17.
5. Indeed, commemorating combines readily with *every* form of remembering. Even a momentary recollection can cue in an experience of commemoration, or highlight it while in mid-course. The same is true of recognition, which may play an important supportive role. Reminiscing can serve an expressly commemorative function, e.g., when it forms part of a eulogy. Notice that in none of these instances can we reduce commemorating itself to the memorial activity with which it is conjoined. Whether as cuing, subserving, expressing, etc., the conjoined activity remains distinguishable from commemorating proper. In the case of body and place memories, we shall see that there is a still more intimate association with commemoration; each is even indispensable to complete commemorating, whose ritualistic aspect almost always requires bodily action in a particular place. Nevertheless, commemoration is not to be understood as a form of body memory or place memory: it remains unreducible to either.
6. It needs to be emphasized that this limpidity is very much an ideal. In a passage I cited in the last chapter Husserl reminded us of the "veiled" character that inheres in recollection itself. My own notion of "aura" is another cautionary note. The ideal of limpidity itself belongs to a Cartesian conception of truth and evidence for truth. As such, it reflects the seventeenth century model of representations in

general as mirroring the external world. This model is taken to task in Richard Rorty's *Philosophy and the Mirror of Nature* (Princeton: Princeton University Press, 1979).

7. The addition of my student's words on the opposite side of the postcard—"The origins of Western thought are indeed difficult to find in this extraordinary world of rubble and stone"—still do not suffice to convert the situation into a commemorative occasion. Such comments, however appropriate, lack certain features of commemorative texts which will be explored in sec. IV.

8. On this aspect of writing, see Hans-Georg Gadamer, *Truth and Method* (New York: Seabury Press, 1975), pp. 145, 351f.

9. On the ritualistic aspects of menus, see Mary Douglas, "Deciphering a Meal," *Daedalus* (Winter 1972):61–81. On cockfights, see Clifford Geertz, "Deep Play: Notes on the Balinese Cockfight," ibid., pp. 1–37.

10. On the notion of *li*, see Tu Wei-ming, *Humanity and Self-Cultivation* (Berkeley: Asian Humanities Press, 1979), chaps. 1, 2; and Herbert Fingarette, *Confucius—The Secular as Sacred* (New York: Harper and Row, 1972), chaps. 3, 4.

11. Included in this category are what Foucault calls the "micropractices" of technique and utilization which have been taken over unthinkingly from the particular cultural tradition in which we find ourselves embedded. On these micropractices and their hermeneutic significance as modes of Heideggerian "fore-having," see Hubert Dreyfus, "Holism and Hermeneutics," *Review of Metaphysics* 34 (September 1980):6–23.

12. Victor Turner, *The Forest of Symbols: Aspects of Ndembu Ritual* (Ithaca: Cornell University Press, 1967), p. 19.

13. Walter F. Otto, *Dionysus: Myth and Cult*, trans. Robert B. Palmer (Bloomington: Indiana University Press, 1973), pp. 41–42.

14. Ibid., p. 43; my italics.

15. For further consideration of these and related aspects of ritual, see my essay, "Reflections on Ritual," *Spring: An Annual of Archetypal Psychology* (1985), pp. 102–9.

16. *Oxford English Dictionary*. This is the second definition of commemoration. *Webster's Third International* says only "to mark by some ceremony or observation."

17. *Oxford English Dictionary*.

18. If I have denied repetition in remembering as a strict re-living of the past, ritualistic repetition—which does not pretend to anything like precise *nachleben*—is not subject to the same severe exclusion.

19. Mircea Eliade, *The Sacred and the Profane* (New York: Harcourt, Brace 1959), p. 69.

20. Mircea Eliade, *The Myth of the Eternal Return* (Princeton: Princeton University Press, 1974), p. 29.

21. See S. Freud, "Obsessive Actions and Religious Practices," in *Standard Edition*, 9:117–27.

22. Turner, *The Forest of Symbols*, p. 45. See also p. 20: "Performances of ritual [are] distinct phases in the social processes whereby groups become adjusted to internal changes and adapted to their external environment."

23. On the relation between repetition and formality, see my essay "Imagination and Repetition in Literature: A Reassessment," *Yale French Studies* 52 (1975), pp. 249–67.

24. "Evidences of human passion and frailty are just not spoken about when the occasion is given up to public commemoration and reanimation of norms and values in their abstract purity" (Turner, *The Forest of Symbols*, p. 38).

25. These are the last lines of Shelley's "Ozymandias."

26. One memorial volume speaks of itself as "a small material remembrance"

(*Robert Palmer Knight 1902–1966—A Memorial* [published privately for the Western New England Institute of Psychoanalysis, 1967]).

27. Plato, *Timaeus* 37 d (Cornford translation).

28. Typically, either eternity is made more timelike (as in Aquinas's view of it as a "*nunc stans*") or time is allowed to rise to the level of eternity as in those rare "moments of vision" *(Augenblicken)* on which Kierkegaard and Heidegger are so insistent. The following pages draw on material from my essay "Commemoration and Perdurance in *The Analects*, Books I, II," *Philosophy East and West* 34 (1984):389–99. On the three temporal modes contrasted above, see A. N. Whitehead, *Science and the Modern World* (New York: Free Press, 1953), pp. 86–87.

29. John Locke, *An Essay Concerning Human Understanding*, ed. J. Yolton (New York: Dutton, 1965), Bk. II, chap. 14, par. 3; my italics.

30. Ibid., chap. 15, par. 11.

31. Heidegger, *Being and Time*, pp. 461–62.

32. Heidegger, "Time and Being" in *On Time and Being*, trans. J. Stambaugh (New York: Harper and Row, 1972), p. 12.

33. The *Oxford English Dictionary* defines "perdurance" curtly as: "permanence, duration."

34. But this latter occurs only gradually: "withstanding wear or decay" *(Oxford English Dictionary)* is indispensable to perdurance.

35. " 'How is it possible to take [a] middleway?' The Master said: 'by means of the *li*, the *li*. Yes, it is by the *li* that one may hold to the mean' " (*Li Chi*, trans. J. Legge, in *The Sacred Books of the East* [Oxford: Clarendon Press, 1885], vol. 27, chap. 28).

36. Confucius, *The Analects*, trans. D. C. Lau (New York: Penguin, 1979), bk. II, chap. 2 p. 63.

37. On swerving and its relation to poetic creativity, see Harold Bloom, *The Anxiety of Influence* (Oxford: Oxford University Press, 1975), pp. 44–45.

38. Indeed, the *Li Chi* maintains the position that "the fundamental principles of the *li* remain unchanged, but their outward concrete manifestations in 'the number of things and observances' ever change with the times" (Fung Yu-lan, *A History of Chinese Philosophy*, trans. Derk Bodde [Princeton: Princeton University Press, 1952], I, 340).

39. "Unless a man has the spirit of the rites, in being respectful he will wear himself out, in being careful he will become timid" (Confucius, *The Analects*, bk. 8, chap. 2 p. 92).

40. "Observe what a man *has to do* when his father is living, and then observe what he *does* when his father is dead" (ibid., bk. 1, chap. 11, p. 60–61; my italics).

41. See Allan Ludwig, *Graven Images* (Middletown: Wesleyan University Press, 1966) and Dickran and Ann Tashjian, *Memorials for Children of Change* (Middletown, CT: Wesleyan University Press, 1974). "Memento Mori" means literally "remember that you have to die."

42. On reactualization, see Eliade, *The Myth of the Eternal Return*, p. 76.

43. Ibid., p. 75.

44. Ibid., p. 82.

45. Cited at ibid.

46. Cited at ibid., p. 83.

47. On the latter notion of supplementing, see Jacques Derrida, *Speech and Phenomena*, trans. D. Allison (Evanston, IL: Northwestern University Press, 1973), pp. 88–104.

48. "*Text* means *tissue*; but whereas hitherto we have always taken this tissue as a product, a ready-made veil, behind which lies, more or less hidden, meaning (truth), we are now emphasizing, in the tissue, the generative idea that the text is made, is

worked out in a perpetual interweaving; lost in this tissue—this texture—the subject unmakes himself, like a spider dissolving in the constructive secretions of its web. Were we fond of neologisms, we might define the theory of the text as an *hyphology* (*hyphos* is the tissue and the spider's web)." (Roland Barthes, *The Pleasure of the Text,* trans. R. Howard [New York: Hill & Wang, 1975], p. 64. See also Jacques Derrida, *Margins of Philosophy,* trans. A. Bass (Chicago: University of Chicago Press, 1982), p. 263n.)

49. The same is true for many nonverbal works of art that are commemorative in their effects: say, the "1812 Overture," Cézanne's paintings of Mt. St. Victoire, Monet's studies of Rouen Cathedral. The addition of labels and titles to these works is not helpful beyond providing bare identification.

50. Confucius, *The Analects,* bk. 4, chap. 7, p. 73.

51. Ibid., bk. 2, chap. 2, p. 63.

52. Fung Yu-lan, *A History of Chinese Philosophy,* p. 56.

53. I have treated this entire situation in more detail in "Commemoration and Perdurance in *The Analects,* Books I and II." Since the role of ancestor worship in the *Analects* is well known, I have ignored it in the text above; but a brief consideration of it is given in section VIII below.

54. The same effect of mutual reinforcement is found in the case of image-*cum*-text; e.g., in gravestones with human faces, skeletons, angels, or animals sculpted on them, in addition to proper names and dates. The Civil War monument referred to earlier for the sake of its eloquent text is crowned by a Union soldier gazing southward with his rifle at rest. Depicted figures often accompany inscriptions on Egyptian and Greek stelae. In all such cases, we witness a complementarity of image and word as conjoined in a single material *commemorabilium*. One factor helps to make up for what the other lacks: simultaneous spatial display on the one hand and verbally encoded information on the other. As in the parallel case of the *ars memorativa,* image and sign empower each other.

55. See Arnold van Gennep, *The Rites of Passage,* trans. M. B. Vizedom and G. L. Caffee (Chicago: University of Chicago Press, 1975).

56. Turner, *The Forest of Symbols,* p. 98.

57. Ibid., pp. 96–97.

58. Victor Turner, *The Ritual Process* (Chicago: Aldine, 1969), p. 101.

59. Ibid., p. 95.

60. In short, there is a suspension of "all attributes that distinguish categories and groups in the social order" (ibid., p. 103).

61. This community is "the repository of the whole gamut of the culture's values, norms, attitudes, sentiments, and relationships. Its representatives in the specific rites—and these may vary from ritual to ritual—represent the generic authority of tradition" (ibid.).

62. "The neophyte in liminality must be a *tabula rasa,* a blank slate, on which is inscribed the knowledge and wisdom of the group, in those respects that pertain to the new status" (ibid.).

63. Ibid., p. 105.

64. Ibid., p. 104.

65. Ibid., p. 101. Turner comments: "Even when a man has become a chief, he must still be a member of the whole community of persons *(antu),* and show this by 'laughing with them,' respecting their rights, 'welcoming everyone,' and sharing food with them" (ibid., pp. 104–5).

66. Ibid., p. 96.

67. "Betwixt and Between: The Liminal Period in Rites de Passage" is the title of the essay from which Turner's developed reflections in *The Ritual Process* take their origin. See *The Forest of Symbols,* pp. 93–111.

68. On this point, see Gillian Feeley-Harnik, *The Lord's Table: Eucharist and Passover in Early Christianity* (Philadelphia: University of Pennsylvania Press, 1981), esp. chaps. 2, 3.
69. S. Freud, *Totem and Taboo* in *Standard Edition,* 13:142.
70. See ibid., pp. 150–51. On the idea of the surrogate victim, see René Girard, *Violence and the Sacred* (Baltimore: Johns Hopkins University Press, 1977), p. 197ff.
71. Freud, *Totem and Taboo,* p. 143; my italics.
72. This formulation is from Freud, *The Ego and the Id, Standard Edition,* 20:29.
73. Hans W. Loewald, "On Internalization," in his *Papers On Psychoanalysis* (New Haven: Yale University Press, 1980), p. 83.
74. Roy Schafer, *Aspects of Internalization* (New York: International Universities Press, 1968), p. 112.
75. S. Freud, "Mourning and Melancholia," *Standard Edition,* 14:257.
76. Loewald, "On Internalization," p. 83.
77. Such an identification is "the earliest expression of an emotional tie with another person" (Freud, *Standard Edition,* 18:105).
78. Freud, *Standard Edition,* 19:36.
79. Ibid., p. 34; my italics.
80. Ibid., p. 48.
81. "By giving permanent expression to the influence of the parents it perpetuates the existence of the factors to which it owes its original" (ibid., p. 35).
82. Other factors are at work as well of course: desexualization of libidinal ties with one's parents, a sublimation of the resultant saving in energy, and an infusion of aggression from the id. The latter factor is increasingly stressed by Freud in the years 1920–1930.
83. Freud, *Standard Edition,* 19:29.
84. Freud, *Standard Edition,* 21:133.
85. See *Standard Edition,* 7:170, 231, 239–40.
86. Freud, *Totem and Taboo,* in *Standard Edition* 13:155. See also p. 158.
87. It could also be shown that, within the vicissitudes of Freud's own writings, there is much the same inversion of interests: as the importance of recollection wanes, the fortunes of non-recollective forms of remembering rise. For a more complete account of these vicissitudes, see my essay "The Changing Fate of Memory in Freud's Work: Commemoration and Memorialization" (forthcoming).
88. On the immortality of the internalized object, see Schafer, *Aspects of Internalization,* pp. 220–36.
89. Freud, *Totem and Taboo,* in *Standard Edition,* 13:151.
90. As Louis Dupré says, "The self can only be remembered" (*Transcendent Selfhood* [New York: Seabury, 1976], p. 76).
91. On identification via mirror images, see Jacques Lacan, "The Mirror Stage as Formative Function of the I" in *Ecrits,* trans. A. Sheridan (New York: Norton, 1977), pp. 1–7.
92. Sigmund Freud, "On Narcissism," in *Standard Edition,* 14:77.
93. Arthur Rimband, letters to Paul Demeny, May 15, 1871.
94. On the body as mediator between sacred and profane, see Ernst Cassirer, *The Philosophy of Symbolic Forms,* trans. R. Manheim (New Haven: Yale University Press, 1955), II, 228.
95. The body of the memorialized person may itself be depicted—as occurs in many stelae and in the case of the Civil War Memorial discussed above.
96. "Ritual" in *Encyclopedia Brittanica,* 15th Edition, vol. XV, p. 866.
97. See Jacques Derrida, *Positions,* trans. Alan Bass (Chicago: University of Chicago Press, 1981), pp. 28, 40, 43, 86.

98. I develop the distinction between "horizontal" and "vertical" communities in my paper, "Commemoration in the Eucharist," in *God: Experience or Origin?*, ed. A. de Nicolas and E. Moutsopoulos (New York: Paragon, 1985), pp. 214–34.

99. Quoted in Jean Cazeneuve, *Lucien Lévy-Bruhl*, trans. Peter Riviere (New York: Harper and Row, 1972), p. 44.

100. Ibid., pp. 41–42; his italics.

101. On this point, see ibid., p. 42.

102. Ibid.

103. Lucien Lévy-Bruhl, *The Notebooks on Primitive Mentality*, trans. Peter Riviere (New York: Harper and Row, 1978), p. 17.

104. Cazeneuve, *Lucien Lévy-Bruhl*, p. 43.

105. See ibid., p. 60: "There is an identity of substance established between a man and what he eats; he becomes, he is what he eats and assimilates."

106. Ibid., p. 51.

107. Lévy-Bruhl, *The Notebooks on Primitive Mentality*, pp. 5–7.

108. Ibid., p. 2.

109. Ibid., p. 14.

110. This duality-unity may itself be regarded as a version of the corpse-and-ghost paradigm mentioned above.

111. Cazeneuve, *Lucien Lévy-Bruhl*, p. 88.

112. This phrase is taken from the first recorded use (1569) of "sempiternall" in the English language, as given by the *Oxford English Dictionary* (and as used in the epigram to this chapter).

113. Lévy-Bruhl, *The Notebooks on Primitive Mentality*, p. 2; his italics.

114. Ibid., p. 18; his italics.

115. Ibid., pp. 14–15.

116. Cazeneuve, *Lucien Lévy-Bruhl*, p. 48.

117. Lévy-Bruhl, *The Notebooks on Primitive Mentality*, p. 1.

118. Moreover, just as we *are* the memories we possess in Locke's view, so we are also defined by the private property we *own:* pieces of property thus being the exact analogues of memorial representations and both being the basis for a radical individualism.

119. Marcel Proust, *Remembrance of Things Past*, trans. C. K. Scott Moncrieff and T. Kilmartin (New York: Random House, 1981), I, 50.

120. Ibid.

121. Ibid., pp. 50–51.

122. Lévy-Bruhl, *The Notebooks on Primitive Mentality*, p. 192; his italics.

123. It could be argued further that the literal bi-presence of Marcel and Léonie in this scene symbolizes, by its very juxtaposition of representatives from two generations, the bi-presence of past and present themselves. The same could be ventured for the ceremonial bi-presence of priest and communicant in the Eucharist. It will be noted that I am using "bi-presence" here in a temporal sense, whereas Lévy-Bruhl originally proposed the idea in referring to a spatial setting (e.g., the case of Grubb and the Indian). But the term easily, and legitimately, invites generalization.

124. Lévy-Bruhl, *The Notebooks on Primitive Mentality*, p. 2.

125. Proust, *Remembrance of Things Past*, I, 51; my italics.

126. Cazeneuve, *Lucien Lévy-Bruhl*, p. 42.

127. On this interpretation, see J. N. Findlay, *Plato: The Written and Unwritten Doctrines* (Atlantic Highlands, NJ: Humanities Press, 1974). Cf. also the following passage from Whitehead: "The potentiality of an eternal object is realized in a particular actual entity, contributing to the definiteness of that actual entity" (in

*Process and Reality*, ed. D. R. Griffin and D. W. Sherburne [New York: Free Press, 1978], p. 23).

128. I say "proto-experiences" to underline the fact that for Plato one does not recollect *personal* experiences *per se*. One recollects only the *kinds* of experience that are necessary to the prior attainment of knowledge, which is itself the primary content recollected.

129. Plato, *Meno* 81 d.

130. That knowing is indeed commemorative is an explicit theme in the writings of Telesio, the Italian Renaissance philosopher: "[the mind] is able to discern the hidden conditions of those things of which but a single one is observed. . . . This power is commonly called understanding *(intelligere)*, but is rather to be named judgment *(existimari)* or better commemorating *(commemorari)*." This passage is cited in J. H. Randall, Jr., *The Career of Philosophy* (New York: Columbia University Press, 1962), p. 205. Randall translates *commemorari* as "remembering together" and comments: "knowing is a remembering together *(commemorari)* the other qualities of an object associated with the one you observe" (ibid.). This statement overlooks the Platonic roots of Telesio's thought.

131. Heidegger's celebrated commemoration of the Greek origins of philosophy could be construed as a commemoration of an equally decisive ending. In his view metaphysics has had a quite determinate beginning—precisely in the Platonic doctrine of Forms—and a very definite ending: in Nietzsche's doctrines of the will to power and eternal recurrence. There is something dramatic, peremptory, and decisive about such an ending—as is conveyed so eloquently in Nietzsche's life and work, which Heidegger commemorates in his four volumes of lectures on this prophetic figure who first saw clearly that "philosophy is ending in the present age" (Heidegger, "The End of Philosophy and the Task of Thinking" in *On Time and Being*, p. 58).

132. Heidegger, "Time and Being," in *On Time and Being*, p. 15.

133. Martin Heidegger, *What Is Called Thinking?*, trans. J. Glenn Gray (New York: Harper and Row, 1972), p. 103.

134. For a remarkable study of evanescing, see William Earle, *Evanescence* (Chicago: Regnery, 1984).

135. On this point, see S. Freud, *Standard Edition*, 1:356; 3:154, 166 n.

136. Nietzsche treats "the will's revulsion against time and its 'It was' " in *Thus Spake Zarathustra*, trans. R. J. Hollingde (Baltimore: Penguin, 1969), Part II, "Of Redemption," pp. 159–63. Heidegger discusses the same point in *What Is Called Thinking?*, pp. 92–96.

137. Whitehead, *Process and Reality*, p. 29. See also p. 82: "the creature perishes *and* is immortal" (his italics).

138. Heidegger, "Time and Being," in *On Time and Being*, p. 13. See also ibid., p. 15: "Futural approaching brings about what has been." The priority of the future is already affirmed in *Being and Time*, sec. 68.

139. Alfred North Whitehead, *Symbolism: Its Meaning and Effect* (New York: Macmillan, 1959), p. 47.

## Part Three—Coda

1. M. Heidegger has pointed to the profound affinities between *Gedächtnis* ("memory") and *Gemüt* ("heart") in *What Is Called Thinking?*, trans. J. Glenn Gray (New York: Harper and Row, 1968), pp. 139–41, 144, 148, 150.

2. All of the above etymologies are taken from the section on "Indo-European

Roots," article on "men-," in *The American Heritage Dictionary of the English Language* (Boston: Houghton Mifflin, 1981), p. 1529.

3. A. N. Whitehead, *Process and Reality*, ed. D. R. Griffin and D. W. Sherburne (New York: Free Press, 1978), p. 63; his italics.

4. Ibid., p. 311; his italics.

5. Ibid., p. 81. See also ibid., p. 312.

6. Heidegger, *What Is Called Thinking?*, p. 5.

## Part Four

### 11. The Thick Autonomy of Memory

1. Among "major forms" I am including the three mnemonic modes of Part Two, the three forms just discussed in Part Three, as well as the following from Part One: primary and secondary remembering, remembering *simpliciter*, remembering-that, remembering-how, and remembering-to.

2. On this notion, see especially Aristotle, *De Interpretatione* 17 a 37–40.

3. See Edward S. Casey, *Imagining: A Phenomenological Study* (Bloomington: Indiana University Press, 1976), Part I, esp. pp. 58–60.

4. Virgil, *Aeneid*, VII, 312. This statement forms the epigram on the title page of Freud's *Interpretation of Dreams*.

5. For a treatment of various senses of autonomy, see Casey, *Imagining*, pp. 177–88.

6. On *Klärung*, see E. Husserl, *Ideas*, trans. W. R. Boyce Gibson (New York: Macmillan, 1962), secs. 67–70.

7. Milan Kundera, *The Unbearable Lightness of Being*, trans. M. H. Heim (New York: Harper & Row, 1985), p. 5.

8. Aristotle, *De Memoria et Reminiscentia* 451 a 15–16 (Sorabji translation).

9. Bertrand Russell, "On Propositions" in *Logic and Knowledge*, ed. Robert C. Marsh (London: Allen & Unwin, 1956), p. 315 and p. 309, respectively.

10. See, for example, C. B. Martin and M. Deutscher, "Remembering" in R. M. Chisholm and R. J. Swartz, eds., *Empirical Knowledge* (Englewood Cliffs, NJ: Prentice-Hall, 1973), pp. 302–31.

11. On the verticalizing movement of imagination, see Gaston Bachelard, *L'air et les songes* (Paris: Corti, 1943).

12. This is not to deny the possibility of hybrid combinations between imagination and memory in which the role of the image is genuinely "possibilizing." This can occur in the midst of recollection itself, as when we employ an actively constructed mental image to remember better "what it might have looked like." Such use of hypothetical imagining still falls short, however, of the fullest form of autonomy of which imagining is capable. On this point, see Casey, *Imagining*, pp. 114–16.

13. See J. Piaget & B. Inhelder, *Memory and Intelligence*, trans. A. J. Pomerans (New York: Basic Books, 1973).

14. Aristotle, *De Memoria et Reminiscentia* 449 a 15; my italics.

15. Nevertheless, this is precisely what Minkowski claims: "Memory creates our experiences"; "it seems equally justified to affirm that memory produces the past as to say that it reproduces it" (*Lived Time*, trans. N. Metzel [Evanston, IL: Northwestern University Press, 1970], p. 149 and p. 151 respectively).

16. E. Husserl, *Experience and Judgment*, trans. J. S. Churchill & K. Ameriks (Evanston, IL: Northwestern University Press, 1973), p. 108.

17. To be more precise, the Indo-European root is now considered to be *mer-* or *smer-*, "to be anxious, to grieve," with the variants *mar-* and *smar-* along with *mor-*, *mur-*, and *smur-*. If this is so, the origin of "mourning" would be even more ancient than that of "remembering." See Eric Partridge, *Origins: A Short Etymological Dictionary of Modern English* (New York: Macmillan, 1959), p. 396. See also C. T. Onions, ed., *The Oxford Dictionary of English Etymology* (Oxford: Oxford University Press, 1966), p. 593. Unless otherwise specified, I shall be drawing on Partridge's book in discussions below.

18. *Com-*, from *cum*, means "with"; but it may also act to intensify the verb onto which it is prefixed.

19. *Oxford English Dictionary*, entry under "remanent."

20. The link is through the *mer-* stem, a variant of the same *mar-* etymon which we have seen to underlie *smárati*, "he remembers." See footnote 18 above. Note also the closely related Welsh *marth*, "sorrow," "anxiety"; the Cornish *moreth*, "grief," "regret"; the Gaelic *smùr*, "sadness"; and the Armenian *mormok*, "regret," "sorrow."

21. See Casey, *Imagining*, pp. 189–90.

22. The Greek adjective *mermeros* is yet another cognate of "memory." The duplication of the *mer-* stem in *mer/meros* is striking; another intensification, a specifically semantic thickening, is here at work. If we were to indulge in what Derrida calls "semantic mirage," we would divide *mermeros* into *merm/eros* and notice once more the rooting of memory in love. (On semantic mirage, see J. Derrida, *Positions*, trans. A. Bass [Chicago: University of Chicago Press, 1981], p. 46.)

23. Martin Heidegger, *Being and Time*, J. Macquarrie and E. Robinson (New York: Harper and Row, 1962), p. 173.

24. This becomes especially evident when we consider memory beyond mind; for celerity is an endemic mental virtue: "thought is quick" (Thomas Hobbes, *Leviathan*, ed. C. B. Macpherson [Baltimore: Penguin, 1968], p. 95).

25. Sigmund Freud, Letter of December 6, 1896 (*Standard Edition*, 1:233; his italics).

26. Harold Bloom, *Poetry and Repression* (New Haven: Yale University Press, 1976), p. 287. See also Bloom's *A Map of Misreading* (Oxford: Oxford University Press, 1975), chap. 4, pp. 63–82.

27. The strongest statement of this circumstance occurs in Freud's "Heredity and the Aetiology of the Neuroses" (1896): "Thanks to the change due to puberty, the memory will display a power which was completely lacking from the [original] event itself" (*Standard Edition*, 3:154).

28. Martin Heidegger, *The Question Concerning Technology*, trans. W. Lovitt (New York: Harper and Row, 1977), pp. 20ff, 37ff.

29. Stanley A. Leavy, *The Psychoanalytic Dialogue* (New Haven: Yale University Press, 1980), p. 94. See also pp. 97, 110–111.

30. Pierre Janet, *L'evolution de la mémoire et de la notion du temps* (Paris: Chahine, 1928), I, p. 87ff.

31. "Etymon" itself means, in its own Greek root (i.e., *etumon*) the *true* sense of a word (*etumos* is "true"). By a revealing reduction, etymon now means a word's strictly historical origin or root.

32. This might seem to make photography a mere instrument in the situation, just another case of "standing-reserve" via "enframing" (in Heidegger's disparaging words). Yet, granting that photography is subject to reductive technological manipulations at every point, this is by no means its only possible fate. It can be, as it is designed to be in the present instance, an agency for *opening* a future of appreciation, for preserving the past in a maximally meaningful way. Here the paradox is that it is precisely the photograph that serves so naturally as a paradigm in passivist

models of memory: a paradox to which I shall return in the concluding pages of this chapter.

33. On the virtuality of remembering in contrast with its actuality, see chapter 2 and section VI below.

34. Heidegger, *Being and Time,* p. 41; his italics.

35. See ibid., pp. 307, 387.

36. T. S. Eliot, "Burnt Norton," Stanza I, *The Four Quartets* in *Collected Poems 1909–1962* (New York: Harcourt, Brace & World, 1963), p. 175.

37. Jacques Lacan, *Écrits,* trans. A. Sheridan (New York: Norton, 1977), p. 86.

38. On this relationship, see Casey, *Imagining,* pp. 103–6.

39. See David Farrell Krell, *On the Verge* (New York: Humanities Press, forthcoming).

40. See Edmund Husserl, *Logical Investigations,* trans. J. N. Findlay (New York: Humanities Press, 1970), II, Investigation VI, secs. 8–12, 36–39.

41. Autonomous remembering is not to be confused with *spontaneous* remembering, although the two can certainly overlap. Spontaneous remembering may include anything from Husserlian primary memory (especially in its "sinking back" character) to Proustian "involuntary memory" (e.g., the tea-tasting episode).

42. But it is wrong to assert, as does R. S. Benjamin, that *in all cases* "a claim to remember is in principle falsifiable or verifiable by observations which are in no way connected with the state of mind of the person making the claim . . . memory claims are verifiable in principle by recourse to publicly ascertainable facts" ("Remembering," in D. F. Gustafson, ed., *Essays in Philosophical Psychology* [New York: Doubleday, 1964], pp. 182–83). This is so only in one subclass of the category of "truth to the that" and does not apply to cases of "truth to the how" at all. Nor is it true that "we treat our memories of such things [as dreams, feelings, thoughts] as though they are verifiable independently" (ibid., p. 183n). As we know that they are *not* verifiable by others, we do not treat them as if they were: we keep them, and their grounds for confirmation or disconfirmation, within the self-system, where possibilities of self-deception are admittedly rife and where others can offer help only indirectly.

43. I borrow this term from Benjamin: see "Remembering," pp. 188–91.

44. Imagining is characteristically indifferent to truth in any of its major senses since it pursues the purely possible and not the actual as such; and thinking, in its inferential, hypothesizing, and speculative moments, is not concerned with the issue of truth as such.

45. For the notion of "remaining over" see Husserl, *Ideas,* I, secs. 31–33; for that of "abiding possession," see Husserl, *Cartesian Meditations,* trans. D. Cairns (The Hague: Nijhoff, 1960), secs. 27, 36.

46. See A. R. Luria, *The Mind of A Mnemonist,* trans. L. Solotaroff (Chicago: Regnery, 1968), esp. pp. 149–59.

47. F. C. Bartlett, *Remembering: A Study in Experimental and Social Psychology* (Cambridge: Cambridge University Press, 1964), p. 208. See also p. 197: "the past operates as an organised mass."

48. Hegel, *The Science of Logic,* section 112 *(Encyclopedia of the Philosophical Sciences),* Addendum; as translated by William Wallace, *The Logic of Hegel* (Oxford: Oxford University Press, 1959), p. 209.

49. For Derrida's interpretation, see his *Edmund Husserl's Origin of Geometry: An Introduction* (Stony Brook, NY: Nicolas Hays, 1978), pp. 76–106. On the repeatability of *eidos* in relation to memory, see my essay "Memory and Phenomenological Method" in W. S. Hamrick, ed., *Phenomenology in Practice and Theory* (The Hague: Nijhoff, 1985), pp. 35–52.

50. See Martin Heidegger, "Der Satz der Identität" in *Identität und Differenz* (Pfullingen: Neske, 1957), pp. 11–34.

51. Reminiscing *in words* provides another instance of a medium—in this case, language—which, despite its aspirations to transparency, brings with it an inherent thickness. Consider only the ways in which various narrative forms may convey the same past event with important nuances of difference. As I have insisted in this chapter, neither words nor images are necessary to remembering. But both constitute valid and vital media of exchange between the remembering present and the remembered past: they, too, form part of memory's thick autonomy.

## 12. Freedom in Remembering

1. Martin Heidegger, *Being and Time,* trans. J. Macquarrie and E. Robinson (New York: Harper and Row, 1962), p. 68.

2. On "mineness," see ibid., pp. 67–69.

3. John Locke, *An Essay Concerning Human Understanding,* ed. J. Yolton (New York: Dutton, 1965), chap. 27, sec. 10.

4. For a contemporary discussion of multiple personality, see B. G. Baum, ed., *The Psychiatric Clinics of North America: Symposium on Multiple Personality* (Philadelphia: Saunders, 1984).

5. On dissociation, see Bernard Hart, *The Psychology of Insanity* (Cambridge: Cambridge University Press, 1920), chap. 4.

6. "[In recollection] the immediate 'I,' already enduring in the enduring primordial sphere, constitutes in itself another as other. [It is a matter of] self-temporalization through de-presentation" (Edmund Husserl, *The Crisis of European Sciences and Transcendental Phenomenology,* trans. D. Carr [Evanston, IL: Northwestern University Press, 1970], p. 185).

7. "Consciousness [i.e., memory] of personal identity presupposes, and therefore cannot constitute, personal identity" (Joseph Butler, First Appendix to *The Analogy of Religion* [cited in J. Perry, ed. *Personal Identity* (Berkeley: University of California Press, 1975), p. 100]).

8. M. Heidegger, *What Is Called Thinking?* trans. J. Glenn Gray (New York: Harper and Row, 1968), p. 3: "Das Gedächtnis ist die Versammlung des Denkens."

9. Heidegger, ibid., p. 151.

10. Heidegger traces this predominance to the fact that *eidos,* Plato's preferred term for "form," originally meant "visual aspect." See his essay, "Plato's Theory of Truth" in *Philosophy in the Twentieth Century,* ed. W. Barrett & H. D. Aiken (New York: Random House, 1962), III, 367–98.

11. I explore this matter further in my essay, "Keeping the Past in Mind," *Review of Metaphysics* 37 (1983), pp. 77–95.

12. Plato, *Meno* 85 d. Sorabji comments: "is not finding knowledge within oneself recollection?" (R. Sorabji, *Aristotle On Memory* [London: Duckworth, 1972], p. 40).

13. See Plato, *Philebus* 34 D: "When the soul that has lost the memory of a sensation or what it has learned resumes that memory within itself *(ex hautou)* and goes over the old ground, we regularly speak of 'recollections'."

14. Thus, a matrix is "a place or medium in which something is bred, produced, or developed"; "a place or point of origin and growth" *(Oxford English Dictionary).*

15. Heraclitus, Fragment 119 (Diels-Kranz). "Fate" translates *daimon,* guardian divinity.

16. Aristotle, *Nichomachean Ethics* 1114 b 17–1115 a 3.

17. Freud, *Standard Edition*, 19:29.

18. Aristotle, *Physics* 210 a 13–25.

19. On encoding specificity, see E. Tulving and D. M. Thomson, "Encoding Specificity and Retrieval Processes in Episodic Memory," *Psychological Review* 80 (1973):352–73.

20. George A. Miller, "The Magic Number Seven, Plus or Minus Two: Some Limits on Our Capacity for Processing Information," reprinted in N. J. Slamecka, ed., *Human Learning and Memory* (New York: Oxford University Press, 1967), p. 233. It is to Miller's credit that he does recognize "limits" on the model he first proposed in 1956. One of these limits is imagery: "Images seem much harder to get at operationally and to study experimentally than the more symbolic kinds of recoding" (ibid.).

21. On this point, see J. Glenn Gray, "Heidegger on Remembering and Remembering Heidegger," *Man and World* 10 (1977):62.

22. I have considered the same three regions in more detail with respect to the freedom of imagination in *Imagining: A Phenomenological Study* (Bloomington: Indiana University Press, 1976), pp. 207–31.

23. S. Freud, *Standard Edition*, 19:50n. Freud underlines the word "freedom."

24. Goethe, "Proverbs in Prose," in *The Permanent Goethe*, ed. Thomas Mann (New York: Dial Press, 1948), p. 640.

25. On Harold Bloom's analysis, the anxiety of influence results in a "misprision" of the works of predecessors. We could just as well say "misremembering" in the circumstance. (See Harold Bloom, *A Map of Misreading* [Oxford: Oxford University Press, 1975], pp. 63–80.)

26. Friedrich Nietzsche, *Beyond Good and Evil*, trans. W. Kaufman (New York: Vintage, 1966), p. 27.

27. On the idea of *im-Griff-behalten*, see Edmund Husserl, *Experience and Judgment*, trans. J. S. Churchill and K. Ameriks (Evanston, IL: Northwestern University Press, 1973), sec. 87.

28. I have pursued this parallel between Husserl and Plato further in my essay, "Memory and Phenomenological Method," in W. S. Hamrick, ed., *Phenomenology in Practice and Theory* (Dordrecht: Nijhoff, 1985), pp. 35–38.

29. On reactivation, see Husserl, *The Crisis of European Sciences and Transcendental Phenomenology*, trans. D. Carr (Evanston, IL: Northwestern University Press, 1970), pp. 353–78.

30. Aristotle, *De Anima* 427 b 16–17.

31. It is striking that the etymology of "monster" includes the Latin *monēre*, "to remind," "admonish." A monster, by its very monstrosity, calls us back to our senses when it does not overcome us utterly. On the concept of the monster, see Catherine Keller, *A Broken Web: Separation, Sexism and Self* (Boston: Beacon Press, 1986), chap. 2.

32. S. Freud, "Remembering, Repeating, and Working-Through," *Standard Edition*, 12:150; his italics.

33. Ibid., p. 148: "descriptively speaking [the goal] is to fill in gaps in memory; dynamically speaking, it is to overcome resistances due to repression."

34. For Freud's own account of his change of views on this question, see ibid., p. 147.

35. On infantile amnesia, see ibid., pp. 148–49, as well as the second of the *Three Essays on the* Theory *of Psychosexuality, Standard Edition*, 7:174–76.

36. It is to be noted, however, that Freud does not equate amnesia with forgetting. An item can be " 'remembered' which could never have been 'forgotten' because it was never at any time noticed—was never conscious" (*Standard Edition*, 12:149).

37. Friedrich Nietzsche, *The Use and Abuse of History*, trans. A. Collins (Indianapolis: Bobbs-Merrill, 1957), p. 7; my italics.

38. Milan Kundera, *The Unbearable Lightness of Being,* trans. M. H. Heim (New York: Harper and Row, 1985), p. 5.

39. Ibid.

40. Eugene Minkowski, *Lived Time,* trans. N. Metzel (Evanston, IL: Northwestern University Press, 1970), p. 156. Heidegger makes a quite comparable claim:

> forgetting is not nothing, nor is it just a failure to remember; it is rather a 'positive' ecstatical mode of one's having been—a mode with a character of its own. The ecstasis (rapture) of forgetting has the character of backing away *in the face* of one's ownmost 'been'. . . . Only on the basis of such forgetting can anything be retained. . . . Just as expecting is possible only on the basis of awaiting, *remembering* is possible only on that of forgetting, *and not vice versa*. (Heidegger, *Being and Time,* pp. 388–89; his italics).

41. For a general treatment, see G. Reed, *The Psychology of Anomalous Experience* (Boston: Houghton Mifflin, 1974).

42. Heidegger, *Being and Time,* p. 89; his italics.

43. Ibid.

44. See M. Merleau-Ponty, *The Visible and the Invisible,* trans. A. Lingis (Evanston, IL: Northwestern University Press, 1968), p. 267 (working note of November, 1960).

45. "Tout participe de la mémoire si l'on se place au point de vue de la mémoire au sens large" (J. Piaget & B. Inhelder, *Mémoire et intelligence* (Paris: Presses Universitaires de France, 1968), p. 476.

46. Black Elk, cited in *Black Elk Speaks,* ed. John G. Neihardt (Lincoln: University of Nebraska Press, 1961), p. 17.

47. See Plato, *Republic* 472: "Perhaps you do not realize that, after I have barely escaped the first two waves, the third, which you are now bringing down upon me, is the most formidable of all" (Cornford translation).

48. The full formulation is "to be, to exist, is to participate." This is the title of the entry of March 23, 1938, in Lucien Lévy-Bruhl, *The Notebooks on Primitive Mentality,* trans. Peter Rivière (New York: Harper and Row, 1978), p. 16–17.

# INDEX